Instructor's Course Planner
to accompany

T5-DIB-189

CHILD DEVELOPMENT

Seventh Edition

John W. Santrock
University of Texas at Dallas

Prepared by

Allen Keniston
University of Wisconsin—Eau Claire

Blaine Peden
University of Wisconsin—Eau Claire

Brown & Benchmark
PUBLISHERS

Madison Dubuque, IA Guilford, CT Chicago Toronto London
Caracas Mexico City Buenos Aires Madrid Bogota Sydney

Copyright © 1996 by Times Mirror Higher Education Group, Inc. All rights
reserved

ISBN 0-697-23556-4

The contents or parts thereof may be reproduced for classroom use with *Child
Development, Seventh Edition,* by John W. Santrock, provided such reproductions
bear copyright notice and the number reproduced does not exceed the number of
students using the text, but may not be reproduced in any form for any other purpose
without permission of the publisher.

Printed in the United States of America by Times Mirror Higher Education Group,
Inc., 2460 Kerper Boulevard, Dubuque, Iowa, 52001

10 9 8 7 6 5 4 3 2 1

Table of Contents

Table of Contents

To the Professor

You are about to undertake the challenging and, we hope, exciting task of teaching about physical, psychological, and social development during adolescence. This instructor's course planner will help you (a) teach basic course content and (b) incorporate additional goals into your course such as active learning and critical thinking by students. To help you teach course content, we have provided lecture suggestions and lists of transparencies from Brown and Benchmark's *Brown and Benchmark's Human Development Transparencies* (2nd ed.) appropriate for each chapter. Also, at the end of the manual you will find lists of audiovisual resources, reference books, references on teaching materials and teaching skills, and suggestions for new teachers and film lists for each chapter. To help incorporate active student learning and critical thinking, we have suggested classroom activities, included critical thinking exercises (with answer keys), identified two or more student research projects, and listed challenging essay and critical thinking questions to accompany each chapter.

In the following paragraphs we describe the features of each chapter of this manual in more detail. Those of you who are familiar with materials for the sixth edition of *Child Development* will soon note that we have essentially modified and built on the excellent manual for the sixth edition prepared by Janet Simons. We have changed formats, included material from other Brown and Benchmark ancillaries, added our own lecture suggestions and classroom activities, added critical thinking exercises, and added a systematic set of "critical thinking essay questions" to each chapter. However, we have also kept most of the material from Dr. Simons's planner. Thus we hope that previous adopters of *Child Development* will find many old friends and acquire many new ones among the suggestions for teaching child psychology that we have assembled here.

LECTURE SUGGESTIONS

We offer at least six and usually several more lecture suggestions for each chapter. Each presents a main idea for a lecture and offers good resources for developing the idea, but it will require additional work on your part to flesh them out and articulate them with your own particular goals and objectives.

In general, the lecture suggestions do not duplicate material in the text. To the contrary, they suggest ways to expand the textbook coverage of a topic or supplement it with interesting new material. We made an effort to focus on developmental themes and to make connections across chapters. Many of the suggestions are ours, but we took many others from instructor's course planners available for other Brown and Benchmark texts.

One feature of these lecture topics is that they attempt to represent three separate objectives. Some lecture suggestions focus on a concept or theory. Others address applications of child psychology, and and still others focus on methodological issues. We hope that these three types of suggestions will help to organize and unify the extremely diverse topics of child psychology.

BROWN & BENCHMARK'S HUMAN DEVELOPMENT TRANSPARENCIES (2ND ED.)

Brown & Benchmark provides *Brown and Benchmark's Human Development Transparencies* (2nd ed.) to adopters of this edition of *Child Development.* The accompanying manual suggests how to use each transparency to stimulate active learning and critical thinking by your students. In the instructor's course planner we have listed the transparencies that seem most appropriate and useful for each chapter.

TEACHING RESOURCES

A wealth of films, books, and journals is available to supplement your teaching. We have reproduced the lists of these relevant to the topics in each chapter assembled by Janet Simons for the course planner to accompany the sixth edition of *Child Development.* These lists appear in the back of the planner.

CLASSROOM ACTIVITIES OR DEMONSTRATIONS

We have suggested at least eight, and usually many more, classroom activities for each chapter. Some directly relate to suggested lectures, others illustrate material in *Child Development,* and still others relate to material not contained in either the text or suggested lectures. The first activity always suggests discussion of the thinking exercises, which are described in greater detail below. We have found that students need and want discussion before, during, and after the time that they have spent working on these exercises. Although you will discover points of your own to discuss, we have suggested lines of discussion that may help students with the exercises.

The second activity for each chapter is to have students present data from their out-of-class research projects. Specific suggestions for classroom activities associated with each project appear at the end of each project description. The typical suggestion is to pool and interpret student data and then to relate the findings to topics in the chapter.

The remainder of the activities listed will vary from chapter to chapter, ranging from demonstrations, structured interactions between you and your students, small group discussions, panel discussions, debates, and role playing. The intent of these is to provide diverse ways to involve students in classroom activity. Some of them require considerable preparation by you or your students, whereas others require very little preparation by either.

CRITICAL THINKING EXERCISES

To the best of our knowledge, the critical thinking exercises for *Child Development* are unique. They apply an idea that we have implemented in a variety of psychology courses over the past eight years and now use routinely in most of our courses as regular assignments. You may wish to use these as graded assignments, structured essay questions, elements of lectures, or bases for discussion. However you choose to use these exercises, we guarantee that they will be thought-provoking!

What are critical thinking exercises? As we define them, they are problems presented in a multiple choice format that require students to identify a best answer, explain why it is the best answer, and explain why the other answers are not as good. We have developed various kinds of problems for students to solve as they read and study the text. For example, many exercises ask students to analyze material in terms of the "nature of development" as presented in Chapter 1. Students may be asked which of several aspects of development are illustrated by material in the text or to identify which of several developmental themes receives greatest emphasis in particular topics. A second type of exercise require students to integrate material within chapters. For example, an exercise for Chapter 17 asked students to identify which of five statements about schools and their influences on adolescents provides the best example of the concept of aptitude-treatment interaction. A third type of exercise requires students to interpret the figures or tables used throughout the text. A fourth type of exercise asks students to apply Santrock's guidelines for "being a wise consumer of information about adolescent development." A fifth type of exercise requires that students recognize the direct or indirect influence of the five theories of development Santrock outlines in Chapter 2. Finally, a fourth type of exercise requires students to learn how to recognize assumptions and distinguish them from inferences and observations. This last type of exercise probably represents what is most widely viewed as critical thinking, but we believe critical thinking also involves using and analyzing information that students study. Importantly, the common activity across all of the exercises is asking students to give reasons for the answers they choose.

If you are interested in knowing more about our experiences with these exercises, send us a request for copies of papers that we have written about them. As indicated, each chapter of this planner includes notes about using the exercises in the concept of student discussions as well as for your own use. Informal observations of student performance on exercises were written to accompany *Children* (2nd ed.), also by John Santrock and published by Brown and Benchmark, and have been included here where applicable. We have also written sample answer keys for each exercise.

The thinking exercises do not appear in the student study guide. One way you could simplify the problem of preparing them for student assignments would be to obtain a copy of this course planner from Brown and Benchmark on a computer diskette, from which you could make copies of the exercises for duplication.

STUDENT RESEARCH PROJECTS

Each chapter contains two student research projects. These projects usually entail relatively simple types of systematic observation that students can do in everyday settings such as playgrounds, stores, schools, or malls. Occasionally they call for interviews, use of questionnaires, or experiment-like manipulations.

We strongly recommend that you use or adapt these activities as assignments in your course. Our strongest reason is that students do not seem to realize how tentative and fragile knowledge is—especially the unstructured, biased knowledge of everyday experience—until they attempt to do research on their own. One of the most challenging tasks for instructors in psychology courses is to break down the dominance of such student responses as "That isn't what I've seen" or "But I know someone who isn't a bit like what you're saying." Several doses of direct contact with structured, purposeful data collection may help these unscientific attitudes.

In any event, doing the research projects will make students aware of the ardors and rigors of data collection, and will also give them firsthand experience with children. Used carefully in conjunction with readings, lectures, and other class activities (such as are suggested at the end of each project description), they can enliven your course.

An important concern is that student projects conform to ethical guidelines for research. To help you make students aware of research ethics, the essay "Ethics, Human Subjects, and Informed Consent" is reprinted in the instructor's course planner.

The research projects appear only in the course planner. As with the critical thinking exercises, you may want to obtain a computer diskette of the course planner from which you can make appropriate copies of the instructions for the projects (which are written to the student, even though they appear in the planner) for your students.

ESSAY AND CRITICAL THINKING QUESTIONS

The last section in each chapter of the course planner contains two sets of questions. The first of these is a "traditional" set of questions intended to test students' comprehension of textbook material. These questions typically require students to define and distinguish terms, show how concepts relate to each other, discuss and evaluate evidence for hypotheses, or apply concepts to aspects of their own lives. The main resource for these questions should be the text (and possibly your lectures) and student's own experiences. There are between 10 and 20 questions for each chapter.

The second set of questions is more rigorous and systematic. They are more rigorous because they require students to go beyond textbook or lecture material. They are more systematic because eight different types of questions occur in every chapter (except Chapter 1). The first question asks students to review one of the books listed in the section "Practical Knowledge about Children" or the resources listed in the section "Resources for Improving the Lives of Children". The second question asks students to analyze material in each chapter in terms of the processes and periods that define "the nature of development" presented in Chapter 1 of the text. The third question asks students to identify material in each chapter relevant to the three fundamental developmental issues, or to consider how these issues might have been addressed if they were not. The fourth question focuses students' attention on information that is not covered in a chapter, and asks students to speculate on why a given topic was omitted. The fifth question asks students to research one of the many quotes from famous people found in the margins of each chapter of *Child Development*. They must find out something about each author and explain why the quote is important, what the quote means, and how it relates to the material presented in the chapter. The sixth question asks students to analyze and interpret topics presented in each chapter in terms of the six major approaches to child development presented in Chapter 2. (We did not write a question like this for Chapter 1.) The seventh question (also not included for Chapter 1) asks students to design a study to answer a question not answered by the text. The focus of these questions is application of "the science base of life-span development" (see Chapter 2). Finally, the eighth question, included for all but Chapter 1, requests that students find an article in a journal, magazine, or newspaper relevant to each chapter's topic, and to evaluate the article following six guidelines Santrock suggests for wise consumers of information.

If you use these questions - particularly the critical thinking questions - we suggest that you spend time teaching your class how to answer essay questions. We also suggest that you explicitly relate material in the textbook on critical thinking to the process of answering these questions. Toward these goals, you may want to use the set of instructions that appear in the next section and which also appear in the student study guide.

Of course, you may use these questions in any way that you like, but the set of critical thinking questions are designed to be take-home assignments that require prolonged reflection and possible library work. The comprehension questions can be used in in-class examinations, but we recommend that they also be used as take-home essays.

SOME FINAL THOUGHTS

We have included a large number and variety of classroom activities and demonstrations, critical thinking exercises, student projects, and essay questions because we strongly believe students should be actively involved in their own learning. If you agree, we hope that these activities will prove useful both as ready-made suggestions for student activity and as guides for activities that you invent to achieve your own course goals and objectives. In fact, we are interested to learn about both your reactions and those of your students to these activities. Please tell us about your experiences by writing us at the Department of Psychology, University of Wisconsin-Eau Claire, Eau Claire, Wisconsin 54702 - 4004 (or send an e-mail letter to either KENISTAH or PEDENBF@uwec.edu). Also, send samples of additional activities, exercises, or assignments that have enhanced your learning, or that represent the kind of learning tools you like. We look forward to hearing from you!

Allen H. Keniston
Blaine F. Peden

Answering Essay And Critical Thinking Questions

Santrock argues that children and adolescents must learn to think critically. For Santrock, critical thinking is "grasping the deeper meaning of problems, keeping an open mind about different approaches and perspectives, and thinking reflectively rather than accepting statements and carrying out procedures without significant understanding and evaluation."

Learning to think critically requires activity rather than passivity on the part of students. To improve your critical thinking skills (e.g., developing problem-solving strategies, seeing things from multiple points of view, expanding your knowledge base, and becoming motivated to use newly acquired critical thinking skills in daily life), you must actively: (a) read, listen, and observe carefully, (b) identify or formulate questions, (c) organize your thoughts on an issue or topic, (d) note similarities and differences, (e) make deductions by reasoning from the general to the specific, and (f) distinguish between logically valid and invalid inferences.

In Chapter 5 Santrock provides a discussion of critical thinking by adolescents. Here he emphasizes that an aspect of critical thinking is being open-minded about issues and thoroughly examining both sides of an issue. Open-minded and thorough answers to questions or solutions to problems require you to present statements that are accurate and true, relevant to the issue, and encompass all relevant issues.

In answering the essay and critical thinking questions you should demonstrate each of these aspects of critical thinking and satisfy the following criteria regarding content, organization, and writing skills. *Appropriate content* includes a sentence that restates the question, and answers to all parts of the question. Additional aspects of content include major points and supporting evidence that are accurate and related to the answer. Provide credit for information from others that you include in your response. Finally, end your response by restating the answer to the question and summarizing major points. *Appropriate organization* requires that your answer to the question appear near the beginning of your response. Major points and supporting evidence should be arranged in an order that is logical and coherent. The answer should be summarily restated at the end of your response. *Appropriate writing* skills require that you use complete sentences, correct punctuation, and other mechanics of good writing.

Ethics, Human Subjects, and Informed Consent

The following section presents information about the ethics involved in doing research with human subjects. It also provides information about what is involved in both a Human Subjects Review Committee Application and in an informed consent form.

It has been our experience that many students today are concerned with issues involving the risks to and the rights of potential subjects in psychological and other research. Many of them have had experience as subjects participating in our research projects. It is in their best interest and ours to provide them with information so that they can understand the issues involved.

ETHICAL PRACTICES IN RESEARCH WITH HUMAN SUBJECTS[1]

There are four issues of major importance in conducting research with human subjects:

1. Informed consent is required from the subject prior to any psychological testing. In doing research with children, written consent of the parents is required. Informed consent means that the purpose of the research and the procedures involved have been explained to the parents and that they understand what is involved and agree to allow their child to participate in the study. The procedures should then be explained to the child at the child's level of understanding, the child's cooperation should be enlisted, and an attempt should be made to maintain the child's interest during his or her participation in the project. Parents must be informed that both they and their child have the right to withdraw from participating at any time for any reason.

2. A Human Subjects Review Committee, by that or some similar name, exists at all institutions that do research with human subjects to evaluate the research projects and to safeguard the rights and the safety of potential subjects. Determinations of such review committees are usually based, in part, upon the possible use of deception and any potential risk to subjects. The concept of informed consent assumes that the real purpose of the experiment has been revealed to subjects and that the subjects are competent to decide whether or not to participate. This condition is violated when the experiment requires deception of the subject. None of the projects in this study guide require deception of the subjects. The second problem is possible risk to subjects. None of the projects presented here involve risk to the subjects. However, they do not provide positive benefits to the subjects either; they are neutral.

3. The requirement for informed consent is violated when coercion is used on subjects because, when coercion is used, subjects are not free to refuse to participate. This freedom to refuse must be guaranteed to the subjects. When working with children as subjects, it is necessary to make the study as playful and gamelike as possible to enlist the interest of children. However, their rights to refuse to participate and to not be coerced must also be respected and protected.

4. Privacy and confidentiality must be guaranteed. It is important to inform the parents that, in any report of the information gained, their child will not be identified by name but only by averages or identifiers that cannot be traced to the individual child. The child's privacy will be protected. This requires that, when you present data in class, you report the data only by age and sex of the child, never by name.

HUMAN SUBJECTS INFORMATION

Your school should have forms available to use for the submission of research studies to the Human Subjects Review Committee on your campus. The kind of information generally required on these forms includes:

1. A description of the purpose of the research and a detailed description of the procedures used, including potential hazards and benefits to the subjects.
2. A copy of the informed consent form that subjects will sign, along with a description of the way in which their consent will be elicited.
3. A description of any possible harm (emotional or psychological) might come from participation in the project.
4. A description of the subjects to be seen, including number, age, and other characteristics.

---

[1]Carroll, M. A., Schneider, H. G., & Wesley, G. R. (1985). *Ethics in the practice of psychology.* Englewood Cliffs, N.J.: Prentice-Hall.

It is also possible that your school allows, as many do, for entire study guides such as this one to be submitted for consideration so that all the research exercises can be considered at once. This is a great convenience. Ask whether your school has such a policy.

INFORMED CONSENT FORM

The informed consent form that parents sign should include several kinds of information:

1. A description of the procedures and the purpose of the study.
2. A statement of the rights of the subject to refuse to participate and to withdraw from participation at any time.
3. A statement guaranteeing the privacy and confidentiality of the results of the study. This usually involves a statement saying that results will not be reported by name and that any identifying information will be omitted from the report.
4. A description of any possible risks or discomforts that the subject might experience.
5. A description of any possible benefits to be expected for the subject. In the exercises presented in this study guide, the benefits tend to simply be the enjoyment of playing some of the games.

It is very likely that your school has such a form already prepared for use by faculty researchers. You can use the same form.

The Nature of Child Development

1 Introduction

SUGGESTIONS FOR LECTURE TOPICS

1. Behaviorist Pioneer John B. Watson

John Broadus Watson, a methodological behaviorist, was born in Greenville, South Carolina in 1878. He did both doctoral and post-doctoral work at the University of Chicago and also taught at this college. His research at the University of Chicago involved the physiology of animal behavior, and his observations of the animals became the foundation for his behavioristic theories.

Watson moved to Johns Hopkins University in 1908, and this setting was where some of his most important writing was done. He advocated both behavioristic ideas and the need for psychology to become an objective, experimental science emphasizing the goals of predicting and controlling behavior. In 1914 he suggested that psychologists should only study overt animal behavior, and his position increased psychological study of rats, pigeons, and other animals. Some contemporary psychologists were resistant to this trend; **Gordon Allport,** for example, stated that psychology was unfortunately becoming the **"psychology of white rats."**

Watson's popularity led to his election to the presidency of the American Psychological Association in 1915. His presidential address was about combining his behavioristic concepts with the classical conditioning concepts of **Ivan Pavlov.**

Watson next turned his attention to applying behaviorism to childrearing, and one of his most famous studies involved the classical conditioning of fears in **"Little Albert."** Watson wrote the "bestselling" childcare book *Psychological Care of the Infant and Child;* many of the concepts in this book are not advocated today, such as letting infants "cry it out," strict schedules, and unemotional parenting.

By 1917, Watson was studying the human sexual response. Because this was the Victorian era, his work was less accepted than the work done later by **Alfred Kinsey** or by **Masters and Johnson.** Unfortunately, Watson chose to include himself and his female laboratory assistant as subjects in his study of the human sexual response during intercourse. His wife sued him for divorce and had all of his research records confiscated and destroyed. Watson was dismissed from Johns Hopkins University and did not find work at another college. He married his research assistant and went to work for a private industry, where he applied behaviorism to public relations and advertising techniques. His research included marketing demographics and the use of subliminal advertising. (*Source:* Simons, J. A., Irwin, D. B., & Drinnin, B. A. 1987. *Instructor's Manual to Accompany Psychology, the Search for Understanding,* St. Paul: West Publishing.)

2. Freud and His Contemporary Philosophers

Many students believe that **Sigmund Freud** was the first to propose the importance of the unconscious, sexuality and aggression, and human irrationality when, actually, the philosophers of his time shared these ideas.

Arthur Schopenhauer was a nineteenth century philosopher who believed that people were irrational beings guided by internal forces of which they possessed only vague awareness. Schopenhauer also believed that sexual behavior was governed by a primary, primitive drive for copulation.

Nineteenth century philosopher **Eduard von Hartmann** believed that the unconscious mind influenced everyday behavior.

Friedrich Nietzsche believed that human beings operated by self-deception. He also stated that the two biological drives of sex and aggression distorted all conscious thought. (*Sources:* Hogan, R. 1986. What every student should know about personality psychology. In V. P. Makosky, *The G. Stanley Hall Lecture Series, Vol. 6.* Washington, D. C.: American Psychological Association.)

3. Stanley Hall (1846-1924)

About the psychologist: Although the word "adolescence" has ancient roots in the Latin word for growth, the word itself is a twentieth century phenomenon—it was coined by G. Stanley Hall, who is considered the founder of adolescent psychology. Hall believed that adolescence was a stormy and stressful developmental stage; current research suggests that a significant minority of the adolescent population has a "stormy adolescence."

Hall is also remembered for his experimental work in child development, and for pioneering the study of aging with a book written when he was nearly 80 years old. Although he began his research with case studies, Hall knew he needed large numbers of subjects in order to have representative data. To acquire the necessary data, Hall devised the questionnaire method, now an important research method in all the social sciences. Although best-known for his study of children and teenagers, Hall was important to the whole of psychology and was one of the founders of the American Psychological Association. Here are some quotes from Hall's *Adolescence* (1904):

". . . every step of the upward way is strewn with wreckage of body, mind, and morals."

"The teens are emotionally unstable and pathic. It is a natural impulse to experience hot and perfervid psychic states, and it is characterized by emotionalism."

"Normal children often pass through stages of passionate cruelty, laziness, lying and thievery."

4. A Look at One Hundred Year Old Predictions

Psychologists often compare historical effects on our development and come up with interesting trends. However, it is a harder task for scientists to understand how development will be affected in the future because people generally do poorly in predicting what events and social policy will occur in the future. This flaw becomes apparent when hearing predictions made in 1893 (in a ten-week series by the American Press Association around the time of the 1893 Chicago World's Fair) about what society will be like in 1993. Although a few have come true, most have not; moreover, we cannot tell which of our predictions will be correct. (*Source:* Walter, D. 1993. *Today Then.* American World and Geographic Publishing.)

"By 1993, the saloon is certain to be outlawed in America."—Thomas Dixon, Jr., minister

"Longevity will be so improved that 150 years will be no unusual age to reach."—Thomas De Witt Talmadge, theologian

". . . women shall have the sole right to say when she shall wear the crown of motherhood."—Mary E. Lease, reformer

"Women will never want the right of suffrage."—Bill Nye, humorist

"In the next century, the time of daily toil will be shortened to four or five hours. All willing hands will be employed."—W. A. Peffer

"Men and children, as well as women, will know how to cook."—John Habberton, editor-author

"By 1993, a traveler will be able to have his breakfast in New York City and his evening meal in Chicago."
    —H. Walter Webb, railroad executive

5.   The Concepts of Development and Interaction

One of the ways in which developmental psychology is distinct from other areas in psychology is its focus on a special kind of behavioral and psychological change. Developmental change is said to be different from other types of change such as learning and maturation.
        Give a lecture that explores the nature of developmental change, its causes, and what distinguishes it from other types of change. Although there are different views about what characterizes developmental change, consider these four features: Developmental change (a) is orderly; (b) is relatively long lasting; (c) produces something that is new or qualitatively different from what was present earlier; and (d) results in superior functioning. Elaborate and exemplify each of these points with brief descriptions of material that you will cover in the course. Motor development is an excellent vehicle, as are Piaget's theory and material on language development.
        After characterizing development, discuss causes of development. Consider these possibilities: (a) heredity; (b) biological maturation; (c) psychological change; and (d) environmental forces. Then address the question of whether any one of these causes is more important than any other. In this context begin a treatment of the concept of interaction as a way to understand development (see class activities below for a useful illustration). Useful

examples include phenylketonuria, language development, Vygtosky's theory of the proximal zone of development, the concept of critical period, gene interactions - in fact, virtually any developmental topic.

6.   Studies of Mother-Newborn Bonding

In the late seventies reform of hospital procedures for handling births received strong impetus from the claims made by pediatricians Klaus and Kennel that mother's needed immediate contact with their newborn babies to bond properly with them. Use this work as the basis of one of your early lectures to illustrate the potential influence of developmental psychology on policies and practices for raising children. Describe the original work, and either describe or discuss appropriate applications of it to or with the class, assuming that the findings were valid.

Then mention that the original work quickly became controversial. Invite the class to criticize it. Eventually, discuss its shortcomings and talk about subsequent research that essentially disconfirmed Klaus and Kennel's findings. An interesting point to pursue, however, is that parents and hospitals alike continue to stress the value early parent-infant contact anyway to their developing relationship. Discuss why.

This lecture provides a good opportunity to illustrate the potential contributions of developmental psychology, the importance of good research methodology, and the place that values have in both research and practice. You may also find it to be a good vehicle for further illustrating concepts and issues you have raised in the other lectures suggested here.

7.   Observation in Child Psychology

Present an overview of the importance of observational methodologies in life-span developmental psychology. Begin by defining the technique. Focus on observation as a means of identifying patterns and regularities in behavior that invite explanation. Relate this to the process of discovery in all of the sciences, drawing on examples from physics, chemistry, biology, and other sciences.

Explore some of the early observational work. Darwin is a good example, whom you may want to parallel with other baby biographers of the late 19th and early 20th century (e.g., Piaget). Identify example regularities such people noticed and felt needed explanation. Comment on how pervasive observational work is in child psychology, and therefore how important it is to understand how it is done. An interesting point to discuss here is the fact that observational work has made something of a comeback in child psychology because researchers are in search of new ideas about various aspects of development.

Finally, explore some of the difficulties of doing observational work. How do observers decide what to look at? How do they record all the information they need? How do they know their observations are accurate? What are the limitations of observational strategies? Depending on time constraints, this may be a good time to deal with such concepts as reliability and validity, or as a point of departure for talking about other research strategies.

BROWN & BENCHMARK'S HUMAN DEVELOPMENT TRANSPARANCIES (2ND ED.)

The transparency set, a supplement to *Child Development*, is accompanied by an annotated manual that describes each of the 141 transparencies. The annotated manual also offers suggestions about how to use the transparencies to engage your students in active learning that will stimulate critical thinking and evaluative skills. The following transparencies are appropriate and useful with Chapter 1: Introduction.

Transparency Number and Title

1   A Garden's Diversity
2   Changes in Ethnic Populations in the United States
3   Daily Statistics
4   Traditional and Life-Span Perspectives of Development
5   The Life-Span Perspective's Characteristics
6   Life-Span Considerations Across Development
10   Biological, Cognitive, and Socioemotional Processes in Life-Span Development
11   Periods and Processes in the Life Span
133   Prenatal Development
134   Infant Development
135   Early Childhood Development
136   Middle and Late Childhood Development
137   Adolescent Development

CLASSROOM ACTIVITIES OR DEMONSTRATIONS

1. You may want to discuss the critical thinking exercises on three different occasions: when you assign them, while students are doing them, and after students have completed them. Chances are that students will not be familiar with these exercises and will need support from you as they get used to doing them.

    When you first assign critical thinking exercises, make sure that students understand that they are to both identify the best answer and the answers that are not as good. Also, they must give their reasons for both types of decision. If you wish, emphasize that their reasoning behind the decisions is really the most important part of the exercises.

    Present the first thinking exercise in class and discuss it with the class. Verify that they know what it means to argue for and against answers. You may want to give tips about how to do that. In particular, stress that you are not interested in opinions or feelings, but that you want logical arguments that apply concepts or evidence to the problem posed in the exercise.

    For the first two exercises for Chapter 1, you may want to review the concepts students need to understand in order to do exercise. You will find that students are often uncertain of the distinction between continuity and discontinuity, for example, and are apt to confuse descriptions of each. In another vein, they will probably have difficulty (at first) understanding what it means to emphasize "a determinant or aspect of development." You may want to work on examples with them.

    For the third exercise, students will be eager to know what the differences are between assumptions, inferences, and observations. You will find it challenging to explain them. While your own understanding of these terms is probably the best place to start, you might suggest the following: Assumptions are guiding beliefs, values, or convictions that motivate or structure a presentation in the book. They are points the author implicitly or explicitly takes for granted and neither attempts to document nor defend with reasons. Inferences are reasoned guesses, predictions, explanations, or conclusions. They typically are interpretations or extrapolations from assumptions or observations; as such, they are bracketed by arguments or references to research findings. Observations are research findings stated in terms of the specific information researchers gather. They typically describe conditions, associations in data, or respondents' performances.

    During the time when students are working on the exercises (presumably out of class), you may want to devote some class time to having them work together. Have them form groups of three and four, and encourage them to share their ideas and argue their points of view. Circulate among the groups to listen to their discussions, and possibly deal with difficulties or confusions they are having with the assignment.

    When students turn the assignments in, again have them form groups to discuss the exercises. This time the objective is for each group to reach a consensus on the answers. Allow 5 to 10 minutes for this activity, then poll the groups to find out what each thought was the best answer. From there, have people present their arguments for and against the alternatives.

    You should find that over the course of the term this becomes a spontaneous activity among your students when they arrive at class. That may make it a "natural" activity, or it may afford you clues about material that students would especially like to discuss.

    These suggestions will not be repeated in subsequent chapters, but they are applicable to each. When appropriate we will suggest specific points you may want to explore with students before, during, or after they have completed assignments.

2. Discuss students' research projects. Suggestions for doing so are listed with the projects suggested below.

3. Here is a way to discuss original sin, tabula rasa, and innate goodness. First have students compare the assumptions and beliefs involved in the three major philosophical views of original sin, tabula rasa, and innate goodness. For each philosophical position discuss, (1) how followers would design educational systems; (2) what advice they would put in a parenting guidebook; (3) what kinds of governmental policy would be backed.

Source: Adapted from King, M. B. & Clark, D. E. 1989. *Instructor's Manual to Accompany Santrock & Yussen's Child Development: An Introduction,* 4th ed., Dubuque, IA: Wm. C. Brown.

---

4. Teaching the concept of interaction, which is fundamental to most of developmental psychology, is one of the more difficult tasks in an introductory course. A demonstration that makes the concept more concrete has been suggested by David Miller. The basic metaphor uses flour as genetic material and different types of cooking as variations in experience.

In the context of a lecture on or discussion of the concept of interaction, exhibit the ingredients of several types of baked goods in class and mix them on paper plates. Explain how the items would be cooked, then pull out examples of each "developmental outcome." Miller reports that students find the "demonstration particularly informative if not amusing" (p. 148). For further discussion and suggestions, see Miller, D. B. (1988). The nature-nurture issue: Lessons from the Pillsbury doughboy. *Teaching of Psychology, 15,* 147-149.

5. Create three lists on the blackboard: 1900-1929; 1930-1959; 1960-1989; have students come up with aspects of life that were common to each of these eras (this task can also be done by each decade if preferred). Suggestions are made here (see next page), but each class will develop a unique list. Have students discuss how these aspects would have influenced one's life. Pick one era and discuss how this era has impact on current times. The Sanoff (1990) article listed below provides ideas on how the 1950's Cold War influences the 1990s.

1900 -1929	1930 -1959	1960 -1989
Sarsaparilla	Cola	Diet Cola
Homemade cookies	Ice cream	Junk food
Roast beef	Macaroni & cheese	Pizza
Honey	Sugar	Artificial sweeteners
Main St. shops	Downtown dept. stores	Suburban malls
Fels Naphtha	Power cleansers	Detergents
Automobiles	Television	Air-conditioning
Potato peeler	Can opener	Food processor
Strolling	Walking	Jogging
Radio		Movies TV/VCR
Raggedy Ann	Shirley Temple	Barbie
Waltz		Swing Rock 'n' roll
Tuberculosis	Polio	V.D.
Croquet	Swimming	Tennis

Sources: Simons, J. 1990. Generational effects: A class activity. Unpublished exercise. Central Iowa Psychological Services; The facts of life, *Good Housekeeping,* February 1990, 112 -114; Sanoff, A. P. 1990 (June 18) The cold war's cultural legacy. *U.S. News & World Report,* 48 -50.

6. Get a class discussion going on expectations about the future. Is life going to get better or worse? Will the economy improve or get worse? Will illnesses be cured? What problems will be alleviated, and what problems will get worse? In the discussion, you might get a sense of whether the class matches a 1989 Gallup poll in which the majority of Americans (54%) expected to have an improvement in their own personal financial picture while only a minority (25%) thought the nation would get better off. Why would such a belief exist?

    What political changes will there be? Over the next 60 years will there be a woman, Black, Asian, Hispanic, or homosexual who is the president of the United States? Will there be contact with intelligent aliens from outer space? Will we solve our concerns with the supply of natural resources such as oil and coal? Will all plant and animal species on earth be identified and catalogued? And, if so, is it because of advances in science or because pollution will kill off so many species? Will there be new entertainment forms such as 3-D holographic movies or lunar space vacation trips?

    To illustrate how quickly Zeitgeist can modify the world, talk about the radical changes in Eastern Europe that occurred in 1989 and 1990; the toppling of the Berlin Wall and internal changes in the political structures of Romania, Poland, East Germany, and so on. Update this struggle, perhaps using the 1990 quote of Romanian prime minister Petre Roman, "From a democracy to a dictatorship, sometimes you need a day. From a dictatorship to a democracy, the way is very much longer."

Chapter 1

Sources: Economic predictions: "Personal future seems brightest." 1989 (October). *Psychology Today,* 16; McKinney, K. 1990 (January). "The oracle at Shattuck." *Omni,* 18; Nordland, R. 1990 (April 30). "Learning to breathe free." *Newsweek,* 38-40.

7.   Have the class discuss their beliefs on whether human development is continuous or discontinuous. Do they believe that infant and early-childhood experiences and qualities predict aspects of adolescence and adulthood? Do they lean toward Freud's concept that adult personality is basically formed by age 6 years?

Are current preferences in art, music, reading, and television influenced by early exposure? Or, is there a lot of discontinuity in human development? Why don't early intelligence scores predict adolescent IQs?

Source: Kagan, J. 1984. *The nature of the child.* New York: Basic.

8.   A survey was done of fourteen child development textbooks published between 1941 and 1980. The following psychologists were cited the most frequently and can therefore be viewed as the foundation of child developmental researchers/theorists: Jean Piaget, Erik Erikson, Arnold Gesell, Harry Harlow, Robert Sears, Rene Spitz, Philip Aries, Karl Lorenz, Sigmund Freud, B. F. Skinner, Noam Chomsky, Wayne Dennis, Barbara Inhelder, Alfred Kinsey, H. Rheingold, Nancy Bayley, John Bowlby, Eleanor Gibson, J. P. Guilford, M. Honzik, Mary C. Jones, and Paul Mussen.

Have students try to identify each of these. What topics did they concentrate on? What kinds of research did they do (e.g., experimental, case studies, correlational)? What theoretical perspective did they hold? Which of them are referenced in their current textbook? Have most/all of them remained important in the last three decades?

You (or the students if they have some psychology background) could speculate on what names would be included if the survey was done on textbooks published in the 1990s. For example, Lawrence Kohlberg, Sandra Scarr, Nancy Eisenberg, David Elkind, James Marcia, Robert Sternberg, Howard Gardner, Carol Gilligan, Eleanor Maccoby, Sandra Bem, John Flavell, and T. Berry Brazelton might be some of the names on an updated list.

Source: Hogan, J. D. & Vahey, M. A. 1984. Modern classics in child development authors and publications. *The Journal of Psychology, 116,* 35-38.

9.   The first suggestion for involving the students in the material is more of an out-of-class assignment but it is very beneficial for giving the material some relevance. Instruct students to spend at least five hours with a child who is 5 years old or younger and at least five hours with an adult who is 60 years old or older over the course of the semester. Ask them to observe the behavior of individuals in the different age groups and keep a journal of their observations. Different age groups can be used; however, most students are relatively good at observing their own behavior and the behavior of their parents, and these two age groups will maximize their exposure to the life span.

Examples of types of visits with children:

1.   special time with their own child
2.   time with a niece or nephew
3.   time with a friend's child
4.   time with a child from a local preschool
5.   time at a preschool playground
6.   time at a mall or Sunday school

Chapter 1

Examples of types of visits with older adults:

1. time with parents or grandparents, if they are over 65
2. phone conversations with grandparents
3. time in a Senior Center
4. time in a mall observing people over 60
5. time with anyone over 60

During the visits with the children, the students are to try to

1. determine what level or stage of development they are experiencing.
2. compare their experience at that age with the experience of the child they are observing.
3. try to understand the child's vision of the future.

During the visits with the adults the students are to try to

1. determine what level or stage of development they are experiencing.
2. compare their experience at 18 to 20 with the older adult's experience at 18 to 20.
3. compare their expectations of being 60 with what the older adult is experiencing.
4. try to compare their vision of the future with the older adult's vision of the future.

Keep the assignment as flexible as possible and encourage students to share their experiences with each other and in the classroom when appropriate. Collect the journals a couple of times during the semester to make sure the students are on the right track and are not waiting until the last week to do the assignment. Most student feedback about the assignment is very positive.

Source: Temple, Lori L. (1992). *Instructor's Course Planner to accompany Life-span Development,* Fourth Edition by John W. Santrock, William C. Brown Communications, Dubuque, Iowa.

---

10. This activity can be used with Chapter 1 or Chapter 2, and as such can be useful for making the transition between these chapters. Notice that students can answer most of the questions with Chapter 1 as the background, but that answers to questions (d) - (h) will be enhanced by reading Chapter 2.

    One week before you want to use this in class, have students find two or three articles on human development from parenting or other popular magazines. They should bring the magazine issue or copies of the specific articles to class and be ready to tell other students (in small groups if desired) the following information about their articles:

    a. Who is the audience for the articles (e.g., parents, teachers, adolescents)?
    b. What is the topic of the article? What are some examples of information provided?
    c. Does the article emphasize heredity (nature) or environment (nurture)?
    d. What theoretical perspective does the author seem to use (e.g., psychoanalytic, behavioral, humanistic, biological, cognitive, ecological)?
    e. Does the article rely on scientific findings, expert opinion, or case example?
    f. Do the conclusions of the articles seem valid?

On articles as a whole, ask students to address these issues.

    g. Which theoretical perspectives seem to be most popular with these magazines?
    h. What topics seem to be getting the most coverage in the magazines?
    i. Are most articles well-done and useful?

Source: Simons, J. A., 1990. Evaluating psychological value of magazine articles. Central Iowa Psychological Services.

CRITICAL THINKING EXERCISES

Exercise 1

Chapter 1 of *Child Development* opens with an essay on how modern times are "the best of times and the worst of times for children." Which of the following philosophical views seems to be implied as a basis for understanding child development by this summary of modern paradoxes in child-rearing? **Circle the letter of the best answer and explain why it is the best answer and why each other answer is not as good.**

A. original sin
B. tabula rasa
C. innate goodness
D. childhood as a unique and eventful period of life
E. a combination of two of these views

Exercise 2

In Chapter 1 of *Child Development* Santrock describes some contemporary concerns in the study of child development. These concerns reflect a larger emphasis on one of the following determinants of development than on the others. Which one is it? **Circle the letter of the best answer and explain why it is the best answer and why each other answer is not as good.**

A. cognitive processes
B. nurture
C. maturation
D. discontinuity
E. change

Exercise 3

Turn to pages 7-8 of Chapter 1 and read the paragraph about the "tapestry of American culture." This discussion about cultural diversity in the United States contains a number of observations, assumptions, and inferences. Which of the following statements constitutes an assumptions rather than an inference or an observation? **Circle the letter of the best answer and explain why it is the best answer and why each other answer is not as good.**

A. Ethnic minority groups comprise 20% of the children and adolescents under the age of 17 in the United States.
B. There will be difficulties in the year 2000 because the balance of ethnicities will change.
C. Ethnic minorities find themselves on the bottom of the economic and social order.
D. Schools, social services, colleges and other programs are not as sensitive as they should be to ethnic differences.
E. Knowing about ethnic differences will make people more sensitive to minority group members

ANSWER KEYS FOR CRITICAL THINKING EXERCISES

Exercise 1

A. Original sin is not the best answer. There is no mention of the inheritance of good and bad characteristics in the discussion; and the focus is on environmental, not hereditary conditions of child development.
B. Tabula rasa is not the best answer, although it is close, because the focus of the essay clearly is on the paradoxical set of environmental influences on contemporary child development. The reason we argue for (E), though, is the idea that these are especially good and bad times for children - adults (and adolescents) are not mentioned, implying (by omission) that modern times have a special influence on children.
C. Innate goodness is not the best answer. Nothing is said about possible enduring adaptive, balancing, and "good" reactions children might have in the face of contemporary developmental challenges.
D. This is not the best answer for the same reason that (B) is not - it is incomplete. This answer does refer to the fact that modern times seem to be especially challenging to individuals at a given developmental level, but omits the stress on environment the "Images" essay conveys.

E.   This is the best answer. As indicated in (B) and (D) above, the essay seems to imply that challenging environmental conditions impinge on an unformed nature in opposite ways, but that the challenge of these contradictions is most severe during childhood.

Exercise 2

A.   Cognitive processes is not the best answer. If this were so, the issues Santrock raised would have concerned how changes in thought, intelligence, or language influence the behavior of a child or the quality of a child's adaptation to the environment. But the contemporary concerns - changes in the family, educational reform, and sociocultural issues - are aspects of the child's environment and how they potentially influence child development.
B.   Nurture is the best answer. As indicated in "A," the focus of the contemporary concerns is children's environments and how they affect children. These are explicitly listed in the text as examples of the "nurture" side of the nature-nurture controversy.
C.   Maturation is not the best answer. Maturation refers to genetic and biological development influences on behavior. This would entail a focus on heredity and, perhaps, genetic engineering as a means of enhancing child development outcomes. But instead the focus is on improving children's environments to enhance developmental outcomes.
D.   Discontinuity is not the best answer. If this were the concern, much would be said about the value of describing child development as a series of stages or about developing the notion of childhood as a distinct stage from adulthood. This is not the sense of the contemporary concerns at all.
E.   Change is not the best answer. If it were, the issue would be that patterns of behavior expressed early in a child's life are not especially predictive of later developmental outcomes. Again, the emphasis is on environmental conditions that promote optimal developmental outcomes.

Exercise 3

A.   This is not the best answer because it is an observation. The statement represents a "fact" determined by census, and therefore it counts as an observation. We need not accept this on good faith or for the sake of argument. We can verify this statement.
B.   This is not the best answer because it is an inference. This is a projection of current population trends among various ethnic groups. Therefore it is a kind of inference: a guess or hypothesis about what will happen in the future. It is not an assumption because it is based on current information, which can be verified. But it is not an observation because it hasn't happened yet! (It is based on an assumption that current fertility rates among the various groups will remain constant, and that no other factors will interfere with reproduction within the various groups, etc.)
C.   This is not the best answer because it is an observation. This is simply a statement that can be verified by a single observation -knowing one individual who is Hispanic but not Catholic.
D.   This is not the best answer because it is an inference. The text asserts that various programs for ethnic minority individuals "need to become more sensitive to race and ethnic origin." The implication of this statement is that these programs are not as sensitive as they should be. This is therefore an inference - a conclusion that we can draw because it is a logical extension of a statement or claim of fact.
E.   This answer is the best one because it is an assumption. Nowhere in the material is it actually stated that knowing about ethnicities will make teachers more sensitive to them. But this appears to be the underlying faith of the author. It is neither given as a fact (a bit of information that we could verify by collecting data) nor as an inference (a conclusion drawn from facts or principles). Rather, it is a basic reason for presenting information about the future population mix of ethnicities. One way of demonstrating that this is an assumption is to pose the question: Would Santrock have included this information in the text if he did not believe this to be true? The likely answer is not whether or not it is actually true that future teachers become more sensitive to different ethnicities as they learn about them. This is actually an open question.

RESEARCH PROJECT 1   MONITORING CONTEMPORARY CONCERNS   IN THE MEDIA

Chapter 1 of *Child Development* indicates that significant contemporary concerns in child psychology are changes in the family, educational reform, and sociocultural issues such as gender roles and ethnic minorities. Monitor a newspaper, radio news program, or television news program for a week and keep a record of stories that reflect each of these concerns. That is, search the paper for news items or listen to news broadcasts, and make a record of stories that reflect these concerns. When you are done, tally the number of stories that reflect each concern. Then write a brief report in which you answer the following questions.

Questions

1. What was the most frequently expressed concern?
2. Were the concerns you encountered in each category focussed on one particular kind of story? Or were there a number of different kinds of news items that reflected a variety of concerns within each category? Explain your answer.
3. Did the stories reflect a life-span or developmental perspective? Or did they reflect some other way of viewing the contemporary concerns about adolescence? Explain your answer.
4. Can you find information in *Child Development* that is related to each story and that helps you to understand it better? Explain your answer.
5. What information do you wish you had in order to understand the story better?

Use in Classroom

Poll the class on their answers to the questions. Find out what the dominant concerns are, what kinds of stories express these concerns, and whether the stories are examples of the life-span or developmental perspective. Be on the lookout for how well students appear to understand text material in terms of the answers they provide, and use their answers as opportunities to affirm their understanding or to emend it.

As a means of introducing the importance of rigorous, systematic enquiry as a means of understanding adolescence, you may find it useful to contrast media presentations with textbook presentations. Have students compare and contrast topics they have found in the media with similar material, and see what they identify as important differences in the respective treatments. This should help set the stage for the subsequent material in Chapter 2 concerning the "wise consumer of information about adolescence."

RESEARCH PROJECT 2   IDENTIFYING THE DEVELOPMENTAL ISSUES IN A RESEARCH REPORT

The knowledge that forms the basis of your textbook is largely found in research reports published in professional journals. While *Child Development* provides you with an encyclopedic coverage of a many topics, you will benefit a great deal by trying to "go the source" for information about as many topics as your time and interest allow. This project suggests a way that you can use *Child Development* to help you understand formal research reports better. See also Research Project 2 in the next chapter for a similar suggestion.

Find a research report in a journal (e.g., *Adolescence, Child Development, Developmental Psychology, Family Therapy, Journal of Marriage and the Family*) on a topic that interests you. Read the article, then write a report about it in terms of the life-span perspective and the nature of development as outlined in Chapter 1 of *Adolescence*. Attach a copy of the first page of the research article (include the abstract which briefly summarizes the entire article) to your report. In addition to including the main points of the study and its findings, answer the following questions.

Questions

1. Does the article address the idea that today is "the best of times and the worst of times for adolescents"? Explain your answer.
2. Does the article help correct a stereotype about adolescents? Explain your answer.
3. Does the article contribute to our understanding of the complexity of adolescent development and sociocultural contexts? Explain your answer.
4. Which aspects of the nature of development does the article address? For example, is the research about cognitive, social, or biological processes? One or more periods of development? Does the article address such issues as maturation and experience, continuity and discontinuity, stability and change. Again, explain your answers.

Use in Classroom

Have students discuss their answers to the four questions in groups in order to discover what themes are widely present in the adolescent development literature. Have them systematically record their answers. This is a good prelude to other activities involving systematic observation, and will provide a quantitative basis for conclusions you may wish to present in class. You may discover, for example, that the concerns Santrock raises in Chapter 1 have not yet become widespread in the adolescent development literature.

ESSAY AND CRITICAL THINKING QUESTIONS

Comprehension and Application Essay Questions

We recommend that you provide students with our guidelines for "Answering Essay and Critical Thinking Questions" when you have them respond to these questions. Their answers to these kinds of questions demonstrate an ability to comprehend and apply ideas discussed in this chapter.

1. Indicate and explain what you regard as the single most important reason for studying child development.
2. Describe each of the three historical views about the nature of the child (i.e., *tabula rasa*, original sin, and innate goodness views). Also explain how one's belief in each view affects what child developmentalists do and study.
3. An important goal of *Child Development* is to provide a current and comprehensive coverage of five contemporary concerns in child development: (a) family issues and parenting, (b) sociocultural contexts, (c) education, (d) health and well-being, and (e) gender. In your own words, explain the nature and importance of each of these five contemporary concerns. Also provide one example from your own life and times that illustrates how each of the five contemporary concerns relates to you personally.
4. What do you believe is the most important social policy issue involving children today? How would you persuade the government to improve citizen's lives related to this particular issue?
5. Explain the meaning of the terms biological, cognitive, and socioemotional processes. Also give an example of each from a source other than Chapter 1.
6. Think about your life during the past 24 hours in terms of the developmental perspective. Demonstrate your understanding of periods of development by indicating one example of how you have, or could have, interacted with individuals from each of the following four developmental periods: infancy, early childhood, middle/late childhood, and adolescence.
7. Explain the controversy regarding: (a) nature versus nurture, (b) continuity versus discontinuity, and (c) early versus later experience. Also, explain why developmentalists do not adopt extreme positions on the three issues.
8. Imagine a career in life-span development. Given your abilities and interests, what you would like to do, with which age group you would like to work, and what factors will encourage or discourage you from pursuing this career.
9. Define generational inequity and explain how it relates to family policy issues.
10. Compare the United States' standings against other countries in the world in terms of "Caring for Children," and suggest ways that the United States could promote better care of its children.

Critical Thinking Questions

We recommend that you have students follow our guidelines for "Answering Essay and Critical Thinking Questions" when you ask them to prepare responses to these questions. Their answers to these kinds of questions reflect an ability to apply critical thinking skills to a novel problem or situation that is *not* specifically discussed in the chapter. These items most appropriately may be used as take-home essay questions (e.g., due on exam day) or as homework exercises that can be answered either by individuals or groups. Collaboratively answered questions encourage cooperative learning by students, and reduce the number of papers that must be graded.

1. At the end of Chapter 1 Santrock indicates books that provide practical knowledge about children and lists resources for improving the lives of children. Choose one of these books or resources and read it or learn as much as you can about it. Then write a brief review in which you (a) characterize the book or resource, and (b) explain how the book or resource relates to material in the chapter.
2. Chapter 1 defines the nature of development in terms of biological, cognitive, and socioemotional processes, and periods or stages. Indicate your ability to think critically by (a) perusing other chapters in your textbook for two examples of each process and two examples of periods or stages, and (b) explaining how and why each example illustrates the appropriate process or period.
3. According to Chapter 1, three fundamental developmental issues concern maturation (nature) versus experience (nurture), continuity versus discontinuity, and early versus later experience. Indicate your ability

to think critically by (a) perusing your textbook for two examples of each of the three defining issues, and (b) explaining how and why each of your examples illustrates the issue in question.

4. One aspect of thinking critically is to read, listen, and observe carefully and then ask questions about what is missing from a text, discussion, or situation. For example, one approach to writing a textbook such as *Child Development* is to study all of the different characteristics of successive developmental periods (e.g., infancy, early childhood, middle/late childhood, and adolescence). An alternative strategy is to study one particular aspect of development (e.g., body weight, cognition, or social interaction) chronologically from infancy through adolescence. Indicate your ability to think critically by (a) perusing your textbook to identify Santrock's approach in this book, and (b) evaluating the pros and cons of what you would learn from each approach.

5. Santrock sets off several quotations in this chapter. Indicate your ability to think critically by selecting one of the quotes and (a) learning about the author and indicating why this individual is eminently quotable (i.e., what was this individual's contribution to human knowledge and understanding), (b) interpreting and restating the quote in your own terms, and (c) explaining what concept, issue, perspective, or term in this chapter that Santrock intended this quote to illuminate. In other words, about what aspect or issue in development does this quote make you pause and reflect?

2 The Science of Child Development

SUGGESTIONS FOR LECTURE TOPICS

1. The Concept of Stage in Child Psychology

The concept of stage has long been useful in life-span developmental psychology. It appears in the earliest developmental theories and continues to be used in modern theories. However, the concept is often misunderstood and misused, and also is often the subject of controversy and debate. For example, Piaget's theory has been criticized on the grounds that cognitive development at all levels proceeds more continuously than his theory suggests.

Give a lecture that begins with an overview of the historical uses of the concept of stage. A starting point might be Hall's idea that the stages of development represent various stages of evolution, followed by a brief description of the stages identified by Gesell. These treatments will establish clearly the strongest meanings of the concept and probably also provide clear generic criticisms of the concept.

Next, distinguish various uses of the concept. These might include (a) description, or a handy way to summarize developmental events typical of given points in the life span; (b) metaphor, which chiefly involves applying analogies (which may be misleading) to periods of life ("adolescence is the spring of life"); (c) genuine theoretical statements, which indicate that there are definite periods of development characterized by the emergence of qualitatively different types of thinking or behaving - developmentally ordered periods that are distinct from others in terms of the underlying organization or principles of personality, thought, or behavior.

Finally, give examples of contemporary uses of the stage concept. You may want to draw on various theories of social cognition that extensively use the concept. Other possibilities include stages of motor development, emotional development, or newer theories of cognitive development. If time permits, you may wish to examine the extent to which the particular application you identify exemplifies one of the other of the three ways in which the stage concept is used.

2. Learning Concepts Applied

Although classical learning theories have not figured large in developmental accounts of age-related behavioral change, they have contributed greatly to techniques for managing and teaching children and to the scientific study of children's behavior. The concepts of classical and operant conditioning continue to be valuable to teachers and parents, and are enjoying a renaissance in educational practice throughout the country. A lecture/demonstration of these would therefore be highly valuable, especially because many of your students may either not know them or may misunderstand them.

Do a basic lecture (or pair of lectures) in which you define the fundamental concepts of classical and operant conditioning. Spice your treatment liberally with sample applications of the concepts to child management or teaching, and invite the class to generate its own examples. Point out how various features of behavioral control that are operating even as you speak (the students are sitting in chairs, oriented to the front of the room, writing down what you have presented on overheads - all examples of stimulus control).

Although the treatment of these concepts seems straightforward, remember that some of the concepts are usually misunderstood. In particular, students usually want to define negative reinforcement as punishment. Take care to differentiate these terms.

This lecture is most effective if you use several demonstrations or other student involvers. A few suggestions appear below, but be tireless and spontaneous in your pursuit of new and innovative ones.

3. Observation in the Work of Ethologists and Behaviorists

Compare and contrast the use of observation in the work of ethologists and behaviorists. This is a valuable exercise for further defining the nature of observational research, as well as defining these approaches to studying children.

For example, ethologists are famous for observing behavior in natural settings, whereas behaviorists are often depicted as confining their observations to laboratory settings. This is a good contrast to draw out the advantages and disadvantages of each strategy; it is also a good point to indicate that the distinction is too simple and not an accurate representation of either approach. For example, consult an educational psychology textbook for examples of natural setting observations carried out by behaviorally oriented researchers/practitioners.

Another productive comparison involves the kind of structure each perspective applies to carrying out observations. For example, both approaches are famous for insisting on concrete, replicable observational techniques that feature operational definitions of to-be-observed behavior. However, they diverge widely in how they structure the sequence of observations. For example, the prototypical ethologist attempts to approach an observation without preconceptions about the meaning or sequence of events, whereas the behaviorist explicitly examines events for antecedent stimuli, target behavior, and consequences. Drawing this comparison out shows how observations are influenced by one's theoretical stance and other observer characteristics, as well as the formal organization of techniques for carrying out observations.

Another useful comparison is the extent to which ethologically motivated observers are willing to draw conclusions about the meaning of behavior in contrast with behaviorally oriented observers. An excellent example here is the study of attachment, which has been a focus of controversy between these points of view.

4.   Early Criticism of Animal Research

The current debate between animal psychologists were often criticized during the Victorian **antivivisectionist movement.** Always the debate has centered on issues of justifying animal research for its implications in application and accumulation of new knowledge vs. views that the research is both trivial and inhumane.

The humane and antivivisection movements originated in nineteenth-century England. In 1822, Parliament approved a bill providing penalties for cruelty to animals, and the **Society for the Prevention of Cruelty to Animals** was founded in London on June 16, 1824. The first state to pass a bill forbidding cruelty to animals was New York, in 1828. The **American Society for the Prevention of Cruelty to Animals** (ASPCA) was founded on April 21, 1866 by Henry Bergh. Meanwhile, the middle of the nineteenth century marked the development of experimental physiology, which relied heavily on animal subjects.

William James, the founder of American psychology, wrote on several occasions about the need for animal experimentation, and also the need to have some regulation and avoid excesses. James wrote, "Vivisection, in other words is a painful duty," and "Man lives for sciences as well as bread . . . To taboo vivisection is then the same thing as to give up seeking after a knowledge of physiology; in other words, it is sacrificing a human intellectual good, and all that flows from it, to a brute and corporeal good."

John Dewey viewed animal experimentation as a duty, both to avoid experimentation upon human beings and for acquiring useful information. Dewey wrote in 1926, "Scientific men are under definite obligation to experiment upon animals so far as that is the alternative to random and possible harmful experimentation upon human beings, and so far as such experimentation is a means of saving human life and of increasing human vigor and efficiency."

John Bascom, who authored the earliest North American comparative psychology text, favored restricting vivisection so that pain was reduced to the lowest possible, experiments did not get repeatedly done, and experiments that were done were on important issues.

Both **John B. Watson** and **Ivan P. Pavlov** were heavily attacked in the media for animal research. Watson did some important studies with white rats to determine the sensory bases used in negotiating mazes. In his research, Watson did surgical operations (always under anesthesia) that included removal of eyes, destruction of the eardrum, removal of olfactory bulbs, and anesthetization of the rats' soles. Media comments included "killer of baby rats"; "I do not see that Prof. Watson has proved anything new by torturing the rat"; and "Now, if the same experiments were tried on the inspired Watson himself the results would be better, as he could tell us all about it. But he prefers to keep his eyes in his own head. So would the rats."

Pavlov justified his work with animals by saying "the human mind has no other means of becoming acquainted with the laws of the organic world except by experiments and observations on living animals." He also said, "When I dissect and destroy a living animal, I hear within myself a bitter reproach that with rough and blundering hand I am crushing an incomparable artistic mechanism. But I endure in the interest of truth, for the benefit of humanity." Yet critics wrote comments about Pavlov such as "The physical researchers probably enjoyed it, so it was not a useless experiment," and "The professor seems to be a humane man. Otherwise he would most likely have tied a tin can to the dog's tail, also."

One of the outcomes of the earlier animal rights and antivivisection movement was that in 1925 the American Psychological Association appointed a committee on animal experimentation to establish research guidelines for animal studies. Today the **APA Committee on Animal Research and Ethics** (CARE) serves the dual purpose of setting standards for animal use in research, and working to ensure the continuance of humane animal research. (*Source:* Dewsbury, D. A. 1990 (March). Early interactions between animal psychologists and animal activists and the founding of the APA committee on precautions in animal experimentation. *American Psychologist,45,* 315-327.)

5.   Subjects' Biases

[Note: To have a demonstration of the biasing effect of a seemingly random number, give half of the class one set of these two problems and the other half the remaining set. Set A: 1. Without figuring the answer out (answering within five seconds), how much is 8 x 7 x 6 x 5 x 4 x 3 x 2 x 1? 2. Given that there are 1,000 annual cases of electrocution, how many people do you think die from fireworks each year? Set B: 1. Without figuring the answer out (answering within five seconds), how much is 1 x 2 x 3 x 4 x 5 x 6 x 7 x 8? 2. Given that there are 50,000 annual deaths from car accidents, how many people do you think die from fireworks each year?]

Research subjects have biases that affect their responses to surveys and other psychological research. The **"better-than-average"** is the tendency of people to believe that they are better than average. For example, in a study of 829,000 high school seniors asked to rate their ability to get along with others, not one person gave a self-rating of below average. In fact, 60 percent ranked their abilities in the top 10 percent and 25 percent ranked themselves in the top 1 percent (Myers, 1980).

The **"self-serving"** bias is the tendency to take credit for one's successes and to explain one's failures as externally caused. Of course, to complicate matters, some people do not take credit for their successes and may overblame failures on lack of effort or ability.

The **"false consensus effect"** is the tendency to use an egocentric bias in perception and to overbelieve that one's own view is held by the majority. For example, subjects were asked if they would give a dollar to someone who had not eaten in two days, and they were also asked to estimate the percentage of other people who would give a dollar. Subjects who indicated that they would give a dollar thought that a majority of people would also give a dollar; similarly, subjects who said they would not give a dollar believed that most people would not give a dollar (Ross et al, 1977).

Amos Tversky and Daniel Kahneman in the 1970s spun a wheel of numbers and then asked subjects to estimate the percentage of African countries that were in the United Nations. When the wheel was on 10, the average estimate was 25 percent, but when the wheel was on 65, the average estimate was 45 percent. What this research study demonstrated was the **blasting effect of a seemingly random number** (Rubin, 1990). This can be a very strong effect. For example, people were asked how many persons die from fireworks each year. If they were told that 50,000 people died in car accidents, the average guess was 331; but, if they were told that there were 1,000 cases of electrocution annually, the average guess was 77 (the actual answer was 6). Persons asked to multiply 8 x 7 x 6 x 5 x 4 x 3 x 2 x 1 gave bigger answers than those asked to multiply 1 x 2 x 3 x 4 x 5 x 6 x 7 x 8 (the right answer is 40,320).

In a study by Daniel Cervone, students were asked how many of 20 puzzles they could solve. They estimated better performance if they were first asked whether the number was above or below 18 than if they were first asked whether the number was above or below 4. Not only that, those who gave higher estimates tried to solve the puzzles longer and did get higher numbers correct. (*Sources:* Myers, D. G. 1980. *The inflated self.* NY: Seabury Press; Ross, L., Greene, D., & House, P. 1977. The `false consensus effect': An egocentric bias in social perception and attributional processes. *Journal of Experimental Social Psychology, 13,* 279-301; Wood, G. 1984. Research methodology: A decision-making perspective. Humans as biased information processors. In A. M. Rogers & C. J. Scheirer, Eds. *The G. Stanley Hall Lecture Series, Vol. 4,* Washington, D.C.: American Psychological Association; Rubin, J. 1990 (June). Weighing anchors, *Omni,* 20, 95.)

6.   The Ecological Approach and the Hutterites

Share information about the Hutterites, a group of 24,000 people living in 230 colonies in Canada and the northern United States. Have students organize this material in terms of the ecological approach.

The Hutterites live communally. Thus, they share farms, buildings, equipment, and dining halls. Their religious beliefs include adult baptism and total pacifism. Clothing is austere (e.g., women's heads, arms, and legs are always covered). Rules are strictly enforced.

A baby born into the commune is viewed as a gift from God. The mother is totally involved in the baby's first 3 months of care. After that, the mother resumes regular duties and the baby is put on a regular schedule of feeding, playing, and time alone. All members of the colony care for the baby, for children belong to the community rather than the parents.

By 3, children are taught strict obedience, and their natural "stubborn wills" are broken by threats and physical punishment. The child could be whipped for refusing to go to any adult and wanting only his biological parents, for quarreling with peers, or for not sharing. Some misbehavior is expected because of the children's nature, but conformity is insisted upon. After any punishment, a child is immediately comforted.

Between 3 and 6 years, the children attend a kindergarten in which they memorize prayers and learn obedience. Quiet cooperative behavior is praised. At 6, the children attend the community school and learn reading, writing, both English and German, religion, and community history. Praise is given for working hard, but not for being a quick learner.

At 15, Hutterites join the adult work force. There is no longer any physical punishment. Young adults must do their work and speak respectfully, yet they are allowed to quietly break minor rules (such as listening to rock music on a transistor radio with headphones). Within a few years, most of these youth decide to become full-fledged members of the colony. (*Source:* Harris, J. & Liebert, R. 1990. *The Child.* Prentice-Hall.)

7.   Crowding Research

Crowding is defined in terms of a high density of people, and can be either detrimental or pleasant. A classic crowding study was done by Calhoun (1962), who put rats into a physical environment designed to accommodate 50 rats and provided enough food, water, and nesting materials for the number of rats in the environment. The rat population peaked at 80, providing a look at cramped living conditions. Although the rats experienced no resource limitations other than space restriction, a number of negative conditions developed:

(1)   The two most dominant males took harems of several female rats and occupied more than their share of space, leaving other rats even more crowded.
(2)   Many females stopped building nests and abandoned their infant rats.
(3)   The pregnancy rate declined.
(4)   Infant and adult mortality rates increased.
(5)   More aggressive and physical attacks occurred.
(6)   Sexual variation increased, including hypersexuality, inhibited sexuality, homosexuality, and bisexuality.

Calhoun's results have led to other research on crowding's effects on human beings, and these research findings have suggested that high density is not the single cause of negative effects on humans. When crowding is defined only in terms of **spatial density** (the amount of space per person), the effects of crowding are variable. However, if crowding is defined in terms of **social density,** or the number of people who must interact, then crowding better predicts negative psychological and physical effects.

Field studies done in a variety of settings such as college dormitories, offshore oil rigs, navy ships, prisons, homes for the aged, and junior high schools, illustrate that social density is associated with negative effects such as social withdrawal and increased psychosomatic complaints. In prison studies, crowded conditions have been associated with increases in health concerns, blood pressure, discipline problems, psychiatric commitments, suicides, violent deaths, and deaths by natural causes.

Crowded individuals adjust their incoming sensations, their attitudes, and their behaviors to reduce the negative aspects of crowding. Women are more likely than men to find high density situations friendly, while men are more likely to experience aggression. This sex difference might be explained by men's greater need for personal space.

Do you believe that Calhoun's studies of crowded rats are applicable to human beings? Create some experiments which involve crowding people. Design a lab experiment or a field experiment. Design a dormitory that minimizes the negative aspects of crowding. (*Sources:* Calhoun, J. B. 1962. A behavioral sink. In E. L. Bliss (Ed.). *Roots of behavior.* New York: Harper & Row; Freedman, J. L. 1975. *Crowding and behavior.* San Francisco: W. H. Freeman; Mueller, C. W. 1984. The environment and social behavior. In A. S. Kahn (Ed.). *Social Psychology.* Dubuque, IA: Wm. C. Brown; Paulus, P. B. & McCain, G. 1983. Crowding in jails. *Basic and Applied Social Psychology, 4,* 89-107.)

8.   An Early Experiment

British adventurer James Lancaster on a return voyage from the East Indies in 1594 noticed that his crew was cured of scurvy, and Lancaster hypothesized that it was lemons that had treated **scurvy,** a disease of bleeding, pain, and anemia.

In 1601, he gave his flagship crew citrus juice each day, while sailors in the other ships did not get the citrus juice. Otherwise the diets were similar from ship to ship. Only the sailors who received citrus juice returned home without scurvy. Lancaster ran a "modern-type" experiment: randomly assigned experimental and control groups, single-blinded experiment, and all other variables held constant. (*Source:* Dobkin, B. 1990 (May). A testing time. *Discover,* 86-90.)

BROWN & BENCHMARK'S HUMAN DEVELOPMENT TRANSPARANCIES (2ND ED.)

The transparency set, a supplement to *Child Development*, is accompanied by an annotated manual that describes each of the 141 transparencies. The annotated manual also offers suggestions about how to use the transparencies to engage your students in active learning that will stimulate critical thinking and evaluative skills. The following transparencies are appropriate and useful with Chapter 2: The Science of Child Development.

Transparency Number and Title

4	Traditional and Life-Span Perspectives of Development
5	The Life-Span Perspective's Characteristics
6	Life-Span Considerations Across Development
12	Conscious and Unconscious Processes: The Iceberg Analogy
13	Erikson's Trust versus Mistrust
14	Erikson's Autonomy versus Shame and Doubt
15	Erikson's Initiative versus Guilt
16	Erikson's Industry versus Inferiority
17	Erikson's Identity versus Role Confusion
18	Erikson's Intimacy versus Isolation
19	Erikson's Generativity versus Stagnation
20	Erikson's Integrity versus Despair
21	Piaget's Stages of Cognitive Development
22	A Model of Cognition
23	A Comparison of the Stage Theories of Freud, Erikson, and Piaget
24	Bandura's Model of the Reciprocal Influence of B, P, and E
25	Bronfenbrenner's Ecological Theory
26	Psychoanalytic Theories
27	Cognitive Theories
28	Ethological Theories
29	Ecological Theories
30	Possible Explanations for Correlational Data
31	Principles of Experimental Strategy
32	A Comparison of Cross-Sectional and Longitudinal Approaches

CLASSROOM ACTIVITIES OR DEMONSTRATIONS

1. Discuss the students' research projects as suggested below.
2. Discuss the critical thinking exercises. For exercise 1, find out if students know who the "observers" are in the quote. They probably will not know, in which case you will want to explain that they were people who introspected about their mental processes in early perception and cognition experiments.

   For exercise 2, students will appreciate a careful review of the differences between correlational and experimental research; they are apt to see Chi's research as experimental work if left to their own devices. They will have little difficulty with the other concepts, but note that Chi's measures do not fit neatly any of those offered, which may entail some discussion of how to interpret Santrock's catalogue of measures.

   For exercise 3, discuss with your class the notion that assumptions are not always directly expressed, but may be very important motivations in researchers' work. That is, assumptions suggest how to solve problems and lead to choices of methods, techniques, or strategies to solve them. You can usefully relate this to the next two discussions as well as the exercise.
3. Divide the class into small discussion groups to consider the following questions: How does one's theoretical view of development affect the kinds of behaviors one notices? What behaviors would be observed by Freud, Piaget, an information processing theorist, Skinner, Bandura, and Bronfenbrenner when watching two adolescents interact in a mall? Ask each group to nominate someone to write down the results of the discussion. Allow some time for discussion and then ask the groups to report. The summary of each group's comments can be the basis for a general class discussion.

Source: King, M. B. & Clark, D. E. 1990. *Instructor's Manual to accompany Children.* Dubuque: Wm. C. Brown Publishers.

4. Have your students describe their relationships with a parent at 16 years of age and currently. How has the relationship changed? What factors in development might account for the changes? How would the different theories--psychoanalytic, behavioral, cognitive, phenomenological, and ecological--account for the differences?

Source: King, M. B. & Clark, D. E. 1990. *Instructor's Manual to accompany Children.* Dubuque: Wm. C. Brown Publishers.

5. Arnold Gesell established his clinic of Child Development at Yale in 1911. He developed the **one-way vision screen technique** to observe infants and children. Gesell's work was pioneering in describing (a) how a normal child grows and (b) how one normal child differs from another. In 1940, Gesell announced the following conclusions about children's development. Have students discuss whether they find Gesell's conclusions to be fairly accurate. Why or why not? Can they cite supporting research, or give everyday examples of these conclusions?

6. This project introduces the various theoretical perspectives, and also allows students to realize how much of the material they already know. On the blackboard, list each of the following perspectives (you may use fewer, or modify labels, to fit how you cover course material) leaving room below each to add comments:

    PSYCHOANALYTIC
    BEHAVIORAL/SOCIAL LEARNING
    COGNITIVE
    ETHOLOGICAL
    ECOLOGICAL

Then one by one have students contribute terms, ideas, and "great psychologists" associated with each. By the end of the exercise, they will be able to see some similarities and dissimilarities for each group. Here is an example of this exercise from one class:

PSYCHOANALYTIC: Freud, Adler, id, ego, superego, sex, early childhood, psychosexual stages, "mom's fault," Erikson, unconscious, defense mechanisms, dreams, Jung, Oedipal complex, birth order, sibling rivalry, inferiority, libido.

BEHAVIORAL: Skinner, Pavlov, reinforcement, punishment, imitation, Bandura, classical conditioning, operant conditioning, modeling, delay of gratification, Watson, token economy, systematic desensitization, behavioral modification, mazes, mechanistic.

COGNITIVE: Piaget, Ellis, memory, information-processing, Binet, Terman, intelligence tests, accommodation, assimilation, language, development, moral development, Kohlberg.

ETHOLOGICAL: Lorenz, split-brain, neurotransmitter, dopamine, genetics, heredity vs. environment, central nervous system, instinct, critical periods, pregnancy, genes, genetic counseling, DNA, autonomic nervous system, stress.

ECOLOGICAL: environment, culture, ethnicity.

What students offer will depend on how many psychology courses some students have had previous to this course. As an instructor, you will learn which theoretical perspectives need the most class coverage, what misconceptions the students have, and what strengths they have coming into the course.

Source: Irwin, D. B. & Simons, J. A. 1984. Theoretical perspectives class activity. Ankeny, IA: Des Moines Area Community College.

7. We are never quite sure that students have grasped the basic components of the theories involved in a discipline or that they know how the theories are the same and how they differ. To check their understanding and their ability to discriminate, use a handout that lists the theories and theorists down one side and the distinguishing characteristics of the theories across the top. The student's task is to indicate where each theorist or theory stands on each of the characteristics. With life-span developmental psychology there are many choices of theorists and many choices for distinguishing characteristics. See the following sample:

Theory	**Characteristic**		
Psychosexual (Freud)	Nature-Nurture	Continuity-Discontinuity	Early/Later Experience
Psychosocial (Erikson)			
Cognitive (Piaget)			
Learning (Skinner)			
Social Learning (Bandura)			
Ecological (Bronfenbrenner)			
Ethological (Hinde)			

Other characteristics that could be used to discriminate between the theories include determinism (yes or no), critical periods (yes or no), and the role of the participant (active or passive). Students find the activity difficult; however, answers to essay questions about the theories show that they seem to learn a lot from the exercise.

Depending on the amount of time available, the class can be divided into groups, each group given one or two theorists, then share the answers. If there is a limited amount of time, use a lecture/discussion format that encourages interaction but moves the discussion along.

8. An important concern in Chapter 2 is sexism in adolescent psychology. An interesting question to raise and discuss is whether sexism even influences the production of textbooks that strive not to be sexist! Explore *Child Development* with students in class for an answer to this question. Divide them into groups of three or four and have each group determine (or guess) the sex of all the individuals quoted in the margins of the text in several chapters. You will find that men outnumber women. Discuss this curious observation. You may also want students to inspect other aspects of the text that may reflect unintended sex biases.

9. Use either Group A or Group B as a handout or transparency in your classes. Ask each student to number the order of the items on the list from the most likely to happen (1) to least likely to happen (8). After providing the correct order and the actual odds, discuss which items surprised students. Discuss whether we use inaccurate odds in making everyday decisions. Tie this activity into the idea that some of the statistics presented throughout the textbook and in instructor's lectures may also be surprising.

GROUP A

A. Your next child would be a boy.
B. A coin will come up heads ten times in a row.
C. You will get hit by lightning.
D. A coin would come up heads.
E. You will be involved in a traffic accident this year.
F. A golf ball would land on a specified blade of grass on a fairway.
G. Your next childbirth would result in twins.
H. You will be dealt a flush in poker.

Group A Answers:

A. A (1 in 1.96)
B. D (1 in 2)
C. E (1 in 10)
D. G (1 in 98)
E. H (1 in 509)
F. B (1 in 1024)
G. C (1 in 2,000,000)
H. F (1 in 1,000,000,000)

GROUP B

- A. A bridge hand will contain one ace.
- B. A coin will come up heads 30 times in a row.
- C. Your next childbirth would be triplets.
- D. A coin would come up heads 7 times in a row.
- E. A bridge hand would contain four aces.
- F. If there are 23 people in a room, 2 would have the same birthday.
- G. You will be killed in an airline accident.
- H. You will be audited by the IRS.

Group B Answers:

- A. F (1 in 1.97)
- B. A (1 in 2.27)
- C. H (1 in 60)
- D. D (1 in 128)
- E. E (1 in 333)
- F. C (1 in 2700)
- G. G (1 in 1,000,000,000)
- H. B (1 in 1,073, 000,000)

Source: Simons, J. A. 1986. "What's the odds on this one? A classroom activity." Ankeny, IA: Des Moines Area Community College; Trefil, J. S. 1984. Odds are against your breaking that law of averages. *Smithsonian,* 66 -75.

10. Use this brief demonstration to generate a discussion about the variety of experimental design in studying a topic.

Ask two students to volunteer for this quick demonstration. Have one student stand still, and have the second student slowly approach this student. The first student should ask the second student to stop when the distance between them "feels too close to be comfortable." Let the first student make small adjustment until the distance between the two students "feels just right." Have a third student measure (with a tape measure) the number of inches between them. Repeat this procedure from the left, the right, and the back. An alternative is to divide the class in threes and have all students take turns as subjects and measurers.

Discuss the results of the demonstration in terms of comfortable **personal space.** How is personal space influenced by culture? Could students redesign this study for cross-cultural research? How might personality characteristics influence personal space? How might you study this aspect? Would specific situation influence personal space comfort? Could students redesign a field experiment to test situational aspects? Might age of subjects influence personal space needs? How could cross-sectional and longitudinal studies be used to look at this aspect? Could natural observation be used in a study of personal space? How? Could correlations and interviews be used? How?

Name some variables (e.g., gender, lighting, alcohol consumption, mood state, audience) that might influence the results on a personal space experiment. Create a hypothesis about the possible effects on personal space of one of the proposed variables. Then design a study to explore this hypothesis.

Source: Simons, J. A., Irwin, D. B., & Drinnin, B. A. 1987. *Instructor's Manual to Accompany Psychology, the Search for Understanding,* St. Paul: West Publishing.

11. Present the following situations to your students and ask them to uncover any possible sampling biases:

1. Teenage males at a movie drive-in, a local tavern, the beach, and the baseball park were surveyed about their driving records and habits. The results led researchers to some interesting conclusions about male adolescent driving abilities and habits.

2. Parents at a PTA meeting were interviewed about the quality of the public school system.
3. A telephone survey assessed a community's attitudes toward A.D.C. recipients.
4. On December 28, children were asked about their impressions of Santa Claus.
5. The elderly population of Palm Springs was sampled on the advantages and disadvantages of being old.
6. The effectiveness of a new and innovative science teaching program in the elementary schools of Ankeny, Iowa was judged by comparing their scientific knowledge on a standardized test with their peers in Brooklyn, New York.
7. Ten different churches' Sunday school classes were asked about their impressions of God, in order to understand how children from 3 to 12 develop a concept of God and religion.

Source: Simons, J. A., Irwin, D. B., & Drinnin, B. A. 1987. *Instructor's Manual to Accompany Psychology, the Search for Understanding,* St. Paul: West Publishing.

12. Newspaper and television stories of research often give vague information about the study and exaggerate cause-and-effect possibilities. Use the following news item (adapted from an actual news story), or one you find in current newspaper, to get your students to become critical evaluators of psychological and medical research reports by the popular press.

CHILDLESSNESS CAN LEAD TO HEART ATTACKS

Recent research suggests that parenthood can be good for your health, because it is related to a lower rate of heart attacks in women. Childless women over 50 are more likely than mothers over 50 to have fatal heart attacks. Researchers examined the medical records of women who died of heart attacks in one Pennsylvania county. Twelve of the 51 heart attack victims were childless. Two previous studies found similar results.

Discussion

1. What is misleading in this article?
2. What information do you wish was included?
3. What other explanations can you think of for the study's findings?
   - Women in one county may not be representative of the nation.
   - Childlessness may reflect a hormonal difference between the two groups of women.
   - Childless women experience great stress from societal pressures to bear children. Over time, this stress increases their risk of heart attacks.
   - More women who bore children may have had their heart attacks before the age of 50 rather than after 50.
   - Women who bore children may not have had better health--maybe they died of other illnesses at a higher rate.
   - Some women do not bear children because of health concerns: Later, these health concerns increase their heart attack risk.

Source: Simons, J. A., Irwin, D. B., & Drinnin, B. A. 1987. *Instructor's Manual to Accompany Psychology, the Search for Understanding,* St. Paul: West Publishing, 56-57.

13. How does zeitgeist affect research? Engage the class in a discussion about how world events may make some research topics popular for a time period. For example, after World War II and Nazi fascism, authoritarian personality and the F-scale was a popular area of research. Social upheavals such as the Vietnam War, Watergate, political assassinations, and inner-city riots might have contributed to the popularity of the research variable internal vs. external locus of control.

The discussion can be expanded to include how research is done—when is cross-cultural research popular? Have assumptions about the causes of cultural, gender, and racial differences changed over the years? How have camcorders and personal computers affected research?

Remember that many students in your class are only taking their first or second psychology course. Because of this, make sure you go into class with some specific examples or some directed questions that aid this discussion. It may be easier to have students speculate about what research topics will grow in importance (e.g., Alzheimers, blended families, drug abuse) because of today's Zeitgeist, than to have them try to figure out a "psychology history" to which they have not yet been exposed. Also, make students aware of the problems with interpreting past writings as if they were written today. Discuss the importance of knowing two kinds of historical influences: (1) **internal history,** or how psychologists influenced each other, and (2) **external history,** or how psychologists were influenced by events outside of psychology. Discuss, for example, what aspects of Victorian society and Victorian medicine influenced Freud. Then discuss what aspects of the current Zeitgeist make Freud relevant or irrelevant today.

Sources: Rotter, J. B. 1990 (April). Internal versus external control of reinforcement: A case history of a variable. *American Psychologists, 45,* 489-493; Wertheimer, M. 1984. History of psychology: What's new about what's old. In A. M. Rogers & C. J. Scheirer, Eds., *The G. Stanley Hall Lecture Series, Vol. 4.* Washington, D. C.: American Psychological Association.

14.   Would knowledge of a people's diet influence how people observe them? Students were given descriptions of fictional cultures with different eating habits and asked to describe each culture. For example, some students were told that "the Chandorans hunted marine turtles and wild boars, and they ate the wild boar and used the turtles' shells." Others were told that "the Chandorans hunted marine turtles and wild boars, and they ate the turtles and used the boars' tusks." According to the students, turtle-eaters were considered better swimmers and more generous; boar-eaters were considered more aggressive and more likely to have beards. In another version, students read about the fictional Hagi. All read that "Hagi hunted elephants and cultivated crops," but half were told "the Hagi sold the crops and ate elephant meat" and the other half were told "the Hagi sold elephant tusks and ate vegetables." Elephant-eaters were expected to have bigger builds and be less graceful than the vegetarian Hagi.

•   How might persons who are doing naturalistic observations in other cultures be initially influenced by the foods that are being consumed?
•   Do we make the same types of assumptions about the effects of food in this country? Are we different (or do we become different) if we eat Southern fried chicken, okra, biscuits and gravy and grits vs. vegetarian or Mexican tacos or Italian pasta? How might you study the effects of food on personality?
•   With other students, brainstorm a variety of ways to study the "you are what you eat" belief.
•   What impressions of Koreans do we form just knowing that the Korean diet includes dog meat? Did you know that many Koreans don't want to stop eating dog, because it is considered to be an aphrodisiac?

Source: The irrational connection between diet and demeanor. 1989 (October). *Psychology Today,* 14; Man wants to bite dog. *Time,* November 13, 1989, p. 57.

15.   Ask students to discuss their experiences in being subjects in polls. Have they participated in a psychology or sociology questionnaire in high school or college? Have they participated in a telephone survey? Have they ever mailed in a survey from a magazine or newspaper? Does anybody admit to lying on a survey? Has anybody ever been confused by the wording of the surveys? How often do they encounter surveys in their reading or television watching? To which polls (e.g., New York Times, Gallup, national television, People magazine) do they pay the most attention? Have polls results (e.g., popularity of political candidates, ratings of movies or television shows) ever influenced their behavior? How accurate do students think most polls are?

Source: Cose, E. 1990 (February 19). Do we ask too much of polls? *Time,* 78.

16. Is it ethical to use the results of unethical research? During World War II, some Nazi doctors performed cruel, mutilating experiments on Jews, Gypsies, Poles, and other political prisoners. In one study, men were immersed in ice water for five hours while physicians recorded their body temperature, respiration rates, pulse rates, and urine and blood contents. Many of the subjects in this study died during the course of this highly unethical experiment. However, results from this particular study have since been used to better understand hypothermia and how long accident victims can survive in cold water.
    Does using this data allow something good to come from horrible experimentation? Or, does using this data condone the original studies?

Source: Simons, J. A., Irwin, D. B., & Drinnin, B. A. 1987. *Instructor's Manual to Accompany Psychology, the Search for Understanding,* St. Paul: West Publishing, 56-57.

17. Have students try to explain psychoanalysis in behavioral terms, i.e., explain how the same behaviors might have been learned.
    The id operates according to the pleasure principle. The goal of the ego is to arrange for the satisfaction of id urges in the real world while avoiding danger. These principles are similar to reinforcement (reward) and the avoidance of punishment. The defense mechanisms are avoidance responses. Repression is motivated forgetting or motivated not-thinking.

Source: Adapted from King, M. B. & Clark, D. E. 1989. *Instructor's Manual to Accompany Santrock & Yussen's Child Development: An Introduction,* 4th ed., Dubuque, IA: Wm. C. Brown.

CRITICAL THINKING EXERCISES

Exercise 1

Chapter 2 presents several different schools of thought about the appropriate subject matter and methods of developmental psychology. The author of the following quote was most likely a proponent of which of the following perspectives:

"I never wanted to use human subjects. I hated to serve as a subject. I didn't like the stuffy, artificial instructions given to subjects. I was uncomfortable and acted unnaturally. With animals I was at home. I felt that, in studying them, I was keeping close to biology with my feet on the ground. More and more the thought presented itself: Can't I find out by watching their behavior everything the other students are finding out by using observers?" **Circle the letter of the best answer and explain why it is the best answer and why each other answer is not as good.**

A. cognitive
B. behavioral
C. eclectic
D. psychoanalytic
E. ecological

Exercise 2

Read the following description of a study that compared memory performances of children and adults:

Do adults remember more than children because they know more about what they are trying to remember? Would children remember more than adults if they knew more than adults did about a topic? These were questions Michelene Chi tried to answer by comparing the memory performances of children and adults with differing levels of knowledge about the information they tried to remember.
    Chi asked children from grades three through eight who were experienced chess players to study either ten numbers or the positions of chess pieces in a chess game for ten seconds. The children then tried to remember all

the numbers or the chess positions, after which they studied the items again for ten seconds. The look-recall cycle continued until the children remembered all the items. Memory performance was measured in two ways: The total number of items remembered on the first trial, and the number of trials that were needed to remember all the items.

Chi compared the children's performances on both tasks to the performances of adults who were novice chess players. The results suggested that knowledge of to-be-remembered material is important to memory. The child chess experts remembered more chess positions and needed fewer trials to achieve perfect recall than did the adult novices. On the other hand, the adults - who presumably knew more about numbers than the children - outperformed the children in both ways when remembering the numbers. (From Chi, M. T. H. (1978). Knowledge structures and memory development. In R. S. Siegler (Ed.), *Children's thinking: What develops?* Hillsdale, NJ: Erlbaum.)

Which of the following sets of terms best describes Chi's research? **Circle the letter of the best answer and explain why it is the best answer and why each other answer is not as good.**

A. cross-sectional, experimental study using interviews
B. longitudinal, correlational study using standardized tests
C. cross-sectional, correlational study using observations
D. longitudinal, experimental study using questionnaires
E. cross-sectional, experimental study using multiple measures

Exercise 3

Read the passage about Jess and his teachers that follows. Which of the following statements is most likely to have been Graubard and Rosenberg's assumption about difficult students, rather than an inference or an observation? **Circle the letter of the best answer, and explain why it is the best answer and why each other answer is not as good.**

Jess and His Teachers

Jess is an eighth grader at a junior high school in California. At 14 years old, he already weighs 185 pounds. He is the school's best athlete, but he used to get some of his biggest thrills out of fighting. Jess knocked out several fellow students with bottles and chairs and once hit the principal with a stick, for which he received a 40-day suspension from school.

Jess's teachers unanimously agreed that he was an impossible case. No one was able to control him. But one week, his teachers began to notice a complete turnabout in Jess's behavior. His math teacher was one of the first to notice the strange but improved behavior. Jess looked at her one day and said, "When you are nice, you help me learn a lot." The teacher was shocked. Not knowing what to say, she finally smiled. Jess continued, "I feel really good when you praise me." Jess continued a consistent pattern of such statements to his teachers and even came to class early or sometimes stayed late just to chat with them.

What was responsible for Jess's turnabout? Some teachers said he attended a mysterious class every day that might provide some clues to his behavior change. In that "mysterious" class, a teacher was training students in behavior modification, which emphasizes that behavior is determined by its consequences. Those consequences weaken some behaviors and strengthen others.

In an experiment, Paul Graubard and Henry Rosenberg (1974) selected seven of the most incorrigible students at a junior high school - Jess was one of them - and had a teacher give them instruction and practice in behavior modification in one 43-minute class period each day. In their daily training session, the students were taught a number of rewards to use to shape a teacher's behavior. Rewards included eye contact, smiling, sitting up straight, and being attentive. The students also practiced ways to praise the teacher, saying such things as, "I like working in this class where there is a good teacher." And they worked on ways to discourage certain teacher behaviors by saying such things as, "I just have a rough time working well when you get mad at me." Jess had the hardest time learning how to smile. He was shown a videotape of his behavior and observed that he actually leered at people when he was told to smile. Although it was somewhat hilarious, Jess practiced in front of a camera until he eventually developed a charming smile.

During the five weeks in which the students implemented their behavior-change tactics, observations indicated that teacher-student interchanges were becoming much more positive. Informal observations and comments after the program ended suggested that positive student-teacher interchanges were continuing. But what happened in the long run? In the case of this experiment, we do not know, but in many cases such behavior modification interventions do not result in long-lasting changes once the consequences for behavior are removed (Masters & others, 1988).

A. The difficult students' behavior was not caused by disturbed personalities or mental abnormalities.
B. The normal reactions of teachers reinforced the disruptive or harmful behavior of difficult students.
C. Students exerted control over their teachers' behavior.
D. Students changed the way that they interacted with their teachers.
E. The improved interaction between students and teachers continued for a short time after the students finished their behavior modification class.

ANSWER KEYS FOR CRITICAL THINKING EXERCISES

Exercise 1

A. Cognitive is not the best answer. The main reasons are (a) the speaker is mainly interested in animals, whereas cognitivists typically (though not exclusively) are interested in people, combined with (b) a focus on observing behavior. Cognitivists are interested in making inferences about the mind and studying conscious mental activity.
B. Behavioral is the best answer. The first reason is the speaker's interest in the objective study of behavior, and the second is the interest in studying animals rather than people. This seems to parallel the development of Skinner's behaviorism - though the speaker is actually John Watson.
C. Eclectic is not the best answer. This researcher focussed on the objective study of animal behavior, and explicitly eschewed alternative methods, in a fashion that indicates he does not believe that all established approaches have something to contribute to his understanding of psychology.
D. Psychoanalytic is not the best answer. Psychoanalysts are interested in people and the inner workings of their thoughts. They also do not typically rely on formal observation as a technique for finding things out, preferring instead various forms of clinical interviews or clinical devices for revealing the nature of personality and personality function.
E. Ecological is not the best answer. Bronfenbrenner's ecological theory is based on an analysis of systems of human behavior, not the observation of individuals - especially not of individual animals.

Exercise 2

A. A cross-sectional, experimental study using interviews is not the best answer. The study is cross-sectional because it compares children to adults. However, the researchers did not manipulate the independent variables (age, chess expertise), but rather selected subjects who had these characteristics. Finally, the researchers did not interview children about their performance, but rather asked them to remember as many items as they could.
B. A longitudinal, correlational study using standardized tests is not the best answer. As indicated in "A," the study used a cross-sectional design. Correlational strategy best describes the research strategy because Chi attempted to show an association (more knowledge is associated with better memory, regardless of age), but Chi did not use standardized tests to measure performance; this was measured with a recall task designed for the study.
C. A cross-sectional, correlational study using observations is the best answer. See "A" for cross-sectional and "B" for correlational study. Although the claim that Chi used observations is not exactly correct, this term better fits the kind of research she conducted than the possibilities mentioned in the alternative answers. For example, one can say that she observed how well children remembered the items by counting the number that they were able to name when asked to remember them.
D. A longitudinal, experimental study using questionnaires is not the best answer. See "B" for longitudinal and "A" for experimental study. Chi did not measure performance in terms of respondents' written responses to questions they had read.
E. A cross-sectional, experimental study using multiple measures is not the best answer. See "A" for cross-sectional and experimental. Identifying the measures as multiple measures is not correct because the term implies the use of several different types of measures, for example, combining interviews and questionnaires, or observations, interviews, and standardized tests.

Exercise 3

A. This answer is the best because it is an assumption. This appears to be a key belief of the researchers who worked with students like Jeff. If they had not believed this, they would not have focused on specific behaviors that students could change which, in turn, might change the way teachers treated them. The statement is not made explicitly in the inset, nor does it seem to be a conclusion of the research, nor is it an observation.

B.   This is not the best answer because it is an inference based on the following reasoning: The article demonstrated that a change in the students' behavior produced a change in the teachers' behavior and that, in fact, the changes reinforced each other. The suggestion is that in "normal" day-to-day interactions the specific pattern of behaviors that people engage in reinforce and maintain each other. For example, the students report things like "I have a rough time working well when you get mad at me." In order to bring about behavioral change one has to intervene in this self-maintaining pattern.

C.   This is not the best answer because it is an inference or a conclusion that one might derive from the research. The teachers' behavior changed when the students changed their own behavior. Since no other factors appear to have generated this change, the inference is that what the students did actually caused the change (controlled it).

D.   This is not the best answer because it is an observation. This is a "fact" - something deliberately done and directly observable. A teacher/trainer taught students to smile, make pleasant comments, and so on. Students' teachers in other classes then noticed these changed behaviors.

E.   This is not the best answer because it is an observation. Teachers reported informally after the study that they continued to see pleasant interactions between the so-called problem students and their teachers.

RESEARCH PROJECT 1   PARENT-CHILD INTERACTION

In this project you will observe a parent-child interaction and interpret it according to psychoanalytic, behavioral, and cognitive theoretical approaches. Go to a local supermarket, store, mall, or theater and watch a mother or father shop with a 2- to 4-year-old child. Describe the interactions you observe, including demands on the part of the child, verbal exchanges between parent and child, and ways in which the parent responds to the demands of the child. Then answer the questions that follow, referring to your observations.

Age _____   Sex _____

Description:

Questions

1.   On what would a psychoanalytic theorist focus in this example? How would the sequence of observed events be explained?
2.   How would a behavioral psychologist analyze the situation? What reinforcers or punishers characterized the interaction? Did specific things occur that would make a behavior more likely to occur in the future? Less likely to occur?
3.   On what would a cognitive theorist focus in this situation? Why?
4.   What is the teenager learning in this situation? What does the teenager already know?

Use in Classroom

Discuss the research project. Have several students present their observations to the class. Are there commonalities to the observations, or is each unique? How would the various theories interpret aspects of the interactions? Do some of the interpretations seem more comprehensive than others? Do some of the interpretations seem more reasonable than others?

RESEARCH PROJECT 2   JOURNAL ARTICLE CRITIQUE

Part of conducting psychological research is reviewing and understanding published research studies. In this research project, you will choose one of the topics that will be covered in this course (e.g., play, gender roles, moral development, effects of television) and find a research report in a journal (e.g., *Adolescence, Child Development, Developmental Psychology, Family Therapy, Journal of Marriage and the Family*) on the chosen topic. Read the article and write a report about the article. Enclose a copy of the first page of the research article (include the abstract which briefly summarizes the entire research study) with your report. In addition to including the main points of the study, give your personal reactions to the research findings.

Questions

1. Can you use the title of the study to identify the independent and dependent variables? (Many titles are in this format: "The effects of IV on the DV.")

2. What did you learn from the introduction section? What is the historical background of the research topic? Which earlier research findings are given as most relevant to this study? What theoretical explanations are emphasized in this section? What is the hypothesis of the present study?

3. What did you learn from the methods section? Who were the subjects? What procedures (e.g., apparatus, directions, assessment tools) were used?

4. What did you learn from the results section? What kinds of statistical procedures were used? What did you learn from charts, frequency tables, and bar graphs? What results did the authors say were statistically significant?

5. What did you learn from the discussion section? How did the authors interpret their results? Did they provide alternative explanations? Did they talk about the limitations of the present research study? What future research studies were suggested?

6. What kinds of ideas did this article make you think about? Can you design a similar study on this topic?

Use in Classroom

Possible modifications of project: (1) Assign specific articles to students; (2) have students choose articles all on one topic; (3) have students choose articles from only one journal; (4) have students read two different articles on the same topic; (5) have students read research articles that address a current social issue (e.g., abortion, teenage pregnancy, racial prejudice), and decide what the research findings would suggest for social policy.

Have students compare journal reading to (1) textbook reading and (2) magazine reading. Which sections were difficult to understand? Which sections of their articles were comprehended? How did the article compare to their expectations?

Were their articles based on basic or applied research? What did the students see as the value of their articles?

ESSAY AND CRITICAL THINKING QUESTIONS

Comprehension and Application Essay Questions

We recommend that you provide students with our guidelines for "Answering Essay and Critical Thinking Questions" when you have them respond to these questions. Their answers to these kinds of questions demonstrate an ability to comprehend and apply ideas discussed in this chapter.

1. What is science? How does a scientific understanding of child development differ from an understanding produced by everyday experiences with people of various ages?

2. Compare and contrast the psychoanalytic theories of Freud and Erikson. Also explain whether Erikson changed psychoanalytic theory in a fundamental way.

3. Explain the Piagetian concepts of organization, adaptation, assimilation, and accommodation. Also indicate how these concepts help explain cognitive change during the development of a child.

4. Explain the computer metaphor for information processing in your own words. Also indicate at least two unique kinds of questions about development prompted by an information processing approach.

5. Think about your life during the past 24 hours from the perspective of behavioral and social learning theories. Provide at least two examples of how (a) rewards, (b) punishments, and (c) observational learning have influenced your behavior during this time frame?

6. Explain and evaluate ethological theory by indicating its strengths, limitations, and what is missing from this approach to child development.

7. Define and distinguish the five systems in Bronfenbrenner's ecological theory. Also provide at least two examples of each system by citing aspects from your own personal life.

8. Explain the meaning of an eclectic theoretical orientation to child development. Also evaluate the pros and cons of such an approach before you explain which approach is most and least agreeable to you personally.

9. Discuss what factors influence your selection of a method (i.e., controlled observation in a laboratory, naturalistic observation, interviews and questionnaires, case studies, standardized tests, cross-cultural studies, physiological research, research with animals, or multimeasure, multisource, and multicontext approach) for scientifically collecting data about child development?

10. Compare and contrast correlational and experimental strategies for research in child development. What do you gain and lose by using a correlational rather than experimental strategy in research?

11. What are the strengths and weaknesses of the cross-sectional and longitudinal approaches to research? In what ways do cross-sectional and longitudinal designs differ from experimental strategies? What kinds of conclusions can you draw from each?

12. Explain how research on development can be sexist. Also discuss ways to reduce sexism in child development research.

13. What precautions must be taken to safeguard the rights and welfare of a child who might be a psychological subject? In your answer, relate each precaution to a specific ethical concern in your answer. In addition, discuss at least two examples of other types of subjects who pose similar ethical difficulties for researchers?

14. Explain how you can become a wise consumer of information about children's development.

Critical Thinking Questions

We recommend that you have students follow our guidelines for "Answering Essay and Critical Thinking Questions" when you ask them to prepare responses to these questions. Their answers to these kinds of questions reflect an ability to apply critical thinking skills to a novel problem or situation that is *not* specifically discussed in the chapter. These items most appropriately may be used as take-home essay questions (e.g., due on exam day) or as homework exercises that can be answered either by individuals or groups. Collaboratively answered questions encourage cooperative learning by students, and reduce the number of papers that must be graded.

1. At the end of Chapter 2 Santrock indicates books that provide practical knowledge about children and lists resources for improving the lives of children. Choose one of these books or resources and read it or learn as much as you can about it. Then write a brief review in which you (a) characterize the book or resource, and (b) explain how the book or resource relates to material in the chapter.

2. Chapter 1 defines the nature of development in terms of biological, cognitive, and social processes, and periods or stages. Indicate your ability to think critically by (a) perusing the alternative theoretical perspectives, and (b) comparing and contrasting any three of the perspectives in terms of these processes and periods.

3. According to Chapter 1, three fundamental developmental issues concern maturation (nature) versus experience (nurture), continuity versus discontinuity, and early versus later experience. Indicate your ability to think critically by (a) perusing the alternative theoretical perspectives, and (b) comparing and contrasting any three of the perspectives on each issues.

4. One aspect of thinking critically is to read, listen, and observe carefully and then ask questions about what is missing from a text, discussion, or situation. For example, Chapter 2 suggests sociocultural and gender criticisms of Freudian theory; however, no other theoretical approach suffers a sociocultural and gender criticism. Indicate your ability to think critically by (a) explaining why only Freudian theory is subjected to a sociocultural and gender criticism, and (b) presenting your own sociocultural and gender analysis (i.e., criticism or commendation) of the other theoretical approaches (i.e., cognitive, behavioral and social learning, ethological, ecological, and eclectic views).

5. Santrock sets off several quotations in this chapter. Indicate your ability to think critically by (a) learning about the author and indicating why this individual is eminently quotable (i.e., what was this individual's contribution to human knowledge and understanding), (b) interpreting and restating the quote in your own terms, and (c) explaining what concept, issue, perspective, or term in this chapter that Santrock intended this quote to illuminate. In other words, about what aspect or issue in development does this quote make you pause and reflect?

6. Chapter 2 indicates that theories help us explain data and make predictions about various aspects of development. Chapter 2 then presents six different theoretical approaches (i.e., psychoanalytic, cognitive, behavioral and social learning, ethological, ecological, and eclectic theory), but notes that no single approach explains the complexity of development. Imagine that you are a psychologist at a nearby college who has several student clients who complain of relationship problems. Indicate you ability to think critically by explaining how you would apply each theoretical perspective while analyzing and treating your client's problems and concerns.

7. At the end of the section about theories of development Santrock concludes that no single theory is capable of explaining the rich complexity of child development. Apply your knowledge about the scientific method by designing a study to determine the relative impact of the different theoretical approaches on the field of child development in the past, present, and/or future: (a) What specific problem or question do you want to study? (b) What predictions would you make and test in your study? (c) What measures would you use (i.e., controlled observation in a laboratory, naturalistic observation, interviews and questionnaires, case studies, standardized tests, cross-cultural studies, physiological research, research with animals, or multimeasure, multisource, and multicontext approach) and how would you define each measure clearly and unambiguously? (d) What strategy would you follow--correlational or experimental, and what would be the time span of your inquiry--cross-sectional or longitudinal? (e) What ethical considerations must be addressed before you conduct your study?

8. According to Chapter 2, your author wants you to become a wise consumer of information about child development by: (a) being cautious about media reports, (b) distinguishing between nomothetic research and idiographic needs, (c) recognizing how easy it is to overgeneralize from a small or clinical sample, (d) knowing that a single study is usually not the defining word about some aspect of child development, (e) remembering that causal conclusions cannot be made from correlation studies, and (f) always considering the source of the information and evaluating its credibility. Indicate your ability to think critically by, first, selecting an article from either a journal, magazine, or newspaper about any topic regarding The Science of Child Development, and, second, evaluating it in terms of these six objectives. If the information in the article is insufficient to evaluate one of these objectives, then specify what kind of information you would need to evaluate the objective.

Biological Processes, Physical Development, and Perceptual Development

---

3 Biological Beginnings

SUGGESTIONS FOR LECTURE TOPICS

1. Interaction Illustrated by the Concepts of Dominance, Recessiveness, Genotype/Phenotype, Canalization, and Reaction Range

The concept of interaction takes some time to master. There are many examples of it in the many topics taught in child psychology, but some of the best for purposes of teaching the idea and its variations are contained in the principles of gene expression. Use these in a lecture that expands on *Child Development's* treatment of the concepts of gene dominance and recessiveness, the relationship between a genotype and its phenotype, and the complementary concepts of canalization and reaction range.

Use the ideas of dominance and recessiveness as an example of interaction between two similar factors, in this case two elements of a heredity. The interaction can be expressed as the fact that the effect of a recessive gene depends on the presence or absence of its corresponding dominant gene.

The genotype/phenotype contrast sets up the case that heredity does not always find direct expression in the outward appearance of organisms. The point can first be bolstered by the already given example of a dominant/recessive gene pairing. However, there are other ways that a phenotype may not directly express its genotype. This fact sets up the examples of canalization and range of reaction.

Canalization and range of reaction indicate that heredity/environment interactions come in different types. These concepts provide a means of discussing the idea that even though the idea of this interaction is "No genes, no organism; no environment, no organism," heredity and environment may play a variable roles in determining individual differences in the expression of traits. In the extremes of canalization, environment plays a "go, no go" role, simply determining whether or not a trait is expressed. At the extremes of reaction ranges, the expression of a given trait is enormously variable in different environments.

A good example for discussing these concepts is Kagan's work on introversion and extroversion, traits that show a large range of reaction. Very recently another has received some attention, the fact that there appears to be a single recessive gene that strongly influences ability to learn aspects of grammar such as past tenses and noun plurals, evidently a strongly canalized trait.

2. Application of Child Psychology: Genetic Engineering

For this lecture venture beyond the normal boundaries of material used for child psychology classes and present Aldous Huxley's vision of the *Brave New World*. Briefly sketch the plot of the book (it is not widely known by students these days), indicating the extent to which knowledge about genetic engineering influences social engineering in the brave new world.

Pause for a moment to solicit class reaction to the book's main idea. Do they think it is absurd? Impossible? Something right-thinking people would prevent? Summarize the class's view before proceeding to the next part of your lecture.

Evaluate the possibility that something like Huxley's vision could be achieved in the near future. Discuss the possibility of human cloning, or the extent to which human characteristics could be manipulated using genetic engineering (consultation with a colleague in biology may be desirable to do this) techniques that are currently available. Finally, present a list of human psychological or behavioral characteristics that have known (or partially known) genetic components. Take a stand on the desirability of perfecting genetic techniques that would ensure control of the expression of these characteristics.

3. Bias in Early Attempts to Measure Intelligence

It seems reasonable to suppose that an antidote to subjectivity in observation is to resort to precise, concrete definitions and procedures for observing and measuring inferred characteristics such as personality traits and intelligence. However, it turns out that even the most objective quantitative means of measurement are open to bias and distortion. This is an important lesson, because students often believe very strongly that much less vigorous descriptive techniques are adequate sources of data about behavior and personality.

Steven Jay Gould provides a beautiful example of this problem in his book *The Mismeasure of Man*. In this book you will find numerous examples of how nineteenth century scientists' conviction that intelligence was an entirely biologically determined, inherited trait blinded them to elementary procedural and calculation errors which happened to confirm their beliefs about such matters as racial and sex differences in intelligence. Compelling material in its own right, this account establishes clearly and straightforwardly the problem of bias in observation, the need for clear, reliable, and valid definitions of behavioral or hypothetical constructs, and the need to make appropriate and wide-ranging comparisons to test hypotheses and their alternatives adequately.

Gould's treatment also highlights the dangers of the strong hereditarian thesis to social policy and practice that are still experienced today. For example, you may wish to compare his treatment to the information presented later in the textbook about the influence of modern research on sex differences in mathematics.

4.   Genomic Imprinting

Not all genes are activated during fetal development; therefore, two individuals with the same faulty gene can have different diseases depending on what is switched on. One switching system is called **genomic imprinting,** a process in which preferential expression is given to either the maternal or paternal gene. Researchers suspect that **methylation** makes biological changes in the gene's DNA by methyl groups attaching to specific subunits of genes. Genomic imprinting may create different timing for the same inherited disease when inherited from a father than from the mother. Future knowledge about genomic imprinting may allow doctors to change imprinting for defective genes. (*Source:* Davis, J. 1990 (June). Printing errors? *Omni*, 24.)

5.   The PCR Machine

In the 1980s, the **PCR machine,** or **polymerase chain reaction** was developed by Kary Mullis. This machine can take one small piece of DNA (such as the small amounts of DNA in hair) and automatically produce a billion faith copies in three hours. The previous system could take months to copy and isolate the one desired gene, whereas now it is an afternoon's work.

The PCR machine has been used to create an extremely sensitive test for the AIDS virus (about one third are also infected; other parents can be relieved and infected infants might benefit from immediate use of AZT). PCR is used to screen for inherited diseases including hemophilia, Tay-Sachs disease, Duchenne's muscular dystrophy, and cystic fibrosis. It is used in much cancer research, such as the work of Michele Manos, who is trying to determine which strains of human papilloma virus are associated with cervical cancer. The PCR machine also plays a large role in the Human Genome Project, the massive research project in which the entire human genetic map is being determined.

Another role for the PCR machine is in forensics. It was used to analyze 8-year-old semen stains and exonerate Gary Dotson from a 1980 rape conviction. Forensics also uses **"DNA fingerprinting,"** but that procedure requires a large, intact sample of body fluids (about 1 in 5 billion have the same DNA fingerprint), but the PCR machine procedure works with small amounts of material. Currently it can analyze only a certain gene in the immune system—a gene that has 21 types. Therefore, it can often rule out suspects (as it did Dotson), but it cannot be used to prove guilt.

The machine can even copy DNA from a mummy's tissues, a preserved hide of an extinct animal, or the living cells of a human embryo. Svante Paabo is a **molecular archeologist** who has used PCR to amplify the DNA remaining in a 2,400-year-old Egyptian mummy and a 7,000-year-old human brain found in a Florida bog. His goal is to draw up genetic profiles of ancient peoples which could be compared with living populations, helping to trace cultural and revolutionary lineages. (*Sources:* Baskin, U. 1990 (July). DNA unlimited. *Discover*, 77-79; Mullis, K. 1990 (April). The unusual origin of the Polymerase Chain Reaction. *Scientific American;* Holzman, D. 1990 (April 23). A new link in the human chain. *Insight*, 48-50; Wingerson, L. 1990. *Mapping our genes*, Dutton.)

6.   Chromosomal Defects—Hereditary Emphysema, Retinoblastoma, and Sickle Cell Anemia

An example of a dominant defect is **retinoblastoma,** a potentially lethal eye cancer that affects children under the age of 4. Retinoblastoma affects 1 in 20,000 births. If caught early, doctors can be 92 percent successful using whole-beam gamma radiation. If caught later the child's life can be saved by enucleating (removing) the eye. Even then, careful monitoring must continue, because some adolescents develop a genetically related bone cancer called **osteosarcoma.**

31   *Chapter 3*

Hereditary emphysema is about 2 percent of 2.1 million cases of emphysema in the United States. It kills more people than any other hereditary disease except cystic fibrosis. A future treatment may be gene therapy; in mouse research, animals infused with a gene that mimics the action of a protein absent in those with hereditary emphysema began producing the protein. This protein protects sensitive lung tissue from **neutrophil elastase,** natural enzyme excreted by white blood cells. The breakdown of lung tissue by neutrophil elastase causes the breathing problems of emphysema patients.

Sickle-cell anemia is a hereditary blood disease characterized by abnormal **hemoglobin,** the protein substance which carries oxygen through the blood. The abnormal hemoglobin associated with sickle-cell anemia is called **hemoglobin S**—named from the crescent shape caused by lack of oxygen in this form of hemoglobin. This elongated-shape form can get stuck in blood vessels affecting blood flow and causing pain that can last for months.

The disease can be fatal, but most sufferers do survive into adulthood. When infants die from the disease, it is usually from getting severe pneumonia. Penicillin can reduce the death rate among infants by 84 percent. In childhood, sufferers may experience a wide range of physical problems, including tissue damage, jaundice, swollen hands, swollen feet, leg ulcers, stunted growth, and pain.

The first sickle-cell anemia case was documented in the United States in 1910. Currently, about 1 in 400 African-Americans (or over 60,000 individuals) is afflicted with the disease, and about 1 in 12 black Americans carry the trait. Carriers do not experience sickle-cell anemia symptoms, but when both biological parents are carriers each child has a 25 percent risk of getting the disease.

Although 30 states have mandated tests for screening sickle-cell anemia in newborns, fewer than 10 states have actually been implementing the testing. This testing is important, because infants do not usually show symptoms for two or three months.

The most promising experimental treatment involves **hemoglobin switching,** which was first attempted in 1976. The procedure involves increasing the level of fetal hemoglobin, composed of molecules not normally susceptible to cell sickling. Researchers are looking for safer drugs to stimulate fetal hemoglobin; hydroxyurea is currently being investigated. Other promising approaches include looking for drugs such as cetiedil, diltiazen hydrochloride, nifedipine, and verapamil hydrochloride, which inhibit cell sickling and/or expand blood vessels. (*Sources:* Angier, N. 1987. Light cast on a darkling gene. *Discover,* March, 85-96; Van Pelt, D. 1989 (October 23). Health briefing. *Insight,* 54; Van Pelt, D. 1989 (October 23). Fast gains to beat sickle-cell pain. *Insight,* 52-53.)

7.   Brain Development and the Blood-Brain Barrier

It is estimated that the brain consists of over 100 billion neurons. To achieve this number, at times the brain in utero must generate more than 250,000 neurons per minute. Like all mammalian brains, the human brain starts as a hollow tube which forms the ventricular system and only gradually develops the features of a mature brain. The cells of the brain are generated along the ventricular wall and then migrate outward to their final destinations. Not only do the brain cells have to travel to their locations, but once there they must form connections with other neurons—some neurons will make up to 15,000 connections.

Once in their proper location in the cortex, neurons differentiate into types of cells and begin to form dendrites and axons (a process called **neuropil**). While neurons are produced and migrate prenatally, much neuropil occurs postnatally. Also postnatally is the process of cell death; initially the brain may have twice as many neurons as needed. Both cell death and neuropil development seem to continue well into adolescence. Research findings suggest that cell death continues in the frontal lobe until about 16 years of age. However, new neurons are rarely produced after birth. Except in the hippocampus, new neurons are not developed postnatally.

The capillaries in the brain make up only 5 percent of its volume, but make up 400 miles of vessels. These capillaries are different from those in the rest of the body, because they form the **blood-brain barrier,** or **bbb,** which keeps the composition of the brain's blood supply more stable and consistent than the blood in the rest of the body. The bbb is important because it restricts fluctuations in amino acids, hormones, and potassium ions. Amino acids and hormones can be neurotransmitters, and potassium ions can change thresholds of neuron firing.

The bbb is an ancient system found in all vertebrates. It allows organisms a buffer from normal chemical fluxes that occur throughout the rest of the body. Without the bbb, eating or exercising could confuse hormones and neurotransmitters so much that organisms would have seizures and die.

The bbb is accomplished through capillaries which have a unique structure. Unlike other capillaries, these have a continuous wall, called the **endothelium,** which is then surrounded by **astrocytes,** one type of **glial cells.** This unique composition is true of all capillaries in the brain except those of the pituitary gland, the pineal gland, the brain stem, and parts of the hypothalamus.

The endothelium is composed of **lipid** molecules; therefore, lipid-soluble molecules (e.g., nicotine, ethanol, heroin, caffeine, valium, codeine) can cross the endothelium easily, while water-soluble molecules (e.g., albumin, sodium, penicillin) cannot. Some non-lipid-soluble molecules which are essential (e.g., glucose, some amino acids) are transported across the endothelium, while other needed substances are synthesized by brain cells.

A second barrier, the **antiluminal membrane,** or "metabolic" blood-brain barrier, exists. Some substances, such as L-dopa, can cross the endothelium but not the antiluminal. Other substances, such as heroin, can cross into the brain, are modified (heroin changes to morphine), and then cannot get back across the antiluminal membrane.

What implications does research on the blood-brain barrier have on medical research? In treating brain tissue diseases, doctors need to get therapeutic substances across the bbb. Some medicines (for example, the antibiotic chloramphenolcol) are lipid-soluble and can enter the brain readily; others are not lipid-soluble (e.g., penicillin), and enter the brain slowly. Research centers on several possible solutions:

1.   Inject the carotid with a hyperosmotic sugar solution (like mannitol), which temporarily lowers the bbb, allowing medicines in. Unfortunately, other unwanted substances can also enter, putting the patient at risk for seizures.
2.   Inject substances into the cerebrospinal fluid.
3.   Modify the substance to get it through the bbb, and then have it change again so it cannot get back through the bbb.

(*Sources:* Kolb, B. 1989. Brain development, plasticity, and behavior, *American Psychologist, 44,* 1203-1212; Goldstein, G. W. & Betz, A. L. 1986. The blood-brain barrier. *Scientific American, 255,* 74-83; Angier, N. 1990 (May). Storming the wall. *Discover,* 67-72; Partridge, W. M. 1987 (November/December). The gatekeeper: How molecules are screened for admission to the brain. *The Sciences.*)

8.   Using Twins to Study the Nature-Nurture Issue with Weight

Is weight determined by heredity of lifestyle? In one report, researchers analyzed weight and height records from the Swedish Adoption/Twin Study of Aging (Stunkard et al., 1990). Using 247 identical and 426 fraternal pairs of twins, twin siblings ended up with similar body weights regardless of whether they were raised together or apart. In fact, the correlation in body-mass index of identical twins reared apart was only slightly less than that of identical twins reared together. They also were more similar in weight to the biological parents than to the adopting parents. When both biological parents were fat, 80% of offspring were fat. Childhood environment was shown not to have an important effect.

Canadian researchers fed 12 pairs of identical twins 1,000 calories above their normal daily intake for 84 days. Weight gains ranged from 4 kg to 13 kg (9 lbs. to 29 lbs.). The difference in the amount gained was much less between twins than between nonsiblings. In other words, considerable variability in weight gain and fat distribution was seen between different twin pairs, but little variability was seen within each pair. Bouchard (1990) concluded, "It seems genes have something to do with the amount you gain when you are overfed." (*Sources:* Chubby? Blame those genes. 1990 (June 4). *Time,* 80; Bouchard, C., et al. 1990 (May 24). The response to long-term overfeeding in identical twins. *New England Journal of Medicine, 322,* 1477-1482; Stunkard, A. J., et al. 1990 (May 24). The body-mass index of twins who have been reared apart. *New England Journal of Medicine, 322,* 1483-1487; Sima, E. A. H. 1990 (May 24). Destiny rides again as twins overeat. *New England Journal of Medicine, 322,* 1522-1524.)

9.   What Is the Role of Animal Research in Learning about Genetics?

Students may offer a variety of opinions about the value of animal research. Hopefully, some individual will know about the role animals have played in learning things about such topics as alcoholism and obesity. Provided here are two examples that you can provide to generate discussion about whether animal research should be encouraged and whether animal research aids in understanding important human concerns. You may also read the McCourt (1990) article to build discussion/lecture material on how animals who have similar diseases to humans help scientists in understanding the genetic background of problems such as cholesterol (the Watanabe rabbit), leprosy (the armadillo), diabetes (the monkfish), and so forth. The diverse examples in this article make for interesting class material. Also appropriate if you are adding this topic is the 1985 National Academy Press which lists the animal models used in Nobel Prize winning work, and the 1990 *MBL Science* report which gives examples of how marine animals can be used to explore human health problems including Alzheimer's, cancer, and birth defects.

Obesity

Scientists have been able to develop a genetically overweight mouse that can weigh ten times as much as a normal mouse. Not only does this mouse allow researchers to examine the differences between obesity and normal weight, this rotund mouse allows researchers to explore the differences between genetic overweight and obesity due to overeating.

In 1987, Spiegelman found that the genetically fat mice were deficient in a protein made by **adipocytes** (fat cells). This protein called **adipsin** is five to ten times lower in genetically fat mice than in either normal weight mice or overeating fat mice (i.e., mice allowed to eat potato chips, bologna, marshmallows, cookies, and candy bars).

Adipsin may turn out to be a regulator of fat in the mice's bodies; since it is produced by fat cells, it circulates in the bloodstream, responds to changes in diet (e.g., when food intake is restricted, adipsin levels rise), and it is a **protease,** a class of enzymes that act as master regulators. Current mouse research involves injecting these genetically fat mice with adipsin to see if weight decreases.

Is there a human equivalent to adipsin? Uncertain at this time, it may turn out that the human correspondent of adipsin is **complement factor D,** which the immune system uses to combat infections. Some researchers believe that this disease protector may also play a role in regulating fat. Future research needs to look into a fat-immune connection. A previous research link in this area was the 1985 identification of **cachectin,** a protein that causes emaciation in many cancer patients while actually fighting the cancer.

Alcoholism

At one time, rats were not good research subjects for the study of alcoholism, because unlike many human beings, rats were not very attracted to drinking alcohol. However, scientists have been able to breed rats that compulsively drink large amounts of alcohol and choose alcohol over food and water. The ability to breed rats that are alcoholic, along with studies of children of alcoholics, has led to intense genetic research to find a gene (or more than one) that may be the root of alcoholism.

By 1990, researchers had identified a gene that might play a role in causing alcoholism. If future research is supportive of this initial work, someday a diagnosis of alcoholism may be based on blood tests, and perhaps a future treatment may include blocking this gene's action.

In a landmark study, researchers have found that a **dopamine D-2 receptor gene** was present in 77 percent of the cadavers of alcoholics and only in 28 percent of the cadavers of nonalcoholics. This gene affects the capacity of cells to absorb **dopamine,** a neurotransmitter that is linked to craving and pleasure-seeking behavior. Of course, alcoholism if not totally due to a single gene; other genes and environment play roles, too, but identification of this possible cause may radically change future diagnosis and treatments. (*Sources:* Block, G. B. 1990 (April). Fat master. *Discover,* 30; Purvis, A. 1990 (April 30). DNA and the desire to drink. *Time,* 88; Cowley, G. 1990 (April 30). The gene and the bottle. *Newsweek,* 59; Blum, K. et al. 1990 (April 18). Allelic association of human dopamine D-2 receptor gene in alcoholism. *JAMA. 263,* 2055-2060; Gordis, E. et al. 1990 (April 18). Finding the gene(s) for alcoholism. *JAMA. 263,* 2094-2095; McCourt, R. 1990 (August). Model patients. *Discover,* 36-41; *Models for Biomedical Research: A New Perspective.* 1985. National Academy Press; Marine animals and biomedical research. 1990 (Spring). *MBL Science.*)

BROWN & BENCHMARK'S HUMAN DEVELOPMENT TRANSPARENCIES (2ND ED.)

Transparency Number and Title

The transparency set, a supplement to *Child Development,* is accompanied by an annotated manual that describes each of the 141 transparencies. The annotated manual also offers suggestions about how to use the transparencies to engage your students in active learning that will stimulate critical thinking and evaluative skills. The following transparencies are appropriate and useful with Chapter 3: Biological Beginnings.

Transparency Number and Title

9   Maximum Recorded Life Spans for Different Species
10   Biological, Cognitive, and Socioemotional Processes in Life-Span Development
33   Facts about Chromosomes
34   Genetic Inheritance Patterns
35   The Genetic Difference Between Males and Females

CLASSROOM ACTIVITIES OR DEMONSTRATIONS

1.   Discuss the critical thinking exercises. For exercise 1, be sure the class understands the genetic principles. They need not fully understand the ramifications of the dominant-recessive genes principle, but it will help to work toward that understanding. Students often do not understand the other concepts well either, and you may want to work through carefully. Their performance on this exercise should be a good indication of their understanding of the concepts. (The class activity suggested below may be a good context for this.)

 The purpose of exercise 2 is to review the material presented in Chapter 1 by applying it; you will discover that many subsequent thinking exercises are similar to this one. The idea is that these developmental issues are not easily mastered, but that doing so is important because they define the nature of developmental psychology (see the last class activity in Chapter 2). If necessary, review this material in class, and possibly work through a topic or two in the text in terms of the issue it illustrates.

 The point of exercise 3 is to make students aware of an important issue in the type of intervention work discussed in Explorations in Child Development 3.1. The idea is that an important piece of information about this work is omitted. Perhaps discuss with students the sorts of information they need to have in order to evaluate these intervention studies.

2.   Discuss the students' research projects as suggested below.

3.   How might the question of heritability of intelligence become an issue in public policy? Suggest to the students that data about parents' (or grandparents') intelligence should be used to determine what kinds of schooling to give to children. For what kinds of social changes might someone coming from a strong genetic position argue? How about a strong environmentalist? What difference does it make whether heritability of intelligence is high or low?

Source: King, M. B. & Clark, D. E. 1990. *Instructor's Manual to accompany Children*. Dubuque, IA: Wm. C. Brown Publishers.

---

4.   If you have the resources and an appropriate class size, you may want to adapt an exercise for demonstrating a genetic environment interaction suggested by Robert Brown. Consult the full article for details. The following is a summary of Brown's abstract:

 This activity is possible using inexpensive equipment and only a few subjects. It uses a complicated design but you need not stress that in your demonstration. In addition to demonstrating the idea of interaction it will also be opportunity to teach about observing behavior. Students observe inbred albino and pigmented mice one at a time in a bright or dim open field and record activity and defecation. In dim light both species are very active; in bright light the albino mice, but not pigmented mice, become less active. Albinos defecate more in both lighting conditions. Clear results may occur with as few as four mice in each of four groups.

Source: Brown, R. T. (1989). Exercise demonstrating genetic-environment interaction. *Teaching of Psychology, 16,* 131-132.

---

5.   Have groups of students roleplay, having roles in different kinds of governments, such as:

   1.   Politicians in a humanitarian, progressive government;
   2.   Politicians in a repressive, prejudicial, and tyrannical government;
   3.   A mad, unscrupulous ruler and his committee of advisers;
   4.   Politicians in a greatly overpopulated country experiencing shortages of food, jobs, and space.

Have them make recommendations or laws for policies involving genetic counseling, reproductive technology, and related issues (e.g., selective breeding, abortion, sterilization, list of desirable characteristics).

Source: Simons, J. A. 1990. Use of genetic counseling by governments: A role play exercise. Central Iowa Psychological Services

6. Ask students to bring in as complete a description as possible of the eye colors of their siblings parents, grandparents, and, if possible, great grandparents. Some students will be unable to get the information, so it might be a good idea to break them into groups and have them use the data of the student with the most complete history. Have the students draw genetic models that explain how they and their siblings got their eye color. If possible, try to get them to draw models that include their grandparents as well as their parents.

    Another activity that can be useful at this time in the course is to force students to adopt a theoretical perspective and argue it with others who have adopted another perspective. The debate over the inheritability of intelligence is a good one. Each student should be assigned to one side of the debate and told to gather at least two pieces of evidence that support their side. The groups can then pool their evidence, select a couple of spokespersons, and let the debate begin. Bringing in a colleague to judge the debate can keep you from having to take sides and may help the students prepare better arguments.

Source: Temple, Lori L. (1992) *Instructor's Course Planner to accompany Life-span Development*, Fourth Edition by John Santrock, William C. Brown Communications, Dubuque, Iowa.

7. A genetic diagnostic test has been developed for the 100,000 Americans with a history of Huntington's disease in their families. The test identifies which individuals have inherited the defective gene. These individuals will usually begin to show symptoms between ages 35 and 45. The symptoms include progressive dementia and loss of body control; after early symptoms of irritability and depression, there are symptoms that mimic "drunkenness" such as slurred speech, slowed thought processes, impaired memory, and diminished problem-solving ability. These individuals also exhibit uncontrolled movements.

    What are the disadvantages and advantages of conducting these simple blood tests?

Disadvantages

1. Some people may be unable to cope with the knowledge that they will inevitably suffer from an incurable disease. Twenty-five percent of individuals diagnosed with early symptoms of the disease attempt suicide.
2. Some families may break up and some people may not be able to concentrate on their jobs.
3. Fetal testing will cause some families to make decisions about abortions that they are uncomfortable making, or they will have to live with the knowledge of which of their children are "doomed."
4. Sibling relationships may change as one is "liberated" from the disease and another is pronounced "doomed."

Advantages

1. Some people will be relieved to know that they will not get Huntington's disease, lifting a lifetime burden from their shoulders.
2. Some people who are informed that they will get the disease may prefer the sure knowledge and plan their lives accordingly, just as many cancer patients would rather know their fates.
3. The 50 percent of family members who will not get the disease can have children without wondering whether they are passing on a "genetic monster." The rest can be more certain about their decisions not to have children.
4. This genetic screening test represents a first step in prevention and successful treatment. Somewhere down the line, potential victims may be treated with medicines or genetic surgery.

Which students would choose to have the test and which would not? For what reasons?

Source: Levin, J., Ajemian, R., & Gorman, C. 1986 (October 20). Do they really want to know? *Time,* 80.

8. Have a class discussion about the possibility of using viruses to perform gene therapy. The Montgomery (1990) article listed below provides a background on the development of a **retroviral truck.**

    Another article briefly describes the first brain cells that were kept alive and grown. The **Johns Hopkins cells** were taken from the brain of an 18-month-old girl who had one third of her right cortex removed due to uncontrollable seizures. Some of the neurons have been kept alive and multiplying for over two years. These cells are being used by scientists working on such diseases as Alzheimer's, Huntington's, and multiple sclerosis.

    The Watson (1990) article describes the potential of the **human genome** project that is directed by **James D. Watson,** who received the Nobel prize in medicine in 1962 for codiscovering the structure of DNA. Over a 15-year period, $3 billion will allow the identification of all 3 billion DNA subunits that make up the genes (only $1 per subunit in the DNA chain). Watson describes the research's knowledge in indicating markers of hereditary diseases, development of drugs to halt the expression of defective genes, and possible gene surgery. Watson also calls attention to the need for laws to keep such advanced genetic research ethical.

    Which techniques do students think will be most useful in the future? Do students approve of gene therapy? What moral and ethical issues arise because of gene therapy?

Source: Montgomery, G. 1990 (March). The ultimate medicine. *Discover,* 60-68; A window on the mind. 1990. (May 14). *Time,* 66; Watson, J. D. 1990 (June). First word. *Omni,* 6.

9. Can acquired characteristics be inherited? In the 1920s, Viennese biologist Paul Kammerer had the following views on **inheritability of acquired characteristics:** "Our descendants will learn more quickly than we will what we know well; will execute more easily what we have accomplished with great effort; and will be able to understand what has injured us almost to the point of death." He thought that if American prohibition laws would have been long-term and strictly enforced, future generations would have been born without any desire for alcohol. He believed that animals adopt the structural formation of their surroundings: Thus the octopus adopts the same texture as the sea bottom, and the grasshopper assumes the characteristics of a blade of grass. Likewise, Negro children raised in Europe would "bleach" and later descendants would have the skin color, skull dimensions, and straight hair of Caucasians. Likewise, Europeans living in Africa would develop in the opposite way.

    Have students discuss the problems with Kammerer's ideas.

Source: Gerow, J. (Ed.). 1988. *Time retrospective: Psychology 1923-1988,* 14.

CRITICAL THINKING EXERCISES

Exercise 1

Many developmentalists believe that an important inherited determinant of personality is temperament. Look ahead to Chapter 11 (Attachment, Temperament, and Emotional Development) to find out how researchers have attempted to identify basic dimensions of temperament and to describe the extent of their stability through individuals' lives. Which genetic principle is best illustrated by this work? Circle the letter of the best answer and explain why it is the best answer and why each other answer is not as good.

A. dominant-recessive genes principle
B. polygenic inheritance
C. genotype/phenotype differences

D. reaction range
E. canalization

Exercise 2

Review "The Nature of Development" in Chapter 1, which describes several important issues in developmental psychology. Which of these issues receives the greatest emphasis in Chapter 3? Circle the letter of the best answer and explain why it is the best answer and why each other answer is not as good.

A. biological, cognitive, and social processes in development
B. continuity versus discontinuity
C. nature versus nurture
D. stability versus change
E. periods of development

Exercise 3

Perspectives on Parenting and Education describes two intervention studies that attempted to maintain or improve the intelligence of disadvantaged infants and children. Which of the following appears to have been an assumption rather than an inference or an observation made by the authors of one or both of these studies? Circle the letter of the best answer and explain why it is the best answer and why each other answer is not as good.

A. At the beginning of the study the individuals in the intervention and control groups were equally intelligent.
B. The IQs of the home-reared children in the North Carolina study declined between 12 and 18 months of age.
C. Getting families to change their children's intellectual environment is difficult if intervention does not begin early
D. In the Texas study, mothers in the intervention group encouraged their children to talk more than did mothers in the control group.
E. In order to maintain or improve the intellectual functioning of disadvantaged infants, early intervention must involve 11 or more contacts with a family.

ANSWER KEYS FOR CRITICAL THINKING EXERCISES

Exercise 1

A. This is not the best answer. The dominant-recessive genes principle refers to a single gene pairing in which one gene determines a quality of the trait governed by the gene. There is a distinctive pattern of probabilities for the expression of each variation of the trait. In any case, temperament is not thought to be controlled by a single gene pair, nor is there a known pattern of probabilities for any given dimension of temperament. The text presents no information on how specific genes influence temperament.
B. This is not the best answer. The important point, as above, is that no information specific to this point appears in the text. The text does indicate, however, that traits such as intelligence are probably based on polygenic inheritance.
C. This is not the best answer. Again, the problem is that no systematic comparisons are presented to indicate the relationship between genotypes and phenotypes for temperament. Given "D" below it is reasonable to suppose, however, that the relationship is not direct.
D. This is the best answer. The text points out that the heritability of temperament seems to decline with age. Also important is that traits such as introversion and extroversion seem to be changeable, within limits. This most clearly corresponds to what is meant by the concept of range of reaction. Different environments seem to produce different expressions of the genetic basis for temperament.
E. This is not the best answer. Canalization refers to traits that show little environmentally caused variability in their expression. Such traits should have uniform heritability during the life span of an individual, but the dimensions of temperament do not.

Exercise 2

A. This is not the best answer. These processes are simply not uniformly discussed in the chapter. The focus of the chapter is one aspect of biological processes, genetic determination. Moreover, this aspect is not discussed much as a continuing influence throughout the development of an individual in the sense of biological maturation.
B. This is not the best answer. The course of development, either prenatally or postnatally, is not described. Thus the issue of continuity or discontinuity of development is not a focus of this chapter.
C. This is the best answer. This is a continuing theme of the chapter. It is expressed most forcefully in the quote from Sandra Scarr near the end: "No genes, no organism; no environment, no organism." From the beginning of the chapter throughout, the point is made that environments interact with genotypes in the course of development. For example, natural selection determines which genotypes survive. In the discussion of genetic principles it is clear that genetic expression is a function, in varying degrees, of environmental influence. Research on intelligence and temperament is driven by the question of how much of the variation in each is determined by heredity and how much by environment.
D. This is not the best answer. There is material on this issue in the discussion of temperament, but the issue is not as pervasive as the nature-nurture issue.
E. This is not the best answer. These simply receive no treatment. The discussion of the biological bases of development is not organized around separate developmental periods, although the notion of different heritabilities at different ages is discussed with respect to intelligence and temperament.

Exercise 3

A. This is an assumption. Nowhere is it mentioned that the groups were comparable at the outset of either study. Yet this would have to be true in order to claim that the interventions were responsible for the relative success of the infants and children who received special attention.
B. This is an observation. It is cited as a result of the study that was used to account for the advantages enjoyed by the intervention group of infants.
C. This is an inference. The statement represents a speculation based on the assumption that established behavior patterns are hard to break.
D. This is an observation. Researchers watched mothers interact with their children after training and noted that intervention mothers talked with their children more.
E. This is an inference. It represents a conclusion based on a review of intervention studies. It is stated as a hypothesis about conditions necessary for interventions to succeed.

RESEARCH PROJECT 1 HERITABILITY OF HEIGHT

The purpose of this project is to demonstrate the concept of heritability by using height as the characteristic. You will do a kinship study of two families (one of the families can be your own) to collect the necessary data. Record the height of all family members over 18 years of age and separate them by sex. Calculate the mean and range of heights of both sexes for both families and compare them. This exercise is intended to give you experience both with a kinship study design and with the concept of heritability for a variable with a clear operational definition. Use the following format to record heights. Then answer the questions that follow.

Person/Sex	Family 1	Family 2	Data	Family 1	Family 2
Self	_____	_____	Average female	_____	_____
Mother	_____	_____	Average male	_____	_____
Father	_____	_____	Tallest female	_____	_____
Grandmother 1	_____	_____	Tallest male	_____	_____
Grandmother 2	_____	_____	Shortest female	_____	_____
Grandfather 1	_____	_____	Shortest male	_____	_____
Grandfather 2	_____	_____			
Sibling	_____	_____			
Sibling	_____	_____			
Sibling	_____	_____			
Aunt	_____	_____			
Aunt	_____	_____			
Aunt	_____	_____			

Person/Sex	Family 1	Family 2
Uncle	_____	_____
Uncle	_____	_____
Uncle	_____	_____
Cousin	_____	_____
Cousin	_____	_____
Cousin	_____	_____
Other	_____	_____
Other	_____	_____
Other	_____	_____

Questions

1. Which family in your sample is, on average, taller for both males and females?
2. Of the taller family, how many females are taller than the females in the shorter family? How many of the males are taller than the males in the shorter family?
3. From your data, does it appear that height is an inherited trait?
4. What is the advantage of examining the heritability of a variable like height rather than a variable such as temperament or intelligence?

Use in the Classroom

Have the class pool their data and examine it for family differences in height. Have them discuss: (a) the evidence for the heritability of height; (b) ideas about environmental differences that might play a role; (c) the reason for separating the data according to sex; and (d) the advantage of using height as a measure rather than intelligence or temperament.

The expectation is that the closer the relative is genetically, the more similar the characteristic measured will be - identical twins, fraternal twins and siblings, parents, (blood) uncles and aunts, cousins, etc.

The data from those in the older generations may be difficult to interpret because 60 or more years ago, different health and nutrition standards may have influenced growth.

The data must be segregated by sex because humans are sexually dimorphic in height. Males are characteristically larger than females.

Height is a good measure to use because it has an easy, noncontroversial, operational definition. Concepts such as intelligence and temperament are harder to define in exact terms and are more controversial.

RESEARCH PROJECT 2   GENETIC COUNSELING AVAILABLE TO YOU

Explorations in Child Development 3.1 tells about how genetic counseling can help expectant couples learn about the possibility that their infants will inherit defects or suffer other genetically-based problems. While the focus sketches the process of counseling, it does not say much about how this service is delivered from community to community.

For this project you will find out and report whether and how genetic counseling services are made available in your community. Form groups of up to four individuals, and divide the following tasks between individuals or pairs. Contact hospitals to learn whether they disseminate information about genetic counseling, and if they do, obtain the pamphlets or handouts that they provide. If there are other services or organizations for expectant couples (e.g., Planned Parenthood, or divisions of social service agencies), find out what they offer. If you can identify individuals in the community who provide such information, contact them to see if they will allow you to interview them about their services. Go to the public library and look up books or other reference materials about genetic counseling.

Once you have determined what information is publicly available, write a report that summarizes (a) how up-to-date the information appears to be; (b) what source of information is most easily and cheaply available; (c) what attitude the materials seem to take toward genetic counseling. For example, Santrock indicates that what couples do about what they find out concerning their infants' chances of suffering a genetic defect is largely their own decision. Does this seem to be true in your community? What range of decisions is available? Are any alternatives discouraged? Finally, can you determine whether these services are uniformly available to all community members? Would anyone be able to use them? Are there significant controversies about their use? What political/ethical/legal issues did you discover? Relate what you find to the claims Santrock makes in *Children* about the quality of prenatal and postnatal care in the United States.

Use in Classroom

Have the teams report their findings to the class. Use a format comfortable to you; an interesting one would be to have teams present their findings as panels. In any case, have the rest of the class carefully attend to the presentations by taking notes in a systematic way. One way to do this would be to have them prepare a data sheet of sorts with categories ready to note answers to the questions posed above.

When all individuals or panels have reported their findings, hold a general discussion of the things people have found out. Are their reports consistent? Why or why not? How well do their efforts correspondent to the material in the text? What implications do their findings have for people seeking genetic counseling in your area?

ESSAY AND CRITICAL THINKING QUESTIONS

Comprehension and Application Essay Questions

We recommend that you provide students with our guidelines for "Answering Essay and Critical Thinking Questions" when you have them respond to these questions. Their answers to these kinds of questions demonstrate an ability to comprehend and apply ideas discussed in this chapter.

1. Explain the concept of natural selection. Also explain the relationship between natural selection and sociobiology.
2. Distinguish between race and ethnicity.
3. Explain the relationship among genes, chromosomes, and DNA. Also indicate how these entities function in reproduction.
4. What is infertility? What causes infertility? Explain what an infertile couple can do to have a baby.
5. Indicate and explain at least three examples of abnormalities in genes and chromosomes.
6. Assume that you have received a number of tests to assess fetal abnormalities. Identify and explain each procedure and what you would learn from it.
7. In your own words, what is a genotype and phenotype? Also explain how these concepts relate to the concepts of dominant and recessive genes.
8. Compare and contrast the concepts of reaction range and canalization.
9. Describe the methods used by behavior geneticists to study heredity's influence on behavior.
10. Indicate how you would explain to a friend that heredity and environment interact in various ways to produce development. Also provide an example of each of the three types of interaction and shared and nonshared environmental influences that you would use to help your friend understand this concept.
11. Imagine that you want to start a family. Explain what you would do before attending a session with a genetic counselor and what kinds of questions you would ask during the meeting.
12. Explain why the desirable attributes of a mate and marriage situation may differ for females and males.

Critical Thinking Questions

We recommend that you have students follow our guidelines for "Answering Essay and Critical Thinking Questions" when you ask them to prepare responses to these questions. Their answers to these kinds of questions reflect an ability to apply critical thinking skills to a novel problem or situation that is *not* specifically discussed in the chapter. These items most appropriately may be used as take-home essay questions (e.g., due on exam day) or as homework exercises that can be answered either by individuals or groups. Collaboratively answered questions encourage cooperative learning by students, and reduce the number of papers that must be graded.

1. At the end of Chapter 3 Santrock indicates books that provide practical knowledge about children and lists resources for improving the lives of children. Choose one of these books or resources and read it or learn as much as you can about it. Then write a brief review in which you (a) characterize the book or resource, and (b) explain how the book or resource relates to material in the chapter.
2. Chapter 1 defines the nature of development in terms of biological, cognitive, and social processes, and periods or stages. Indicate your ability to think critically by identifying material in this chapter that illustrates developmental processes and periods. If there is little or no information in this chapter about

developmental processes and periods, identify and explain how developmental processes and periods could be used to guide the analysis of any topic in the chapter.

3. According to Chapter 1, three fundamental developmental issues concern: (a) maturation (nature) versus experience (nurture), (b) continuity versus discontinuity, and (c) early versus later experience. Indicate your ability to think critically by identifying material in this chapter that illustrates each of the three fundamental developmental issues. If there is little or no information in this chapter about fundamental developmental issues, identify and explain how these issues could be used to guide the analysis of any topic in the chapter.

4. One aspect of thinking critically is to read, listen, and observe carefully and then ask questions about what is missing from a text, discussion, or situation. For example, what is missing from this chapter's discussion of in vitro fertilization in light of a January 6, 1992, Associated Press article titled "America's First Test-Tube Baby Turns 10?" Indicate your ability to think critically by (a) listing as many developmental questions as you can about in vitro fertilization, and (b) speculating why Santrock does not discuss this topic more fully.

5. Santrock sets off several quotations in this chapter. Indicate your ability to think critically by selecting one of the quotes and (a) learning about the author and indicating why this individual is eminently quotable (i.e., what was this individual's contribution to human knowledge and understanding), (b) interpreting and restating the quote in your own terms, and (c) explaining what concept, issue, perspective, or term in this chapter that Santrock intended this quote to illuminate. In other words, about what aspect or issue in development does this quote make you pause and reflect?

6. Chapter 2 indicates that theories help us explain data and make predictions about various aspects of development. Chapter 2 then presents six different theoretical approaches (i.e., Freudian, cognitive, behavioral and social learning, ethological, ecological, and eclectic theory), but notes that no single approach explains the complexity of development. Indicate your ability to think critically by (a) perusing this chapter for topics influenced by at least one of the six theoretical approaches, and (b) explaining which theoretical approach dominated the topic in question. If the presentation is entirely atheoretical, identify and explain how one of the theoretical approaches could be used to guide the analysis of the topic in question.

7. Santrock discusses the role of the genetic counselor in this chapter. Apply your knowledge about the scientific method by designing a study to determine whether and how prospective and expectant parents benefit from consultations with a genetic counselor: (a) What specific problem or question do you want to study? (b) What predictions would you make and test in your study? (c) What measures would you use (i.e., controlled observation in a laboratory, naturalistic observation, interviews and questionnaires, case studies, standardized tests, cross-cultural studies, physiological research, research with animals, or multimeasure, multisource, and multicontext approach) and how would you define each measure clearly and unambiguously? (d) What strategy would you follow--correlational or experimental, and what would be the time span of your inquiry--cross-sectional or longitudinal? (e) What ethical considerations must be addressed before you conduct your study?

8. According to Chapter 2, your author wants you to become a wise consumer of information about child development by: (a) being cautious about media reports, (b) distinguishing between nomothetic research and idiographic needs, (c) recognizing how easy it is to overgeneralize from a small or clinical sample, (d) knowing that a single study is usually not the defining word about some aspect of child development, (e) remembering that causal conclusions cannot be made from correlation studies, and (f) always considering the source of the information and evaluating its credibility. Indicate your ability to think critically by, first, selecting an article from either a journal, magazine, or newspaper about any topic regarding Biological Beginnings, and, second, evaluating it in terms of these six objectives. If the information in the article is insufficient to evaluate one of these objectives, then specify what kind of information you would need to evaluate the objective.

4 Prenatal Development and Birth

SUGGESTIONS FOR LECTURE TOPICS

1. Principles of the effects of teratogens

Continue the treatment of the concept of interaction with a lecture about the principles governing the effects of teratogens. You will also find that this material provides opportunities to expand and clarify other developmental constructs as well.

A good source of these principles is the third edition of Hetherington and Parke's (1986) *Child Psychology: A Contemporary View*. Six principles listed and discussed there (pp. 108-111) include (a) The effects of a teratogen vary with the developmental stage of the embryo; (b) Because individual teratogens influence specific developmental processes, they produce specific developmental deviations; (c) Both maternal and fetal genotypes can affect the developing organism's response to teratogenic agents and may play an important role in the appearance of abnormalities in offspring; (d) The physiological or pathological status of the mother will influence the action of a teratogen; (e) The level of teratogenic agent which will produce malformations in the offspring may show no or mild detrimental effects on the mother; and (f) One teratogen may result in a variety of deviations, and several different teratogens may produce the same deviation.

As you present each principle, relate it to the concept of interaction and other developmental concepts. For example, the first principle is an example of interaction in which developmental level mediates the influence of a specific experience. This seems to be related to the concepts of critical/sensitive period, fixation, and developmental readiness. The third principle provides a complicated example of heredity/environment interaction, and an example of dyadic interaction--albeit at the physiological level.

Another way to organize your presentation on teratogens is according to the principle applicable to each teratogen's effects. Alternatively, you could assign that task to the students in the class, who would use teratogens that you describe or those discussed by Santrock in the textbook.

2. Dangers of Drug Use during Pregnancy

Information about the teratogenic effects of "everyday drug use" is very important to students as present or future parents. You may wish to underscore this with a lecture that explores this issue in greater depth than is possible in the text. Place special emphasis on the potential dangers of even normal everyday drug use, in particular the use of caffeine (coffee), nicotine (cigarettes), and alcohol.

Some important points to sketch include: (a) There are graded effects of these teratogens, such that increasingly it is risky to talk about "safe" levels of use. For example, taking just one drink a day increases risks for developmental disorders associated with alcohol use. Fetal alcohol syndrome is not an all-or-nothing outcome, but has more and less severe variants. (b) Effects may be direct or indirect. Alcohol use may lead to organic abnormalities; nicotine use may lead to temperamental difficulties in babies that influence the quality of their interactions with their caregivers. (c) Risks can be vitiated by discontinuing use of the drug. It is not reasonable to continue using a drug on the grounds that harm has already been done and cannot be reversed. (d) Risks may be variable at different times during prenatal development, a point related to the immediately preceding point. (e) The drug use habits of both parents can affect the fetus, either directly or indirectly. Indirect smoke could be a worry (we know, however, of no research on this point yet); the quality of care and support a husband can provide to his pregnant wife could influence the outcome of the pregnancy.

An important addition to your lecture could be a treatment of how mothers (and fathers) can deal with drug use habits that may endanger their unborn baby. Identify and cite specific programs in your area designed to help drug-using parents.

3. Images of Prenatal Development

A compelling way to bring home the value of observation as a research technique and, at the same time, prenatal development as a pivotal period in human development is to present and discuss images of prenatal development. A particularly interesting approach here would be an historical overview of the means by which scientists have been able to learn about the prenatal period. Consult older texts for pictures and discussions of life before birth. If neither you nor your students are too bothered by the idea, see if you can obtain specimens of human embryos or fetuses from your Biology Department, or a cooperating hospital. If you can compare these to specimens of other animals, you may enjoy a spontaneous discussion of the similarities and differences between the prenatal forms of humans versus other mammals.

Culminate your lecture with a series of in vivo photographs, movies, or a videotape such as *The Everyday Miracle of Birth*. Discuss how the ability to obtain such images has changed our conception of prenatal development and capacities, and influenced the quality of care available to pregnant women and their unborn babies. You may also find it important to talk about how the availability of such information has influenced views and arguments about abortion, or the psychological life of babies before birth.

4. Legal issues involving pregnancies

Each advancement in reproductive technology poses difficult moral and social issues which will eventually be considered in state and federal laws, and in the courtroom. For example, one legal issue concerning **artificial insemination with donor sperm (AID)** is whether or not the offspring have a right to know the identity of the genetic father. Practicality suggests that AID children would benefit from access to genetic and medical information about their biological father's family, and that knowledge of the donor's identity would help prevent the possibility of marriage between two persons with the same donor.

On the other hand, offspring might wish to contract their genetic fathers, but end up intruding on another family's right to privacy. In one Australian study of 67 sperm donors, about 60 percent indicated that they would not mind being contacted by an adult child conceived with their donated sperm; however, those who wish to make contact may not neatly match up with those who feel comfortable being contacted. Could an AID child demand to be part of his genetic father's will, or could the donor demand to have visitation rights with his child?

Moreover, there are few regulations over the use of donor sperm. Perhaps there should be limits on the number of inseminations done using the sperm from one donor. What would be an appropriate number—five offspring? 20 offspring? As number of offspring from one donor increases in a small geographical area, the chance increases that these AID children will meet each other. There have been cases in which medical doctors have broken confidentiality and intervened when they have known that AID children with the same genetic father had become intimate or planned to get married. What other controls should be placed on the donor? Should there be mandated psychological screening of donors? Should wives of married donors provide informed consent for the procedure?

In another court case, a woman is suing a sperm bank for artificially inseminating her with the wrong sperm. In 1985, a couple stored the husband's sperm because he would become infertile from chemotherapy for cancer. The following year, the husband's health grew worse and the wife decided to have the baby as soon as possible believing that "having his child was the bond that would link us together." However, DNA tests on the child and on the husband's remaining deposits at the sperm bank confirm no genetic link between the two. How responsible would you hold the sperm bank personnel for this error?

While many ethical decisions have not been legislated and are left to the medical profession and couples involved, both the United Kingdom and Australia passed laws in the 1980s that stated that when both husband and wife have given consent to the AID procedure, the child is considered a child of the marriage.

The United Kingdom and Australia have also passed legislation on IVF and surrogate pregnancy procedures. The **Australia Infertility Act of 1984** permits IVF to be performed only in approved hospitals on behalf of married couples who have had unsuccessful prior infertility treatments and have had counseling. In contrast, one problem in the United States is the profusion of infertility centers which often provide misleading statistics about their success rate with IVF and other procedures.

Similar to Australian law, the **United Kingdom's Surrogacy Arrangements Bill of 1985** prohibits the recruitment of women as surrogate mothers, and prohibits the advertising of surrogacy arrangements. In the United States, where more than 500 babies have been born to surrogate mothers, ground rules for surrogate pregnancies are being hammered out slowly and painfully in the courtrooms. One celebrated case involved the rights of surrogate mother Mary Beth Whitehead over **"Baby M,"** the baby she bore for the Sterns couple.

One actual court case in 1989 involved what to do with seven frozen fertilized eggs of a divorcing couple in which the woman wanted custody for future implantation and the man wanted say on the future of the embryos, because he did not want to father children in a single-parent situation (Sanders, 1989). How would you decide this case? At the Circuit Court level, a judge gave custody to the mother because "human life begins at conception" and "it is to the manifest best interests of the child or children in vitro that they be available for implantation." Critics believe that the judge should not have made a statement about when life begins, but should have weighed the respective interests of each spouse. What do you think?

In addition to legal issues involving the new ways to conceive babies, growing concern exists about human embryo research. As of 1987, 25 states had laws barring nontherapeutic fetal research. Some scientists believe that embryo research is needed both to improve IVF and embryo transfer knowledge and to improve knowledge in the areas of cancer cell research and drug testing. Two proponents of embryo research have said, "The minimal characteristic needed to give the embryo a claim to consideration is sentence, or the capacity to feel pain and pleasure. Until the embryo reaches that point, nothing we can do to the embryo can harm it." (Singer & Kuhse, 1987; p. 136).

A strong opposing position to embryo research is presented by George Annas (1987) who said, "Unrestricted embryo experimentation could also lead to a less rosy future. A future in which "motherhood" is abolished and made-to-government-specification children are the norm. A future in which prefabricated human embryos are frozen and sold in supermarkets and through mail order catalogues. A future in which a woman could order twins or triplets, and a future in which a daughter could give birth to her genetic sister, who could, in turn, give birth to her genetic mother.

We can also picture a world in which human embryos are fabricated not for reproduction but purely for experimental purposes. The embryos could be used for such things as testing the toxicity of new drugs, chemicals, and cosmetics, much the way in which rabbits' eyes are now used. Are these developments we should look forward to and encourage? Fairy tales we can afford to ignore? Or real dangers we should attempt to avoid by reasonable legislation and regulation?" (p. 138)

What do you think? What should and can be done? Compare your views with those of others in your class. (*Sources:* Andrews, 1984 (December) Yours, mine and theirs. *Psychology Today,* 20-29; Annas, 1987. The ethics of embryo research: Not as easy as it sounds. *Law, Medicine & Health Care, 14,* 138-140; Hartmann, 1987. *Reproductive rights and wrongs.* New York: Harper & Row; Kantrowitz, B., Kaplan, D. A., Hager, M. & Wilson, L. 1990 (March 19). Not the right father. *Newsweek,* 50-51. Kirby, 1987. Medical technology and new frontiers of family law. *Law, Medicine & Health Care, 14,* 113-119.; Singer & Kuhse, 1987. The ethics of embryo research. *Law, Medicine & Health Care, 14,* 133-137; Waller, 1987. New law or laboratory life. *Law, Medicine & Health Care, 14,* 120-140.; Woodward, 1987. Rules for making love and babies. *Newsweek,* March 23, 42-43; Sanders, A. L. 1989 (October 2). Whose lives are these? *Time,* 19.)

5.   Ectopic pregnancies

Ectopic pregnancy is pregnancy in any location other than in the uterus (e.g., Fallopian tubes, ovaries, cervix, peritoneal cavity). Ninety-five percent of ectopic pregnancies occur in one in the fallopian tubes. From 1970 to 1980, the rate of ectopic pregnancies in the United States increase from 4.5 to 10.5 of 1,000 reported pregnancies. About 40,000 ectopic pregnancies occur each year. Ectopic pregnancies cause 5.7 percent of all maternal deaths.

Several conditions of the fallopian tubes can retard or prevent passage of the fertilized ovum and result in ectopic pregnancy; (1) **Salpingitis** is caused by sexually transmitted diseases or by a postpartum or postabortion infection. In this condition, the cilia of the fallopian tubes are reduced and the tube itself is constricted, resulting in a slower movement of the fertilized ovum through the fallopian tube. (2) Infections following abortion, puerperal sepsis, salpingitis, or appendicitis, or infections due to intrauterine devices or endometriosis complications can result in **peritubal adhesions.** (3) **Postoperative scarring** can delay the progress of the fertilized ovum in the fallopian tube. (4) **Transmigration** occurs either when an "ovum is fertilized before it is in the fallopian tube, or when a fertilized ovum enters the uterus and then continues to move into the opposite fallopian tube." (5) Some ectopic pregnancies occur after **tubal sterilization,** especially when the tubal cauterization technique was used. Sometimes recanalization allows passage of the sperm, but the fertilized egg cannot pass through. (6) About 10-20 percent of all pregnancies that occur with an **intrauterine device (IUD)** in place are ectopic.

Although most ectopic implantations are in the fallopian tubes, 5 percent are implanted elsewhere. The second more common site of ectopic pregnancy is **abdominal pregnancy.** If the embryo is properly nourished, it continues to develop, occasionally to term. More often, the infant dies before the fortieth week. **Cervical pregnancy** occurs in one of every 15,000 pregnancies. This location results in profuse bleeding in the early months of pregnancy. Maternal mortality is high with this type of pregnancy, and hysterectomies sometimes must be performed to control hemorrhage. **Ovarian pregnancy** is also rare and almost always requires partial or complete removal of the involved ovary. Ectopic pregnancies in the fallopian tubes may go on from 4 to 16 weeks before causing rupture, depending on the specific location of the implantation. Severity of symptoms and risk for profuse bleeding and death also vary with the location without the fallopian tube.

No specific type of pain is characteristic of ectopic pregnancy, but over 90 percent of patients report abdominal pain. Twenty-five percent of cases have the classic triad of abdominal pain, vaginal spotting, and amenorrhea. Before tubal rupture, the majority of patients have adnexal tenderness.

Ectopic pregnancy needs to be differentially diagnosed from corpus luteum cyst, follicular cyst, twisted ovarian cyst, salpingitis, and appendicitis. The doctor can use the HCG testing, pelvic ultrasonography, and laparoscopy to improve diagnostic abilities and detect ectopic pregnancies before rupture. The treatment of choice is conservative surgery, preferably by basic laparoscopy for all unruptured tubal ectopics. (*Source:* Fayez, J. A. 1990 (January). Ectopic pregnancy: Early detection and treatment. *Hospital Physician,* 21-30.)

6. A History of Abortion

Check your knowledge about the history of abortion by taking this short true-and-false quiz (next page):

1. The first time abortions were legal in all states was after the Supreme Court made its decision in *Roe vs. Wade* in 1973.
2. Abortion techniques were first developed in the nineteenth century.
3. As today, nineteenth-century feminists were strong advocates of a pro-choice position and resisted attempts to make safe, early abortions illegal.
4. Currently, China has one of the lowest rates of abortion.
5. From the time of the early Church, Christians have opposed the use of abortions.
6. Adolf Hitler encouraged the widespread use of abortions.

The scoring of this quiz is fairly simple, for all six statements are false. Most individuals consider only the last three decades when thinking about abortion, but the history of abortion goes back many centuries. Chinese medical texts printed in 2737 B.C. included abortion techniques, and ancient Greeks, Romans, and Hebrews all permitted some abortions in their cultures. From the beginning, there have been several cycles of permitting abortions and then severely restricting abortions, and the proponents and opponents of legalized abortions often change.

Early Christians believed that abortions were not murder as long as they were performed before the soul entered the body. It was not until 1869 that the Roman Catholic Church took a strong anti-abortion position, when Pope Pius IX declared that followers would be **excommunicated** for *any* abortion, even those performed to save the life of the pregnant woman. Some church officials hold this opinion in the 1990s, too. New York Cardinal John J. O'Connor proposed excommunication for politicians who supported legal abortions or helped to make public funds available for abortion.

Few legal restraints existed in England from 1307-1803, and from 1607-1828 in America. In general, common law allowed abortions if performed before quickening. After quickening, abortion was considered a misdemeanor. English law changed in 1803 when King George III decided that abortions before quickening were punishable by a fine, whipping, imprisonment, or oversea deportation up to 4 years. Abortion after quickening was considered murder, punishable by death. By 1861, all women who had abortions could receive life imprisonment.

In 1821, Connecticut became the first state to pass a law that forbade abortions after quickening. New York state passed a stricter law in 1829 and allowed abortions only to preserve the mother's life. Other states began to pass more restrictive laws, too. After the Civil War, the anti-abortion drive was most strongly supported by upper-class, white, Anglo-saxon Protestants who wanted to raise the birthrates among Americans to counterbalance the high birthrates among immigrants. Other anti-abortion supporters during this era were anti-obscenity crusaders and feminists. Early feminists perceived abortions as a byproduct by women's suppression and suggested abstinence as an alternative. In 1871, the *New York Times* called abortion "the evil of the age." The combined efforts of these groups worked; by 1900, all abortions were illegal except those in which the pregnant woman's life was endangered.

During the twentieth century, great variation has existed in the legal status of abortions. In 1920, the Soviet Union became the first country to relegalize first-trimester abortions. Even today, abortions are the most common form of contraception in the Soviet Union. In the 1940s Hitler used the threat of the death penalty to keep German women from having abortions. China legalized abortions in 1957, the United Kingdom in 1968, the United States in 1973, India in 1975, and France in 1979.

Through the 1980s, the two countries with the strictest restrictions against abortion were Iran and Romania. Romania even had "birth squads" that visited childless couples and encouraged them to become parents. Married Romanian women were subjected to mandatory monthly medical exams; if the exam determined that a woman was pregnant, she could be imprisoned if she did not deliver a baby in nine months. This practice in Romania led to an outbreak of infants with AIDS that was detected shortly after the downfall of dictator Nicolae Ceausescu. Because birth control and sex education were outlawed in order to boost the population, many infants were sick or orphaned and received blood transfusions with dirty needles. In these settings, about one third of all young children were infected.

Attitudes about abortion and beliefs about whether abortions should be legalized are often forced into the either-or positions of pro-choice or anti-abortion, but the issue is much more complex. Some people believe that abortions should be allowed for any reason during the first trimester. Others believe abortions should only be used if the mother's health is threatened. The majority of people—over 80 percent—believe that abortions should be allowed when the fetus has a major genetic or developmental defect. However, prenatal diagnoses of these defects often cannot be made until the second trimester, which many people think is too late for an abortion. It is difficult to resolve the conflict between wanting to permit only first-trimester abortions and knowing that a 5-month-old fetus has a neural tube defect, Tay-Sachs disease, or Down Syndrome.

The above conflict represents the conflict between two reasons for having abortions: (1) to end an unwanted pregnancy, and (2) to end the pregnancy of a defective fetus. The first reason can be decided early in pregnancy; the second reason usually cannot. While a high percentage of the population believes that defective fetuses may be aborted, the timing of these abortions occurs when potential parents have already grown attached to the developing fetus and are full of delightful expectations about the baby.

Abortions can also be used to enforce government policy, as evidenced by the **one-child policy** in China. The current population of China is over one billion individuals, and government officials wish to reduce the population to 700 million within 100 years. The Chinese are encouraged to get married later, to pledge to have only one child (cash subsidies are given for pledging), to get sterilized, and to abort later pregnancies. In fact, some women may be forced to have abortions. From 1900 to 1987, the global population grew from just over 1 billion to 5 billion. Some experts expect the population to grow to over 10 billion by 2110. Perhaps along the way other countries will decide to encourage or even enforce abortions for women.

Another concern is who makes the decision to have an abortion. Some feminists believe that the decision to have an abortion should be made solely by the pregnant woman. Others want the husband or boyfriend to be involved in the decision, and to be able to prevent a woman from having an abortion. Health professionals, lawmakers, judges, and parents may be part of the decision-making in some cases. Should a pregnant teenager need her parents' consent if she wishes to have an abortion? The permission of her 15-year-old boyfriend? His parents? The courts?

During a five-year period in which Minnesota had a parental consent law, 99.9 percent of minors who used the judicial bypass system were ruled mature enough to make the decision alone. Meanwhile, the court system became crowded with these cases, and the teen birthrate increased 38 percent in Minneapolis alone. Some abortions took place in the second trimester instead of the first because of delays in the judicial bypass system. The Supreme Court has given states permission to have laws that required a pregnant teenager to inform a parent before an abortion.

What conditions would you put on the right to an abortion? For what reasons should a woman be able to get an abortion? Which individuals should be part of the decision-making process. Are there any conditions or circumstances under which women should be forced to have an abortion?

How do attitudes toward abortion shift as technology provides new means for abortion procedures? **Mifepristone** or **RU486,** an orally administered medication, can effectively (96 percent of the time) terminate pregnancies within 49 days of amenorrhea (Silvestre, et al., 1990). (*Sources: Planned Parenthood of Mid-Iowa,* Fall 1989; Purvis, A. 1990 (February 19). Romania's other tragedy. *Time,* 74; Woodward, K. L. & Talbot, M. 1990 (June 25). An archbishop rattles a saber. *Newsweek,* 64; Silvestre, L. et al. 1990 (March 8). Voluntary interruption of pregnancy with mifepristone (RU486) and a prostaglandin analogue: A large-scale French experience. *New England Journal of Medicine, 322,* 645-648.)

7.   Examples of Cross-Cultural Birth Practices and Beliefs

- West Africa: Women are expected to give birth without making any sounds; girls who cry out are called cowards and are expected to have longer labors.
- Latin American peasants: Massaging to direct the baby down, and using long pieces of cloth bound across the upper abdomen in the belief that babies might otherwise travel upwards instead of descending into the vagina.
- East Africa: Women in long labors have their vaginas packed with cow dung to encourage the baby to want to be born (i.e., the baby will believe it is being born into a wealthy family).
- Cuna Indians of Panama: The shaman sings the baby out of the woman's body.
- Zuñi Indians: Birth takes place on a hot sand bed 20" across and 5" high covered by a sheepskin. The sand bed is symbolic of Mother Earth.
- The Zia of New Mexico: The father dips eagle feathers in ashes and throws the ashes in the four directions. Then he draws the ashy feather down the pregnant woman's sides and center of the body while praying. The father's sister places an ear of corn near the pregnant woman's head and blows on it during the next contraction to aid the father's prayer.
- India: A budded flower is placed near the pregnant woman and her cervix is encouraged to dilate as the flower's petals open.
- Manus of New Guinea: The husband and wife are to confess any hidden angers toward each other so that the childbirth process can proceed normally. A hot coconut soup is used to comfort the mother.
- Jamaica: Childbirth is quickened if the mother smells the sweaty shirt of the father.

(*Source:* Examples come from Ch. 5 of Kitzinger, S., 1980. *Women as mothers: How they see themselves in different cultures,* NY: Vintage Books.)

8.   Medical Advances: Pregnancy in Diabetic Women

Although diabetes still poses serious, even fatal problems for pregnant women and developing fetuses, the statistics have changed dramatically in the twentieth century. Maternal morality among diabetics fell dramatically after the discovery of **insulin** in 1922. However, for decades, stillbirths and neonatal deaths from pregnancies complicated by diabetes continued to be higher than 1 in 3. Now, the mortality has dropped to only three percent. Two major reasons for this decrease: (1) technology that tells if the fetus' existence is endangered; through quick delivery, and using neonatal intensive care units, many survive; (2) self-monitoring of glucose levels is now practical.

However, the number of **congenital anomalies** in the offspring of diabetic women has remained three times higher than those of offspring of nondiabetic women. It seems that **maternal hyperglycemia** during the first eight weeks of gestation when organs are forming is the major cause.

A Diabetes in Early Pregnancy Study found that when diabetic women begin monitoring glucose levels *prior* to a planned pregnancy, the rate of spontaneous abortions and birth defects was not much higher than for other pregnancies. With prior monitoring, 4.9 percent of offspring had major malformations; for those who began monitoring after the twenty-first day after conception, the birth defect rate was 9 percent.

Pregnant diabetic women with markedly elevated glucose readings had a 45 percent spontaneous abortion rate; when initial levels were near normal the rate was 15 percent. In other words, the time to prevent birth defects and spontaneous abortions for diabetic women is *before* conception. (*Source:* Coustan, D. R. 1988 (December 22). Pregnancy in diabetic women. *The New England Journal of Medicine, 319,* 1663-1665.)

9.   CMV Transmission

CMV stands for cytomegalovirus, a virus that can be dangerous to the unborn children of pregnant women. Experts are especially concerned about CMV being passed from infants and young children to pregnant care providers since CMV can be passed in the children's saliva and urine. Risk occurs, for example, when day care workers change diapers, have contact with mouth toys, kiss near the mouth or on the hands, or share food, drinking glasses, or utensils with children. Frequent hand washing, immediate disposal of diapers, and wiping changing area and counter tops with soap and bleach and water can help stop the spread of CMV.

In a study by Jody Murphy of the University of Iowa, 100 day care providers and 112 children were tested for CMV. At the commencement of the study, six percent of the children in family home day care and fifteen percent of those in large day-care centers were excreting CMV in urine. Among family home day care providers, forty-three percent did not have evidence of CMV infection at this time. The study is an on-going long-term CMV study, but during the early phase of the study, five percent of the uninfected providers had become infected with CMV. (*Source:* Cushman, D. (May 18, 1993). Day care providers and parents must consider CMV transmission. *Des Moines Register.*)

BROWN & BENCHMARK'S HUMAN DEVELOPMENT TRANSPARENCIES (2ND ED.)

Transparency Number and Title

The transparency set, a supplement to *Child Development*, is accompanied by an annotated manual that describes each of the 141 transparencies. The annotated manual also offers suggestions about how to use the transparencies to engage your students in active learning that will stimulate critical thinking and evaluative skills. The following transparencies are appropriate and useful with Chapter 4: Prenatal Development and Birth

Transparency Number and Title

38   The Germinal Period
39   The Placenta and the Umbilical Cord
40   The First Trimester
41   The Second Trimester
42   The Third Trimester
43   Teratogens and their Effects
44   Drug Use During Pregnancy

CLASSROOM ACTIVITIES OR DEMONSTRATIONS

1.   Discuss the critical thinking exercises. Exercise 1 continues the theme of applying the issues from "The Nature of Development" in Chapter 1. Review these as necessary; again, you may want to work with a few examples from topics in Chapter 4.
      Exercise 2 provides a review of previously learned material. Students do not usually have to remember the major research methods and time sampling techniques of developmental psychology; our experience is that they do not remember them long after the first unit. When possible, then, it is a good idea to apply that information to material that they are studying. You may find that they want to review the definitions of correlational and experimental strategies, and of cross-sectional and longitudinal designs. Note also the study by Field and others will give them trouble because it is not really a longitudinal study. The problem that will stump students is the time frame, not the formal definition of the technique. This is a good opportunity to talk about appropriate time frames for different studies that use the longitudinal strategy.
      Exercise 3 continues to provide practice in identifying inferences, assumptions, and observations. A good discussion prior to this exercise would involve asking students whether they are beginning to develop their own criteria or procedures for discriminating these different sorts of propositions. They may find the material for this exercise difficult because it is largely descriptive; have people be on the lookout for the sorts of conditional statements and qualifications that mark inferences. A key to identifying the assumption in this passage is that it is the belief that seems to underlie most prepared or natural childbirth techniques.
2.   Discuss the students' research projects as suggested below.
3.   Hand out copies of the following questions about fetal alcohol syndrome and have your class answer them. After providing them with the correct answers, discuss (a) whether students under- or overestimated FAS; (b) their misconceptions about the risks of FAS; and (c) strategies for reducing the number of babies affected by FAS.

1.   About _____ American babies are born each year with alcohol-related defects.
      A.   5,000   B.   15,000 C.   25,000
      D.   40,000 E.   50,000
2.   Of babies affected by alcohol, _____ are severely enough affected to be called Fetal Alcohol Syndrome (FAS) babies.
      A.   2, 000 B.   6,500 C.   12,500
      D.   18,000 E.   25,000
3.   FAS is responsible for _____ percent of all cases of mental retardation in this country.
      A.   5   B.   10   C.   15   D.   20   E.   35
4.   Which group has the biggest risk for having a child with FAS?
      A.   Black B.   Caucasian   C.   Native American ·
      D.   There are no differences in FAS rates among ethnic groups.
5.   Drinking during the first trimester does not lead to FAS.
      A.   True   B.   False
6.   Motor development can be impaired for breast-feeding babies whose mothers drink alcohol.
      A.   True   B.   False
7.   Some studies suggest that some injuries to the fetus from alcohol may be corrected in the womb if a mother gives up alcohol before her third trimester.
      A.   True   B.   False
8.   Barbiturates, opiates, and alcohol have similar effects on developing fetuses.
      A.   True   B.   False

Answers:

1.   E.   Actually, this is a conservative number.
2.   C.   Damage includes facial deformities, mental retardation, and heart abnormalities.

3.	D.	FAS is the primary threat to children's mental health, much greater than either Down syndrome or spina bifida.
4.	C.	The risk for Blacks is 6.7 times that of whites; for Native Americans it is 33 times more likely than the Caucasians.
5.	B.	Although risk may be minimal during the first two weeks, during the rest of the first trimester the organs are developing and much damage can be caused.
6.	A.	Alcohol can be ingested in the breast milk.
7.	A.	Scandinavian, Boston, and Atlanta studies all indicate that some correction may occur. At least size and healthiness improves, but there is no evidence that intelligence is repaired.
8.	B.	Barbiturates and opiates affect the nervous system; alcohol can affect any cell.

Source: Simons, J. A. 1989. Quiz on Fetal Alcohol Syndrome: A Classroom Quiz. West Des Moines, IA: Central Iowa Psychological Services; Dorfman, A. 1989 (August 28). Alcohol's youngest victims. *Time,* 60.

4. Just asking the question "When does life begin?" can generate lots of emotional responses from the class. We suggest you read the article, and ideally the book, listed below before generating this discussion, because Clifford Grobstein presents a well-balanced and scientifically based presentation on the issue. His idea that there are six individualities (genetic, developmental, functional, behavioral, psychic, and social) that develop at different rates is one that deserves mention in a discussion or as a lecture topic. Presented here are a few of Grobstein's ideas taken from the *Psychology Today* article:

- **Genetic individuality** begins at conception, but **developmental individuality** does not begin until implantation two weeks after conception. Until this time, Grobstein uses **pre-embryo.** Pregnancy does not begin until implantation occurs. (Note: Under this idea, IUDs and "morning-after" pills like RU486 do not cause an abortion but prevent a pregnancy.)
- At least two-thirds of all fertilized eggs do not go through full pregnancy.
- **Behavioral individuality** begins when movement occurs, six weeks or later. This early movement is reflexive only because the rudimentary brain does not yet have neurons.
- From 8 to 20 weeks the central nervous system is extremely immature and probably indicates that there is no awareness, a criterion for **psychic individuality.** Until about 30 weeks after conception you don't see brain wave patterns that are characteristic of EEGs in persons. Between 20 and 30 weeks is the "iffy" time period for when awareness begins.
- **Social individuality** begins after birth.

Source: Hall, E. 1989 (September). When does life begin? *Psychology Today,* 42–46; Grobstein, C. 1988. *Science and the unborn,* New York: Basic Books.

5. In August 1989, 23-year-old Jennifer Johnson was found guilty of delivering a controlled substance to a minor; the minor was her baby who was born a cocaine addict. She could have received a 30-year sentence, but she was sentenced to a year of house arrest in a drug rehabilitation center and 14 years of probation.

    Do you think that mothers who use drugs during pregnancy should face criminal prosecution? Might this policy keep some pregnant women from getting good prenatal care and delivering the baby in a hospital setting? Is fetal abuse the equivalent of child abuse? What alternative solutions can you suggest?

    How far should the prosecution go? Research, for example, suggests that mothers who smoke tobacco during pregnancy and up to the time their children are 5 years old increase the risk of their offspring getting asthma. Should smoking mothers also be prosecuted?

    How responsible is a drug-using male in infertility and newborn health problem situations? Cocaine usage also lowers sperm count, increases abnormally shaped sperm, and decreases sperm mobility. Infertility problems may last more than 2 years after a man quits using cocaine. Do you think a wife should be able to sue her husband for infertility problems caused by use of cocaine?

    In your discussion, inform students of typical effects of cocaine in personality and physical aspects of offspring. For example, babies whose mothers used cocaine during pregnancy had significantly lower cardiac output, lower stroke volume, and higher mean arterial blood pressure with a higher heart rate (Van de Bor et al., 1990).

Sources: Cocaine babies: The littlest victims. 1989 (October 2). *Newsweek,* 55. Van Pelt, D. 1990 (April 30). Smokers' offspring more prone to asthma. *Insight,* 47; Van Pelt, D. 1990 (May 7). Sperm abnormalities among cocaine users. *Insight,* 50; Van de Bor, M. et al. 1990 (Jan). Decreased cardiac output in infants of mothers who abused cocaine. *Pediatrics,* 85. 30–32.

---

6. Pro-choice legislator in West Virginia Charlotte Pruitt introduced some bills restricting male reproductive rights to illustrate how abortion restrictions amount to unequal treatment of women and men in reproductive matters. She said, "If women's rights and bodies are going to be violated, then men's should be too."

    Her proposed bills would require that:

    (1)   Men who failed to keep up with child support payments be sterilized;
    (2)   A husband must get his wife's permission before undergoing a vasectomy;
    (3)   Husbands must be counseled about vasectomy as an alternative if their wives are considering tubal ligation.

    Do you think Pruitt has made her point? Why or why not? Do you approve of any of her proposals that she herself labels "absolutely outrageous"?

Source: Powell, M. 1990 (March 5). Bills take aim at double standard. *Insight,* 49.

---

7. Have students role-play presenting information to a hospital board advocating changes in hospital policy to facilitate bonding between mother and infant and father and infant. First, ask all students to present changes (as well as continued practices) in hospital operations that would serve to promote bonding. Then have a group of students present evidence to support bonding practices and have a second group of students present evidence to support parent-infant separation (or against making any changes to increase bonding opportunities).
    A short example of positions:
    Pro-bonding: Bonding is important. Both the infant and the mother need the close contact. For the infant, it facilitates attachment. For the mother, it increases involvement, reduces the artificiality of the hospital setting, and reduces the chance of postpartum blues. For the father, it makes him part of the infant's life from the first moments and increases his sense of involvement. It is good for the family.
    Anti-bonding: There is no evidence for the importance of bonding. It is more important to clean up and test the neonate to assure its physical health. Attachment can certainly wait a few hours. Besides, the mother will probably drop off to sleep immediately. The inclusion of fathers increases the risk of infection. Fathers have no real biological role to play. Everyone knows they are less important to the infant than the mother.

Source: Adapted from King, M. B. & Clark, D. E. (1989). *Instructor's Manual to Santrock and Yussen's Child Development: An Introduction,* 4th ed. Dubuque, IA: Wm. C. Brown Publishers.

---

8. Ask class members to list reasons why couples have children (i.e., What value do children serve?). Compare their suggestions to those offered by Hoffman and Hoffman:

    1.   adult social status and identity
    2.   expansion of the self, tie to a larger entity, sense of immortality
    3.   morality, religion, good of the group, altruism, normality
    4.   primary group ties, affiliation

5.   stimulation, novelty, fun
6.   creativity, accomplishment, competence
7.   power, effectiveness, influence
8.   social comparison, competition
9.   economic utility

Source: Hoffman, L. W. & Hoffman, M. L. (1973). The value of children to parents. In J. T. Fawcett (Ed.) *Psychological perspectives on population* (pp. 19-76), New York: Basic Books.

9.   From the book material or from their personal experiences, have students list and describe medical technology that is part of modern childbirthing. Have them discuss the advantages and disadvantages of this medical technology. Share the results of the following study:
     Semmelweis Clinic in Vienna has emphasized nonintervention or "low-tech" childbirthing (e.g., little fetal monitoring and cesarean section). Other maternity clinics in Vienna are interventionist, "high-tech" birth centers. In the 1970s and 1980s, Semmelweis has had a cesarean-section rate of only 1.3 percent and a forceps rate of 3.1 percent. Semmelweis's maternal death rate is 0.5 per 10,000 births; in the other Vienna clinics the rate is 1.1 per 10,000 births. In the 1980s, Semmelweis had a significantly lower postneonatal mortality rate compared to the other clinics.

Source: Rockenschaub, A. (1990, April). Technology-free obstetrics at the Semmelweis Clinic. *Lancet, 335*, 977-978.

10.   Ask students about their preferences for daughters or sons, and the reasons for their preferences. Are there differences in preferences between (a) parents and non-parents; (b) young, middle, or older adults; (c) females and males; (d) different ethnic or racial groups? If differences do exist, how might they be explained?
      Enhance the discussion with examples of gender preferences in other cultures. For example, Bumiller (1990) writes about the Indian blessing "May you be the mother of a hundred sons." India is a culture that puts much pressure on women to produce sons instead of daughters. Daughters represent huge financial problems for families, as there will be a need to go into debt for a dowry. Girls receive less education, less medical care, and less food than do boys. Women's work includes field work, housework, cooking, tending cows, making cow-dung cakes for fuel, and hauling water. Girls are often married before their adolescence, and beatings are a fairly routine aspect of marriage.

Source: Bumiller, E. 1990. *May you be the mother of a hundred sons.* New York: Random House; Shapiro, L. 1990 (June 25). Millions of daughters. *Newsweek, 57.*

11.   Americans love their VCRs and some like to record every important event in their lives. What is your opinion about an imminent father taping the birth of his child? How about taping a wedding (or, in some cases, after the real wedding shooting a camera-version of the wedding)? Is it appropriate to tape Granny's funeral?
      Use the humor-based source below as part of your discussion.

Source: Slattery, D. P. 1989 (November 13). An Orwellian Wedding. *Newsweek, 10.*

12.   The text presents a great deal of information on the effects of potential teratogens on prenatal development. Divide the class into small groups and have them compose a letter to a pregnant friend advising her on what she should do (or not do) during her pregnancy. The students should provide evidence to justify their advice. (To shorten this project, assign one type of teratogens per group, for example, medicines, illegal drugs, diseases, environmental hazards.) Tell her how risks vary from early through late pregnancy.

Based on the information provided in the text, the advice to the pregnant friend would include: no alcohol (fetal alcohol syndrome); no illegal drugs (cocaine babies, addictions); no unnecessary medicines (thalidomide-type risks); no cigarettes (lower birth weight, higher risk of death); avoid diseases such as rubella and sexually transmitted diseases; avoid radiation including X-rays; eat a balanced diet. During the embryonic period when organogenesis is in progress, teratogens are the most likely cause of anatomical defects. During the fetal period, teratogens are more likely to affect organ functioning or stunt growth than they are to cause anatomical defects.

Source: Adapted from King, M. B. & Clark, D. E. 1989. *Instructor's Manual to Santrock and Yussen's Child Development: An Introduction,* 4th ed. Dubuque, IA: Wm. C. Brown.

13.   Have the class discuss the future prospects of doing surgery for birth defects on the fetus. Should fetal surgery be done only in cases in which otherwise the fetus would die, or should it be an option to help minimize severe disabilities?

    For example, animal research is being done to learn how to successfully cover exposed spinal cord with a skinlike material. In the future, **spina bifida** may use a similar fetal surgery technique to minimize damage.

    Actual successful surgery on 24-week-old fetuses has been performed since 1990 on fetuses who have an opening in the diaphragm, which separates the abdomen and chest. This condition, which affects 1 in 2,500 fetuses, is fatal 75 percent of the time, because the opening allows the stomach, intestines, and so on to move into the chest and keep the lungs from growing properly. In the fetal surgery, surgeons open up the uterus, remove the amniotic fluid, cut into the fetus, and move the abdominal organs into their proper place. Then, they close the chest with a Gore-Tex patch, enlarge the fetus's abdomen with more Gore-Tex, and finally return the amniotic fluid.

Sources: Van Pelt, D. 1990 (June 25). Fetal surgery tested for spina bifida. *Insight,* 51; Begley, S. 1990 (June 11). The tiniest patients. *Newsweek,* 56-57.

CRITICAL THINKING EXERCISES

Exercise 1

Chapter 4 illustrates a number of the issues discussed in "The Nature of Development" presented in Chapter 1. Which of the following topics taken from Chapter 4 correctly illustrates the Chapter 1 topic paired with it in terms of prenatal or postnatal development of the fetus or infant? **Circle the letter of the best answer and explain why it is the best answer and why each other answer is not as good.**

A. germinal, embryonic, and fetal periods: stability
B. embryonic development: maturation
C. teratology: biological determinants and influences
D. miscarriage/abortion: discontinuity
E. to work or not to work: cognitive processes

Exercise 2

Explorations in Child Development 4.1 in your text describes two intervention studies done with low-birthweight and preterm infants. These studies are important because they evaluate ways to improve the care of infants. An important aspect of evaluating these studies, however, is identifying the research techniques used in them. Which of the following pairs of terms best represents this intervention research? **Circle the letter of the best answer and explain why it is the best answer and why each other answer is not as good.**

A. correlational, cross-sectional
B. correlational, longitudinal
C. experimental, cross-sectional

D. experimental, longitudinal
E. both correlational and experimental, and cross-sectional and longitudinal

Exercise 3

Methods for supervising and assisting childbirth have changed considerably in the past two decades. Your text describes the basics of today's methods as well as a number of new and experimental practices. An interesting feature of current practices is that they represent a renewed assumption about the process of childbirth that did not get much emphasis in the more physician-controlled practices of previous years. Which of the following is a statement of assumption, rather than an inference or an observation? **Circle the letter of the best answer and explain why it is the best answer and why each other answer is not as good.**

A. Most current methods are based on Grantley Dick-Read's concepts.
B. The father may not be the best coach during labor.
C. Active breathing is associated with less pain during delivery.
D. Women know how to give birth.
E. Including siblings in the birth presents sibling rivalry.

ANSWER KEYS FOR CRITICAL THINKING EXERCISES

Exercise 1

A. No, these do not illustrate the concept. Prenatal development is a period of rapid and radical change, not stability. These phases better illustrate periods of development.
B. This illustrates the concept. Embryonic development is perhaps the best illustration of a clear, orderly sequence of changes that most likely are dictated by a genetic blueprint. An indication of this is that this period of prenatal development is least susceptible to damage from teratogens; if there is too much environmental interference, the organism aborts.
C. This does not illustrate the concept. Teratogens do influence biological development, but they are environmental influences.
D. No, these do not illustrate the concept. The concept of discontinuity is that development produces qualitatively new and different features, often in what appears to be a progression of stages. These events represent an end to development.
E. No, this does not illustrate the concept. Parents' decisions to work or not work is certainly a cognitive process, but the influence of the decision on the developing infant is social, shaping the parental practices that dictate the infant's environment and parents' relationships with the infant.

Exercise 2

A. No, these studies are not correlational nor are they cross-sectional. Infants were assigned to experimental or control conditions, and the same groups were studied over time. That makes the work experimental and longitudinal.
B. See A.
C. See A.
D. See A.
E. See A.

Exercise 3

A. This is an observation. It is based on comparison of various techniques and their acknowledged debt to the work of Dick-Read.
B. This is an inference. It represents a reasoned judgment based on the idea that men do not experience childbirth.
C. This is an observation. Physicians have noted this about women who practice active breathing when they deliver their babies.
D. This is the assumption. It is stated plainly in the text without justification, argument, or evidence. It is also not clear precisely what the statement means!
E. This is an inference. It is based on the notion that children grow worried and jealous when their parents exclude them to devote time and attention to their newborn sister or brother.

RESEARCH PROJECT 1 WHY DO SOME PREGNANT WOMEN SMOKE, DRINK AND DO DRUGS?

Despite the fact that the dangers of drinking alcohol, smoking, and other drug use to fetal development are now well known and widely publicized, women continue to use these substances while they are pregnant. This research activity (suggested in Salkind, S. S. (1990). Child development. Fort Worth: Holt, Rinehart, & Winston) attempts to find out why.

Have students invite a group of female friends who smoke or drink to talk to you about whether they will do these things when they are pregnant. Then have them ask their friends whether they know that smoking and drinking endanger prenatal development and about what they know in detail. Have them talk about the dangers (they may need to do some teaching!), and then ask again whether their friends will drink and smoke. You may want to suggest to students that they tape record the answers, but make sure they prepare an interview schedule no matter how they choose to record answers.

RESEARCH PROJECT 2   FATHERHOOD

How actively are fathers participating in the births of their children these days? Find out by carrying out an interview project suggested in a child development text by Neil Salkind (Salkind, N. (1990). Child Development. Fort Worth: Holt, Rinehart, & Winston).

Invite two first-time, expectant fathers and two fathers of children under the age of two. Interview these men using the following sets of questions:

Expectant fathers:

1. What are your feelings about becoming a father?
2. How have you been involved in your wife's pregnancy?
3. What part will you play in your child's birth? What part would you like to play?
4. What do you think being a "good father" means?
5. How will having a child change your life?

Fathers:

1. What part did you play in the birth(s) of your child (children)? What were your feelings about this experience?
2. What are the three biggest challenges you face as a father?
3. What do you think a "good father" is?
4. How has having a child changed your life?
5. What advice would you give a new father?

Write a brief report indicating what you were trying to find out, describe your sample and how you interviewed the fathers and soon-to-be fathers, and then summarize similarities and differences between the two pairs of men. Relate what you learn to material on fathers' participation in childbirth that is in the text.

ESSAY AND CRITICAL THINKING QUESTIONS

Comprehension and Application Essay Questions

We recommend that you provide students with our guidelines for "Answering Essay and Critical Thinking Questions" when you have them respond to these questions. Their answers to these kinds of questions demonstrate an ability to comprehend and apply ideas discussed in this chapter.

1. Describe development during the germinal, embryological, and fetal periods. Also indicate and explain what factors might contribute to complications at specific times during gestation.
2. What is organogenesis, and why is this concept important to the process of development?
3. Discuss medical, ethical, psychological, and personal issues pertinent to the decision to have an abortion.
4. What is a teratogen? Also indicate at least two examples of teratogens and their specific effects.

5. Compare and contrast the risks to expectant mothers who are either teenagers, twenty-something, or thirty-something.
6. Describe the stages of birth, and also explain three birth complications.
7. Imagine that you are about to give birth. What questions about cesarean sections and the use of drugs during delivery would be important to you? What reasons would lead you to accept or reject a cesarean section and drugs such as tranquilizers, sedatives, and analgesics during delivery?
8. Imagine that you are an expectant parent. What would you do and learn in a parent education class on pregnancy, prenatal development, and the three most common childbirth strategies?
9. Why and how have fathers and siblings become more involved in childbirth? Also discuss the pros and cons of this involvement.
10. How do preterm and low-birth-weight infants differ?
11. What would you learn about your newborn from the Apgar and Brazelton Neonatal Behavioral Assessment Scales?
12. Explain why some claim that the postpartal period should be termed the fourth trimester.
13. A newborn baby often raises a question as to whether the mother will return to work outside the home or stay home with the baby. Explain how the advice of Eisenberg, Murkoff, and Hathaway would help you make this decision.
14. Summarize the evidence for and against the claim that touch and massage improves the growth, health, and well-being of infants and children?

Critical Thinking Questions

We recommend that you have students follow our guidelines for "Answering Essay and Critical Thinking Questions" when you ask them to prepare responses to these questions. Their answers to these kinds of questions reflect an ability to apply critical thinking skills to a novel problem or situation that is *not* specifically discussed in the chapter. These items most appropriately may be used as take-home essay questions (e.g., due on exam day) or as homework exercises that can be answered either by individuals or groups. Collaboratively answered questions encourage cooperative learning by students, and reduce the number of papers that must be graded.

1. At the end of Chapter 4 Santrock indicates books that provide practical knowledge about children and lists resources for improving the lives of children. Choose one of these books or resources and read it or learn as much as you can about it. Then write a brief review in which you (a) characterize the book or resource, and (b) explain how the book or resource relates to material in the chapter.
2. Chapter 1 defines the nature of development in terms of biological, cognitive, and social processes, and periods or stages. Indicate your ability to think critically by identifying material in this chapter that illustrates developmental processes and periods. If there is little or no information in this chapter about developmental processes and periods, identify and explain how developmental processes and periods could be used to guide the analysis of any topic in the chapter.
3. According to Chapter 1, three fundamental developmental issues concern: (a) maturation (nature) versus experience (nurture), (b) continuity versus discontinuity, and (c) early versus later experience. Indicate your ability to think critically by identifying material in this chapter that illustrates the three fundamental developmental issues. If there is little or no information in this chapter about fundamental developmental issues, identify and explain how the these issues could be used to guide the analysis of any topic in the chapter.
4. One aspect of thinking critically is to read, listen, and observe carefully, and then ask questions about what is missing from a text, discussion, or situation. For example, this chapter discusses the psychological effects of abortion on the mother, but not the father. Indicate your ability to think critically by (a) speculating about why Santrock neglected to discuss the psychological effects of abortion on fathers, and (b) evaluating whether this seeming oversight represents a case of sexism in developmental research that should be avoided, according to the author's claim in Chapter 2.
5. Santrock sets off several quotations in this chapter. Indicate your ability to think critically by selecting one of the quotes and (a) learning about the author and indicating why this individual is eminently quotable (i.e., what was this individual's contribution to human knowledge and understanding), (b) interpreting and restating the quote in your own terms, and (c) explaining what concept, issue, perspective, or term in this chapter that Santrock intended this quote to illuminate. In other words, about what aspect or issue in development does this quote make you pause and reflect?

6. Chapter 2 presents six different theoretical approaches (i.e., Freudian, cognitive, behavioral and social learning, phenomenological and humanistic, ethological, and ecological), but notes that no single approach explains the complexity of development. Imagine that you are a developmental psychologist with several clients who have considered having an abortion. In some cases, the individuals obtained an abortion, and in other cases, the individuals did not obtain an abortion. Indicate your ability to think critically by explaining how you would apply each theoretical perspective in analyzing and treating your clients.

7. According to an Associated Press article on February 20, 1992, the issue of the effects of drugs on prenatal development arose after Jeffrey Dahmer was sentenced to life imprisonment for 15 slayings. In brief, the claim was made that Dahmer's mother ingested four sedatives (meprobamate, mephobarbital, phenobarbital, and secobarbital) and the female sex hormone progestin one month after becoming pregnant. The article suggested that these drugs could have affected Dahmer and were somehow related to his slaying the victims, having sex with their corpses, and eating their flesh. Apply your knowledge about the scientific method by designing a study to determine the effects of prenatal effects of sedatives and hormones on personality development and behavior. Clearly specify (a) What specific problem or question do you want to study? (b) What predictions would you make and test in your study? (c) What measures would you use (i.e., observation, interviews and questionnaires, case studies, standardized tests, physiological research, or multimeasure, multisource, and multicontext approach) and how would you define each measure clearly and unambiguously? (d) What strategy would you follow--experimental or correlational, and what would be the time span of your inquiry--cross sectional or longitudinal? (e) What ethical considerations must be addressed before you conduct your study?

8. According to Chapter 2, your author wants you to become a wise consumer of information about child development by: (a) being cautious about media reports, (b) distinguishing between nomothetic research and idiographic needs, (c) recognizing how easy it is to overgeneralize from a small or clinical sample, (d) knowing that a single study is usually not the defining word about some aspect of life-span development, (e) remembering that causal conclusions cannot be made from correlation studies, and (f) always considering the source of the information and evaluating its credibility. Indicate your ability to think critically by, first, selecting an article from either a journal, magazine, or newspaper about any topic regarding Prenatal Development and Birth, and, second, evaluating it in terms of these six objectives. If the information in the article is insufficient to evaluate one of these objectives, then specify what kind of information you would need to evaluate the objective.

5 Physical, Motor, and Perceptual Development in Infancy

SUGGESTIONS FOR LECTURE TOPICS

1. Nature and Nurture in Infant Motor Development

In *Development in Infancy* T. G. R. Bower presents an excellent treatment of the classic nature-nurture controversy about the causes of motor development. Use this material as the basis for a lecture on what we know about the relative contributions of maturation and experience to infant locomotion. A useful starting point is the belief prevalent during the first half of this century that motor development was largely a maturational phenomenon. Gesell figured largely in this debate, and discussion of it helps to clarify his belief in the maturational basis of psychological development more generally. Gesell also performed interesting, if not definitive, experiments on the issue.

Much more recent information has been gathered about cross-cultural differences in patterns and rates of motor development, experiments in which reflexes have been exercised, and clinical attempts to deal with the motor development of blind infants (e.g., the classic work of Denis on institutionalized babies). All of this can be used to show that motor development appears to result from a variety of interactions between developmental level and environmental stimulation. In developing your argument you will also find opportunities to illustrate the concepts of canalization and range of reaction as well as the possibility of hereditary influences on motor development.

2. Testing Infants' Vision and Hearing

Research on infant capacities has produced scientific information and provided clinical procedures that have improved our ability to assess basic infant capacities. In this lecture you could begin with the initial infant scales of development, which tended to focus on motor development as a reflection of the dominance of that topic early in infant research. Proceed to cover those techniques that allow physicians and others to assess infants' vision and hearing. Consult a local pediatrician or family practitioner to learn about these. Also consider asking those professionals to give a guest lecture or demonstration.

This is an important application of infancy research. The medical profession's long-held assumption that infants had very few sensory, cognitive, and perceptual capacities may have both prevented earlier discovery of these capacities and perpetuated medical practices that are not developmentally optimal. Your text, for example, discusses the issue of sensitivity to pain and the usual practice of not anesthetizing male infants when they are circumcised. You may wish to build on that example to discuss pertinent assumptions made about other medical procedures with infants.

3. Opportunities for and Limitations of Infant Observation

Early in the history of child psychology, the method of choice in studies of infants was free observation. Particularly famous observers were Charles Darwin and Jean Piaget. Darwin's work on facial expression inspired modern work in that area at all age levels. The work of Piaget has established a standard of observational excellence and serves as a challenge to those who wish to improve it.

In this lecture, illustrate the technique of free observation with examples of work by Darwin, Piaget, or others (baby diaries were very popular in the late nineteenth and early twentieth centuries). Establish why these observations are celebrated and valuable sources of information about infants, and trace the questions and hypotheses that have stemmed from this work.

Next, discuss the limitations of free observation as a means of finding out about infants. Bower provides a start here with the comment that what you see is limited by the need to make inferences about the meaning of behavior (a problem especially when behavior fails to suggest a capacity) and by the sorts of observations made possible by the environments in which we usually observe babies. This will establish the need for more structured observations and careful examination of environmental influences. You should be able to make the case that readily observable aspects of infant behavior are reliably and validly established by relatively simple observational methods. For example, Shirley's documentation of the sequence of motor development is still the standard work. However, more inferential claims have become increasingly complicated. There are diverse examples to trace. Consider as possibilities the study of infant depth perception, the development of the object concept, or the discovery of interactional synchrony. There is also a wealth of work on infant memory and perceptual capacities.

This lecture may afford many opportunities for critical thinking and discussion by the class. You may also be able to work discussion of students' informal experiences with infants or specific assignments to observe infants into your presentation.

4.   Additional Information on Extremely Low Birth-Weight at Five Years

A longitudinal study conducted in Western Ontario looked at the status of 78 **ELBW** (extremely-low-birthweight) babies born between 1980 and 1982, and observed those who survived. At 5, these ELBW survivors were given extensive tests to assess intelligence, functioning, and neurologic status.

Nine percent of the ELBW children had neurosensory impairments (one was blind from retrolental fibroplasia; six had cerebral palsy). Overall, they had average cognitive ability (about 60 percent had normal IQ scores). However, less than half of the ELBW children scored in the normal range in tests of motor function and visual-motor integration (e.g., copying complex geometric figures).

About half of the ELBW subjects had both normal IQ and normal neurosensory status, although several of these were deemed to have some risk for future learning disabilities. About one fifth of the total group subjects were already receiving special school assistance. (*Source:* Saigal, S., et al. 1990 (March). Intellectual and functional status at school entry of children who weighed 1000 grams or less at birth: A regional perspective of births in the 1980s. *Journal of Pediatrics, 116,* 409-416.)

5.   Dealing with Respiratory Problems

One of the biggest problems with premature infants is lung damage, primarily due to lack of **surfactant,** which keep the inside surfaces of lungs from sticking together. One new procedure that might help preemies born as early as 20 weeks after conception is to infuse the lungs with **perfluorocarbon,** an oxygen-carrying liquid. Perfluorocarbon uniformly expands the lungs better than conventional gas respiration techniques. In the future, perfluorocarbon may be useful in treating children's and adult's respiratory distress too (Van Pelt, 1989).

Two 1990 studies looked at the short- and long-term effects of surfactant replacement therapy. In one study (Soll et al., 1990), 155 premature newborns received either **Survanta** (a bovine surfactant extract) or air placebo within minutes after birth. At 24 hours, those who received Survanta were requiring less oxygen. Measures at seven days and 28 days revealed no differences in clinical measures. The surfactant group had fewer cases of pneumothoraces but more necrotizing enterocolitis. The smallest premature infants received the most benefit from the treatment.

The second study (Ware et al., 1990) looked at the long-term safety of surfactant. By following 41 premature infants for 24 months, the researchers found no differences in physical growth, cognitive testing, and motor skills. However, those infants who had received surfactant had fewer allergy manifestations. Both studies suggest that surfactant therapy is beneficial and safe, but the positive effects are only moderate. (*Sources:* Van Pelt, D. 1989 (August 28). Oxygen-bearing liquid for preemies' lungs. *Insight,* 53; Soll, R. F. et al. 1990 (Kime). Multicenter trial of single-dose modified bovine surfactant extract (Survanta) for prevention of respiratory distress syndrome. *Pediatrics, 85,* 1092-1102; Ware, J. et al. 1990 (June). Health and developmental outcomes of a surfactant-controlled trial: Follow-up at 2 years. *Pediatrics, 85,* 1103-1107.)

6.   Cry Assessment

Parents with small infants sometimes seem to know what their crying baby needs even before they check the diapers and feeding time schedules. One clue that parents may use in determining what their baby wants is the way their baby is crying. Research (Wolff, 1969) suggests that all babies use three styles of crying: **anger cry** (loud and prolonged vocalization), **hunger & basic cry** (rhythmic and repetitive vocalization), and **pain cry** (sudden onset, initial long cry, and extended breath holding). More recently, medical researchers have explored whether crying styles indicate more than immediate needs and emotions.

Barry Lester has suggested that medical cues can be derived from the crying patterns of neonates. For example, a pattern called **"cri du chat,"** a steady crying at approximately 800 cycles, is a distinctive cry of brain-damaged infants. This steady cry is quite a contrast to normal infants' crying, which starts at 200 cycles and rises to 600 cycles, holds steady, and then drops off (Angier, 1984; Lester & Boukydis, 1985).

Researchers have been able to differentiate 80 measures of infant crying, but frequency (pitch) is the most important aspect that facilitates adult recognition of infant needs (Zeskind & Marshall, 1988). Malnourished infants have high-pitched, arrhythmic crying which is low in intensity but high in duration (Angier, 1984). Infants with Down syndrome have pain cries that are lower in pitch than those of normal infants (Zeskind & Marshall, 1988). Male neonates undergoing circumcision undergo an increase in the pitch of their cries (Porter et al., 1988).

Asphyxiated babies have shorter cries, higher fundamental frequencies, and less stable cry signals (Campos et al., 1983).

Researchers believe that high pitches and variability of the frequency are means to assess subtle differences in neurological functioning. For example, infants who have great variability in cry pitch needed more visits with health-care personnel during their first month after hospital discharge (Zeskind & Marshall, 1988). Eventually, analysis of crying sounds may become part of standard neonatal exams (Turkington, 1984).

Not only do professionals use crying for assessment; newborns themselves pay attention to the crying of other infants. One study found that neonates who heard the tape-recorded cry of a 5-day-old infant cried more than neonates who heard a synthetic cry or no sounds (Simner, 1971). Moreover, full-term newborns were able to distinguish between another infant's crying, an older child's crying, a chimpanzee's crying, and their own crying. Calm newborns ignored their own cries and those of an older child and a chimpanzee, but not those of other newborns. Crying infants continued to cry in response to another infant's crying, but stopped crying when they heard their own cry (Martin & Clark, 1982). (*Sources:* Angier, N. 1984. Medical clues from babies' cries, *Discover,* (September) 49-51; Campos, J. J., Barrett, K. C., Lamb, M. E., Goldsmith, H. H., & Stenberg, C. 1983. Socioemotional development. In P. H. Mussen (Ed.). *Handbook of Child Psychology,* 4th ed. 2. New York: Wiley; Lester, B. M. & Boukydis, C. F. Z. 1985. *Infant crying: Theoretical and research perspectives,* New York: Plenum; Martin, G. B. & Clark III, R. D. 1982. Distress crying in neonates: Species and peer specificity. *Developmental Psychology, 18,* 3-9; Simner, M. L. 1971. Newborn's response to the cry of another infant. *Developmental Psychology, 5,* 136-150; Turkington, C. 1984. Psychologists help spot danger in crib. *APA Monitor,* December, 38; Wolff, P. H. 1969. The natural history of crying and other vocalizations in early infancy. In B. Fuss (Ed.). *Determinants of infant behavior.* Vol. 4. New York: Wiley; Zeskind, P. S. & Marshall, T. R. 1988. The relation between variations in pitch and maternal perceptions of infant crying. *Child Development, 59,* 193-196.)

7.   Two Explanations for Brain Lateralization during Infancy

1.   **No-change hypothesis** (Kinsbourne & Hiscock, 1983). According to this hypothesis, brain lateralization is present early in life. Young infants have preferred postural positions (typically to the right) and a hand preference. PET scans of young infants reveal larger speech centers in the left hemisphere, and 15-week-old infants exhibit a right ear advantage in hearing.
2.   **Progressive hypothesis** (Aoki & Siekevitz, 1988). According to this hypothesis, brain lateralization increases in early childhood. Evidence for this idea includes the great neuroplasticity of infant brains, which allows one part of the brain to perform more than the task it was designed to do. Children under 5 years old have incredible ability to adapt to damage to the left hemisphere by having the right hemisphere assume language responsibilities. Older individuals, such as persons recovering from a stroke, have some incomplete recovering due to plasticity. (*Sources:* Aoki, C. & Siekevitz, P. 1988 (December). Plasticity in brain development. *Scientific American,* 56-64; Kinsbourne, M. & Hiscock, M. 1983. Normal and deviant development of functional lateralization of the brain. In P. H. Mussen (Ed.). *Handbook of Child Psychology (Vol. 2). Infancy and Developmental Psychology.* M. M. Harth & J. J. Campos (Vol. ed.). New York: Wiley.)

8.   Development of Stereopsis Infants

Stereopsis in infants is depth perception due to the disparity of images brought in by the two eyes. The average age of emergence of stereopsis is 14 weeks.

Held believed that stereopsis involved the segregation of neural pathways, and the prestereopsis, vision involves the overlap of the patterns brought in by both eyes. Shimajo studied this hypothesis using infants from the third through the twenty-fourth week.

Shimajo displayed (1) vertical lines to both eyes and (2) vertical lines to one eye and horizontal lines to the other eye. The first pattern should be preferred when vision is stereoptic because the second pattern would then be contradictory and confusing. However, since infants prefer checkerboard patterns to vertical lines, prestereoptic infants should prefer the second pattern (the overlapping of the two eyes' patterns would create a checkerboard). Indeed, Shimajo found that 25 of 27 infants who were younger than 13 weeks preferred the second pattern, but older infants preferred the first pattern. (*Sources:* Siegler, R. S. 1989. Mechanisms of cognitive development. *Annual Review of Psychology, 40,* 333-379; Mehler, J. & Fox, R. 1985. *Neonate cognition: Beyond the blooming conclusion.* Hillsdale, N.J.: Erlbaum.)

9. Reye's Syndrome Alert

Some infants and young children (and older individuals) get **Reye's syndrome** toward the end of a viral illness, such as chicken pox or the flu. Reye's syndrome can be misdiagnosed as encephalitis, meningitis, diabetes, poisoning, drug overdose, or sudden infant death.

Symptoms of Reye's syndrome are (1) relentless vomiting; (2) listlessness; (3) drowsiness; (4) personality change; (5) disorientation or confusion; (6) combativeness; (7) delirium, convulsions, or loss of consciousness.

Using aspirin or aspirin-containing medications to treat symptoms of viral illness *increases* the chance of developing Reye's syndrome. In fact, aspirin should not be used by individuals under the age of 19 years. Anti-nausea medicine may mask the symptoms of Reye's syndrome.

Two liver function tests can be done to test for the possibility of Reye's syndrome. When treated early, 90 percent recover. (*Source:* National Reye's Syndrome Foundation.)

BROWN & BENCHMARK'S HUMAN DEVELOPMENT TRANSPARENCIES (2ND ED.)

Transparency Number and Title

The transparency set, a supplement to *Child Development*, is accompanied by an annotated manual that describes each of the 141 transparencies. The annotated manual also offers suggestions about how to use the transparencies to engage your students in active learning that will stimulate critical thinking and evaluative skills. The following transparencies are appropriate and useful with Chapter 5: Physical, Motor, and Perceptual Development in Infancy.

Transparency Number and Title

10	Biological, Cognitive, and Socioemotional Processes in Life-Span Development
11	Periods and Processes in the Life Span
48	Infant Reflexes
49	Developmental Changes in Height and Weight from Birth to Eighteen Months
50	Developmental Milestones in Gross Motor Development
51	The Development of Gross Motor Skills in Infancy
52	The Development of Dendritic Spreading
134	Infant Development

CLASSROOM ACTIVITIES OR DEMONSTRATIONS

1. Discuss the critical thinking exercises. Exercise 1 continues the activity of examining illustrative material presented in the text. While this activity is similar to the previous one, it involves more interpretation. You may want to discuss with students how inferences can be drawn from the tables and figures beyond what is indicated in text or captions.

The point of exercise 2 is to have students attend to the difference between sensation and perception and to examine the sorts of inferences researchers make about infant perceptual capacities based on infant behavior. Both of these issues are good topics for discussion prior to having students do this exercise. The distinction between sensation and perception is not clear to people working in the field, and some researchers do not feel it is productive to make the separation. Nevertheless, an interesting way to apply the distinction is to discuss whether infants' discrimination between stimuli or their reaction to stimulating events represents some sort of innate, reflexive response or whether it is based on active interpretation. You can guide students' solutions to this exercise by having them try to decide which of the results for each of the senses described in the text most convincingly indicate active perceptual processes.

Exercise 3 continues to provide practice with the distinctions between inferences, observations, and assumptions. An interesting feature of this one is that the passage used for it bases its conclusion on something that we actually do not know - normal patterns of parent-infant interaction. So we are obliged to assume that these include the kinds of face to face interactions said to provide adequate exercise.

2. Discuss the students' research projects as suggested below.

3. In small groups, have students plan a day-care program for infants that would facilitate motor perceptual development and that is based on suggestions from current research findings on infant motor and perceptual development. They could do this in two parts. First, they could review research findings that are relevant to the task. Second, they could plan the day-care program.

Source: King, M. B. & Clark, D. E. 1990. *Instructor's Manual to accompany Children.* Dubuque: Wm. C. Brown Publishers.

4. When doing the unit on infancy attempt to bring an infant into the class. One of the students very often has an infant in his or her family or knows someone who does; most often a phone call is all it takes to get the parent to bring the baby to the class. Before the infant arrives, be sure to have covered the Apgar, the Brazelton Neonatal Assessment Scale, and the Denver Developmental Screening Test in lecture. Tell the students before the demonstration that it will be their task to determine the age of the child as well as their developmental scores. It is best if each student gets a copy of the screening devices ahead of time. They should be familiar enough with the tasks that they can form their questions before the class period begins.

    Have the parent bring the infant in about 20 minutes into a 50-minute lecture period and then run the infant through some of the components of each of the screening devices. The infant, if awake, will tolerate between 10 and 20 minutes of manipulation before deciding that it is too young to be in college. Conduct the behavioral tests but only at the direction of the students. Let them tell you what tests to do.

    After the infant leaves or refuses to play anymore, have students try to determine what its scores would be on the various measures. If the infant is unresponsive or asleep during the class period, allow the students to ask questions. Students may ask the parent how the infant behaves under different circumstances. To close the activity ask the class to give its best guess as to the specific age of the infant and its scores. Ask the parent to reveal the infant's actual age and, if known, the baby's latest score on the screening device of the pediatrician's choice.

    If your department or library does not have a copy of the screening devices, a local pediatrician may be convinced to part with a copy of what they use and to offer some quick instruction on how to use it. They might even volunteer to come in and give the screening.

5. *To circumcise or not to circumcise - that is the cutting question.*

    Have the class come up with the advantages and disadvantages of circumcision. Take a vote on position (any differences by students' gender, age, or parenting status?).

Against circumcision:

- Surgery has a little risk, as do all surgeries; after-surgery care is important for avoiding infection.
- Physical trauma occurs because most circumcisions are performed without anesthesia.
- There is no evidence that a circumcised male is less likely to acquire or transmit venereal disease.
- Cancer of the penis is quite rare.

For circumcision:

- Parents can make certain that after-surgery care is properly done and infection is avoided.
- Parents can request safe local anesthesia for the baby during the procedure.
- Circumcised males have easier hygiene to practice.
- Circumcised men are less likely to contract cancer of the penis.

Source: Squires, S. 1990 (June). Medinews, *Ladies' Home Journal,* 94.

6. *The direct perception and constructivist views.*

    Have students present the main assumptions of the direct perception and constructivist position and also attempt to relate these two positions back to earlier philosophical ideas (e.g., constructivist position is related to John Locke's tabula rasa and empiricism). Also, have students offer research findings that support each position.

Source: Adapted from King, M. B. & Clark, D. E. 1989. *Instructor's Manual to Santrock and Yussen's Child Development: An Introduction,* 4th ed. Dubuque, IA: William C. Brown Communications.

7.   *Evaluating Gesell's 1940 conclusions about early development*
            Arnold Gesell established his clinic of Child Development at Yale in 1911. He developed the one-way vision screen technique to observe infants and children. Gesell was a pioneer in describing (1) how a normal child grows and (2) how one normal child differs from another. In 1940, Gesell gave the following conclusions about children's development. Have students discuss whether they find Gesell's conclusions to be fairly accurate. Why and why not? Can they give research or everyday examples of these conclusions?

•   The first five years of life are the most important in an individual's education.
•   Early childhood upbringing (what he called "developmental supervision") is primarily a medical problem.
•   Parent training is as important as child training.
•   Children should not be forced to read at 6 if they are not ready.
•   Something should be done about homes in which children are scolded, threatened, shouted at, slapped, or beaten.
•   A child is not a miniature adult but a growing being who changes radically during these years.

Source: Gerow, J. 1988. *Time Retrospective,* 26.

8.   Have students in small groups compose a letter to a new parent. In this letter have them provide information about games to play with the baby which will reveal the perceptual abilities of the baby. Base your games on current research findings and tasks from the Brazelton Scale.
            One game that can be suggested is an imitation game. Try to get the infant to imitate facial gestures. Sticking out one's tongue should get the most responses.
            A second game can be based on the principles of habituation and orientation.
            Another game could be based on the looming effect. Other appropriate options include hide-and-seek or peek-a-boo.

Source: Adapted from King, M. B. & Clark, D. E. 1989. *Instructor's Manual to Santrock and Yussen's Child Development: An Introduction,* 4th ed. Dubuque, IA: Wm. C. Brown Publishers.

CRITICAL THINKING EXERCISES

Exercise 1

Chapter 6 contains a number of tables and figures that illustrate various topics. Some of these are listed below, paired with an interpretation of the information they present. Which interpretation is most accurate? **Circle the letter of the best answer, and explain why it is the best answer and why each other answer is not as good.**

A. Figure 5.1: Reflexes that disappear involve patterns of gross motor behavior.
B. Figure 5.3: Growth in height and weight slows down during the first two years of life.
C. Figure 5.4: Most infants can walk by themselves before they are 1 year old.
D. Figure 5.6: The number of brain cells increases dramatically during the first two years of life.
E. Figure 5.7: There is no evidence that 2-month-old infants can discriminate between colors.

Exercise 2

In this chapter, Santrock distinguishes between the concepts of sensation and perception and then takes the reader on a tour of the sensory and perceptual capacities of human infants. For which sense do we appear to know the most about the perceptual capabilities of infants? **Circle the letter of the best answer, and explain why it is the best answer and why each other answer is not as good.**

A. vision
B. hearing
C. smell
D. taste
E. touch

Exercise 3

Explorations in Child Development 5.1 makes a case against having infants participate in exercise classes. Which of the following is an assumption underlying this advice, rather than an inference or an observation? **Circle the letter of the best answer, and explain why it is the best answer and why each other answer is not as good.**

A. More infants are suffering bone fractures and other injuries today than in the past.
B. Adults do not usually know babies' physical limits.
C. Infants achieve no aerobic benefits from exercise.
D. There is a variety of infant exercise programs.
E. Today's parents regularly touch and play with their infants.

ANSWER KEYS FOR CRITICAL THINKING EXERCISES

Exercise 1

A. This is not accurate. The grasping reflex, for one, involves fine motor behavior.
B. This is accurate. The family of curves in this figure all "bend downward," which indicates that the rate of change in growth is slowing down.
C. This is not accurate. The figure shows a broad band of time during which infants begin to walk unaided. This time frame extends well past 1 year of age.
D. This is not accurate. The figure illustrates the increasing richness of connections between neurons, not an increase in the number of neurons. Dendrites are nerve processes that connect neurons, not separate nerve cells.
E. This is not accurate. Although the differences are small, 2-month-old infants appear to fixate on red, yellow, and white discs for different amounts of time. This suggests that they can discriminate between these colors.

Exercise 2

A. Vision is the best answer. We know of several kinds of visual discriminations that infants can make (e.g., striped vs. gray fields, stages of face perception, depth perception, and coordination of vision and touch). These all seem to require different kinds of interpretations of visual stimuli and involve a greater variety of interpretations compared with the other senses.
B. Hearing is not the best answer. Facts are presented about auditory discrimination, the coordination of hearing and vision, and hearing sensitivity. The first two are arguably aspects of perception, but the last seems more an example of sensation (registering the occurrence of a stimulus). So "vision" is a better answer.
C. Smell is not the best answer. We know about a small number of smell discriminations that infants can make. These qualify as perceptions, but we have fewer examples of different olfactory perceptions than visual perceptions.
D. Taste if not the best answer. Again, we mainly know about various discriminations that are possible. Some of these discriminations, however, appear to be based on responses newborns make to very specific taste stimuli, which may indicate that "true" perception is involved.
E. Touch is not the best answer. Much of the information about touch comes from studies of reflexes; hence, it is unclear whether perception is involved. Nothing is indicated about touch discriminations, and the only perceptual phenomenon noted is the coordination of touch and vision.

A. This is an observation. It is based on reports by pediatricians of the types of infant injuries they see.
B. This is an inference. It is an attempt to explain how adults injure their infants when exercising them. However, the passage presents no direct information about what adults know about infants' physical capacities.
C. This is an inference. It is based on the claim in the passage that infants' limbs cannot be stretched enough to provide truly aerobic exercise. However, no direct information about whether exercise for infants is aerobic or not appears in the passage.
D. This is an observation. It presumably is based on a canvass of the types of programs that have been made available to parents.
E. This is the assumption. It is stated as a condition (the reference to couch potatoes) of the conclusion that infants need no special exercise beyond what they ordinarily get in day-to-day interactions with their parents. However, no information about parents' normal interaction patterns with the infants is presented.

RESEARCH PROJECT 1   GROSS MOTOR ACTIVITY

This project provides an observational exercise for examining the gross motor activity of children. Pair up with another student in the class and go to a local daycare. Observe two infants, one about six months old and the other about one year old. For each infant, describe five gross motor behaviors the infant performs while you are observing. (See your text for sample behavior to note.) Then answer the questions that follow.

Infant 1	Infant 2
Sex___Age___	Sex___Age___
Behavior 1 ( )	Behavior 1 ( )
Behavior 2 ( )	Behavior 2 ( )
Behavior 3 ( )	Behavior 3 ( )
Behavior 4 ( )	Behavior 4 ( )
Behavior 5 ( )	Behavior 5 ( )

Questions

1. What were the five behaviors you observed?
2. In general how can these behaviors be characterized or described for the six-month-old? For the one-year-old?
3. How did the infants differ in the way they performed the behaviors?
4. From your observations of the two infants and five behaviors, what do you see as the course of development of gross motor behavior between sixth months and one year? How do your specific findings compare with the general descriptions reported in the text?

Use in Classroom

Have the students discuss the results of the research project. Divide the class into small groups after the observations have been made and ask them to discuss general trends that appear in the observations when examining data from more than one infant at each age. Are there any sex differences that show up in the development of gross motor activity? Are any differences evident because of the choice of behavior that was observed? If so, what might account for those differences?

RESEARCH PROJECT 2   REFLEXES

For this research project, you will need the permission of parents of a young infant (one to four months old) and an older infant (six to twelve months old) to examine their infant's reflex repertoire. In order to test the two infants, you will need to clear this project through the human subjects review board at your school and get a signed informed consent form from the baby's parents. You may work in groups of 2 to 4 to make it easier to locate and gain access to the appropriately aged infants. Be certain to indicate age by months because your results will vary if you use a 2-month vs a 4-month baby or a 6-month vs an 11-month baby.

For each infant, perform the stimulation necessary to elicit the reflexive behavior. Note which of the reflexes are present (P) or absent (A) for each infant. You may mark these responses in the chart below. After performing the demonstration with each infant, answer the questions.

Reflex	Stimulation and reflex	Infant 1 Sex___ Age___	Infant 2 Sex___ Age___
Placing	Backs of infant's feet are drawn against a flat surface's edge: Baby withdraws foot	P/A	P/A
Walking	Hold baby under arms with bare feet touching flat surface: Baby makes steplike motions that appear like coordinated walking	P/A	P/A
Darwinian (grasping)	Stroke palm of infant's hand: Baby makes strong fist; if both fists are closed around a stick, the infant could be raised to standing position	P/A	P/A
Tonic neck	Baby is laid down on back: Infant turns head to one side and extends arms and legs on preferred side and flexes opposite limbs	P/A	P/A
Moro (startle)	Make a sudden, loud noise near infant: Infant extends legs, arms, and fingers, arches back, and draws back head	P/A	P/A
Babinski	Stroke sole of baby's foot: Infant's toes fan out and foot twists in	P/A	P/A
Rooting	Stroke baby's cheek with one's finger: Baby's head turns, mouth opens, and sucking movements begin	P/A	P/A

Questions

1. How many of the reflexive behaviors were exhibited by the younger infants? By the older infants?
2. Which reflexes dropped out early?

3.   What responses seem to replace each of the reflexive behaviors in the older infants?
4.   What might be the adaptive value of each reflex in the newborn's repertoire?

Use In Classroom

Gather the reflex data and discuss the above questions based on all the data that is available. Discuss the reasons for why reflexes drop out.

ESSAY AND CRITICAL THINKING QUESTIONS

Comprehension and Application Essay Questions

We recommend that you provide students with our guidelines for "Answering Essay and Critical Thinking Questions" when you have them respond to these questions. Their answers to these kinds of questions demonstrate an ability to comprehend and apply ideas discussed in this chapter.

1.   Explain how it is possible for developmentalists to study newborns and infants and learn about their early competencies.
2.   How would you explain the importance of reflexes and their development to a friend?
3.   Identify and describe the general patterns in the development of infant motor capabilities during the first year.
4.   Compare and contrast the development of gross and fine motor skills during infancy.
5.   Describe the various states of infant consciousness. Also explain their relationship to sleep and waking?
6.   Discuss the pros and cons of breast- versus bottle-feeding.
7.   Define and distinguish sensation, perception, and intermodal perception. Also explain why they make interesting problems for study by developmentalists and what practical problems their study might solve?
8.   Apparently infants can imitate facial expression nearly at birth, but have 20-200 to 20-600 vision at birth. Provide a rationale for understanding this apparent inconsistency.
9.   Explain what we know about the ability of infants to hear.
10. Do infants feel pain? Also indicate evidence that challenges the traditional practice of not administering anesthetics to infants having operations.
11. Evaluate the pros and cons of exercise classes for infants.
12. Explain why what is good food for an adult is not necessarily good food for an infant.

Critical Thinking Questions

We recommend that you have students follow our guidelines for "Answering Essay and Critical Thinking Questions" when you ask them to prepare responses to these questions. Their answers to these kinds of questions reflect an ability to apply critical thinking skills to a novel problem or situation that is *not* specifically discussed in the chapter. These items most appropriately may be used as take-home essay questions (e.g., due on exam day) or as homework exercises that can be answered either by individuals or groups. Collaboratively answered questions encourage cooperative learning by students, and reduce the number of papers that must be graded.

1.   At the end of Chapter 5 Santrock indicates books that provide practical knowledge about children and lists resources for improving the lives of children. Choose one of these books or resources and read it or learn as much as you can about it. Then write a brief review in which you (a) characterize the book or resource, and (b) explain how the book or resource relates to material in the chapter.
2.   Chapter 1 defines the nature of development in terms of biological, cognitive, and social processes, and periods or stages. Indicate your ability to think critically by identifying material in this chapter that illustrates developmental processes and periods. If there is little or no information in this chapter about developmental processes and periods, identify and explain how developmental processes and periods could be used to guide the analysis of any topic in the chapter.
3.   According to Chapter 1, three fundamental developmental issues concern: (a) maturation (nature) versus experience (nurture), (b) continuity versus discontinuity, and (c) early versus later experience. Indicate your ability to think critically by identifying material in this chapter that illustrates each of the three fundamental developmental issues. If there is little or no information in this chapter about fundamental developmental issues, identify and explain how these issues could be used to guide the analysis of any topic in the chapter.

4. One aspect of thinking critically is to read, listen, and observe carefully and then ask questions about what is missing from a text, discussion, or situation. For example, your author includes a list of activities for the visual and tactile stimulation of infants; however, there is no comparable list for any other sensory modality. Indicate your ability to think critically by (a) speculating about why your author only listed activities for visual stimulation, and (b) devising your own list of age-appropriate activities for at least two other sensory modalities.

5. Santrock sets off several quotations in this chapter. Indicate your ability to think critically by selecting one of the quotes and (a) learning about the author and indicating why this individual is eminently quotable (i.e., what was this individual's contribution to human knowledge and understanding), (b) interpreting and restating the quote in your own terms, and (c) explaining what concept, issue, perspective, or term in this chapter that Santrock intended this quote to illuminate. In other words, about what aspect or issue in development does this quote make you pause and reflect?

6. Chapter 2 indicates that theories help us explain data and make predictions about various aspects of development. Chapter 2 then presents six different theoretical approaches (i.e., Freudian, cognitive, behavioral and social learning, ethological, ecological, and eclectic theory), but notes that no single approach explains the complexity of development. Indicate your ability to think critically by (a) perusing this chapter for topics influenced by at least one of the six theoretical approaches, and (b) explaining which theoretical approach dominated the topic in question. If the presentation is entirely atheoretical, identify and explain how one of the theoretical approaches could be used to guide the analysis of the topic in question.

7. At the 1992 meeting of the American Association for the Advancement of Science, Michelle Lampl (University of Pennsylvania) reported that contrary to the belief that growth is gradual, babies between the ages of 3 and 15 months literally grew overnight up to three-quarters of an inch. Carl Fackler, an orthopedic surgeon, said that he was intrigued by the report, but felt a larger study was needed to determine its factual correctness. Apply your knowledge about the scientific method by designing a study to determine whether tiny tots grow gradually or in spurts: (a) What specific problem or question do you want to study? (b) What predictions would you make and test in your study? (c) What measures would you use (i.e., controlled observation in a laboratory, naturalistic observation, interviews and questionnaires, case studies, standardized tests, cross-cultural studies, physiological research, research with animals, or multimeasure, multisource, and multicontext approach) and how would you define each measure clearly and unambiguously? (d) What strategy would you follow--correlational or experimental, and what would be the time span of your inquiry--cross-sectional or longitudinal? (e) What ethical considerations must be addressed before you conduct your study? Note that M. Lampl, J. D. Veldhuis, and M. L. Johnson published their results in an article titled "Saltation and Stasis: A Model of Human Growth" that appeared in the October 30, 1992 issue of *Science* (Volume 258, pages 801-803).

8. According to Chapter 2, your author wants you to become a wise consumer of information about child development by: (a) being cautious about media reports, (b) distinguishing between nomothetic research and idiographic needs, (c) recognizing how easy it is to overgeneralize from a small or clinical sample, (d) knowing that a single study is usually not the defining word about some aspect of child development, (e) remembering that causal conclusions cannot be made from correlation studies, and (f) always considering the source of the information and evaluating its credibility. Indicate your ability to think critically by, first, selecting an article from either a journal, magazine, or newspaper about any topic regarding Physical, Motor, and Perceptual Development in Infancy, and, second, evaluating it in terms of these six objectives. If the information in the article is insufficient to evaluate one of these objectives, then specify what kind of information you would need to evaluate the objective.

6 Physical Development in Childhood and Puberty

SUGGESTIONS FOR LECTURE TOPICS

1. The Development of Attention and Reaction Time

The development and control of attention probably results from changes at a variety of levels. On the one hand, studies suggest that the brain is becoming more mature and myelination more complete. On the other hand, children are becoming cognitively more sophisticated and able to employ limited sorts of conscious control over their attention.

In this lecture, first sketch the development of attention during the toddler years. You may wish to review material in the text, but flesh it out either with more detail from the studies cited or with additional studies. Characterize the typical child's attentional capacities during play, in interactions with adults, and while watching television. Discuss how such factors as fatigue, distractibility, and ability to understand what is happening influence attention. Consider the nature of the stimuli typical of these situations as well.

Next, outline the development of reaction time or other indices of basic information processing during this period (e.g., span of apprehension). You should be able to suggest a parallel between improvements in information processing efficiency on the one hand, and deployment, maintenance, and control of attention on the other.

Finally, present work that suggests that young children's attention can be improved if they are taught attentional strategies, such as talking to themselves in ways that direct their attention away from distracting stimuli. In development these points speculate about how efficient information processing may be necessary for adequate cognitive control.

Summarize your lecture by reviewing the various levels of information processing and cognitive control. You may wish to use a diagram or flow chart of some sort to organize these levels and suggest relationships between them. The result will be an organized presentation of information that relates basic brain development to enhanced cognitive functioning, as well as a scheme that will prove useful later in presentations about information processing approaches to cognition.

2. Teaching Toddlers to Draw

Should children be taught to draw? Or should they be allowed simply to draw however they wish, letting their motor, perceptual, and cognitive skills develop and enhance their drawing skills naturally?

Tackle these questions in a lecture that relates fine motor development during toddlerhood to children's drawing abilities. You may with to invite a day-care or kindergarten teacher to present information on typical experiences with drawing provided to young children, and have them comment on whether they are concerned with using training to enhance drawing abilities.

You may wish to open your (or your guest's) presentation to class discussion. Are there reasons why we might want to teach children to draw? Can drawing skills be trained? What is the nature of individual differences in drawing skill at these ages? Are these predictive of later skill? Were great painters talented scribblers as toddlers? You may find that this information is very interesting to students. Many suspect that drawing is something each of us wish we could do better if we only had the talent. But perhaps early training could enhance our subsequent artistic skills.

3. Systematic Studies of Young Children's Drawings

Children's drawings also provide an opportunity to discuss another observational approach to child development, the systematic study of things that children create. The work of Rhoda Kellogg is an excellent resource here. Get a copy of her *Understanding Children's Art* and prepare several overheads to illustrate children's drawings at several ages during early childhood. Begin a lecture/discussion by viewing these drawings in succession.

After broadly characterizing the developmental progressions apparent in the drawings, discuss how changes in the pictures might be analyzed or quantified. Review Kellogg's approach, but consider whether others are also appropriate. You should be able to show that the drawings can be assessed both quantitatively and qualitatively. For example, drawings will increase in number and accuracy of detail, but they will also increase in their organization and complexity. Patricia Greenfield has suggested that they, in fact, show changes in organization that parallel changes in language and cognitive development, exhibiting greater organization and hierarchical relationships between elements.

Conclude with a discussion of the value of drawings as measures of child development. Present in some detail one or two views, or sketch the range of interpretation given to drawings. You may wish to conclude this class with an assignment that requires students to get their own samples of drawings and subsequently to evaluate and interpret them using approaches such as Kellogg's.

4.   Nature and Nurture in Adolescent Development

Popular lore contends that biology looms large as a direct determinant of developmental behavior at the onset of adolescence. Hormones are said to create new sex drives, moods, and aggressive tendencies; some even suggest that girls become innately more interested in babies. Brain changes are said to lead directly to mental development. However, according to the 1984 *Minnesota Symposium on Child Psychology,* the issue is by no means so clear. Entrance into adolescence is also accompanied by radical changes in school experience, regard by adults, and individual children's expectations about how they ought to feel and what they ought to experience. Biological change is thoroughly confounded with social, cognitive, and personality change.

     Discuss this problem in a lecture. Give reasons why interpreting behavioral changes as the direct result of biological changes is probably too simple, likely erroneous, and possibly even pernicious (e.g., do boys really have a powerful sex drive that must be released?). Outline Anne Peterson's schema for direct and indirect effects, and give real examples of both if you can find them. You may conclude that evidence for direct effects usually is confounded with other factors and that the evidence for indirect effects is more compelling. For example, the classic literature on early versus late maturers is a powerful hint that indirect effects are important. Another source is Laurence Steinberg's treatment of changes in parenting at puberty.

     You may begin or conclude with the note that this is a classic issue in adolescence. Refer to the biological versus cognitive views of the period and the theoretical and practical consequences of taking either point of view.

5.   Application of Child Psychology: Books for Adolescents on the Development of Their Bodies

Find a book written for young adolescents that is designed to teach them about their bodies. Make appropriate overheads of representative illustrations, and extract representative passages to show how the book teaches about the diverse physical and physiological changes of pubescence.

     Next, compare the book's information with more formal presentations given in textbooks. Is the information accurate? Up-to-date? Does the book attempt to make the material suitable and palatable to young teens, or does it distort or misrepresent the information in any way?

     Finally, analyze the approach taken by the book's authors to determine how well they apply what is known about cognitive, emotional, and personality development in their presentation. Speculate on the likely effect the book would have on its consumers according to your analysis. Would they benefit from it? Would their questions likely be answered? If necessary, make recommendations about how the book could be improved.

6.   The Research of James Tanner

Some of the best research on adolescence is James Tanner's research on physical and physiological development during adolescence. Tanner's work has been the standard reference for better than 20 years. He performed meticulous, detailed descriptive studies that have provided standards for determining developmental age, typical growth rates and causes of atypical growth rates, and the precise nature of biological changes that occur throughout adolescence.

     Use Tanner's work both as a model of excellent research and for the information it provides about adolescent physical and physiological development. His books contain a wealth of photographs, tables, and graphs that can be used to illustrate the uses of data as well as trends in growth and development. This information also illustrates the concept of stages of growth, qualitative versus quantitative change, and stable versus changing characteristics. As such, it can serve as an important reprise of these basic developmental concepts as you near the end of the course.

7.   Organ Growth and Changes

Of course, all bodily systems are becoming more complex and larger from birth on. Here are a small number of physical bodily changes that occur in the early years:

•   **Ossification** is the process by which cartilage is turned into hard bone. At birth, the only ossified bones are in the face and cranium. During childhood, girls are ahead of boys, and blacks are ahead of whites in the ossification process.

•   Muscles grow at twice the pace of bone growth. The increased size and strength of the muscles allow toddlers to engage in better motor abilities and play activities.

•   Infants have thin skin layers and limited ability to produce pigmentation. Therefore, infants are more susceptible to blistering, chafing, and sunburn than are older children and adults. In addition, sweat glands of infants are not yet fully functioning.

•   During the first year, the heart doubles in weight and shifts from an almost horizontal to a more vertical position. In the first months, walls of the left ventricle become thicker than the right because the left ventricle is more crucial in pumping blood to the rest of the body.

•   Weight of the lungs doubles from birth to six months and triples from birth to the first year.

•   Salivary glands mature at about the third month, and at this time there is an increase in drooling. (*Sources:* Ashburn, S. S. 1986. Biophysical development of the toddler and the preschooler. In C. S. Schuster & S. S. Ashburn. *The process of human development: A holistic life-span approach,* 2nd ed. Boston: Little, Brown & Co.)

8.   Synatogenesis

Synaptogenesis is the production of synaptic connections in the brain. The greatest numbers of synapses are produced in late prenatal and early postnatal periods. Density increases during the first two years of life, resulting in an overproduction of synapses. So, from 2 years to 7 years, there is a pruning of synaptic connections.

From 6 months to 7 years, children have more synapses than do adults. This high number may lead to a higher ability to learn object permanence and delay-response problems, and aid progress in walking and speaking.

Environmental factors also influence the amount of synaptogenesis. Rats in cages that allow exploration and enriched cognitive experiences end up with 25 percent more synapses per neuron in the upper visual cortex than do rats in conventional cages.

Greenenough suggests that initial over production of synapses is largely maturationally regulated, but how pruning of synapses takes place is largely dependent on experience. Normal experiences result in typical connections, but abnormal experiences result in atypical connections. (*Sources:* Siegler, R. S. 1989. Mechanisms of cognitive development. *Annual Review of Psychology, 40,* 353-379; Greenenough, W. T. 1985. Differential rearing effects on rat visual cortex synapses. I. Synaptic and neuronal density and synapses per neuron. *Brain Research, 329,* 195-203.)

9.   Body Changes in the Preschool Years

Here are a few other facts about physical growth during the preschool years:

•   By 4 years, preschoolers double their birth length.

•   At 3 years, children's brains are three-fourths of their adult size; by 5 years, children's brains are about 90 percent of their adult size.

•   Preschoolers' skin becomes less soft as the water content of their skin decreases, and they develop fine hair on their legs and lower arms.

•   By their third birthday, salivary glands are adult-sized.

•   Changes in the brain allow preschoolers to have much better body temperature regulation than they did as infants and toddlers.

•   Preschoolers continue to have more **ossification** of their bones, but this process is not complete until early adulthood. Therefore, children in their early childhood years are more prone to bone, joint, and muscle injuries than are older children.

•   From birth until 5 years, children's hearts quadruple in weight.

•   During the preschool years, children's hair tends to become thicker, darker, and less curly.

•   Children in the play years have legs and feet whose appearance is affected by their early walking activities. Early walkers, for example, are more likely to have bowed legs and to be flat-footed. Flat footedness can be helped by allowing the young children to be barefoot most of the time. (*Source:* Schuster, C. S. & Ashburn, S. S. 1986. *The process of human development: A holistic life-span approach,* 2nd ed., Boston: Little Brown.)

10.   Preschoolers' Attitudes about Medical Personnel and Illness

The equipment and uniforms of medical personnel, and the formality of the offices of doctors and dentists, may scare small children. Parents should recognize their children's feelings as legitimate, and try to reassure their children. It is helpful to familiarize children with the typical procedure that doctors do. Presence of parents during appointments often reassure small children. It is also helpful to calmly inform small children about a half day before the appointment that they are visiting the doctor or dentist (Salk, 1983).

About 4,000,000 children stay overnight in a hospital each year. About 80 percent of pediatric hospitals and 49 percent of general hospitals have preadmission programs for children to help children learn about hospital procedures and to ally their fears. Parents can get a staff pediatric specialist at other hospitals to arrange an individualized pre-op hospital tour. Using hospital play, demonstrating typical procedures such as taking blood pressure, and being sensitive yet realistic in describing medical procedures helps children deal with hospital experiences (Richmond, 1989).

Towards the end of the play years, most children have come to believe that illness is caused by their behaviors or non-behaviors. They view sickness as a punishment for not obeying the rules (Elkind, 1981). Young children who are not feeling well need reassurance from their parents and other adults that they are not bad children. (*Sources:* Elkind, D. 1981. Recent research in cognitive and language development. In L. T. Benjamin, Jr. *The G. Stanley Hall Lecture Series, Vol. 1.* 65-88; Salk, L. 1983. *What every child would like his parents to know,* NY: Simon & Schuster. Richmond, S. 1989 (October). When your child goes to the hospital. *Changing Times,* 116.)

11.   Juvenile Hyperthyroidism and Pituitary Dwarfs

When biological aspects of the growth program are deficient, impairment of growth occurs. In juvenile **hypothyroidism** ("hypo-" means "under," so hypothyroidism involves too little hormonal activity in the thyroid), for example, an 11-year-old may have the bone age of 6 years and the average height of a 7-year-old. This 4- to 5-year height deficit translates to more than nine inches. Treatment over a few years at this age can help to narrow the gap between this child with juvenile hypothyroidism and the average child (Fisher, 1988; Rivkees et al., 1988).

In **pituitary dwarfs,** the pituitary gland produces an inadequate amount of **growth hormone.** Growth hormone stimulates the liver to produce **somatomedins,** which in turn stimulate bone growth. Researchers have also found that adults produce more growth hormone when fasting (i.e., growth hormone is produced during fasting to mobilize fat while **insulin** is produced during feasting to increase fat storage), when under stress, or when running. Therefore, the main role of growth hormone may be to conserve muscle tissue at the expense of fat tissue.

While growth hormone is legitimately used to treat pituitary dwarfs, some parents get their normal-height children injections of growth hormone to make them taller, and hopefully more successful in sports and in getting prestigious jobs. After all, executives and bank presidents are usually taller than their employees, and even bishops average more height than priests.

Until recently, growth hormone was produced from the pituitaries of cadavers; 50,000 were processed each year to supply nearly 6,000 patients. However, since 1985 a genetically engineered version has been created, with the resulting cost now being closer to $10,000 a year for three injections a week. (*Sources:* Fisher, D. A. 1988. Catch-up growth in hypothyroidism. *New England Journal of Medicine,* March 10, 632-634; Rivkees, S. A., Bode, H. H., & Crawford, J. D. 1988. Long-term growth in juvenile acquired hypothyroidism: The failure to achieve normal adult stature. *New England Journal of Medicine, 318,* 599-602; Kolata, G. 1986. New growth industry in human growth hormone. *Science, 234,* 22-24.)

12.   Asthma

Asthma is a common respiratory illness that still goes underdiagnosed and undertreated. Many children (more boys than girls) who have asthma are diagnosed as having recurrent bronchitis or pneumonia. Of the 9.6 million asthmatic Americans, 3.2 million are children. About 10-12 percent of all children have asthma. In fact, about 80 percent of individuals who develop asthma exhibit some symptoms before the age of 5.

Asthma is airway obstruction from degranulation of mast cells in the lung's lining. The airways are affected by a variety of possible conditions, including an inherited genetic predisposition to asthma, viral infections, ingested allergens (e.g., milk, eggs), inhaled allergens (e.g., pollen, mold) pets, exercise, climatic changes (e.g., humidity), cigarette smoke, noxious fumes, and emotional stress. One study (Weitzman et al., 1990) that looked at the effects of passive smoking on asthma analyzed data from 4,331 children. Asthma was reported in 2.3 percent of children whose mothers did not smoke, 2.9 percent of children whose mothers smoked up to half a pack a day, and 4.8 percent of children whose mothers smoked at least half a pack a day.

Treatment during the acute phase is to create bronchodilation. Long-term treatment involves preventing or reducing the inflammatory process.

Many children with asthma (80-90 percent) wheeze, but wheezing can be an indicator of other heart or pulmonary problems. A minority of children have cough-variant asthma, in which a persistent cough instead of wheezing is the primary symptom.

Over 70 percent of asthmatic children have a mild case. In these cases, the asthma occurs seasonally or in response to a known stimulus. About 7 percent have severe asthma that requires frequent hospitalizations or emergency room visits.

Contrary to widely held beliefs: (1) Asthma does not typically mean frailty and no gym class. In fact, 11 percent of the athletes on U. S. Olympic teams have asthma. (2) Asthma is not outgrown, but about half of mildly asthmatic children experience a remission of symptoms during puberty. (3) Emotions are rarely the cause of asthma.

Typical symptom descriptions include episodes of: wheezing, cough, shortness of breath, chest pain, fatigue, loss of appetite, and upper respiratory tract infections. For children 5 and older, pulmonary function studies can be performed to document the degree of airway dysfunction or obstruction.

The first step in treatment is to stabilize the airways. Bronchodilation can be done using **inhaled beta$_2$-agonists. Theophyllines** may be used because of their effect on respiratory muscle function. In some cases **corticosteroids** are used for a few days because of their direct anti-inflammatory properties.

Cromolyn sodium may be used in a maintenance program to stabilize the mast cell membrane and prevent its degranulation. Severe asthma may require large doses of bronchodilators and steroids.

One study of asthma (Weiss, 1990) compared hospital discharges and deaths due to asthma from 1982 through 1986. During this five-year period, there were nearly half a million hospitalizations annually for asthma. Hospitalizations were more common for those under 5 years and older than 65 years. Hospitalization rates for nonwhites were almost three times higher than for whites. During this time period, there were 18,114 deaths due to asthma, or an average annual mortality rate of 1.52 per 100,000 population. Mortality rates differed by age with 0.17 per 100,000 for children younger than 5 years to 6.71 per 100,000 for those at least 65 years old. Mortality rates for nonwhites were twice as high as for whites.

The researcher found that for persons aged 5 through 24 years, hospitalizations peaked in September through November and deaths peaked in June through August. For individuals older than 64 years, however, both hospitalizations and deaths were more common during December through February. (*Sources:* Hen, Jr., J. 1989 (Winter). Asthma: Dispelling the myths. *PA Practice,* 14-16; Weiss, K. B. 1990 (May 2). Seasonal trends in U. S. asthma hospitalizations and mortality. *Journal of the American Medical Association, 263,* 2323-2328; Weitzman, M. et al., 1990 (April). Maternal smoking and childhood asthma. *Pediatrics, 85,* 505-511.)

13.   Epilepsy

Epilepsy involves recurring seizures caused by abnormal, excessive, synchronous discharges of cerebral neurons. More than 6 percent of the population have experienced at least one epileptic seizure, but the overall prevalence of epilepsy in the United States is 1-2 percent. The highest incidence of epilepsy is in children under the age of 4; the incidence falls from 5 to 9 years, but climbs again from 10 to 20 years before declining throughout adulthood.

Epileptic seizures have three phases: **prodrome** (or **aura**), **ictus** (or **seizure**) and **postictal state.** The aura is a consciously remembered motor, sensory, visceral, or psychological aspect that warns of an imminent seizure, e. g., headache, unpleasant smells, dizziness, or a sense of déjà vu. Aspects of the prodrome and two other phases help to classify seizure disorders. There are three major categories: partial, generalized, and unclassified. Correct diagnosis of the type of seizure is the key to effective medical management of epilepsy.

Partial seizures are characterized by local onset, focused in a specific area of the body. Partial seizures are more common than generalized seizures. **Simple partial seizures** are brief (about 30 seconds). Characteristics may involve twitching to massive jerking of a limb, loss of sensation in a limb, sweating, pupillary dilation, déjà vu, dream states, fear, and anger. In this type of disorder, no loss of consciousness occurs.

Some partial seizures progress to a more generalized form; these seizures start with twitching and spread along the anatomic arrangement of the motor strip from face to arm to leg (called the **"jacksonian march"**). Sometimes this type of seizure progresses to a grand mal seizure and there is loss of consciousness. In the minority of cases, a transient paralysis (**Todd's paralysis**) that lasts up to hours may occur following the seizure activity.

One-fifth to one-fourth of seizures in children are **complex partial seizures,** which last up to eight minutes. These seizures involve hallucinations, cognitive and emotional changes, psychomotor automatisms (including blinking, mumbling, smacking the lips, picking at clothes), and impairment of consciousness. Some complex partial seizures progress to generalized seizures.

Generalized seizures are bilateral and symmetrical. The best-known kind of generalized seizure is the **tonic-clonic** or **grand mal** seizure, which is experienced by just over one-tenth of epileptics. These tonic-clonic seizures are characterized by sudden loss of consciousness preceded by an aura. The tonic phase involves body rigidity, an "epileptic cry," and the rolling up of the eyes; the clonic phase involves rapid jerking of the head and extremities followed by slower jerking, incontinence, and breathing through clenched teeth. The tonic-clonic seizure lasts about one to two minutes, typically followed by a postictal state of unarousable coma (up to five minutes), confusion, disorientation, and deep sleep (one to two hours). Grand mal seizures are associated with significant mortality rates and are treated as a medical emergency.

Absence seizures, also known as **petit mal seizures,** are characterized by abrupt onset and no aura. They usually last two to fifteen seconds, but can occur 100 times a day, or up to 30 times in one hour. During the absence seizures, the patient stares while eyelids flutter rhythmically. Recovery is immediate, although there is amnesia for the event. Absence seizures usually appear between the ages of 4 and 10 and become less frequent with age, often disappearing by age 20.

Atonic seizures and **myoclonic seizures** occur almost exclusively in children. Atonic seizures produce loss of body tone; myoclonic seizures produce violent contraction of the neck, trunk, and upper extremities. Falls associated with both of these types may cause serious injuries, and patients may wear helmets to prevent serious head injuries.

Infantile spasms are myoclonic-like seizures that usually begin around 4 to 6 months. They involve jackknife seizures that come in a series. The incidence of mental retardation in infants with this disorder approaches 85 percent.

Epilepsy is a condition with many possible etiologies, such as congenital or developmental birth defects, anoxia or other birth injury, genetic metabolic defects, central nervous system infections, tumors, abscesses, head injury, toxins, and degenerative disease. (*Source:* Stajich, J. M. 1989 (November). Common neurological disorders. Part I: Vascular syndromes and epilepsy. *Physician Assistant,* 13-30.)

14.   Adolescents and Steroids

Have your class discuss what they know about **anabolic steroids,** whether they know of users (if not a personal friend, the Canadian track star Ben Johnson might be mentioned), and what they would do to reduce steroid usage among adolescents. Somewhere between 6 and 15 percent of high school boys have tried steroids or are current users. Anabolic steroid use among college athletes increased from 4 percent in 1985 to 5 percent in 1989. Would you want schools to do random drug testing of athletes (or all students) to reduce steroid use?

The first healthy persons to use anabolic steroids were not athletes, but Hitler's SS troops in World War II, to increase their aggressiveness. In 1954, a medical report mentioned that Russian athletes were using the steroids and by 1956 American athletes had **methandrostenolone (Dianabol)** available.

Two major patterns of taking anabolic steroids emerge among athletes. One technique is the **"stacking principle,"** or the simultaneous use of different anabolic steroid preparations to saturate many receptor sites. The second technique is a **cycling** method, which involves using different steroids over a six- to twelve-week period. Some do this style in a belief that it minimizes negative effects. It also means that specific steroids can be scheduled to meet different needs for competition.

Athletes use anabolic steroids to increase lean body mass, strength, and aggressiveness, and to reduce recovery time between workouts. Side effects during steroid use can include: increased muscle mass, dramatic mood swings, sleep disturbance, altered libido, male pattern baldness, acne, and facial hair in both female and male users. Side effects for males include **gynecomastia** (breast development), impotence, and lowered sperm count. Side effects for females include masculinization, **cliteromegaly** (enlarged clitoris), and **hirsutism** (male pattern of body hair). Adolescents who use anabolic steroids can experience precocious puberty. More serious effects (which may be irreversible) for both males and females include: impeded growth, early heart attack or stroke, liver failure or liver cancer, psychological addiction.

Abnormal aggression, mood swings, and psychiatric dysfunctions are also associated with anabolic steroid use. In a study of 41 football players and body builders who had used steroids, nine had the DSM-IIIR criteria for full affective syndrome and five had psychotic symptoms during the steroid usage. In a study of 100 health club athletes who used steroids, 90 percent reported episodes of aggressive and violent behavior.

In 1984, a report came out that 59 Soviet Olympia competitors and users of steroids had died. The study was poorly monitored, and in fact, some now believe that the report was a politically-inspired hoax rather than a valid scientific report. It may be that steroids cause medical complications, but not as many severe and fatal ones as assumed just a few years ago. (*Sources:* Sobel, D. 1989 (October). Health watch: Teens and steroids. *Ladies Home Journal,* 110; Windsor, R. E. 1988 (September 15). Anabolic steroid use by athletes: How serious are the health hazards? *Postgraduate Medicine, 84,* 37-49.)

15.   Acne and Its Treatment

Acne affects mostly teenagers, but it can occur in young children and in adults. Most adults with acne had acne in adolescence, but some do develop acne in their twenties and thirties.

Acne has several etiologies, including heredity and hormones. These factors trigger excessive oil production, causing oil ducts to become plugged, forming pimples and blackheads. Bacteria in the oil ducts aggravates acne.

Today, many medications are available to reduce the clogging of oil ducts and reduce the bacteria in the ducts. **Benzoyl peroxide** is available over-the-counter or in stronger forms by prescription. This medicine is applied on the skin and helps to reduce bacterial levels.

A prescription is needed for **Retin-A,** which will split apart skin cells that clump together in an oil duct. If using this medication, one must avoid sun exposure, use sunscreens, and wash only with mild soaps.

Certain antibiotics can be prescribed to reduce the levels of bacteria in the skin.

Hormone therapy can be used, because fluctuating levels of ovarian hormones can cause acne flare-ups, especially premenstrually. Prescribing an estrogen-containing oral contraceptive may work here. When women develop acne for the first time in their twenties or later, the problem is more likely to be due to increases in androgen. Control of this type of acne may involve oral contraceptives, cortisone-related medications, or androgen-blockers.

The most potent prescription medication for treating acne is **accutane,** which reduces oil production, plugging of the oil ducts, and bacteria in the skin. However, this drug is known to cause birth defects so it must be avoided with anyone who is pregnant or might become pregnant soon. When accutane is used, it is the sole treatment; the other possible solutions can be used in combination.

Assessment should also be done as to whether or not the person with acne is using any medications or cosmetics that can aggravate the situation. Oral contraceptives containing progestins and some anticonvulsant drugs, for example, may make acne worse. Cosmetics should be labeled **"noncomedogenic,"** which means that clinical tests have shown them to not contribute to skin problems. (*Source:* Sobel, D. 1990 (March). Acne treatments that could work for you. *Good Housekeeping,* 241.)

16.   Physically Unfit Teens

Although some adolescents are quite physically fit and plan their lives around exercise, good nutrition, and other good health habits, many adolescents are physically unfit. Some teenagers have bad health because of unhealthy choices—using drugs, smoking cigarettes, eating junk foods, leading inactive lives—but others are unfit largely due to the nonadoption of good health habits.

Between 1966 and 1986, there was a 39 percent increase in obesity among twelve- to seventeen-year-olds. Obesity tends to be resistant to change. About 70 percent of obese adolescents become obese adults. Only a minority of teenagers are obese because of binge-eating patterns; most obese teenagers overeat by a few too many calories consistently while underexercising (*Science,* 1986).

Heavy television viewing by adolescents is associated with obesity and other physical problems. For every hour of television viewing, the prevalence of obesity among teens goes up 2 percent (Dietz & Gortmaker, 1985). Television viewing encourages snacking and paying attention to food ads that push sugary or fatty foods while discouraging healthful exercise (*Science,* 1986).

Adolescents also model other adult behaviors that build unhealthy lifestyles. Many teenagers, for example, learn Type A behaviors of speed and impatience and hard-driving competitiveness from adult models. Within families, sons are especially likely to pick up this rapid, push style from their fathers (Weidner et al., 1988).

Schools can become part of the solution by providing more consistent and practical physical fitness education for all students. Currently among fourteen-year-olds, only 25 percent can do ten pull-ups and only 25 percent of all girls can do one pull-up. Twenty-five percent of all adolescent boys and 50 percent of all girls need longer than a half-hour to walk two miles (President's Council on Physical Fitness and Sports, 1987).

The best solution, however, is for adolescents and their parents to choose better health habits. For example, teenagers can limit their television viewing, eating fewer calorie-rich snacks, and cut down on alcohol, cigarettes, and other drugs. Teenagers can engage in regular physical exercise (such as walking, aerobics, bicycling, or swimming), eat nutritious foods regularly, switch to snacks such as raw vegetables, and get enough sleep and relaxation. (*Sources:* President's Council on Physical Fitness and Sports. 1987. *1985 School Population Fitness Survey.* Washington, D.C.; *Science.* 1986. Obese children: A growing problem. *Science, 232,* 20-21; Weidner, G., Sexton, G., Matarazzo, J. D., Perieira, C., & Friend, R. 1988. Type A behavior in children, adolescents, and their parents. *Developmental Psychology, 24,* 118-121.)

17.   Marijuana Use and Abuse

Cannabis sativa or marijuana has been cultivated for at least 5,000 years, but its use has never been as prevalent as in the last few decades. A 1985 National Institute on Drug Abuse survey reported that 62 million Americans had tried marijuana with 29 million using within the last year. In 1986, 5.1 million high school students (12 to 17 years old) had used marijuana (4.3 million in past year; 2.7 million in past month). In 1987, 16 percent of employed persons between 20 and 40 years old used marijuana within a month of when the survey was done. A 1988 study found detectable blood levels of marijuana in one-third of 1,023 patients treated for shock/trauma following accidents in Baltimore. In other words, marijuana is the most frequently used illicit drug in the United States.

While many persons think of marijuana as a harmless mind-altering substance, cannabis contains more than 400 chemicals, including 61 cannabinoids, 11 steroids, 20 nitrogenous compounds, 50 hydrocarbons, 103 terpenes, and benzopyrene. The effects on the body of most of these components is still unknown.

The primary psychoactive agent is **THC, or tetrahydrocannabinol.** In the 1970s THC content of marijuana ranged from 1 to 3 percent of the marijuana, but in the 1980s, more potent varieties of marijuana raised the THC content to between 5 and 15 percent. Tetrahydrocannabinol is fat soluble and it binds tightly to proteins in the blood. Therefore, THC is quickly taken up by tissues that are well supplied with blood: the liver, spleen, lungs, kidneys, testes, and ovaries. THC reaches the brain within 14 seconds of being smoked. The half-life of THC is about 56 hours in first-time users and 28 hours in long-term users. THC may remain in body tissues for 30 days or more; in fact, cannabinoids may be found in the urine for up to 30 days after marijuana use.

Most marijuana users report pleasant subjective effects of euphoria, joy, and light-heartedness. Users may believe that they are more creative, philosophical, innovative, and carefree. However, some users report unpleasant subjective effects such as anxiety, jitters, paranoia, hallucinations, and loss of energy and will.

The greater potency of marijuana means that more users may experience toxicity, tolerance, and physical dependence. For those users who are physically dependent, withdrawal symptoms may occur within several hours to several days after last use. Withdrawal symptoms may include chills/shakes, restlessness, confusion, fearfulness, malaise, cannabis craving, sweating, insomnia, nausea, irritability, attention deficits, increased blood pressure, increased respiration, sleep disturbances, and vomiting.

Medical consequences of high doses or long-term use of marijuana mostly affect the pulmonary system, the central nervous system, and the reproductive organs. Just a few of the medical complications of cannabis use are: tachycardia, laryngitis, bronchitis, tremors, decreased REM sleep, panic attacks, paranoias, memory impairment, lower sperm count, altered menstrual cycles, and fetal organ malformation and growth retardation. Perception of distance and time are impaired in a marijuana-intoxicated state, contributing to motor vehicle accidents. Marijuana makes it more difficult to learn new information. (*Source:* Bartholomew, S. 1990 (January). Marijuana abuse: Clinical implications. *Physician Assistant,* 45-52.)

18.   Cocaine's Physical and Psychological Problems

Cocaine bought on "the streets" has typically been "cut" (mixed) with other substances four to eight times. "Cuts" include mannitol, lactose, sucrose, caffeine, phenylpropanolamine, ephedrine, amphetamine, procaine, lidocaine, and benzocaine. These "cuts" add volume and therefore profits to the dealers, but they also add medical risks to the ones inherent in the cocaine itself. Besides health and legal risks, cocaine creates financial problems. The street value of cocaine is more than six times the price of gold (National Institute on Drug Abuse, 1986).

Since smoking cocaine gained popularity, the incidence of myocardial ischemia, hypertensive episodes, and angina have climbed as complications of intravenous, freebased, and intranasal cocaine use. Cardiovascular manifestations are characterized by tachycardia and hypertension (Buchanan, 1989).

In the 1980s, the number of cocaine-related strokes climbed especially among adults in their twenties. Cocaine is now considered one of the leading causes of stroke in young people. Cocaine-caused strokes involved more intracerebral or subarachnoid hemorrhages (78 percent) than cerebral infarctions (22 percent), unlike other caused strokes. (Emergency Medicine, 1990). A headache or any focal neurological deficit following cocaine use could be a sign of intracranial hemorrhage (Buchanan, 1989).

Seizures are more common after intravenous or freebased administration of cocaine than from intranasal use. The seizures probably result from the cocaine's blockage of the reuptake of norepinephrine and dopamine in the cerebral cortex. Mostly cocaine-induced seizures are transient (Buchanan, 1989).

Hyperthermia, caused by increased muscle activity, seizures, and vasoconstriction-induced impaired heat dissipation, plays a significant role in fatal cocaine intoxication. Cocaine may also directly affect hypothalamic thermoregulatory centers. Hyperthermia can lead to acute renal failure.

Psychological effects of cocaine intoxication are many. The user usually experiences increased feelings of power, special entitlement, and of being "in control." These feelings develop because cocaine acts on the pleasure center in the brain. However, the effect is temporary, because the presence of cocaine depletes the production of dopamine in the brain so that when cocaine is not present the user "comes down." Following cocaine binges, users often become significantly agitated and depressed, and suicide attempts are common. Personality changes associated with long-term cocaine use include exaggerated interest in detail, hypersensitivity to peripheral sensory cues, heightened anxiety, and paranoid thinking (Jorgensen et al., 1989). (*Sources:* National Institute on Drug Abuse. 1986. Cocaine use in America. *Prevention Networks,* April, DHHS Publication No. (ADM) 86-1433. Washington, DC: U. S. Department of Health and Human Services; Lerner, M. A. 1989 (Nov. 27). The fire of `ice.' *Newsweek,*

37-40. When coke leads to stroke. 1990 (April 15). *Emergency Medicine,* 35-38; Buchanan, J. F. 1989 (November). Cocaine intoxication: Presentation and management of medical complications. *Physician Assistant,* 187-193; Jorgensen, G. Q., White, Jr., G. L., & Woolley, D. E. 1989 (November). Psychological implications of cocaine dependence. *Physician Assistant,* 88; Farrar, H. C. & Kearns, G. L. 1989 (Nov.). Cocaine: Clinical pharmacology and toxicology. *Journal of Pediatrics, 115,* 665-675.)

19.   Progeria

Progeria refers to medical conditions in which there is premature or accelerated aging. Two examples of progeria are the Hutchinson-Gilford syndrome and Werner's syndrome.

With the **Hutchinson-Gilford syndrome,** patients who are ten years old may display the physical signs associated with persons older than 70. Sufferers look old and wizened, are bald, are dwarfs, and have generalized atherosclerosis. These patients usually die of coronary artery disease before the age of 20 years. The syndrome affects both males and females and individuals of various races and intelligences. The Hutchinson-Gilford syndrome is believed to be caused by an autosomal recessive trait.

About one in 1,000,000 babies is born with **Werner's syndrome.** About 200 individuals with this disease are living in the United States. With persons with Werner's syndrome, advanced aging occurs during their twenties, and if they survive into their forties they are biologically very old (average life expectancy of Werner's patients is 47). These patients are short, have thin limbs, a beak-shaped nose, receding chin, and juvenile cataracts. Sexual maturity is delayed.

They are predisposed to diabetes, osteoporosis, atherosclerosis, and calcified blood vessels.

An average person's cells would divide 50 times in a lab dish, but Werner's syndrome individuals' cells would divide only 10 to 20 times in this condition. Researcher Sam Goldstein found that 40 or 50 genes are contributing to this pattern, including some genes that are unique to Werner's syndrome. However, patients with Hutchinson-Gilford syndrome do not exhibit a decrease in the number of cell doublings.

These individuals are susceptible to cancer, heart disease, and osteoporosis. (*Sources:* Begley, S., Hager, M., & Murr, A. 1990 (March 5). The search for the fountain of youth. *Newsweek,* 44-48; Brown, W. T. 1987. Progeroid syndromes. In G. L. Maddox (Ed.). *The encyclopedia of aging.* New York: Springer; Cohen, G. D. 1988. *The brain in human aging,* New York: Springer.)

BROWN & BENCHMARK'S HUMAN DEVELOPMENT TRANSPARENCIES (2ND ED.)

Transparency Number and Title

The transparency set, a supplement to *Child Development,* is accompanied by an annotated manual that describes each of the 141 transparencies. The annotated manual also offers suggestions about how to use the transparencies to engage your students in active learning that will stimulate critical thinking and evaluative skills. The following transparencies are appropriate and useful with Chapter 6: Physical Development in Childhood and Puberty.

Transparency Number and Title

3	Daily Statistics
10	Biological, Cognitive, and Socioemotional Processes in Life-Span Development
11	Periods and Processes in the Life Span
65	Average Height and Weight of Girls and Boys from 2-6 Years of Age
66	Growth Curves for the Head and Brain and for Height and Weight
67	Recommended Energy Intakes for Children Ages 1 through 10
68	The Development of Fine Motor Skills in Early Childhood
98	Pubertal Growth Spurt
99	Sexually Active Adolescents
100	Adolescents and Alcohol
135	Early Childhood Development
136	Middle Childhood Development
137	Adolescent Development

CLASSROOM ACTIVITIES OR DEMONSTRATIONS

1. Discuss the critical thinking exercises. Exercise 1 differs from previous exercises in that it requires students to use information they learn in Chapter 6 to evaluate a program for children. Or more broadly, this material could be used to have students evaluate the sports programs of their own elementary school years, be they school programs, city athletic leagues, or YMCA programs.

   The "trick" in this exercise is using the material in ways that are relevant to the aims and goals of the Chinese sports schools. For example, alternative "E" is certainly true, but it is irrelevant. The schools are designed to foster special talent, so handicapped individuals are deliberately excluded. The same idea is true for choice "A," because the school only admits children who are advanced in motor development compared to their peers. Discuss with students the notion that criticism can occur on different levels and have different purposes. In the case of the sports schools, Santrock seems to be more concerned with the fates of the children who attend them rather than with broader social or political issues.

   Exercise 2 requires students to focus on graphic illustrations of material presented in the text. Students will still have questions about all of the alternatives. For example, for alternatives "A", "B", and "D" they will need to know how a graph displays rates of change. "C" requires careful attention to all the material in the figure, and "E" requires students to draw inferences about the percentages of individuals who have had intercourse.

   Exercise 3 is another one in which students have to identify an explicitly stated assumption. By now they may be adept at doing this. They are more likely to have difficulty realizing that there are no observations in this exercise! Statements "A," "B," and "E" are all generalizations or extrapolations from other statements. For example, the text reports that girls do not run the 50-yard dash as fast today as they did in 1975, then suggests that they are not as fit today as they were then. Likewise, a correlation between watching a great deal of television and getting little exercise is reported, but one must infer a causal basis for this pattern. You may wish to focus discussion on these statements on the question of whether they are soundly based, and explore how claims like these can become controversial simply because they are inferential and may reflect strong value biases.

2. Discuss the students' research projects as suggested below.

3. Fernald and Fernald (1990) have developed a class activity that is well liked by students and provides a good bridge between Sections 2 and 3 of the text. The activity illustrates several principles of development such as the cephalocaudal and proximodistal principles, prompts discussion of issues such as the relative roles of maturation and experience in development, and gets students thinking about how to measure relative degrees of development.

   You may want to use part or all of the following page to do this exercise. Give a copy to each student and have them spend 10 to 15 minutes in small groups to complete the exercise. Then discuss their ideas about what the correct order should be. There is usually agreement on the items that develop first, with decreasing agreement on later items. Discuss the reasons for this pattern of agreement and disagreement.

The correct order is as follows:

2 months	Turns head to follow moving object
9 months	Sits alone for 1 minute; says "da-da"
1 year	Walks while holding on to something
1 year 3 months	Walks alone; says several words
1 year 6 months	Climbs stairs; says many words
2 years	Runs; uses simple word combinations
3 years	Puts on shoes
4 years	Laces shoes
5 years	Names penny, nickel, and dime
6 years	Describes the difference between a bird and a dog
7 years	Tells time to quarter hour
8 years	Tells how a baseball and an orange or an airplane and a kite are alike

You may want to present this order to the class or, if you are more discovery oriented, require them to find it out on their own. Likewise, you may wish to pursue their answers to the questions on the worksheet, or you may simply want to have them deal with these issues in class discussion: How are the cephalocaudal and proximodistal principles illustrated by the order? Which items appear to develop mainly through maturation and which develop through training? Is there an age-related pattern? Finally, you may want to discuss whether these items would be appropriate for an intelligence test. Discuss definitions of intelligence and relate them to these items.

1. Study the list of verbal and motor accomplishments given below and list the order in which you think each accomplishment occurs:

Order of   Motor and Verbal Ability
Development

_____   Walks alone; says several words
_____   Describes the difference between a bird and a dog
_____   Turns head to follow moving object
_____   Names penny, nickel, and dime
_____   Climbs stairs; says many words
_____   Laces shoes
_____   Sits alone for 1 minute; says "da-da"
_____   Tells how a baseball and an orange or an airplane and a kite are alike
_____   Puts on shoes
_____   Tells time to quarter hour
_____   Runs; uses simple word combinations
_____   Walks while holding on to something

2. Study the order of accomplishments that you have identified. Describe any rules or patterns that you think apply to the order. Justify your conclusions with appropriate examples from the above list.

3. Which of the above accomplishments do you think come about chiefly through maturation? Which involve training? Do you see any trends here? Identify them and justify your conclusions with appropriate examples.

Source: Fernald, P. S. & Fernald, L. D. (1990). Early motor and verbal development. In V. P. Makosky, C. C. Sileo, L. G. Whittemore, C. P. Landry, and M. L. Skutley (Eds.). *Activities handbook for the teaching of psychology.* Washington: American Psychological Association.

---

4. Have the students plan a school lunch program for young children based on the information presented in Chapter 6. What kinds of menus would both provide balanced nutrition and be tasty enough to be appealing as well as fairly easy to prepare? What are the tradeoffs between those factors?

Source: King, M. B. & Clark, D. E. 1990. *Instructor's Manual to accompany Children.* Dubuque: Wm. C. Brown Publishers.

---

5. Have students break into small groups. Have them pretend that they are parents of a 7-year-old who is overweight and who never exercises. What might they do to help their child become better physically conditioned? Have them design a plan that would help their child.

Source: King, M. B. & Clark, D. E. 1990. *Instructor's Manual to accompany Children.* Dubuque, Wm. C. Brown Publishers.

---

6. Have students (possibly in small groups) use information on preschoolers gross and fine motor skill development to plan preschool program activities that would facilitate both types of motor skills development. What activities would be appropriate for 3-year-olds? For 5-year-olds?

For gross motor skills the program might incorporate a game such as follow the leader, in which the leader ran, skipped, hopped, walked backwards, skipped rope, and performed similar activities for the legs. For the arms the program could incorporate throwing a ball, bowling (with a light ball), and skipping rope. Fine motor activity could be promoted by work such as drawing with crayons. You could also incorporate work with puzzles, cutting and pasting, shaping clay, and playing with small blocks or dolls.

Source: Adapted from King, M. B. & Clark, D. E. (1989). *Instructor's Manual to Santrock and Yussen's Child Development: An Introduction,* 4th ed. Dubuque, IA: Wm. C. Brown.

7.   Children with serious illnesses are usually better off when families deal with their illness directly and openly. One overwhelming conclusion of a study of 117 childhood cancer survivors and their families was that they believed they were best off to tell the child about the cancer early on in honest terms the child could comprehend, and to provide the child with a sense of mastery over the disease.

Do you agree with the results of this study? Are there situations in which you would not tell a child that he or she has a serious illness? How would you deal with the possibility of death?

Source: Hurley, D. 1987. A sound mind in an unsound body. *Psychology Today,* August, 34-43.

8.   Have the class talk about how parents should talk to children about AIDS. At what age should parents first talk to children about AIDS? How should parents adjust what they say by children's age? Should schools and parents work together on this topic?

Children under 5 don't understand adult sexual behavior, so if they ask direct questions, then it is good to reassure them that they are healthy. From 5 to 7, answer children's direct questions. It is important to alleviate unfounded or exaggerated fears and to let them know they wouldn't get AIDS by being near the AIDS patient, a doctor's needle, a water fountain, or by giving blood. They may wish to know how some babies are born with AIDS, and they need a simple explanation. From 8 to 10, parents can begin to deal with tough morality and causation issues. Give appropriate information. From 11 on, adolescents may not ask their parents much so it is very important that parents willingly provide information.

Source: Koch, J. B. 1989 (Oct). Talking to your children about AIDS. *Psychology Today,* 62-63.

9.   A way to illustrate the classic findings about the relationship between early or late maturation and aspects of personality and social development among adolescent boys is to do what we call "The Stars and the Nerds" activity. This activity is fun and nearly always stimulates student discussion about the relationship between physical and psychological development at puberty, as well as their spontaneous application of the material to their own lives.

Begin by asking the class to think about the most popular boy in their seventh-, eighth-, or ninth-grade class. Have students try to form an image of the person that they can then describe to you. Give them a minute, then solicit their physical and psychological descriptions. Write their answers on a chalkboard or on an overhead under the "Star" heading.

You may have occasion to ask for clarification or additional comments on the meaning of the characteristic or observation. You should find that students have fun thinking of these characteristics and describing the individuals they have in mind.

When you finish collecting descriptions of the "stars," announce that you now want a description of the class "nerd," or least popular boy. Arrange student responses under the "Nerd" heading as you collect them. This phrase will undoubtedly pass with a certain amount of hilarity, which generally should contribute to, rather than detract from, the exercise.

Finally, ask students to study the paired sets of characteristics and comment on any pattern among the respective lists of psychological and physical characteristics that they notice. You should find indications that (a) the popular boy was an early maturer and the unpopular boy was a late maturer, and (b) the popular boy enjoyed a considerable range of personal and social advantages compared to the unpopular boy. Comment on the extent to which this mirrors the classic and contemporary work on early versus late maturation. If you have time you may want to repeat the activity for students' recollection of popular versus unpopular girls (or do it this way in the first place), and find out whether the results are similar. The literature suggests that they should not be.

10. Have the class divide into groups. Have the groups think up situations in which adolescents would be affected differently by the onset of puberty. Discussion should be related to information presented in the text. Have each group present their examples to the class for general discussion.

Source: King, M. B. & Clark, D. E. 1990. *Instructor's Manual to accompany Children.* Dubuque, Wm. C. Brown Publishers.

11. Divide the class into small groups, and give each group a different problem to discuss (e.g., an adolescent juvenile delinquent, a child with an alcohol abuse problem, an adolescent with anorexia nervosa, a pregnant teenager). How would they, as parents, respond to a child with that difficulty? Have each group present their plan to the class.

Source: King, M. B. & Clark, D. E. 1990. *Instructor's Manual to accompany Children.* Dubuque, Wm. C. Brown Publishers.

12. Have students discuss what they would do if they were a high school teacher and suspected that a student of theirs was potentially suicidal. What obligations would they have to the student? What kinds of things could they do to help that individual? Should people have the right to take their own lives?

Source: King, M. B. & Clark, D. E. 1990. *Instructor's Manual to accompany Children.* Dubuque, Wm. C. Brown Publishers.

13. Adolescence is a recently added developmental stage (a word coined by G. Stanley Hall at the beginning of the twentieth century). Ask students to "brainstorm" the societal changes and influences that produced the need for an adolescence stage. How did the industrial revolution create a need for an adolescence stage? What effects did the need for more education have on the teenage years? Could modern society exist without an adolescence stage? How might society change if teenagers were allowed to compete as equals with adults in the workforce? What are the advantages and disadvantages of adolescence? Why does society hurry individuals through childhood and then suspend them in a prolonged period of adolescence?

Source: Simons, J. A., Irwin, D. B., & Drinnin, B. A. 1987. *Instructor's Manual to Accompany Psychology: The Search for Understanding.* St. Paul: West Publishing.

14. Currently there are fairly accurate tests (urine tests, radioimmunoassay for metabolites of pot) for diagnosing marijuana use. Do you think parents and school officials should use these tests to ensure that adolescents stay off marijuana? Why? Should your college do random drug testing for marijuana (and other drugs)?

In 25 states, high school athletes have their urine tested for drug usage. School administrators in Arkansas have used blood tests, breathalyzer tests, and polygraph tests on high school students. In Delaware, drug-sniffing canines are used in the schools. Although the Fourth Amendment to the Constitution outlaws spot searches, in New Jersey it is legal for schools to do spot searches of lockers, gym bags, and purses.

Sources: Lester, D. & Collins, M. (1988). *Psychological Reports, 62,* 304; Bentayou, F. (1990, April), Children, behave, *Omni,* 33.

15.   Take a private class poll on what punishments should be given to casual users. The percentage supporting the punishments that are provided here were from a Gallup poll conducted September 7-8, 1989. Discuss student reactions to the class or Gallup poll.

       Do you support the following punishments for casual users?

Suspend driver's license for 1 to 3 years (77%)
Seize cars used to buy or carry drugs (82%)
Inform employers (68%)
Publish name in newspaper (62%)
Require community service (87%)
Environmental work camps or boot camps (71%)
Fines up to $10,000 (67%)
A period of house arrest (68%)
At least some jail time (74%)

Source: Gallup poll in Morganthau, T. 1989 (September 18, 1989). *Newsweek,* 22-24.

16.   Have your students answer the following questions and discuss the answers together:

   1.   How much did out-of-wedlock childbearing increase from 1980 to 1987?
         A. 10%   B. 40%   C. 70%   D. 110%
         E. Actually decreased 20%
   2.   Bearing a child while in high school significantly increases the likelihood of dropping out of school before graduation.
         A. True B. False
   3.   The peak year (up until 1987) for teenage childbearing was
         A. 1957.   B. 1967.   C. 1977.   D. 1987.
   4.   About _____ percent of girls get pregnant at some time between the ages of 13 and 19.
         A. 5   B. 10   C. 25   D. 40   E. 55
   5.   Of the 462,312 adolescent births in 1987, how many were to girls younger than fifteen?
         A. 1,000   B. 10,000   C. 50,000   D. 100,000   E. 150,000
   6.   Adolescent births in 1987 make up _____ percent of the total number of births in the United States.
         A. 2   B. 12   C. 22   D. 32   E. 42,000
   7.   During the 1920s, the adolescent childbearing rate was _____ the rate in 1990.
         A. higher than   B. lower than   C. equal to
   8.   _____ pregnant Black teenagers end the pregnancy with an abortion compared to pregnant white teenagers.
         A. About the same percentage of   B. A higher percentage of
         C. A lower percentage of
   9.   In 1970, 50 percent of babies born out-of-wedlock were relinquished for adoption; in 1990, the percentage was _____.
         A. 70%   B. 50%   C. 25%   D. 10%   E. 1%
   10.   _____ of teenage mothers are on welfare at the time of their baby's birth.
         A. Three-fourths B. One-half   C. One-fourth   D. One-eighth   E. One-twelfth
   11.   According to a 1986 study, after ten years, _____ of teenage marriages intending to legitimate babies were intact.
         A. 1/16   B. 1/4   C. 1/2   D. 3/4   E. 8/9

12.   Teenage mothers who relinquish their babies for adoption have higher self-esteem than teenage mothers who keep their babies.
        A. True B. False

Answers:

1.   B. Still, half of the teenagers who give birth are married.
2.   B. Dropout rates are not influenced by pregnancy. However, dropouts who have babies are less likely to return to school.
3.   A. In 1957 the fertility rate was 97.3 births, per 1,000 females; by 1977, it had dropped to 52.8 births per 1,000 ; by 1987, it was 51.1 births per 1,000.
4.   B. Half give birth, 40 percent choose abortion, and the rest miscarry.
5.   B. This number has held constant for the past decade. A significant number of pregnancies among very young adolescents are due to rape or incest. Two-thirds of teen births are to women age 18 to 19.
6.   B. In 1973, 20 percent of all births were to teen mothers.
7.   C. However, more of the teenage moms today stay single.
8.   C. Forty-four percent of nonwhites compared with 64 percent of whites, according to a 1989 Alan Guttmacher Institute report.
9.   D. In fact, this may be the one major reason why teenage childbearing is now seen as an epidemic compared with previous decades.
10.   C. And, the majority are back in the workforce by the time their youngest child is 3.
11.   D. Although it is somewhat lower for Blacks.
12.   B. The two groups have about equal levels of self-esteem.

Source: Simon, J. A. 1990. Teenage Pregnancy Quiz. Unpublished classroom activity. West Des Moines, IA: Central Iowa Psychological Services; Allen, C. L. 1990 (April 30). Teenage birth's new conception. *Insight,* 8-13.

CRITICAL THINKING EXERCISES

Exercise 1

This chapter initially sketches life for children who attend sports schools in China to prepare for the Olympics. Although Santrock does not explicitly criticize these sports schools, the tone of his treatment conveys his disapproval of them. Which of the following topics presented in Chapter 12 provides a basis for the most severe criticism of sports schools in China? **Circle the appropriate letter, and explain why it is the best answer and why each other answer is not as good.**

A. The training program in the sports schools does not conform to the developmental timetable for gross and fine motor skills.
B. Children in the sports schools are required to be too active.
C. The training programs do not implement sound nutritional policies for children.
D. The training programs are too stressful for children.
E. There is no place for handicapped children in the program.

Exercise 2

Santrock illustrates what we know about physical development with data that invite us to draw our own conclusions. Each of the following statements is a conclusion that one might draw. Which conclusion is best supported by the data in the designated table or figure? **Circle the appropriate letter, and explain why it is the best answer and why each other answer is not as good.**

A. Figure 6.1: The rate of increase in height between 3 and 6 years of age slows down.
B. Figure 6.2: Between 3 and 6 years of age, brain and head growth occur at a constant rate.

C. Figure 6.6: Age at menarche has ceased to decline since 1960.
D. Figure 6.7: The rate of growth among males is most rapid at age 14.
E. Figure 6.11: On the average, girls engage in sexual intercourse for the first time one year later than do boys.

Exercise 3

In this chapter Santrock discusses the importance of exercise to children's health. Which of the following statements underlying this presentation constitutes an assumption, rather than an inference or an observation? **Circle the letter of the best answer, and explain why it is the best answer and why each other answer is not as good.**

A. Many children do not get enough exercise because they watch television.
B. Typical school fitness programs do not engage children in enough exercise.
C. Children imitate the exercise patterns exhibited by adults.
D. The physical fitness of children and adolescents dropped between 1980 and 1989.
E. Long distance running is too strenuous for young children.

ANSWER KEYS FOR CRITICAL THINKING EXERCISES

Exercise 1

A. No, this is not the basis of the criticism. The programs do not require that children do what they are not able to do. In all likelihood, only children who are relatively advanced are accepted into the programs.
B. No, this is not the basis of the criticism. Children in middle to late childhood are said to need a great deal of activity. Although challenging, the sports schools probably provide a superb physical regimen.
C. No, this is not the basis of the criticism. There is not enough information in the material about the sports schools about the children's diets to assess this claim.
D. Yes, this is the basis for the criticism. The physical training is hard and injury-producing. There are few opportunities for rest and relaxation, particularly after setbacks. Children suffer punishment and occasional humiliation. The description of the children's experience appears to directly contradict Santrock's recommendations concerning how parents (adults) should be involved in children's sports, particularly in terms of the kinds of pressures they should avoid applying and a too early specialization in sport for the children.
E. This is not the basis for the criticism. The main reason is that the point is irrelevant. The schools are not intended to serve all children, but rather they admit only children showing exceptional sports talent. Furthermore, there is no information in Chapter 6 about best ways to include handicapped children in sports.

Exercise 2

A. This is not an accurate statement. The data actually show steady, regular increases in height from ages 3 to 6. The differences between each successive age are nearly equal. If the average heights for each age are graphed as a function of age, the result is roughly a straight line.
B. This is not an accurate statement. The portion of the curve in the figure corresponding to head and brain growth between 3 and 6 years of age bends slightly downward, indicating that growth slows down.
C. This is not an accurate statement. Although scientists generally believe that the decline has leveled off in modern industrialized countries, the graphs in Figure 6.6 do not consistently show this; two do and three do not. Overall the decline looks steady and linear with no indication that the downward trend will stop.
D. This is not an accurate statement. The graph shows an acceleration of growth among males during the early teen years, but growth rates earlier in infancy and childhood are much faster.
E. This is the most accurate statement. Figure 6.11 indicates that for most ages, the percentage of girls who have had intercourse roughly equals the percentage of boys who had intercourse one year earlier. Given the assumption that there are equal numbers of boys and girls having intercourse overall, this means that the average age of initiation into intercourse is about one year later for girls than for boys.

Exercise 3

A. This is an inference. It is an interpretation of the observation that children who do not watch television are more fit than children who watch a lot of television. The evidence is correlational.

B. This is an inference. This statement is a generalization, and as such it is an inference. It is based on specific data from the School Fitness Survey.

C. This is the assumption. Santrock states it as a principle without argument or factual justification. He uses this statement to recommend that adults become better models for exercise that promotes physical fitness.

D. This is an inference. The specific observation the proportion of 6- to 17-year-olds who earned satisfactory performance ratings on their ability to sprint, and to do sit-ups, push-ups, and long jumps declined from 1980 to 1989. Assuming these are measures of fitness, one could conclude (infer) that today's children and adolescents became less fit.

E. This is an inference. The specific observations are that (a) some (few) children are competing in marathons; and (b) physicians are seeing more injuries in children of the type that used to be seen only among adults. An interpretation of these observations is that long distance running is too strenuous for children. No direct, observed connection between these two observations is available.

RESEARCH PROJECT 1   GROSS MOTOR ACTIVITY OF CHILDREN

This project provides an observational exercise for examining the gross motor activity of children. Pair up with another student in the class and go to a local playground. Observe two children, one about 4 years old and the other about 8 years old. For each child, describe five gross motor behaviors that the child performs while you are observing. These can include running, climbing, skipping, jumping, hopping, walking, throwing, catching, etc. Describe the same five behaviors for each child, noting differences in the way they perform the behaviors. Use the data sheet on the next page for recording your observations. Then answer the questions that follow.

DATA SHEET

Child 1   Child 2

Sex _____ Age _____   Sex _____ Age _____

_____

Behavior 1 (   ):   Behavior 1 (   ):

Behavior 2 (   ):   Behavior 2 (   ):

Behavior 3 (   ):   Behavior 3 (   ):

Behavior 4 (   ):   Behavior 4 (   ):

Behavior 5 (   ):   Behavior 5 (   ):

_____

Questions

1. What were the five behaviors you observed?
2. In general how can these behaviors be characterized or described for the 4-year-old? for the 8-year-old?
3. How did the children differ in the way they performed the behaviors?
4. From your observations of the two children and five behaviors, what do you see as the course of development of gross motor behavior between 4 and 8 years? How do your specific findings compare with the general descriptions reported in the text?

Use in Classroom

Have the students discuss the results of the research project. Divide the class into small groups after the observations have been made and ask them to discuss general trends that appear in the observations when examining data from more than one child at each age. Are there any sex differences that show up in the development of gross motor activity? Are any differences evident because of the choice of behavior that was observed? For example, did students who observed jumping and hopping find different trends in their data than did students who observed running, climbing and throwing? If so, what might account for those differences?

RESEARCH PROJECT 2   CURRENT EXERCISE LEVELS

In this exercise, interview three people about their current exercise levels. (If you are between 18 and 20 years old, you may use yourself as one of the subjects.) One subject should be 5 years old, one 10 years old, and one 18 to 20. Use the interview questions on the data sheet, record each person's responses, and then answer the questions that follow.

DATA SHEET

	Person 1 Sex___Age___	Person 2 Sex___Age___	Person 3 Sex___Age___
1. How often do you exercise a week?			
2. What kinds of activities do you do?			
3. How much time do you spend exercising each week?			

Questions

1. In what kinds of activities does the 5-year-old engage? How much time a week does the 5-year-old spend exercising? How often does the 5-year-old exercise?
2. In what kinds of activities does the 10-year-old engage? How much time a week does the 10-year-old spend exercising? How often does the 10-year-old exercise?
3. In what kinds of activities does the 18-year-old engage? How much time a week does the 18-year-old spend exercising? How often does the 18-year-old exercise?
4. What differences do you find in activity level between the three different ages? Are there differences in the kinds of exercise engaged in at the different ages? If so, what are these?
5. Could variables other than age determine differences between your subjects reported activity levels? What are these?

Use in Classroom

Have the students present their data from the research project. Examine the data for age and sex differences in patterns of exercise. What activities do males and females perform? How do these differ at different ages? Is amount of exercise a function of age or of sex? What other variables might account for differences between individuals besides age and sex?

One might expect males to be more active than females, and regular exercise to increase with age. The latter trend might be from a conscious decision to exercise. However, it could be that children are more active than adolescents and therefore exercise more. Individual variation can include parental models, reinforcement for participating in sports, and aspirations to excel in a sport.

RESEARCH PROJECT 3   COLLEGE STUDENTS AND THE USE OF ALCOHOL

In this project, you interview five friends about their history of alcohol use. (If you want, you can respond to the questions yourself, as one of the five individuals.) Use the interview questions on the data sheet, record each person's responses, and then answer the questions that follow.

DATA SHEET

	Person 1	Person 2	Person 3	Person 4	Person 5
	Sex ___	Sex___	Sex___	Sex___	Sex___
Questions:	Age___	Age___	Age___	Age___	Age___

1. How often do you have a drink?
2. At what age did you first drink?
3. When you take a drink, how much do you drink?
4. Do you ever get drunk?
5. If you answered "yes" to question 4, how frequently?

Questions

1. What is the average frequency of drinking in your subjects? What is the range among individuals? Are there large individual differences in frequency of drinking? Are there age or sex differences?
2. What is the average age at which your subjects first drank? What is the range among individuals? Are there large individual differences in the age at which they started drinking? Are there age or sex differences?
3. On the average, how much do these subjects consume when they drink? What is the range among individuals? Are there large individual differences in the amount they drink? Are there age or sex differences?
4. How often, overall, does this group get drunk? What is the range among individuals? Are there large individual differences in frequency of drunkenness? Are there age or sex differences?
5. How do your data compare with data on alcohol use in adolescents presented in the text? Do your data support or refute the text?

Use in Classroom

Have students present and pool their data in class. Identify trends in the data, and discuss the findings.

ESSAY AND CRITICAL THINKING QUESTIONS

Comprehension and Application Essay Questions

We recommend that you provide students with our guidelines for "Answering Essay and Critical Thinking Questions" when you have them respond to these questions. Their answers to these kinds of questions demonstrate an ability to comprehend and apply ideas discussed in this chapter.

1. Describe physical and motor changes from early childhood through late childhood.
2. Discuss ways that parents and other adults can enhance children's health and safety.
3. Explain what it means to take a developmental perspective on children's health, and give examples.
4. List six nutritional and physical fitness facts that parents of preschoolers should know; explain how they can use these facts.
5. Explain how poverty is a factor in children's health.
6. Attack or defend this proposition: If parents want their children to become great sport stars, they must be aggressively involved in their children's sports participation from as early an age as possible.
7. What is puberty? How does it affect the psychological development of children?
8. Compare the typical outcomes for an early-maturing male vs. a late-maturing male, and an early-maturing female vs. a late-maturing female.
9. Compare adolescent female sexual scripts with adolescent male sexual scripts. How do these sexual scripts affect communication between adolescent males and females?
10. Explain whether we do or do not understand the causes of homosexuality (or heterosexuality).

Chapter 6

11. Define AIDS, including information about how it is transmitted. How is AIDS influencing sexual behavior among teenagers?
12. In your opinion, which of the following is the most serious adolescent concern in our society: drugs and alcohol, pregnancy, suicide, or sexually transmitted diseases? Why?
13. Compare and contrast the eating disorders of anorexia nervosa and bulimia.

Critical Thinking Questions

We recommend that you have students follow our guidelines for "Answering Essay and Critical Thinking Questions" when you ask them to prepare responses to these questions. Their answers to these kinds of questions reflect an ability to apply critical thinking skills to a novel problem or situation that is *not* specifically discussed in the chapter. These items most appropriately may be used as take-home essay questions (e.g., due on exam day) or as homework exercises that can be answered either by individuals or groups. Collaboratively answered questions encourage cooperative learning by students, and reduce the number of papers that must be graded.

1. At the end of Chapter 6 Santrock indicates books that provide practical knowledge about children and lists resources for improving the lives of children. Choose one of these books or resources and read it or learn as much as you can about it. Then write a brief review in which you (a) characterize the book or resource, and (b) explain how the book or resource relates to material in the chapter.
2. Chapter 1 defines the nature of development in terms of biological, cognitive, and social processes, and periods or stages. Indicate your ability to think critically by identifying material in this chapter that illustrates developmental processes and periods. If there is little or no information in this chapter about developmental processes and periods, identify and explain how developmental processes and periods could be used to guide the analysis of any topic in the chapter.
3. According to Chapter 1, three fundamental developmental issues concern: (a) maturation (nature) versus experience (nurture), (b) continuity versus discontinuity, and (c) early versus later experience. Indicate your ability to think critically by identifying material in this chapter that illustrates each of the three fundamental developmental issues. If there is little or no information in this chapter about fundamental developmental issues, identify and explain how these issues could be used to guide the analysis of any topic in the chapter.
4. One aspect of thinking critically is to read, listen, and observe carefully and then ask questions about what is missing from a text, discussion, or situation. For example, *Child Development* presents no information about normal sexual behavior among children. Indicate your ability to think critically by (a) listing as many questions as you can about sexual behavior among children, and (b) speculating why Santrock does not discuss this topic more fully.
5. Santrock sets off several quotations in this chapter. Indicate your ability to think critically by selecting one of the quotes and (a) learning about the author and indicating why this individual is eminently quotable (i.e., what was this individual's contribution to human knowledge and understanding), (b) interpreting and restating the quote in your own terms, and (c) explaining what concept, issue, perspective, or term in this chapter that Santrock intended this quote to illuminate. In other words, about what aspect or issue in development does this quote make you pause and reflect?
6. Chapter 2 indicates that theories help us explain data and make predictions about various aspects of development. Chapter 2 then presents six different theoretical approaches (i.e., Freudian, cognitive, behavioral and social learning, ethological, ecological, and eclectic theory), but notes that no single approach explains the complexity of development. Indicate your ability to think critically by (a) perusing this chapter for topics influenced by at least one of the six theoretical approaches, and (b) explaining which theoretical approach dominated the topic in question. If the presentation is entirely atheoretical, identify and explain how one of the theoretical approaches could be used to guide the analysis of the topic in question.
7. This chapter begins with a discussion about China's policy of discovering and training potential Olympic athletes at very young ages. Apply your knowledge about the scientific method by designing a study to determine the relationship between involvement in competitive sports at a young age and developmental outcomes: (a) What specific problem or question do you want to study? (b) What predictions would you make and test in your study? (c) What measures would you use (i.e., controlled observation in a laboratory, naturalistic observation, interviews and questionnaires, case studies, standardized tests, cross-cultural studies, physiological research, research with animals, or multimeasure, multisource, and multicontext approach) and how would you define each measure clearly and unambiguously? (d) What strategy would you follow-- correlational or experimental, and what would be the time span of your inquiry--cross-sectional or longitudinal? (e) What ethical considerations must be addressed before you conduct your study?

8. According to Chapter 2, your author wants you to become a wise consumer of information about child development by: (a) being cautious about media reports, (b) distinguishing between nomothetic research and idiographic needs, (c) recognizing how easy it is to overgeneralize from a small or clinical sample, (d) knowing that a single study is usually not the defining word about some aspect of child development, (e) remembering that causal conclusions cannot be made from correlation studies, and (f) always considering the source of the information and evaluating its credibility. Indicate your ability to think critically by, first, selecting an article from either a journal, magazine, or newspaper about any topic regarding Physical Development in Childhood and Puberty, and, second, evaluating it in terms of these six objectives. If the information in the article is insufficient to evaluate one of these objectives, then specify what kind of information you would need to evaluate the objective.

Cognition, Learning, Information Processing, and Language Development

7 Cognitive Development and Piaget's Theory

SUGGESTIONS FOR LECTURE TOPICS

1. The Life of Jean Piaget

Jean Piaget lived from 1896 to 1980. He was a Swiss psychologist who did ingenious work in cognitive development. His scientific interests developed early with childhood interests in how machines worked and how animals lived. His first publication was on rare sparrow observations at the tender age of 11 years. During his high-school years he worked in a natural science museum and wrote papers on mollusks. As an adult he was considered an expert on the classification of mollusks. Perhaps it is this interest in mollusk classification that led to his exploration of how children classify objects.

Jean Piaget got a doctorate degree in biology before turning his interests to psychology and psychoanalysis. He considered himself the founder of **genetic epistemology,** or the experimental science of the acquisition of knowledge.

Before engaging in his own cognitive research, he worked in Alfred Binet's laboratory. But his own interests were quite different from Binet's in measuring individual differences in intelligence. His own research looked at development in six areas: circular reactions, imitation; understanding of time, space, and causality; and object permanence. His research involved careful observation of children while they engaged in tasks.

Piaget's theory became popular in Europe in the 1930s, but at that time American psychology was heavily influenced by behavioral theory. In the United States, Piaget's popularity came in the 1960s. His impact is felt in parenting ideas, educational strategies, and current cognitive research. (*Sources:* Evans, R. I. 1981. *Dialogue with Jean Piaget.* Trans. Eleanor Duckworth, New York: Praeger; Harris, P. L. 1983. Infant Cognition. In P. H. Mussen (Ed.). *Handbook of Child Psychology (Vol. 2), Infancy and Developmental Psychobiology.* M. M. Harth & J. J. Campos (Vol. ed.). New York: Wiley.)

2. Cognition Observed: On How to Identify What Infants Are Thinking About

How can we tell what infants are thinking? Or, alternatively, how can we determine what sorts of information an infant can process? What mental capacities do infants have? Review the procedures that various researchers have used to study infant cognition. You may wish to begin with Piaget's classic observations and the conclusions he drew about the progression of intellectual development during infancy. If you have already given lectures on the procedures used to study newborns and on the opportunities and limitations of observational research, this part of your lecture will be a review and extension of those topics.

Having treated Piaget, select a sample of perceptual or cognitive capacities and present techniques used to learn about them. Important processes include attention, perception, and memory. Good treatments of strategies used to pursue these issues are found in Bower's *Development in Infancy,* and there are more recent books by Vogel and Bornstein.

One way to focus your presentation would be to take the case of infant memory. Sketch inferences about memory from Piaget's work, then consider how more recent studies have qualified and revised Piaget's findings. Discuss the importance of the full range of approaches to this topic, from Perlmutter's use of mothers' reports (see text) to the careful, systematic procedures used by researchers such as Rovee-Collier.

3. Research Findings on Object Permanence

- Infants younger than 4 months watched as a screen blocked a toy. When the screen was removed, half the infants again viewed the toy and the other half saw no toy remaining. Those infants who were in the no-visible toy condition exhibited more surprise, suggesting a rudimentary sense of object permanence (Bower, 1982).
- 4-month-old infants looked longer at impossible events (Baillargeon, 1987).
- 5-month-old infants reached out in the dark to touch an object visible a few seconds before (Bower & Wishart, 1972).

- Infants younger than 6-1/2 months did not withdraw an object they were grasping under a cloth. They had not yet co-located visual and tactile information (Harris, 1983).
- 7-month-old infants watched as an object was moved from A to B. The immediate response was to look at B. However, with more than a second's delay, the infants searched location A for the object. At one year, infants looked at location B even after a ten-second delay (Diamond, 1985).
- 7-month-old infants do better at locating objects hidden by two-dimensional objects (e.g., screen, cloth) than at locating objects hidden by three-dimensional objects (e.g., cups, boxes). By 10 months, there was no difference (Dunst et al., 1982).

(*Sources:* Bower, T. G. R. 1982. *Development in infancy,* 2nd ed., San Francisco: W. H. Freeman; Baillargeon, R. B. 1987. Object permanence in 3-1/2 and 4-1/2 month old infants. *Developmental Psychology, 23,* 655-664; Bower, T. G. R. & Wishart, J. G. 1972. The effects of motor skill on object permanence. *Cognition, 1,* 165-174; Harris, P. L. 1983. Infant cognition. In P. H. Mussen (Ed.). *Handbook of Child Psychology (Vol. 2). Infancy and Developmental Psychobiology.* M. M. Harth & J. J. Campos (Vol. ed.). New York: Wiley; Diamond, A. 1985. Development of the ability to use recall to guide action, as indicated by infants' performance on AB. *Child Development, 56,* 868-883.; Dunst, C. J., Brovks, P. H., & Dorsey, P. A. 1982. Characteristics of hiding places and the transition to stage IV performance in object permanence tasks. *Developmental Psychology, 18,* 671-681.)

4.   Preschoolers' Conception of Distance

Piaget found that preschoolers made many errors on the three types of distance judgment tasks. For example, young children usually judged that two paths that were originally identical became different if subjected to some irrelevant conservation transformation. In a second problem, 84 percent of children under 4-1/2 years old judged that two lines that began and ended at the same points were equal in length even though the lines differed in directness of path. In a third task, the interval AC was compared with the same interval with a third point, B, placed between the first two points. Young children often judged length ABC to be smaller than length AC.

Some more recent studies, however, have found young children capable of accurate judgments on some distance tasks. For example, preschoolers can be tested on their understanding of two distance principles: (1) the **direct-indirect principle** is the concept that a straight route between two points is always the shortest route; (2) the **same-plus principle** is the concept that if two routes are the same to a point, and then only one route continues, the route that continues is the longest. Preschoolers performed better on distance transformations that involved one of these principles (74 percent) than they did a principle-irrelevant task (19 percent). (*Sources:* Bartsch, K. & Wellman, H. M. 1988. Young children's conception of distance. *Developmental Psychology, 24,* 532-541; Piaget, J., Inhelder, I., & Szeminska, A. 1960. *The child's conception of geometry.* London: Routledge & Kegan Paul.)

5.   Children and Holidays

Children enjoy holiday customs starting in the preschool years. However, it takes time for children to understand the meaning of holidays. In a Playskool poll of children aged 4 to 6 years, many did not understand why Thanksgiving was celebrated. Reflecting the preoperational stage of cognitive reasoning, their explanations were often "confused" and mixed facts and erroneous material together, e.g., "It's when Benjamin Franklin discovered pumpkins," or "It's when the Pilgrims invited the Italians for dinner." Each year parents should give explanations about important holidays to their children. (*Source:* Little, M. A. 1989 (November). Mother & child: Kids and Thanksgiving. *Good Housekeeping,* 80.)

6.   Are Young Children As Limited As Piaget Claimed? The Work of Gelman, Shantz, and Others

Piaget's work is especially important for convincingly showing that children do not think the same way as adults. He documented the differences in diverse ways and created a comprehensive theory that unified his findings and placed them in developmental perspective. Nevertheless, many modern researchers now feel that Piaget's methods for delineating children's cognitive capacities actually underestimate children's capabilities and lead to a view of children as deficient rather than competent thinkers. These researchers have worked hard to demonstrate cognitive capacities in children at earlier ages than Piaget reported them to occur. Their findings suggest that Piaget's theory must be modified.

Develop this theme in a lecture that first shows how Piaget came to believe that children's minds work differently from those of adults. Describe his early observations of systematic errors on intelligence test items, and proceed to illustrate how most of his tests reveal cognitive errors in the thought of toddlers.

Choose one of Piaget's tasks and discuss how it may impose information processing difficulties on a child. Relevant work toward this end has been done by Carolyn Shantz, Thomas Trabasso, Rochel Gelman, John Flavell, and others. These researchers have shown how task analyses of Piaget's tests indicate that alternative information processing hypotheses, as opposed to Piaget's structural-functional analyses, could account for young children's failure. Thus, for example, young children may fail transitive inference tasks because they forget information, not because they lack logical capacities (see Trabasso's work).

Work through one or two examples. Then discuss with the class the impact it ought to have on an understanding of children's thinking and on applications of research to education. For example, is it an appropriate implication that educators can begin to teach children at earlier ages? How does that fit with recommendations made in the textbook? Engage the class in an appreciation of both Piaget's work and that of the information processing researchers.

7.   Self-referential sentences

Not until individuals are in the formal operations stage can they find humor in self-referential sentences (and the effect is better in written than oral form). Here are some examples of these sentences:

    This sentence contradicts itself—or rather—well, no, actually it doesn't.
    This sentence contains exactly three errors.
    You can't have "your cake" and spell it "too."
    Well, how about that—this sentence is about me!
    When you are looking at it, this sentence is in Spanish.
    The sentence would be seven words long if it were six words shorter.
    I have been sentenced to death.
    These irrational statements are also better understood once in the formal operations stage:
    As long as I have you, I can endure all the trouble you inevitably bring.
    Remember me? I'm the one who never made any impression on you.
    Why does trouble always come at the wrong time?
    Due to circumstances beyond my control, I am master of my fate and captain of my soul.
(*Sources:* Hofstadter, D. R. 1985. On self-referential sentences. *Metamagical themas: Questing for the essence of mind and pattern.* New York: Basic Books; Hofstadter, D. R. 1985. Self-referential sentences: A follow up. *Metamagical themas: Questing for the essence of mind and pattern.* New York: Basic Books.)

8.   Cultural and Experiential Influences in the Development of Formal Operations

Piaget's theory suggests that no special experience is necessary for formal operations to emerge. Biological changes in the brain coupled with normal "cognitive experience" are said to be the key determinants of formal operational thinking.

Nevertheless, there is considerable evidence to suggest that, in fact, special experiences play an important role in the emergence of formal operational thinking. The primary reason for this belief is that formal operations seems to be prevalent only in cultures that provide their youth with secondary schooling. In addition, the achievement of formal operations within a culture may be limited to areas of special interest to individual teenagers.

Present a lecture that evaluates Piaget's original findings and theoretical claims about the emergence of formal operations in light of cross-cultural work. A good source is research done by Jacqueline Goodnow over the past 30 years. Additional material is found in work done by Pierre Dasen.

You may wish to present this information in conjunction with information about the incidence of formal operations within a modern, industrialized country. The data suggest that formal operations are neither universally achieved nor are they uniformly expressed in all adolescents' thinking. An irony in this work is that, in contrast to his work on children, Piaget seems to have overestimated the cognitive maturity of adolescents.

You could conclude this lecture in different ways. One is to evaluate the idea that formal operations is a discrete, unitary stage of mental development. Another is to sketch an information processing analysis of a selected formal operations task (you might review Sternberg's work on analogies) and to discuss how cultural variables such as schooling might influence various stages of problem solving. In either case, indicate how Piaget's claims need to be modified to encompass the data.

9.   Tests of Formal Operations

Students often find the concept of formal operations difficult. One solution is to present to them diverse examples of problems that only people who have formal operations are supposed to be able to solve. One source is John Renner's book, *Research, Teaching, and Learning with the Piaget Model*, or you may want to demonstrate one or more of Piaget's tasks.

Your presentation could focus on actually having students solve some of the problems, or it could offer an analysis of the skills each task requires. If you and your students are up to it, you may want to show how Piaget's INRC group is represented in each task.

If you have students solve a number of tasks, you will probably be able to show that not all formal operational tasks are equally easy, either tasks of the same or tasks of different types. This could provide a ready basis for the suggested lectures or simply give foundation for discussion about whether the problem lies in the measurement or in the theory used to interpret the measures.

Another tack would be to discuss the extent to which measures of formal operations represent real problems that adolescents have to solve at school and in their personal lives. This will lead to a discussion of the validity of these devices as measures of mental skills used in everyday life.

BROWN & BENCHMARK'S HUMAN DEVELOPMENT TRANSPARENCIES (2ND ED.)

Transparency Number and Title

The transparency set, a supplement to *Child Development*, is accompanied by an annotated manual that describes each of the 141 transparencies. The annotated manual also offers suggestions about how to use the transparencies to engage your students in active learning that will stimulate critical thinking and evaluative skills. The following transparencies are appropriate and useful with Chapter 7: Cognitive Development and Piaget's Theory.

Transparency Number and Title

21	Piaget's Stages of Cognitive Development
27	Cognitive Theories
53	Piaget's Six Substages of Sensorimotor Development
54	Piaget's Description of the Main Characteristics of Sensorimotor Thought
69	Concept Formation
70	The Three Mountains Task Devised by Piaget and Inhelder
71	Piaget's Conservation Task
72	Domains of Conservation
73	Preoperational Thought's Characteristics
74	Vygotsky's Zone of Proximal Development
75	An Interactionist View of Language
76	Developmentally Appropriate and Inappropriate Practice: I
77	Developmentally Appropriate and Inappropriate Practice: II
84	Classification
85	Characteristics of Concrete Operational Thought
101	Characteristics of Formal Operational Thought
111	Schaie's Stages of Cognitive Development
128	Intellectual Development in Adulthood

CLASSROOM ACTIVITIES OR DEMONSTRATIONS

1.   Discuss the critical thinking exercises. Exercise 1 is a straightforward exercise in recognizing concrete operational thought and distinguishing it from preoperational and formal operational thought. The interesting point is that students have difficulty differentiating nonstandard examples of concrete operational thinking from the other levels. Thus they are inclined to identify "B" as formal operational, "C" as concrete operational, and to confuse "E" with all three levels. To prepare students for this exercise you may want to discuss the distinguishing attributes of the three levels of mental development and both present many examples as well as have students generate examples.

At first you may believe that Exercise 2 is too easy, because generally Santrock states criticisms of the Piagetian findings or concepts listed right after he discusses the concepts of findings. However, our experience is that students do not attend to these criticisms well, or pause to reflect on them and understand their significance. This exercise will require them to do that; you may want to tell your students so directly. Also, a couple of the alternatives are based on material that is separated in the text. We suggest that when you have students do this exercise that they focus on explaining why a given pairing is accurate or confused. Possible working through one of the "wrong" alternatives with them will give them a better sense of the task.

Exercise 3 is straightforward in all but one way: Students have considerable difficulty deciding whether "C" is an inference or an observation. They want to call it an observation but suspect that they should not. Help them to discover how words like "fanciful" and "inventive" imply how children's drawings come to be the way they are, rather than describing children's drawings. This can be an excellent discussion about the nature of traits and trait description in general. You can also use the answer to "E" to further illustrate the perils of making inferences. Finally, you may want to review problems with the study of perception and object permanence in infants as parallels to the one here, and to link it to the more general problem of underestimating children's mental development raised in Chapter 7.

2. Discuss the students' research projects as suggested below.
3. What are the advantages and disadvantages of basing theoretical ideas on natural observations of one's own children? Why did Piaget prefer this technique to more controlled laboratory experiments? Why do his critics think that Piaget's methodology was poor? How does psychology benefit from both Piaget's techniques and more precise experiments?

Source: Gratch, B. & Schatz, J. A. 1988. Another look at Piaget's books on infancy. *Human Development, 31,* 245-255.

---

4. Have students plan an infant day-care program based on Piaget's theory of sensorimotor development. What behaviors and abilities develop during this time period? What activities might help to promote the development of these behaviors and abilities? What decor might be facilitating?

Sensorimotor development includes a mastery of the coordination of sensation with simple motor behaviors. The child also comes to have some appreciation for physical causality and object performance. The child's gross and fine motor performance should be stimulated. Think of these tasks as related to the substage of sensorimotor development.

Examples:

1. Developing the skill of reaching can be promoted by hanging objects just out of reach and allowing the child to reach for them. These objects should be small enough for an infant to grasp comfortably.
2. Fine motor control can be stimulated by providing puzzle boards and objects with which to play.
3. The development of the object concept can be stimulated by hiding toys and allowing the child to search for them.
4. Children can learn about causality by giving them strings tied to objects. A child pulls on the string to get the object.

Source: Adapted from King, M. B. & Clark, D. E. (1989). *Instructor's Manual to Santrock and Yussen's Child Development: An Introduction,* 4th ed. Dubuque, IA: Wm. C. Brown.

---

5. Divide the class into small groups. Ask the students to design a curriculum for decreasing egocentric responding on spatial tasks in preoperational children. During the first part of the discussion, have the students specify what problems normally characterize this period. After this initial discussion, have them identify what activities might promote change.

Source: King, M. B. & Clark, D. E. 1990. *Instructor's Manual to accompany Children.* Dubuque, Wm. C. Brown Publishers.

---

6.   Have groups of students work on designing possible computer activities that could be used to promote concrete operational reasoning in preoperational children. It is important to specify what changes take place between the two stages, identify what activities might promote these changes, and then to design ways to translate these activities into computer games.

Children learn concrete operational reasoning by interacting with physical objects, practicing moving objects around, and counting objects. How can these activities be translated to the computer screen? Design possibilities for both conservation tasks and hierarchical classification tasks.

Source: Simons, J. A. (1990). *Computers and Piaget.* West Des Moines, IA: Central Iowa Psychological Services.

7.   Assign students the task of asking preschoolers the following questions and bringing back responses that include typical limitations of preoperational thinking such as egocentrism, animism, irreversibility, and artificialism.

1.   How did you learn to talk?
2.   Where does the sun go at night?
3.   Why is the sky blue?
4.   Why do dogs bark?
5.   Why does it rain?
6.   Where do babies come from?
7.   Who are you going to be when you grow up?
8.   Why do you eat breakfast in the morning instead of at night?
9.   Why do you have toes?
10.   Why are you ticklish?
11.   How do birds fly?
12.   What is your favorite toy?

Source: Simons, J. A., Irwin, D. B., & Drinnin, B. A. (1987). *Instructor's Manual to Accompany Psychology, the Search for Understanding.* St. Paul: West Publishing.

9.   Ask students to define big and little, and how they know the difference. Ask them what the difference is between a big button and a little mountain. Ask them to guess at what age children can deal with being told that a small plate is probably bigger than a big button. Ask them when they think young children can correctly give big shoes and little shoes to appropriate family members. Will a preschooler tell them that a big insect is a big animal? Have them propose some ways of studying (in naturalistic observation, case study, and experiment) children's developing concepts of size of things.

Describe some of the experiments done with preschoolers and adults in the source listed below. Two-year-olds did pretty well with shoe sizes, and 3-year-olds were accurate on sizes of buttons and plates.

Source: Sera, M. D., Troyer, D., & Smith, L. B. 1988. What do two-year-olds know about the sizes of things? *Child Development,* 59, 1489-1496.

10.   Describe each of the following research studies, and have students try to predict the findings and then give the results:

A.   Third graders were shown two identical glasses filled equally full of colored liquid and asked to predict what would happen if the contents of one glass were poured into a wider glass. (Get a prediction here.) About 90 percent predicted that the level would be lower in the wider container. However, a tube was secretly connected to the third container. As water was poured into the wide container, extra water was added. The wider container actually filled up to a higher level than the narrower container. How did the third graders answer the question: "Is there the same amount of water in the two containers?" (Get predictions and reasons here.)

Over half replied that the wider container had more water. Forty-two percent said that the amount of liquid was the same. Explanations included "a trick glass that makes things look big."

B. In one experiment, 6-year-olds and 9-year-olds were shown a small bit of an animal picture, not enough for them to predict what the animal was. They were then asked to predict whether another person could identify the animal from the same amount of information. What did the children say? (Get predictions and reasons here.)

Forty-four percent of the six-year olds said the other person would be able to identify the animal. Almost all of the nine-year-olds correctly realized that the other person also would not be able to identify the animal.

C. Researchers asked first and fourth graders to imagine that they were playing with a friend (some were told the friend had been at their house before, and some were told the friend had never been over before) in the kitchen and they were asking the friend to get a particular toy from their bedroom. How well did the children do in giving toy-finding instructions? (Get predictions and reasons here.)

Interestingly, both first and fourth graders provided more information to the friend who had never visited the house. Overall, however, fourth graders gave more precise information about the toy. Both this example and the one above shows the gradual improvements in middle childhood in the ability to judge how much information other people have and how much they need.

Sources: Olson, D. R. & Astington, J. W. 1987. Seeing and knowing: On the ascription of mental states to young children. *Canadian Journal of Psychology, 41,* 399-411; Sonnenshein, S. 1988. The development of referential communication: Speaking to different listeners. *Child Development, 59,* 694-702.

---

11. Adapt Piagetian ideas into the discovery method of learning for elementary school, junior high, and high school, making adjustments for changes in thinking abilities.

Source: Gerow, J. 1988. *Time Retrospective: Psychology 1923-1988,* 52-53.

---

12. Ask groups of four to six students to design a curriculum for promoting formal operational reasoning in concrete operational children. During the first part of the discussion, the students should specify what changes normally take place between those two stages. After the initial discussion, the students should identify what activities might promote those changes.

Source: King, M. B. & Clark, D. E. 1990. *Instructor's Manual to accompany Children.* Dubuque, Wm. C. Brown Publishers.

---

13. Have the class role-play early adolescents in a variety of situations in which adolescents might cater to an imaginary audience. The students can either think up situations themselves or use some of the following:

a. Girl going to party notices a stain on her pants.
b. Boy is to give book report in front of class but is not prepared.
c. Boy is to have class picture taken and just got braces on the day before.
d. Girl is at restaurant with arguing parents when boy she likes walks in.

Source: King, M. B. & Clark, D. E. 1990. *Instructor's Manual to accompany Children.* Dubuque, Wm. C. Brown Publishers.

14. Have students work in small groups for the following two tasks. Group members will attempt to solve Piaget's pendulum task and Piaget's chemical task and then analyze their problem-solving process for aspects of formal operational reasoning. (You can also do this as a large group demonstration in which you do the tasks as suggested by class members.)

Pendulum Task: Have a pendulum with various lengths of string and a number of equal weights. Group members are to identify the variable(s) that determine the speed of the pendulum swing. The possible variables to manipulate are length, weight, height of the drop, and force of the drop.

Chemical Task: Have five numbered flasks with each containing one of the following colorless chemicals: water, hydrogen peroxide, potassium iodine, acid, and thiosulfate. Have the students determine which combination of chemicals produces a mixture with the color yellow.

Each task is a combination problem. They are solved by systematically manipulating each of the variables and all of the possible combinations of variables to identify the correct solution. In the chemistry task, the solution to the problem is to try each chemical until the solution to the problem is found. For the pendulum problem, the problem solver must manipulate the length of the string, the number of weights, the force with which the weight is swung, and the height from which the weight is dropped.

Source: Adapted from: King, M. B. & Clark, D. E. (1989). *Instructor's Manual to Accompany Santrock & Yussen's Child Development: An Introduction,* 4th ed. Dubuque, IA: Wm. C. Brown Publishers.

CRITICAL THINKING EXERCISES

Exercise 1

Indicate which of the following cases best illustrates **concrete operations.** *Hint:* There is more than one example of concrete operational thinking. **Circle the appropriate letters, and explain why they are the better answers and why each other answer is not as good.**
A. Katie is asked, "Do you have a brother?" She says, "Yes." Then she is asked, "Does he have a sister?" She answers, "No."
B. Ray says, "A fly is like both insects and birds. It's like birds because it flies, but it's like insects because it has six legs."
C. Tim is working on analogies. He declares, "Biking is to pedaling as riding in a car is to stepping on the gas pedal because they both make the vehicle go!"
D. Bobby states, "I understand how this nickel and these five pennies are the same as this dime."
E. Her teacher asks Mary, "How can the scale be brought back into balance?" Mary replies, "The only way to do that is to remove the weight that made one pan sink lower than the other."

Exercise 2

One of the marks of the greatness of Piaget's theory is that it has been so thoroughly examined and so roundly criticized. The theory identified problems for researchers so well that John Flavell declared that "We owe him the present field of cognitive development . . ." (see page 213 of Child Development). Thus one of the challenges of understanding Piaget is knowing when current research has qualified one of his claims, and understanding why a new finding questions or invalidates an aspect of Piaget's theory. Listed below are Piagetian concepts or claims of fact paired with a statement that may or may not accurately reflect a criticism or contradiction of that concept or claim of fact. Only one pairing is accurate; the rest represent a confusion. Find the most accurate pairing. **Circle the letter of the best answer, and explain why it is the best answer and why each other answer is not as good.**

A. During the first year of life infants cannot represent information mentally (symbolically): Eight-month-olds search for objects behind screens 70 seconds after they are hidden.
B. Three- and four-year-olds are highly egocentric: Three- and four-year-olds' drawings are highly fanciful and inventive.
C. Preoperational children fail conservation tasks: Children do not pass all conservation tasks at the same time within a stage of development.
D. Preoperational thought is animistic: Children can take the perspective of others on some tasks but not on others.
E. Formal operational thought is not complete until late in adolescence: Children can be trained to reason at higher levels.

Exercise 3

In this chapter Santrock presents a sample and some interpretations of preschool children's art. Which of the following statements underlying this presentation constitutes an assumption, rather than an inference or an observation? **Circle the letter of the best answer, and explain why it is the best answer and why each other answer is not as good.**

A. When they are 3 years old, children draw scribbles that resemble pictures.
B. Children know more about the human body than they are capable of drawing.
C. Preschool children's drawings are fanciful and inventive.
D. Children both distort and omit the details of what they are trying to draw.
E. Children's drawings reflect levels of cognitive development despite the fact that children's motor skills are limited.

ANSWER KEYS FOR CRITICAL THINKING EXERCISES

Exercise 1

A. This is not an example of concrete operational thinking. In this example, Katie fails to understand that sibling relationships are reciprocal. According to Piaget this is a sign of preoperational thinking.
B. This is an example of concrete operational thinking. In this example, Ray is able to understand that flies have attributes that place them in more than one category (creatures that fly and creatures with six legs). According to Piaget this is a concrete operational skill.
C. This is not an example of concrete operational thinking. In this example, Tim declares that he understands the equivalence of two abstract relationships. Piaget claims this is a formal operational ability.
D. This is an example of concrete operational thinking. In this example, Bobby is working with two concrete representations of money and is able to add the values of the nickels and pennies to confirm their equivalence to the dime. The equivalence also implies reversibility. All of these points characterize concrete operational thinking according to Piaget.
E. This is an example of concrete operational thinking. In this example, Mary shows reversibility. However, she can only think of one solution to the problem and fails to realize that there are several ways to balance a scale. Piaget identifies this as concrete operational thinking.

Exercise 2

A. This is the best answer. The fact that eight-month-olds search for a hidden object after even a short delay implies an ability to retrain some mental representation of the object-as-present behind a screen. This finding also directly contradicts Piaget's observations of infants confronted with a similar but more demanding search task.
B. This is not the best answer. The fact that young children's drawings are fanciful and inventive is not necessarily a contradiction of the claim that young children are egocentric. In fact, our judgement about their drawings is that these children are seeing the world differently from the way that we see it, but leave us in doubt about exactly what they are seeing because they do not explain their ideas clearly to us (this idea is illustrated in Explorations in Child Development 7.2). The main point is that fancy and invention may indicate either egocentrism or abstraction, and so is moot concerning whether children's thinking is egocentric.

C. This is not the best answer. The fact that children do not pass all conservation tasks leads to the criticism of Piaget's concept of cognitive stages; in a strong version of the theory, children should be able to solve all puzzles that require the mental operations of one stage. This point, however, is irrelevant to the question of whether preoperational children could pass concrete operations problems.

D. This is not the best answer. Again, the point is basically incorrect. Animistic thinking is not based on perspective-taking skills. Piaget argued that it represented elements of preoperational children's thinking about the nature of things; the relevant criticism is that animistic thinking may more accurately reflect limited specific rather than errantly global thinking about the world.

E. This is not the best answer. There is no necessary connection here. The first statement represents a revision in Piaget's claims about the timing of formal operational thought that came about chiefly from evidence of later development, not in any way from training studies. In fact, most of the training studies have had to do with concrete operational thinking.

Exercise 3

A. This is an observation. It is a descriptive statement characterizing children's drawings.

B. This is an inference. It is one hypothesis about the meaning of children's drawings; Piaget actually claimed just the opposite. The inference is based on the fact that children can talk about more body parts than they typically draw; they can name body parts they have not included in a drawing.

C. This is an inference. Words like "fanciful" and "inventive" represent guesses or judgments about the process that generates children's drawings. They attempt to provide an explanation for the fact that children's drawings are not very realistic.

D. This is an observation. We can see the distortions and omissions directly. If a 3-year-old draws a "tadpole human," we see that this is a distorted picture of a person and that it lacks many details. The same points apply to the children's drawings of a game of catch described in the text.

E. This is the assumption. At the end of the inset, Santrock mentioned that perceptual and motor skills limit what children can draw; nevertheless he discussed how pictures reflect cognitive development. Thus he assumes that children's drawings reflect cognitive levels of development despite fine motor skill limitations.

RESEARCH PROJECT 1   OBJECT PERMANENCE

For this project, in which you may work in groups of two to four, you need an infant from two of the following four age groups: 4 to 8 months, 8 to 12 months, 12 to 18 months, and 18 to 24 months. In order to perform the object permanence task with these two infants, you need to clear your project through the human subjects review board at your school and get a signed informed consent form from the infants' parents. With each infant, perform each of the following three tasks and record the infants' responses:

(Data sheet begins on the next page.)

Infant Responses:

	Infant 1	Infant 2
Task Description	Sex _____ Age _____	Sex _____ Age _____

1. Show each infant an interesting object (e.g., ball or rattle). Then cover it with a piece of cloth. Note the response.

   Now move the cloth so that part of the rattle is exposed. Note the response.

2. Show the child the rattle again. Now move it so that it disappears behind a screen. Note the response.

   Now do the task again, but this time have the toy go behind one screen and then another one located close by. Note the response.

3. Show the infant the rattle, then cover it with a small box. Move the box behind the screen. Let the rattle remain behind the screen, but bring the box back into view. Note the response.

Questions

1. How do the younger and older infants respond in task 1? Do both seem to understand that the rattle is under the cloth? When part of the rattle is exposed, does the baby exhibit surprise? Reach out for the rattle?
2. In the second task, which infants realize the rattle is behind the screen? Can either baby follow the action when the rattle is moved to a second screen?
3. How do each of the infants respond when the rattle is in the box? When the box no longer contains a rattle, does either of the infants look behind the screen?
4. How does object permanence change as infants get older? Do your observations agree with Piaget's findings about object permanence?

Use In Classroom

Have students present data in class from the research project, pooling the data for the four age groups of infants. Discuss how the younger and older infants responded to the three tasks. How does object permanence improve during infancy? Do the class's observations agree with Piaget's findings?

RESEARCH PROJECT 2   CONSERVATION TASKS

The purpose of this exercise is for you to see an example of a preoperational and a concrete operational reasoner. Pair up with another class member and test two children, a four- to five-year-old child and an eight- to nine-year-old child, using several of Piaget's tasks. Administer two conservation and two classification tasks to each child, and then compare the children's responses with each other and attempt to interpret those responses in view of Piaget's theory. In order to test the two children, you will need to clear this through the human subjects review board at your school and get a signed informed consent form from the children's parents. A description of the tasks, the data sheet for recording the observations, and a list of questions to answer follows.

Conservation Task 1: Conservation of number task. Make two sets of ten identical items with each set a different color (e.g., one set of ten blue poker chips and one set of ten white poker chips). First place one row of ten same-colored items in front of the child. Ask the child to make an identical row with the other set. Ask the child if the two rows have the same amount of items or if one row has more. Do not go on until the rows are identical in number and arrangement and the child agrees that the two rows are the same. Now spread one row out and push the other row together so that the display looks as follows:

OOOOOOOOOO

o o o o o o o o o o

Ask the child if the rows are the same or if one row has more. Ask the child why it is the same or why one has more and which one, if either, has more. If the child says one row has more, ask the child where the more came from. Record all responses.

Conservation Task 2: Conservation of liquid task. Pour into two identical glasses an identical amount of juice. Ask the child if the two glasses have the same amount, and adjust the volume in each glass until the child agrees that both have the same. Now pour the liquid from one glass into a taller, thinner glass. Ask the child if the amount of juice is the same in both glasses or if one has more. If the child thinks one has more, ask which one. Have the child justify the judgment of having the same or different amount. Record all responses.

Classification Task 1: Classification of groups. Present the child with cutouts of big and small triangles, circles, and squares. Some of the shapes should be red, some blue, and some green. Ask the child to put together those things that go together. Record how the child sorts the objects. Now ask the child if there is another way to put the objects together. Record the second sort.

Classification Task 2: Present the child with a set of wooden beads, with ten red and two blue. (You can substitute poker chips or M&Ms.) Ask the child if there are more red beads or more blue beads. If the child were to make a train with the red beads and another train with the blue beads, which train would be longer? Now ask the child if there are more red beads or more wooden beads. If the child were to make a train with the red beads and another train with the wooden beads, which train would be longer?

Use the data sheet on the next page to record your results.

DATA SHEET

Task	Child 1 Sex___Age___	Child 2 Sex___Age___
Conservation Task 1:		
Creation of row		
Response		
Justification		
Conservation Task 2:		
Response		
Justification		
Classification Task 1:		
First ordering		
Second ordering		
Classification Task 2:		
Response : red > blue?		
Response: red > wooden?		

Questions

1. Which tasks did the four- to five-year-old child solve? How would you characterize the nature of the child's responses to the questions?
2. Which tasks did the eight- to nine-year-old child solve? How would you characterize the nature of the child's responses to the questions?
3. How would you characterize the differences between the performance of the younger and older child on these tasks?
4. What do these observations tell you about Piaget's theory? How would the children be classified into Piaget's stages based on their responses to your problems?

Use in Classroom

Have students present data in class from the research project. Pool the data for the two age groups, and compare mean performance for each age group. What kinds of behaviors were seen in the 4- to 5-year-olds? What kinds of justifications did they give for their answers? What kinds of answers did they give? How did the 8- to 9-year-olds differ from them? How do the class data bear on Piaget's theory?

The expectation is that the 4- to 5-year olds will not be able to do either the simple classification task or the class inclusion task. The 4- to 5-year-olds are also nonconservers for liquid and probably for numbers. The 8- to 9-year-olds will be able to do all the classification and conservation tasks.

RESEARCH PROJECT 3   PIAGET'S PENDULUM PROBLEM

Pair up with a classmate. One of you is to present the other with Piaget's pendulum task. Then reverse roles and one of you will present the other with Piaget's chemical task. Then test an 11-year-old on the two tasks.

For the pendulum task, provide a frame for a pendulum as well as various lengths of string and a number of weights of equal size. Instruct your subjects to assemble the pendulum and to identify the variable(s) that determine the period of the pendulum swing. The possible variables to manipulate are length, weight, height of the drop, and force of the initial push. Record on the data sheet the variables that the subjects manipulate and the way in which subjects organize the manipulations.

For the chemical task, provide water, hydrogen peroxide, potassium iodine, acid, and thiosulfate in five numbered flasks. All of the chemicals are initially clear liquids. The subjects must determine which combination of chemicals produces a mixture with the color yellow. Record on the data sheet the variables that the subjects manipulate and the way in which subjects organize the manipulations.

Both tasks present combination problems, which are solved by systematically manipulating each of the variables and all of the possible combinations of variables to identify the correct solution. These tasks test for aspects of formal operational reasoning. After making the observations, answer the questions that follow.

DATA SHEET

Task	Subject 1	Subject 2
	Sex ___ Age ___	Sex ___ Age ___
Pendulum Task		
Chemical Task		

Questions

1. How did the students solve the tasks? How would you characterize the responses? Did the students systematically manipulate the variables?
2. How did the 11-year-old solve the tasks? How would you characterize the 11-year-old's responses? Did he or she systematically manipulate the variables?
3. What differences did you observe in performance of the younger and older adolescent? How would you characterize their performances according to Piaget's theory? Did you find evidence of formal operational reasoning in either, both, or neither of your subjects? How would you account for your findings? What is the nature of the difference between performances of the younger and older adolescent?

Use in Classroom

Have the students combine their data, identify trends in the results, and relate their results to Piaget's theory.

ESSAY AND CRITICAL THINKING QUESTIONS

Comprehension and Application Essay Questions

We recommend that you provide students with our guidelines for "Answering Essay and Critical Thinking Questions" when you have them respond to these questions. Their answers to these kinds of questions demonstrate an ability to comprehend and apply ideas discussed in this chapter.

1. Explain how adaptation, organization, and equilibration explain cognitive change during a child's development, and illustrate your main points with an example.

2. Describe how the cognitive capacity of infants changes throughout the sensorimotor period.
3. Explain why Piaget referred to the initial stage of cognitive development as the sensorimotor period.
4. What is the relationship between each of the substages in Piaget's theory of the sensorimotor period? How does the infant get from one stage to the next?
5. Present Piaget's view on the development of object permanence, and one contrasting view.
6. What is the "new perspective on cognitive development in infancy"? How does it relate to Piaget's ideas about cognitive development during infancy?
7. What does Piaget mean by the "operations?" Also explain how preoperational thought differs from sensorimotor thought.
8. Describe limitations of thought during the preoperational stage.
9. Compare and contrast the preoperational and concrete operational stages.
10. Explain the four characteristics of concrete operational thought according to Piaget.
11. Describe the tasks of conservation and classification.
12. Compare and contrast the concrete operational and formal operational stages.
13. Explain the concepts of adolescent egocentrism, imaginary audience, and personal fable. Include at least two original examples of each in your response.
14. How is cognitive development different in industrialized vs. developing countries? Why? How can the differences be minimized?
15. Explain Vygotsky's zone of proximal development and Rogoff's concept of apprenticeship.

Critical Thinking Questions

We recommend that you have students follow our guidelines for "Answering Essay and Critical Thinking Questions" when you ask them to prepare responses to these questions. Their answers to these kinds of questions reflect an ability to apply critical thinking skills to a novel problem or situation that is *not* specifically discussed in the chapter. These items most appropriately may be used as take-home essay questions (e.g., due on exam day) or as homework exercises that can be answered either by individuals or groups. Collaboratively answered questions encourage cooperative learning by students, and reduce the number of papers that must be graded.

1. At the end of Chapter 7 Santrock indicates books that provide practical knowledge about children and lists resources for improving the lives of children. Choose one of these books or resources and read it or learn as much as you can about it. Then write a brief review in which you (a) characterize the book or resource, and (b) explain how the book or resource relates to material in the chapter.
2. Chapter 1 defines the nature of development in terms of biological, cognitive, and social processes, and periods or stages. Indicate your ability to think critically by identifying material in this chapter that illustrates developmental processes and periods. If there is little or no information in this chapter about developmental processes and periods, identify and explain how developmental processes and periods could be used to guide the analysis of any topic in the chapter.
3. According to Chapter 1, three fundamental developmental issues concern: (a) maturation (nature) versus experience (nurture), (b) continuity versus discontinuity, and (c) early versus later experience. Indicate your ability to think critically by identifying material in this chapter that illustrates each of the three fundamental developmental issues. If there is little or no information in this chapter about fundamental developmental issues, identify and explain how these issues could be used to guide the analysis of any topic in the chapter.
4. One aspect of thinking critically is to read, listen, and observe carefully and then ask questions about what is missing from a text, discussion, or situation. For example, this chapter presents material on culture and the development of concrete operations, but does not do so for sensorimotor thought. Indicate your ability to think critically by (a) listing as many questions as you can about the cultural correlates of the development of formal operations, and (b) speculating why Santrock does not discuss this topic more fully.
5. Santrock sets off several quotations in this chapter. Indicate your ability to think critically by selecting one of the quotes and (a) learning about the author and indicating why this individual is eminently quotable (i.e., what was this individual's contribution to human knowledge and understanding), (b) interpreting and restating the quote in your own terms, and (c) explaining what concept, issue, perspective, or term in this chapter that Santrock intended this quote to illuminate. In other words, about what aspect or issue in development does this quote make you pause and reflect?
6. Chapter 2 indicates that theories help us explain data and make predictions about various aspects of development. Chapter 2 then presents six different theoretical approaches (i.e., Freudian, cognitive, behavioral and social learning, ethological, ecological, and eclectic theory), but notes that no single approach explains the complexity of development. Indicate your ability to think critically by (a) perusing

this chapter for topics influenced by at least one of the six theoretical approaches, and (b) explaining which theoretical approach dominated the topic in question. If the presentation is entirely atheoretical, identify and explain how one of the theoretical approaches could be used to guide the analysis of the topic in question.

7.   What is the relationship between culture and the development of formal operations. Apply your knowledge about the scientific method by designing a study to answer this question: (a) What specific problem or question do you want to study? (b) What predictions would you make and test in your study? (c) What measures would you use (i.e., controlled observation in a laboratory, naturalistic observation, interviews and questionnaires, case studies, standardized tests, cross-cultural studies, physiological research, research with animals, or multimeasure, multisource, and multicontext approach) and how would you define each measure clearly and unambiguously? (d) What strategy would you follow--correlational or experimental, and what would be the time span of your inquiry--cross-sectional or longitudinal? (e) What ethical considerations must be addressed before you conduct your study?

8.   According to Chapter 2, your author wants you to become a wise consumer of information about child development by: (a) being cautious about media reports, (b) distinguishing between nomothetic research and idiographic needs, (c) recognizing how easy it is to overgeneralize from a small or clinical sample, (d) knowing that a single study is usually not the defining word about some aspect of child development, (e) remembering that causal conclusions cannot be made from correlation studies, and (f) always considering the source of the information and evaluating its credibility. Indicate your ability to think critically by, first, selecting an article from either a journal, magazine, or newspaper about any topic regarding Cognitive Development and Piaget's Theory, and, second, evaluating it in terms of these six objectives. If the information in the article is insufficient to evaluate one of these objectives, then specify what kind of information you would need to evaluate the objective.

8 Information Processing

SUGGESTIONS FOR LECTURE TOPICS

1. Information Processing Analysis of Piagetian Tasks.

One way to make the transition from Piaget's theory of cognitive development to information processing approaches is to show how information processing psychologists have analyzed some of Piaget's tasks. there are numerous examples to be drawn from each of the four stages. You may wish to draw on each, focus on concrete and formal operations, or deal exclusively with formal operations.

Begin your lecture with a review of the criticisms of Piaget's theory that students have just studied in Chapter 4. Much of this critique has been developed by individuals arguing from an information processing perspective; you could draw in the works of Rochel Gelman, Thomas Trabasso, Jerome Bruner, and many others. In any event, the main point to make is that Piaget's tasks call on diverse aspects of information processing, and age difference in performing them could be do to failure in any one of them rather than failure to attain some generalized set of cognitive operations.

Illustrate your point with a specific example. A good one is Trabasso's classic analysis of transitive inference (a good choice, because you can devise tests of transitive inference that your students will fail). Present Trabasso's analysis in some detail, as well as some of the experiments he and Peter Bryant carried out to test their ideas. There are many other possibilities, but we particularly also recommend Robert Sternberg's analysis of performance on analogies (see suggestion 3 below).

Conclude your lecture by taking a stand on how the cognitive processing research related to Piaget's work, and vice-versa. You may wish to argue that it points up severe deficiencies that invalidate the old master's contribution. Alternatively, you may wish to develop the position that Piaget has unearthed puzzles that continue to fascinate and challenge subsequent generations of researchers.

1. Memory Observed: Research on Metamemory

Not too long ago research on memory had a strict behavior cast to it. But over the past two decades, research on memory development has increasingly focused on mental manipulations of information called memory strategies. The logical extension of this work (as it seems in retrospect) was the suggestion that older people tend not only to be more strategic when they have to perform memory tasks, but tend to have better understanding about how memory works: to use which strategies, what sorts of memory tasks they perform well or badly, and so on. This sort of knowledge is called metamemory.

Researchers have tried to find out about the development of metamemory by devising a means to get children to tell them what they (the children) know about memory. A classic reference here is the 1975 *Society for Research in Child Development* monograph titled "An Interview Study of Children's Knowledge about Memory," by M. Kreutzer, C. Leonard, and J. Flavell. Use the information in this monograph to cover some of the ways researchers find out what children think about memory processes.

Metamemory research has been very active but has not gone unscathed by criticism. In the 1980s, critical reviews of the work appeared in the journal *Child Development*. You may wish to consult these as a basis for making a critical analysis using the descriptive data of self-reports to study mental processes.

3. Do We Know How to Teach Children How to Read?

A continuing and interesting dilemma for anyone who would teach children to read is that no one really knows the best way to do it. Dominant contenders are the phonics method and the whole-word method, but there is no conclusive evidence to recommend one method over the other. Although there are proponents of each approach, the general solution suggested by the text is a pragmatic mixing of elements of both that seem to help.

In a lecture on this issue, outline each of the dominant theories, and show how they translate into classroom practices. Then present the evidence that shows why neither of these theories or approaches is "right." A good source could be any of several volumes of *The Kappan,* which has monitored this debate in articles published over the past several years.

Having done this, suggest the importance of the issue that reading involves many cognitive processes, many of which may not be captured in the whole-word/phonics debate. Project SAIL is a contemporary program being conducted in Maryland schools that illustrates this point. It has shown great potential as a pragmatic application of what is known about reading processes. Michael Pressley is an energetic spokesman for the project and one of the main researchers and evaluators of this program; he is beginning to publish extensively about it in reading journals. You may even be able to obtain videotapes from him that can be used to illustrate various components of the process.

4.   Emotions and Memory Abilities

Emotions have a strong effect on the ability to recall events in early childhood (Todd, 1985). High levels of fear and anxiety make it more difficult for young children to remember new information (Hill, 1972; Master et al., 1979). Even children as young as 3 years know that their emotional state can affect their ability to remember well. The majority of preschoolers believe that they can learn more easily when happy than when sad, when alert than when tired, and when they are quiet rather than noisy (Hayes et al., 1987). However, 5-year-olds have a tendency to overestimate their overall abilities to remember objects (Yussen & Levy, 1975). (*Sources:* Hayes, D. S., Scott, L. C., Chemelski, B. E., & Johnson, J. 1987. Physical and emotional states as memory-relevant factors: Cognitive monitoring by young children. *Merrill-Palmer Quarterly, 33,* 473-487; Hill, K. T. 1972. Anxiety in the evaluative context. In W. W. Hartup (Ed.). *Young child* . Washington, D.C.: National Association for the Education of Young Children; Masters, J. C., Barden, R. C., & Ford, M. E. 1979. Affective states, expressive behavior, and learning in children. *Journal of Personality and Social Psychology, 37,* 380-390; Todd, C. M. 1985. *Long-term recall of everyday events by preschool children.* Unpublished doctoral dissertation. University of Minnesota, Minneapolis, MN; Yussen, S. R. & Levy, V. M. 1975. Developmental changes in predicting one's own span of short-term memory. *Journal of Experimental Child Psychology, 34,* 490-509.)

5.   Verbal Rehearsal Strategies

Improvements in verbal rehearsal strategies continue well past the middle childhood years. For example, subjects of various ages were asked to recall a list of words. Recalling some of the words would earn the subjects 10 cents per word and other words would earn only one cent each. Fifth graders rehearsed 10-cent and one-cent words equally. Eighth graders only slightly rehearsed 10-cent words more. College students, however, spent twice as much time rehearsing the words that earned them 10 cents each than words that earned only a penny each. Only the college students were able to use a strategy that maximized income. (*Source:* Kail, R. 1984. *The development of memory in children,* 2nd ed. NY: W. H. Freeman.)

6.   Motor Skill Memory

When was the first time you jumped rope? Blew soap bubbles? Roller skated? Rode a bicycle? Played hopscotch? Can you remember these events? If you do, you are atypical. However, you probably still remember how to do each of these skills if you learned them at some time in your life. So, although you don't remember the learning, you do remember the motor skill. How do you remember motor skills?

It appears that the ability to learn and recall motor skills is located in the **cerebellum,** the area of the brain under the back side of the cerebrum and behind the brain stem. The cerebellum accounts for only one eighth of the brain's weight. Whenever a motor skill is learned, part of the cerebellum's nerve cell system changes physically.

Once thought to only control balance and keep movements smooth and rapid, the cerebellum also helps the brain to learn and remember motor skills. The cerebellum has four types of cells, and some research suggests that **H-VI Purkinje cells** are most important during learning. In the cerebellum, Purkinje cells are inhibitory, and their most common reaction when stimulated during learning is to decrease their response. (*Source:* Phillips, K. 1990 (May). You must remember this. *Omni, 30,* 112.)

7.   Laughter theories

Little psychological research has been done on laughter or humor, but the following theories have been developed to explain laughter:

1.   **Superiority theory** is the oldest and most often cited theory of laughter. Superiority theory focuses on emotions as the cause of laughter. Laughter is self-congratulatory or a feeling of a sense of "superior adaptation". That is, individuals laugh because they feel they are better off than other people or because they feel they are better off than they once were. Some individuals believe this type of humor is less prevalent than it once was because of

the modern moral development that objects to enjoying others' suffering. Would people still be amused by a day of watching the Christians and lions?

2. **Incongruity theory** focuses on ideas. According to this theory, amusement is an intellectual response to dealing with unexpected, inappropriate, or illogical situations. People laugh because something they perceive does not fit the usual pattern.

3. **Relief theory** focuses on biology, or laughter as a way to vent nervous energy. Freud, for example, thought that repressed sexuality and hostility often led to humor. Others suggest that any prohibition is a potential source of laughter. Dirty jokes fit this category well.

4. **Psychological shift theory** suggests that laughter is the physical activity caused by feeling a pleasant psychological shift. Not only does it account for humor that fits each of the first three theories, but it also accounts for laughter produced by nonhumorous occasions, e.g., tickling, peekaboo for a baby, watching a magic trick, or winning a game.

Analyze your own humor and laughter. Why do you laugh? What things do you find humorous? Do you joke at others' expense? At unusual situations? About taboo situations? How has your sense of humor changed since you were a small child? Do you find offensive any styles of humor that your friends enjoy? On which type of humor do various popular television shows rely? Which popular comedians rely on each of the types of theories? (*Source:* Ludovici, A. 1933. *The secret of laughter.* New York: Viking; Morreall, J. 1983. *Taking laughter seriously.* Albany, New York: State University of New York.)

8. Developmental Stages of Dreaming

According to David Foulkes, children have different dream content than do adults. Not until they are 8 or 9 do children have dreams that are similar to adults' dreams. The changes in dream content during the first several years of life are compatible to thinking process changes as proposed in theories such as Jean Piaget's.

Fetuses only 23 weeks old experience REM sleep, the sleep pattern in which dreams are frequent, but of course, the dream content cannot be studied until children have some language ability. It seems that 3- and 4-year-olds have dreams in "bits and pieces", comparable to viewing a slide story or seeing pictures in a storybook. Their dreams have little emotional content and rarely are they in their own dreams. On the other hand, preschoolers are prone to nightmares.

At 5 and 6, children begin dreaming in stories that have some action and movement, but they themselves are not featured in their own dreams. Around 7 or 8, the children begin to place themselves in their dreams; brighter children tend to begin this earlier than is typical. By 9, dreamers star in their own dreams.

Despite limitations, children older than 5 can be instructed in successful **lucid dreaming** in which they learn to influence the action of their own dreams. One advantage is that children who have recurring scary dreams can learn to change the dream into a pleasant one. (*Source:* Begley, S. 1989 (August 14). The stuff that dreams are made of. *Newsweek,* 41-44.)

9. Visual vs. Auditory Memory

Older children remember more than younger children, *except,* that is, when the memory task is purely visual. In one study, children were shown picture books containing 40 colored pictures of common objects and animals. There were four pictures on each page—one in each quarter of the page. After viewing the pictures, the children were shown a second copy and asked to indicate what its page location had been (top to bottom, left or right). Many 3- and 4-year-olds were good at this task, and 5- and 6-year-olds did as well as college students.

In a second study, 5-year-olds and 11-year-olds were tested on a picture-remembering task. The younger subjects most often confused pictures that looked alike (e.g., a pencil and a toothbrush), and the older subjects were more likely to confuse things that sounded alike (e.g., rap and rat).

As children get older, they use language to help them remember. This means that they begin using more elaborate memory strategies such as rehearsal, categorization, and elaboration. However, the visual memory of preschoolers is quite good. Perhaps that is why one of the first games children enjoy is Memory. (*Sources:* Ellis, N. R., Katz, E., & Williams, J. E. 1987. Developmental aspects of memory for spatial location. *Journal of Experimental Child Psychology, 44,* 401-412; Hitch, G. J., Woodin, M. E., & Baker, S. 1989. Visual and phonological components of working memory in children. *Memory and Cognition, 17,* 175-185.)

10.   Memory Learning of Brain Cells

A team at Berkeley is learning a great deal about how individual neurons learn and remember. By using a cancer gene inserted into mouse brain cells, they induce division resulting in a supply of identical HT4 cells that can be grown in cultures and provide limitless duplicate cells for research. In studies, Daniel Koshland and others have found that serotonin, one of the neurotransmitters, is important in long-term memory. For example, when HT4 cells are exposed to minute quantities of serotonin, they have increased, but short-lived, output of excitatory amino acids. If subjected to one high dose of serotonin, the effects lasted for the entire five-hour life of the cell. In other words, a huge dose created what appears to be a lasting long-term memory. Another way to create a permanent change is to give the cells simultaneous smaller doses of serotonin and glutamate (an excitatory acid) repeatedly. Either way, it seems that the serotonin receptor must be activated to create a rise in a molecule called cyclic AMP. Glutamate receptors activate protein kinase C, an enzyme that keeps cyclic AMP high. When cyclic AMP levels are elevated, long-term memory stage appears to occur. Based on current knowledge, cellular long-term storage seems a lot like the way our holistic long-term memory works. Things can get into the long-term memory if they are strong, powerful events (e.g., witnessing a bad car crash) or if people work at learning something hard and often (e.g., learning one's multiplication tables). Of course, more research must be done to understand the relationship between the cellular process and the process in the whole human being. Other needed research includes seeing whether cells other than the HT4 respond the same way, and if so, whether researchers will then be able to find the cells that have just learned a certain function by finding neurons with the highest level of cyclic AMP. (*Source:* Nadis, S. 1993 (1993). Test-tube obedience training: Nerve cells in a dish obey like Pavlovian dogs. *Omni,* 10.)

BROWN & BENCHMARK'S HUMAN DEVELOPMENT TRANSPARENCIES (2ND ED.)

Transparency Number and Title

The transparency set, a supplement to *Child Development*, is accompanied by an annotated manual that describes each of the 141 transparencies. The annotated manual also offers suggestions about how to use the transparencies to engage your students in active learning that will stimulate critical thinking and evaluative skills. The following transparencies are appropriate and useful with Chapter 8: Information Processing

Transparency Number and Title

22   A Model of Cognition
27   Cognitive Theories
69   Concept Formation

CLASSROOM ACTIVITIES OR DEMONSTRATIONS

1.   Discuss the critical thinking exercises. In a preview to Exercise 1 you may want to indicate that all of the processes are conceivably involved in understanding the passage, but that one of them is prerequisite to the operation of the others. That is, the others will avail a reader very little if one of them is not in operation. Also, point out to your class that there is no material that will directly tell them the answer, but that one of the concepts is contained in a description in the text that indicates a clue *by analogy*.

    Exercise 2 involves mainly a review of research strategies that scientists use to find things out. We find that if we do not consistently ask students to make these kinds of judgements they become inaccurate in their ability to identify the types of research that produce various findings. To the extent that this weakens their ability to evaluate what they are reading, students lose out. Prior to this exercise remind students of the value of identifying the kinds of research that underly findings in this chapter, which is unusually good about providing such details. You may find that you need to work systematically through the identifying features of experiments, correlational studies, and so forth.

    The main purpose of Exercise 3 is to highlight the underlying logic to the argument concerning the idea that children's concepts function as theories. Suggest to your students that the argument is basically a syllogism, and that they are basically looking for its premise. Although a bit abstract, this exercise may make them realize that such study as the philosophy of science, which may seem fairly remote from child psychology, has an important bearing on what child psychologists think they are coming to understand when they study cognitive development. There is more than a little opportunity in that point to remind students of Piaget's motivation in studying cognitive development, and to note certain parallels between the ideas contained in this section on concepts as implicit theories and ideas that are basic to Piaget's theory.

2. Discuss the students' research projects as suggested below.

3. Have students discuss what skills children should have before they learn to read. Have them discuss which activities help young children learn these skills. Have them give their opinion on the advantages and disadvantages of beginning to learn to read before attending school. Use the following information to aid the content of discussion.

Three skills help young children read at the beginning of first grade:

1. First, young children need to know the alphabet. Children who do not know how to identify both upper-case and lower-case letters by the middle of kindergarten are likely to have trouble with first-grade reading.
2. A second needed skill is the ability to break up words into their component sounds. A child who cannot do this by first grade will get behind in reading skills.
3. The third skill is really an attitude, a love and interest in reading.

Most good readers come from homes that have books and other reading material, parents who enjoy and model reading, and have been read to on many occasions. These children also have above-average vocabularies and do well on IQ tests. Exposure to reading and the love of reading is sufficient, and experts do not recommend parental pressure or early reading training.

Sources: Walsh, D. J. Price, G. G., & Gillingham, M. G. 1988. The critical but transitory importance of letter-naming. *Reading Research Quarterly,* 23, 108-122; Ellis, N. & Large, B. 1988. The early stages of reading: A longitudinal study. *Applied Cognitive Psychology,* 2, 47-76; Bradley, L. 1988. Rhyme recognition and reading and spelling in young children. In R. Masland & M. Masland (Eds.). *Pre-school Prevention of Reading Failures,* Parkton, MD: York Press. Scarborough, H. S. 1989. Prediction of reading disability from familial and individual differences. *Journal of Educational Psychology,* 81, 101-108; Jackson, N. E. 1988. Precocious reading ability: What does it mean? *Gifted Child Quarterly,* 32, 200-204.

---

4. Have students discuss what they remember when they learned to read a clock? How did they deal with the time segments in school? Did they always lose track of time? Do they remember how long car trips seemed to take, or how endless sermons were? How did anticipation about holidays affect time? Ask them if all children learn that time is an important variable. Use the following information to enliven discussion and introduce new points and questions:

Middle-class children are introduced to an organized sense of time early in life - they tend to see parents go to work at certain times and return at a certain time, meals are scheduled, bedtime is regular, and alarm clocks are used to get them up on time for school or church. Children reared in poverty do not see adults going to work at regular times, and they are less likely to have consistent meal or bed times. As a result, they can be overwhelmed by the school day being divided into segments. They have difficulty conforming to schedules before having built a solid sense of time.

During middle childhood, children gradually improve their ability to estimate time periods. By second grade, most can name the days of the week; most third graders can name the months of the year; by fifth grade they can start with any day (month) and figure out which day (month) is three from now; by tenth grade they can start at any day (month) and count backwards.

Sources: Taylor, E. 1989 (February 27). Time is not on their side. *Time,* 74; Friedman, W. J. 1986. The development of children's knowledge of temporal structure. *Child Development,* 57, 1386-1400.

---

5. Ask students to describe memories about judging their abilities and performances as a child. When did they learn to assess their own cognitive reasoning? Their memory abilities? What effects did an increase in accuracy of judgment of performance have?

For example, older school children are better than younger children at judging their performance on a multiple-choice exam. What are the effects of this? Does it lead to better use of study time? More efficient judgment of abilities? Depression after a test due to estimate of poor performance? More test anxiety? More competition?

Young children are likely to overestimate the accuracy of their cognitive judgments. If, for example, they were to guess the number of jelly beans in a jar without being able to take them out and count them, many 5-year-olds would confidently state that they got the right number. School-aged children, however, will recognize that their guesses are unlikely to be exactly right.

Source: Pressley, M., Levin, J. R., Ghatala, E. S., & Ahmad, M. 1987. Test monitoring in young grade-school children. *Journal of Experimental Child Psychology, 43,* 96-111.

6. Around the age of 7, children begin to monitor communication from others to check what was actually said. In fact, only half of 7-year-olds are "good monitors." "Poor monitors" fail to notice ambiguities in messages and assume that they know what the speaker actually said. Obviously, these "poor monitors" can have trouble in school because they "mishear" teachers' directions and comments.

    Have your students come up with some possible techniques to try to help "poor monitors" learn to monitor better. Their suggestions can include things teachers can modify in order to improve the possibility of being heard correctly by the "poor monitoring" students.

Source: Bonitatibus, G. 1988. Comprehension monitoring and the apprehension of literal meaning. *Child Development, 59,* 60-70.

7. After presenting the following research findings on selective attention, have students discuss why so many students did poorly in open classroom schools. Also, have them debate whether children should be allowed to do homework with a radio on or in front of the television.

    •   Second graders had more trouble than sixth graders concentrating on a task while music played.
    •   The task was to sort cards into two piles based on a small or large middle square. First-graders were slowed down more than fifth graders by other geometric figures printed on the cards.
    •   The task is to memorize one of three words printed on a card. School-age students did worse than college students when any one of the words was printed in red.

Sources: Lorch, E. P. & Horn, D. G. 1986. Habituation of attention to irrelevant stimuli in elementary school children. *Journal of Experimental Child Psychology,* 41, 184-197; Ackerman, B. P. 1987. Selective attention and distraction in context-interactive situations in children and adults. *Journal of Experimental Child Psychology,* 44, 126-146.

8. Have students plan a lesson to teach a group of preschool children and a group of third-grade children memory strategies that would aid in their assigned learning tasks. Use the information on memory strategies presented in the text. They should begin by listing the various memory strategies. They should then list the cognitive abilities of preschool and third-grade children. They should next plan a lesson plan strategy for teaching the two age groups in planning their lesson.

    Spontaneous maintenance rehearsal appears at about five years. Children from 5 to 10 can be taught this form of rehearsal. The youngest ones can be taught to repeat the material to be remembered. Organization, which appears spontaneously around 10, can be taught to children. The youngest children could be taught to put to-be-remembered material into piles. Elementary school children can use imagery in the form of the keyword method. Third-grade students could probably be coached in semantic elaboration because they show spontaneous inferencing.

Source: Adapted from King, M. B. & Clark, D. E. (1989). *Instructor's Manual to Accompany Santrock and Yussen's Child Development: An Introduction,* 4th ed. Dubuque, IA: Wm. C. Brown.

9. Present the following list of words to the class. Instruct half the class to think of an opposite word and the other half of the class to count the number of vowels in each word. Present the list at the rate of one every five seconds. Test recall for the list in each group, and see if recall is different for the two groups.

Son	Old	Book
Pale	Less	Coffee
Water	Good	Clock
Order	Desk	Painting
Green	Girl	Door

The group that was instructed to think of opposite words will remember more words. They have engaged in semantic elaboration. This deeper level of processing leads to better incorporation into a long-term memory.

Source: Adapted from King, M. B. & Clark, D. E. 1989. *Instructor's Manual to Accompany Santrock & Yussen's Child Development: An Introduction,* 4th ed., Dubuque, IA: Wm. C. Brown.

10. You can easily demonstrate the value of chunking to short-term memory performance by using the following two sets of numbers:

$$1\ 4\ 9\ 1\ 6\ 2\ 5\ 3\ 6\ 4\ 9\ 6\ 4\ 8\ 1$$

$$1\quad 4\quad 9\quad 16\quad 25\quad 36\quad 49\quad 64\quad 81$$

Of course, these are the same digits, but the first set is arranged to seem either as a long number of 15 digits, or 15 individual digits, whereas the second set more clearly arranges the digits as 9 separate numbers. You may also have noticed that these are the numbers 1 through 9 squared!

In any event, prepare overhead of each of these number strings for use in an in class experiment. You may do the experiment in any way that is convenient to you, but we suggest that you have half the class view one set, and half the class the other, in a very brief (say, 2 second) exposure (while one half is viewing have the other half close their eyes). Immediately after students see the numbers have them write down as many numbers as they can. Thirty seconds is usually enough time for recall. Next, have students count each *individual digit* that they were able to remember. For example, writing 36 would count as two digits. When students have done that, collect data from at least 10 students from each viewing condition. Write the reported number of digits remembered in two columns on blackboard or overhead, and calculate means for each group.

Discuss the results. You will usually get a very big difference between groups; sometimes we have had completely non overlapping distributions of scores. Have students suggest reasons why the group with the grouped numbers did so well compared to the group without grouped numbers. If anyone remembered all 15, ask them how they did it.

This is a very effective demonstration of the benefits of chunking, as well as a potent indicator that there are different levels of chunking and problems in defining the concept of a chunk. Clearly, variables such as knowledge and expertise define what individuals perceive as a chunk. You should be able to use these points to discuss a variety of reasons that children's memory is "smaller" than adults' memory, as well as the odd demonstration of superior memory among children.

For an added dimension, use the squares of the numbers 1 to 10, but omit one of them, say, 49. You may have someone in the class include it in their performance anyway, which will give you an opportunity to discuss how ideas and expectations about to-be-remembered information can distort or impair memory performance.

11.	There are many ways to demonstrate the efficacy of memory strategies. Here is one that is somewhat unusual because it demonstrates a retrieval strategy: Tell your students that you are about to do a demonstration of the processes of attention and habituation (or some other basic process). Say that you will do this by having them write down a set of numbers and letters, during which they are to pay as close attention to what they are doing as they can. Twit them a bit, suggesting that they will quickly discover the difference between attention and habituation. Use the following set of letters and numbers (taken from the Keniston and Flavell reference below): 6XDL3BU1QYA0E5COHKI9FJ2WNPS.

When you are done reading the numbers and letters, have students put their papers away and then do something, anything, for 30 seconds. Perhaps you could have someone characterize the difference between attention and habituation in terms of what they have just done. In any event, when 30 seconds have passed ask your students to get out a clean sheet of paper and try to remember which of the letters they have just written down. Give them at least 30 seconds to remember as many as they can, and then to count the number of letters they have remembered. Do not be overly concerned about intrusions.

Ask if anyone remembered 10 or fewer letters. If anyone did, ask them to slowly read their list while you write on a blackboard or overhead. Get at least two such lists from people who remembered relatively few letters. Then find out who remembered the largest number of letters, and have them read to you their lists.

What should be plain is that the students who remembered more letters did so by systematically going through the alphabet "in their heads" and writing down the letters they recognize having written down earlier. Their recall protocol may show one or many such transits. In general, the large memory performances should be more alphabetical. Furthermore, if you ask students to describe how they went about remembering the letters, those who produced the shorter lists should report something like "I just let the numbers come to me," whereas those remembering the longer lists should mention an alphabetical strategy.

Discuss these results in light of various themes from the book. At minimum the demonstration shows the value of memory strategies. It also shows how knowledge may be used to benefit memory. You can also use the task to discuss the concepts of encoding, storage, and retrieval, and to illustrate how experimenters isolate one of these sets of processes by controlling others (e.g., in the present case, by using an incidental recall task using well-learned material to isolate retrieval differences). Use the reference listed below to present developmental data obtained with the task, and as a further example of the sorts of task analyses researchers do to study memory development.

Source: Keniston, A. H., & Flavell, J. H. 1979. A developmental study of intelligent retrieval. *Child Development, 50,* 1144-1152.

CRITICAL THINKING EXERCISES

Exercise 1

Read the following passage from the research of Bransford and Johnson (1973):

The Procedure is quite simple. First, you arrange things into different groups. Of course, one pile may be sufficient, depending on how much there is to do. If you have to go somewhere else due to lack of facilities, that is the next step; otherwise, you are pretty well set. It is important not to overdo things. That is, it is better to do too few things at once than too many. At first the whole procedure will seem complicated. Soon, however, it will become just another facet of life. After the procedure is completed, one arranges the materials into different groups again. Then they can be put into their appropriate places. Eventually they will be used once more, and the whole cycle will have to be repeated. (*Source:* Bransford, J.D., and Johnson, M.K. (1973). Consideration of some problems in comprehension. In *Visual information processing*, W.G. Chase (Ed.). New York: Academic Press.)

Which concept best explains the difficulty you have with understanding this passage? **Circle the letter of the best answer, and explain why it is the best answer and why each other answer is not as good.**

A. schema
B. attention
C. elaboration
D. metacognitive knowledge
E. content knowledge

Exercise 2

Santrock and Siegler describe research about many different aspects of the development of information processing in Chapter 8. It is important that the reader understands the types of research they describe in order to appreciate and evaluate the information correctly. Below you will find brief references to research Santrock and Siegler describe paired with a type of research. Only one of these pairings is correct. Which is it? **Circle the letter of the best answer, and explain why it is the best answer and why each other answer is not as good.**

A. The capacity of short-term memory increases with age (p. 249): experimental research
B. The faster that infants habituate to stimuli at 6 months of age, the higher their IQs at 6 to 9 years of age (p. 250): correlational research
C. The percentage of children who make lip movements in studies of free recall increases with age (p.253): case study
D. Children given a keyword strategy to remember the names of state capitals remembered more names than children not given such a strategy (p. 254): observational study
E. A 4-year-old's knowledge of dinosaurs can be described as a semantic network (pp. 256-257): correlational research

Exercise 3

In the section on conceptual development in Chapter 8 of *Child Development*, Santrock and Siegler explain the idea of concepts as implicit theories. Which of the following statements represents an assumption that underlies this material, as opposed to an inference or an observation? **Circle the letter of the best answer, and explain why it is the best answer and why each other answer is not as good.**

A. Children's concepts resemble scientific theories.
B. Cause-effect relationships are found in both children's and scientist's theories.
C. Infants that see one object apparently pass through another look for a long time at the space where the even occurred.
D. The distinctive features of a theory are explanations of relations between its parts, a prominent role for cause-effect relationships, and hierarchical organization with respect to other theories.
E. Children begin life with three grand theories.

ANSWER KEYS FOR CRITICAL THINKING EXERCISES

Exercise 1

A. This is the best answer. The various statements do not seem to be related to each other, nor are there clues in the passage to clarify what their relationship is. One has to impose an organizational schema, a schema that will indicate what role each statement plays in the event that is being described (doing the laundry).
B. This is not the best answer. The difficulty is not that a reader does not pay attention to each individual statement. In fact, a motivated reader will probably devote a great deal of attention to such a passage, even focussing on the material to the exclusion of other stimuli in an effort to understand. However, simply committing attention to the passage will not render it more understandable.
C. This is not the best answer. Elaboration will not guarantee understanding, because there are few if any clues about how best to elaborate these sentences. Some prior indication is needed, such as would be provided by a schema. With an appropriate schema in hand, useful and clarifying elaboration could take place.
D. This is not the best answer. Metacognitive knowledge by itself would mainly indicate to a reader that he or she is not understanding the passage. On the other hand, metacognitive knowledge might provide a clue to what is missing. Sure cognitive monitoring would prompt the question, "What is this passage about?", which might lead to a search for appropriate candidate schemas that would lead to insight.

E. This is not the best answer. Content knowledge cannot be activated until an appropriate knowledge domain is activated by a schema. Once that happens, however, content knowledge can provide useful elaboration, which would lead to better understanding.

Exercise 2

A. This is not the best answer. The type of research that has generated this finding has been comparisons of the memory span performances by children of different ages. This is essentially a correlational design.
B. This is the best answer. These statements indicate a relationship between measures of different cognitive performances at different points in individual's lives.
C. This is not the best answer. The research which forms the basis of this observation is essentially a comparison how children of different ages deal with free recall tasks. Measures taken and recorded were concentrated on aspects of memory-related behavior alone; no comprehensive gathering of data about numerous aspects of individual's lives was undertaken. A specific question was asked in a comparative (correlational) study.
D. This is not the best answer. This was not an observational study inasmuch as the measures assessed aspects of memory performance rather than recordings of behavior. Furthermore, the implication in the text (though the text is not clear on this point) is that the work was experimental rather than descriptive, because the researchers wanted to claim that the keyword strategy caused better memory performance.
E. This is not the best answer. Only one 4-year-old is described, therefore there can be no correlation. Although the data collected about the individual were very limited, this finding is best described as a case study.

Exercise 3

A. This is not the best answer. Although this claim is stated at the beginning of the section, it is stated as a hypothesis that the authors then attempt to support with evidence. Thus it is an inference.
B. This is not the best answer. This is stated as the result of a specific comparison of children's concepts and scientific theories. Thus it is an observation.
C. This is not the best answer. This statement describes what an observer sees an infant do under the specified circumstances. That makes it an observation.
D. This is the best answer. This is a definition of a theory that serves as the premise, or assumption, of the entire passage. In effect, the passage relies on a syllogism that states "All theories have these characteristics, children's concepts have these characteristics, hence children's concepts are theories."
E. This is not the best answer. This is an hypothesis tendered by Henry Wellman and others about the most general, organizing concepts that are present among children's concepts.

RESEARCH PROJECT 1

The function of this project is to provide a demonstration of memory span. Pair up with a classmate and test four individuals: a 3-year-old, a 6-year-old, a 9-year-old, and a classmate. The task is a digit span task. Present a list of digits to each subject at the rate of one per second, and have each subject repeat as many digits as he or she remembers. One of you will present the digits and the other will record the subject's response. Use the following work sheets for data collection and then answer the questions that follow.

DATA SHEET

Task	Child 1	Child 2	Child 3	Adult
	Age___	Age___	Age___	Age___
	Sex___	Sex___	Sex___	Sex___
Digits	Response:	Response:	Response:	Response:

2
74
196
2389
64157
326890

Task	Child 1	Child 2	Child 3	Adult

7509621
92503184
849276304

<u>Number of correct</u>
<u>digits out of:</u>

one
two
three
four
five
six
seven
eight
nine

Questions

1. How many digits would a 3-year-old remember? Was it the same number regardless of the number of digits presented? How many could the 6-year-old, the 9-year-old, and the classmate remember? Was the number different depending on the number presented? In what way was the number different?
2. Did you find age differences for memory span? What is the nature of the differences observed? Could anything besides memory span account for the differences? (Consider possible sex differences, if applicable, or differences in the child's understanding of his or her role in the task.)
3. From your data, what statement could you make about the development of memory span from 3 years to adulthood? What qualifications, if any, would you need to make about your statement, based on the limitations of your data?

Use in Classroom

Have students present their data from the research project in class. Have them discuss the developmental trend that appears in the class data. How does memory span for digits change with age? Are there any variables besides age that could account for the data?

You would expect digit span to be about 2, 4 to 5, 6 to 7, and about 7 with the increasing age groups.

RESEARCH PROJECT 2   DOES CRITICAL THINKING GET BETTER WITH PRACTICE?

This project will afford you data about whether your experience of the critical thinking exercises written for *Child Development* has enabled you to perform those exercises. The basic idea is simple: Compare class performance to the performance of students who have not had any previous experience with the exercises.

Persuade five students you know who have not tried to do critical thinking exercises like the ones you have been doing complete Critical Thinking Exercise 3 for Chapter 7 of *Child Development*. Use Exercise 3 because you have had more experience of this type of exercise than of the others, and because it is relatively easy to copy the material from the textbook that is the basis of the exercise. You may allow your respondents any amount of time to complete the exercise you like, but we recommend that you give them no more than 45 minutes and that you supervise them in whatever manner is comfortable to you.

Obtain an answer key from your instructor and score the exercises (you will be learning what grading is like as well as learning about research!) Your instructor will also give you five randomly selected (and anonymous) scores from your class's performance on the assignment. Arrange both the scores of your respondents and your class's scores in an appropriate table, which also shows means and (if you know how to calculate them) and standard deviations for the data. When you have prepared your table, write a brief report about your findings that answers at least the following questions:

Questions

1. What did you expect to find out? Why?
2. Who were your respondents? Briefly indicate as much as you can about their age, sex, years in college, and anything you can add about their experience as "critical thinkers" (you may wish to interview them briefly about that).
3. What was your procedure?
4. What were your results?
5. Did your results confirm or disconfirm your expectations? How do you explain them?
6. Criticize this project: Is it a true experiment? Why or why not? Is the comparison an appropriate test of the hypothesis (e.g., are extraneous or confounding variables appropriately controlled)?
7. What would be your next step?

Use in the Classroom

Have some of your students briefly report their findings; get a sense about whether there is a consensus of results. You may also want to pool some or all of the data in order to make a comparison based on a larger sample. Discuss the various ways that students have collected their data, and consider whether these variations produced different findings. Discuss the results in terms of the intent and value of the critical thinking assignments, and in terms of what we wish we knew about how to train critical thinking skills in our students.

ESSAY AND CRITICAL THINKING QUESTIONS

Comprehension and Application Essay Questions

We recommend that you provide students with our guidelines for "Answering Essay and Critical Thinking Questions" when you have them respond to these questions. Their answers to these kinds of questions demonstrate an ability to comprehend and apply ideas discussed in this chapter.

1. Define the information processing approach, and illustrate its identifying features with an example from Chapter 8.
2. Compare and contrast the information processing and Piagetian approaches to cognitive development. Illustrate their similarities and difference with specific examples drawn from Chapters 7 and 8 of *Child Development*.
3. Compare and contrast the three time frames of memory, supplying an examples of everyday phenomena that suggest the existence of each, and indicating how each seems to develop.
4. Define and outline the development of schemas. What role may they play in other aspects of cognitive function and development?
5. Are the basic cognitive processes related to each other? If so, how? Do they play a role in other cognitive functions? What?
6. Compare and contrast any two memory strategies, with an aim toward recommending how each can be applied appropriately to education.
7. Discuss how both metacognitive knowledge and content knowledge can play a role in memory performance.
8. Define concepts and discuss the role they play in children's understanding of the world.
9. Sketch the development of children's understanding of the concept of mind.
10. Discuss developmental and individual differences in children's understanding of biological concepts.
11. What are the different forms of spatial representation? Does the ability to use them occur in a developmental sequence? If so, what is the sequence?
12. What develops with respect to children's understanding of number?
13. Explain how children use rules to solve balance beam problems; cite relevant evidence.
14. Explain the sense in which imitation is an example of problem-solving among infants.
15. Compare and contrast any two of means-end analysis, scientific reasoning, and reasoning by analogy.
16. According to Chapter 7, what level of cognitive development would a child have to reach to use any of the problem solving strategies described in Chapter 8? Explain your answer.
17. Discuss how social contexts influence children's problem-solving, and explain whether this conforms to Vygotsky's or Piaget's ideas better.
18. Describe the development of any one of the academic skills presented in Chapter 8.

19. Discuss how development of basic processes may be involved in the development of any one of the academic skills discussed in Chapter 8.
20. Discuss how strategies, metacognitive knowledge, or content knowledge may be involved in the development of any one of the basic academic skills discussed in Chapter 8.

Critical Thinking Questions

We recommend that you have students follow our guidelines for "Answering Essay and Critical Thinking Questions" when you ask them to prepare responses to these questions. Their answers to these kinds of questions reflect an ability to apply critical thinking skills to a novel problem or situation that is *not* specifically discussed in the chapter. These items most appropriately may be used as take-home essay questions (e.g., due on exam day) or as homework exercises that can be answered either by individuals or groups. Collaboratively answered questions encourage cooperative learning by students, and reduce the number of papers that must be graded.

1. At the end of Chapter 8 Santrock indicates books that provide practical knowledge about children and lists resources for improving the lives of children. Choose one of these books or resources and read it or learn as much as you can about it. Then write a brief review in which you (a) characterize the book or resource, and (b) explain how the book or resource relates to material in the chapter.
2. Chapter 1 defines the nature of development in terms of biological, cognitive, and social processes, and periods or stages. Indicate your ability to think critically by identifying material in this chapter that illustrates developmental processes and periods. If there is little or no information in this chapter about developmental processes and periods, identify and explain how developmental processes and periods could be used to guide the analysis of any topic in the chapter.
3. According to Chapter 1, three fundamental developmental issues concern: (a) maturation (nature) versus experience (nurture), (b) continuity versus discontinuity, and (c) early versus later experience. Indicate your ability to think critically by identifying material in this chapter that illustrates each of the three fundamental developmental issues. If there is little or no information in this chapter about fundamental developmental issues, identify and explain how these issues could be used to guide the analysis of any topic in the chapter.
4. One aspect of thinking critically is to read, listen, and observe carefully and then ask questions about what is missing from a text, discussion, or situation. For example, your author suggests that developing and using critical thinking skills is a desirable developmental outcome. Indicate your ability to think critically by selecting any major section of chapter 8 and evaluating it in terms of the author's list of the active thinking processes necessary for critical thinking (see page 272).
5. Santrock sets off several quotations in this chapter. Indicate your ability to think critically by selecting one of the quotes and (a) learning about the author and indicating why this individual is eminently quotable (i.e., what was this individual's contribution to human knowledge and understanding), (b) interpreting and restating the quote in your own terms, and (c) explaining what concept, issue, perspective, or term in this chapter that Santrock intended this quote to illuminate. In other words, about what aspect or issue in development does this quote make you pause and reflect?
6. Chapter 2 indicates that theories help us explain data and make predictions about various aspects of development. Chapter 2 then presents six different theoretical approaches (i.e., Freudian, cognitive, behavioral and social learning, ethological, ecological, and eclectic theory), but notes that no single approach explains the complexity of development. Indicate your ability to think critically by (a) perusing this chapter for topics influenced by at least one of the six theoretical approaches, and (b) explaining which theoretical approach dominated the topic in question. If the presentation is entirely atheoretical, identify and explain how one of the theoretical approaches could be used to guide the analysis of the topic in question.
7. This chapter discusses various aspects of cognitive development in childhood. Apply your knowledge about the scientific base of child development by designing a study to determine whether formal instruction in reading should be delayed until age 7: (a) What specific problem or question do you want to study? (b) What predictions would you make and test in your study? (c) What measures would you use (i.e., controlled observation in a laboratory, naturalistic observation, interviews and questionnaires, case studies, standardized tests, cross-cultural studies, physiological research, research with animals, or multimeasure, multisource, and multicontext approach) and how would you define each measure clearly and unambiguously? (d) What strategy would you follow--correlational or experimental, and what would be the time span of your inquiry--cross-sectional or longitudinal? (e) What ethical considerations must be addressed before you conduct your study?
8. According to Chapter 2, your author wants you to become a wise consumer of information about child development by: (a) being cautious about media reports, (b) distinguishing between nomothetic research and

idiographic needs, (c) recognizing how easy it is to overgeneralize from a small or clinical sample, (d) knowing that a single study is usually not the defining word about some aspect of child development, (e) remembering that causal conclusions cannot be made from correlation studies, and (f) always considering the source of the information and evaluating its credibility. Indicate your ability to think critically by, first, selecting an article from either a journal, magazine, or newspaper about any topic regarding Information Processing, and, second, evaluating it in terms of these six objectives. If the information in the article is insufficient to evaluate one of these objectives, then specify what kind of information you would need to evaluate the objective.

9 Intelligence

SUGGESTIONS FOR LECTURE TOPICS

1. The Origins of Intelligence Tests

Textbooks often give a brief account of the beginning of the intelligence testing movement. The sixth edition of *Adolescence* does also, but you could add to its treatment. Doing so is an excellent introduction to the topic, and a good way to bring forth most of the classic concerns with the enterprise and with the concept of intelligence.

You could begin your lecture with a brief treatment of Galton's idea of the inheritance of intellect. Briefly summarize Galton's ideas (these are usually outlined in introductory psychology texts), and then discuss Galton's idea that intelligence could be measured in terms of elementary cognitive functions such as reaction time; and that intelligence represented a biological trait much like any other. You might conclude with Galton's observations that genius seemed to run in families, the inferences he drew from that, and his interesting recommendations about the value of eugenics. This might be a good time to let the class discuss the ideas you are presenting!

Continue with a few examples of other early attempts to measure intelligence (you could draw on Stephen Jay Gould's *The Mismeasure of Man*). The main point is to show that most early attempts foundered, which is also an opportunity to review concepts such as reliability and validity.

Make the high point of your lecture a presentation of Binet's success. You could emphasize any of the following points: (a) the practical basis of Binet's work (the French government's commission); (b) Binet's empirical approach (development and norming of items that discriminated between children of different ages); (c) the essentially developmental basis of Binet's work (something often overlooked in discussion of the intelligence); (d) Binet's belief that intelligence was learned and remediable; (e) Binet's concerns with the need for an objective, reliable, and valid measure. All of these points feature in contemporary controversies about intelligence, and presenting them allows you to cast contemporary issues in a historical context.

You could conclude your lecture with examples of how IQ tests came to be used after Binet developed the first successful one. For example, one of the first big users was the United States Army, who also figured large in the development of group intelligence tests. The tests also played a role in attempts to control immigration in the early 20's into the United States

2. Measuring Infant Intelligence

A problem of long-standing interest is the question of whether individual differences in infant intelligence can be measured and whether they have predictive value. A lecture on this topic would be an opportunity to explore how basic values influence what researchers consider to be good and important questions, a chance to illustrate and elaborate the stability/change issue, and a further vehicle to discuss how modern methodological advances have contributed both to our scientific and, potentially, applied knowledge of infants.

First, explore the reasons why it would be valuable to identify individual differences in infants. In doing this you may wish to review the reasons why Binet developed the intelligence test. It would be interesting to point out that Binet was optimistic that if he were able to identify intellectual deficits early in the life of a child, he would be able to develop intervention techniques to enhance the child's intelligence. You may wish to explore the rather different historical development of uses of the intelligence test to speculate on the fate of similar rationales for developing infant intelligence tests.

Second, briefly trace the history of attempts to develop developmental scales for infants, expanding on the textbook's coverage. In this treatment it would be important to indicate that these early tests never yielded impressive correlations with later intelligence, yielding an opportunity to review the meaning and uses of correlational findings. Note that recent fine-grain analyses of performance on Bayley scales have shown that some subscales on this test predict later language ability. Finally, present the evidence that rate of habituation in very young infants correlates with later measured intelligence.

Finally, speculate about the meaning of this correlation. Does it mean that intelligence is basically a biological trait? Or does it suggest that differences in information processing capacity lead to differential rates of learning and remembering? Is rate of habituation a cause of intellectual development or is it related to something else? If you can, it would be valuable to interpret these findings in terms of several theories of intelligence (e.g., Jensen's, Gardner's, Sternberg's).

You may wish to conclude with a speculative treatment concerning possible applications of these findings.

3.   Product and Process in the Study of Intelligence

In recent years, theorists and researchers like Lauren Resnick and Robert Sternberg have emphasized the important process versus product distinction in the study of intelligence. They point out that traditional intelligence tests focus on the products of intelligence and as such are limited indices of intellectual processes. Although Binet, the creator of the first successful intelligence test, hoped to go beyond the product orientation, that remains the dominant legacy of the tests. Perhaps an unfortunate concomitant (though unintended) legacy is the view that intelligence is a fixed quantity rather than a dynamic, changing process.

Modern researchers have been dissatisfied with this state of affairs and have attempted a process-oriented approach to the analysis of intelligence. Present a lecture that outlines this approach. A good, seminal reference is Resnick's 1976 book, *The Nature of Intelligence,* or any of a number of works by Robert Sternberg. Begin by presenting the limitations of intelligence tests as devices for revealing the nature of intelligence. Basically, the tests permit us only to guess about the nature of the processes that underlie intellectual performance and do nothing to outline how these processes may accrue or change with age. Then outline what it might mean to take a process approach. This basically involves reviewing the information processing approach, which may mean reviewing material that you have presented in previous lectures (i.e., always a good idea!).

The culmination of the lecture is an analysis of any standard intelligence test item. Sternberg's analysis of analogies is an excellent example. A fun prelude to it is to have the class solve this analogy: Washington is to 1 as Lincoln is to (5, 10, 15, 50). This is Sternberg's own example; students' correct and incorrect guesses help to illustrate through personal experience the validity of Sternberg's componential analysis.

Sternberg also shows how his componential analysis illuminates development. It turns out that children cannot carry out a crucial step, which uniformly results in failure; adolescents, by contrast, pass it. Sternberg also presents data on the success of training people to perform the various mental steps needed to solve analogies.

4.   Spatial Orientations Intelligence

Children as young as 6 can infer spatial relationships in familiar environments. Six-year-olds are as likely as older children to use permanent, reliable environmental cues (e.g., bridges, street signs, store fronts) instead of transient, unreliable cues (e.g., "house for sale" sign, parked car). Six-year-olds have some skill in providing general directions to neighborhood landmarks not visible from their own homes (Herman et al., 1987).

However, even 11-year-olds have difficulty determining spatial environments in large, unfamiliar environments (Herman et al., 1987). Even though older children have trouble negotiating their way in strange environments, most airlines do not provide "child escort service" after the age of 11. Perhaps schools need to provide more direct training on spatial conceptual abilities and on strategies for negotiating one's way in unfamiliar settings.

Spatial orientation abilities are often viewed as skills in which males are better than females. However, preschoolers and school-aged children exhibit few sex differences. The relationship between gender and spatial development really shows up in late adolescence (Cohen, 1986). Perhaps differential treatment toward males and females in childhood results in significant differences in abilities from late adolescence on. Although older children are allowed to go farther from home than are younger children, at all ages boys are permitted greater distances than are girls (Herman et al., 1987). The greater physical distance experiences may be one aspect of improving males' spatial orientation abilities over time. Formal instruction in a variety of spatial orientation skills, such as map reading, might be helpful in reducing gender differences in this area. (*Sources:* Cohen, H. G. 1986. A longitudinal study of the development of spatial conceptual ability. *Journal of Genetic Psychology, 148,* 71-78; Herman, J. F., Heins, J. A., & Cohen, D. S. 1987. Children's spatial knowledge of their neighborhood environment. *Journal of Applied Developmental Psychology, 8,* 1015.)

5.   Racism, IQ Tests, and Immigration Laws

In the 1920s, beliefs about racial differences in intelligence influenced the **immigration quotas** from different countries. Psychologists expressed racist attitudes in their articles and books about intelligence. For example, the prominent psychologist **Robert Yerkes,** in 1923, wrote an article called "Testing the Human Mind" for *The Atlantic*. In this article he claimed that the **WWI testing program of the army** showed that Southern European immigrants had low intelligence. Yerkes wrote, "Certainly the results of psychological examining in the United States Army established the relation of inferior intelligence to delinquency and crime, and justify the belief that a country which encourages, or even permits, the immigration of simple-minded, uneducated, defective, diseased, or criminalistic persons, because it needs cheap labor, seeks trouble in the shape of public expense."

In that same year, psychologist **Carl Brigham** published *A Study of American Intelligence* in which he divided the U.S. population into four racial groups of declining ability:

1. *The Nordic Race.* Belgium, Denmark, Holland, Norway, Sweden, England, Scotland, Canada.
2. *The Alpine Race.* Austria-Hungary, France, Germany, Russia, Poland, European Turkey. (Germans were rated much higher than others in this group because they were a mixture of the Nordic and Alpine Races.)
3. *The Mediterranean Race.* Greece, Ireland, Italy, Wales, Asia, Turkey.
4. *The Negro Race.*

The quota system in the **Immigration Act of 1924** was unfavorable to Southern and Southeastern Europeans partly on the basis of the belief that these immigrants had inferior intelligence. Some psychologists, including Robert Yerkes, who developed the army intelligence tests, campaigned for immigration restriction. (*Source:* Marks, R. 1981. *The idea of IQ.* Lanham, MD: University Press of America.)

6.   Characteristics of Gifted Children

How would you describe gifted individuals? Many believe that gifted children are odd, physically inept, glasses-wearing loners. Actually, most gifted children are above average in physical development, social skills, and psychological adjustment. However, many gifted children *are* near-sighted and therefore wear glasses.

The first longitudinal study of gifted children was begun in California in the 1920s by Lewis Terman. Terman studied 1500 children with IQs from 140 to 200. In middle childhood they scored well in a variety of measures from achievement to social and physical skills. They even were 2.5 centimeters taller than their peers. Followed throughout their lives, most of the male subjects (almost 90 percent) went to college; many of them became doctors, lawyers, writers, and researchers. Because of the time period (they were born in the 1910s), most of the women became housewives. As adults they had below average rates of alcoholism, mental health problems, physical health problems, criminal records, and divorce.

Recent studies also conclude that gifted children are average to superior to their peers on social and emotional adjustment. They score lower on aggression and hostility and higher on perseverance and need for achievement.

Some gifted children have problems in school because they find it boring. After all, textbooks and curriculum are geared to the average child. School systems sometimes try enrichment programs, acceleration programs, and other special programs to try to challenge gifted children. (*Sources:* Reiss, S. M. 1989. Reflections on policy affecting the education of gifted and talented students. *American Psychologist, 44,* 399-408; Stamps, L. E. & Clark, C. L. C. 1987. Relations between the Type A behavior pattern and intelligence in children. *Journal of Genetic Psychology, 148,* 529-531; Olszewski-Kubilius, P. M., Kulieke, M. J. & Krasney, N. 1988. Personality dimensions of gifted children and adolescents, *Gifted Child Quarterly, 32,* 347-352; Halpern, J. J. & Luria, Z. 1989. Labels of giftedness and gender-typicality: Effects on adults' judgments of children's traits. *Psychology in the Schools, 26,* 301-310; Benbow, C. 1988. Sex differences in mathematical reasoning ability in intellectually talented preadolescents: Their nature, effects, and possible causes. *Behavioral and Brain Sciences, 11,* 169-183.)

7.   Birth Order, Family Size, and Intelligence

Birth order has a small but detectable effect on intelligence and school achievement. Firstborns tend to be more verbal, have slightly higher IQ scores, and are higher achievers.

Children in small families do better in school and stay in school longer. Even controlling for SES, children with many siblings do not do as well in school. Children with many siblings are more likely to drop out of school. One explanation is that large families provide fewer opportunities for a child to interact with a parent—each ends up with less verbal stimulation and less attention. This leads to lower verbal intelligence and fewer school successes.

For given family size, children who are born close together have a slight decrease in IQ compared to sibling space of three or more years. Twins, for example, average 5 lower IQ points over single births. (*Source:* Blake, J. 1989. Number of siblings and educational attainment. *Science, 245,* 32-36.)

8.   Thurston's Seven Primary Mental Abilities

Louis Leon Thurstone, mathematician and psychologist, was an assistant of Thomas Edison, an originator of tests used by the U.S. Army in World War I, an engineer professor, a psychology professor, and a president of the American Psychological Association. His wife Thelma was a research collaborator with him.

Thurstone did not believe that intelligence should be measured in one general term. So he engaged in six years of research with 56 tests which he gave to 240 students whose IQs were above average. When he analyzed the resultant data, he concluded that intelligence was made up of seven separate mental abilities: numbers, words, visual imagery, memory, perception, induction, (finding a rule governing a set of facts), and verbal reasoning.

Thurstone also concluded that persons who rank high in one of the abilities are likely to have high scores in the other abilities. However, there were frequent cases of superior individuals doing poorly on one or more sections. Several bright persons, for example, had poor memory.

Thurstone also found that the work people like to do is likely to match their particular mental abilities. Many vocational counselors believe that matching abilities and interests to career plans leads to the highest levels of job satisfaction. (*Source:* Gerow, J. *Time Retrospective: Psychology 1923-1988,* 18.)

9.   Superbabies

Superbabies are advanced-achieving infants who are trained to perform precociously by their parents. Every generation has taken pride in having offspring who walk or talk early, but today's parents may take a lot of time and effort into increasing infant knowledge. Parents who are more educated, older, and economically well-off are the most likely to work on having a superbaby. The parents themselves are often competitive and successful. They are often aware of animal studies that show advantages of enriched environments and the impressive results of longitudinal studies of Sesame Street and Head Start. (However, these studies show the advantages of enrichment over deprivation and do not address the advantages of enrichment over typical home environment.) They also know that scientists have found that fetuses can hear, and some ambitious parents start prenatal education.

Some parents create their own infant education program, while others dole out money for programs such as Glenn Doman's Better Baby Institute, which has been around since the 1960s. Parents can take a one-week intensive training program in how to use flash cards three times a day with infants. For example, babies may be shown a picture of an apple along with APPLE, or a picture of Mona Lisa along with LEONARDO DA VINCI.

Critics are concerned that superbabies may learn to mimic and memorize rather than excel in curious creativity. In other words, drilling does not equal comprehending. Infants may also adopt the notion that learning is stressful, and may become worried that they will fail their parents' expectations. Superbaby learning may impede other skills in the arenas of social, physical, and emotional learning. Critics also suggest that much of the parental efforts may be a waste of time. First, brain maturation is necessary for some learning. Second, infants learn well from everyday situations. (*Sources:* Chess, S. & Thomas, A. 1987. *Knowing your child.* New York: Basic; Elkind D. 1981. *The hurried child: Growing up too fast too soon.* Reading: Addison-Wesley; Kagan, J. 1984. *The nature of the child.* New York: Basic; Langway, L. 1983 (March 28). Bringing up superbaby. *Newsweek,* 62-68; Meyerhoff, M. K. 1988 (August). Avoiding the superbaby syndrome. *American Baby,* 18-22.)

10.   Savant Syndrome

Savant syndrome is a rare (a few hundred cases worldwide) serious mental handicap in which individuals are retarded and yet have a spectacular area of intelligence in one of the following areas: music, visual arts, mathematical ability, mechanical wizardry, or mnemonic skills such as calendar calculation.

The condition was first described by J. Langdon Down in 1887. It was then called **idiot savant;** however, these individuals have IQs of 40 or more, and **idiot** refers to an IQ of 25 or less.

Various explanations have been offered over the years; eidetic imagery, inherited ability, sensory deprivation and social isolation leading to boredom and the adoption of trivial preoccupations, or reliance on concrete thinking. Treffert suggests that the savant syndrome is caused by dysfunction of the cerebral cortex due to postnatal, or more likely, prenatal injury to the brain's left hemisphere. The right hemisphere compensates somewhat in language and motor skills. Most savants have unusual talents generally associated with the right brain.

Additional tidbits:

*   One in 10 autistic children demonstrates savant skills.
*   One in two savants exhibit clinical symptoms of early infantile autism.
*   The brain's right hemisphere completes development first.
*   85 percent of all savants are male.
*   Savants seem to use a memory circuit governed by the basal ganglia, rather than the hippocampus.

(*Source:* Robotham, R. 1989 (September). Islands of genius. *Omni, 18,* 110.)

BROWN & BENCHMARK'S HUMAN DEVELOPMENT TRANSPARENCIES (2ND ED.)

Transparency Number and Title

The transparency set, a supplement to *Child Development*, is accompanied by an annotated manual that describes each of the 141 transparencies. The annotated manual also offers suggestions about how to use the transparencies to engage your students in active learning that will stimulate critical thinking and evaluative skills. The following transparencies are appropriate and useful with Chapter 9: Intelligence

Transparency Number and Title

36	Genotypes and Environments
86	Test Construction and Evaluation
87	The Normal Curve and Stanford-Binet
88	Sample Subtests of the Wechsler Intelligence Scale for Children
89	Approaches to Children's Learning and Cognitive Development: Part I
90	Approaches to Children's Learning and Cognitive Development: Part II
91	Perkins's Snowflake Model of Creativity
96	Visuospatial Ability of Males and Females
127	Fluid and Crystallized Intellectual Development Across the Life Span

CLASSROOM ACTIVITIES OR DEMONSTRATIONS

1. Discuss the critical thinking exercises. The main point of Exercise 1 is to promote students' awareness of how developmental issues are involved in the study of intelligence as the field is represented in Chapter 9. You may find that students are a little rusty in their ability to identify these issues, so prior to assigning or working on the exercise find out if they can remember them and how they are manifest in developmental research and thinking. You will also find it useful to briefly review the issues themselves. One of the excellent things about studying intelligence is that it shows that the issues are often very important to people, for example, the question of whether intelligence is mainly determined by heredity. The answer one gives to that question in particular has very important consequences to one's view of education, as students will also find out in one of the last activities suggested below.

    Exercise 2 mainly aims to promote integration of material students study in Chapters 7, 8, and 9. You could suggest to them that the key success with the exercise is the language Sternberg uses to describe his theory. This language is very much derived from the tradition that influenced him.

    There are many potential issues to explore with Exercise 3. You may find it useful and beneficial to suggest to students that the discussion of heredity-environment interactions in Chapter 2 is directly relevant to identifying the assumption in the exercise. Review that material if students cannot recall it or explain it. The exercise also lends itself to a discussion of the nature of the evidence that Jensen cited to support his case, and the overall logic of behavior genetic research.

2. Discuss the students' research projects as suggested below.

3. Have students discuss whether developing intelligence scales for infants that could accurately predict later intellectual abilities is important. Why or why not? Speculate about the types of assessment ideas that would be included in such a scale. What would be the advantages and disadvantages of a system that allowed intellectual potential to be measured in a 3-month-old fetus?

Source: Simons, J. A., Irwin, D. B., & Drinnin, B. A. 1987. *Instructor's Manual to Accompany Psychology, the Search for Understanding,* St. Paul: West Publishing.

---

4. If possible, get a Stanford-Binet and a WISC-R. Most students have taken an intelligence test but, at the time, did not really know what they were doing. Describe each subscale and then read representative examples from the tasks. Ask students to help determine the average levels of performance for different ages on each task. Make clear which tasks are performance tasks and which are verbal. Drop some hints about how the two categories of tasks are affected by increasing age.

    In the best scenario, arrange to have three children of different ages come in and ask them to do some of the tasks. Keeping the attention of three youngsters in front of a classroom of 20 or 30 can be a bit much, so pick your children wisely and try to avoid children in the early middle childhood period. If you are able to bring the children in, have the students attempt to guess their ages by their performance on the tasks.

Source: Temple, Lori L. (1992) *Instructor's Course Planner to accompany Life-span Development,* Fourth Edition by John W. Santrock, William C. Brown Communications, Dubuque, Iowa.

5. Have the students in small groups write a letter to an imaginary sister or brother whose 5-year-old child was just given an IQ test and received a score of 65. The parents have been told that the child will be placed in a class for the mentally retarded. Have the students advise their sibling.

   You should not accept such a decision based only on an IQ test. Some specific local problem, such as illness, or the death of a friend or pet might cause the deficiency. The child may not have paid much attention during the test. IQ scores at young ages do not have great predictability of IQ scores over the years. Parents should insist on (or even obtain themselves) a more extensive evaluation. Work with the child to encourage and promote the sorts of skills the test indicates are missing. Remember a correlation as high as .8 only accounts for 64 percent of the variability, so there is plenty of room for the score to change even in one year. Know your state laws, because your state may not permit such an assignment on the basis of an IQ score alone.

Source: Adapted from King, M. B., & Clark, D. E. 1989. *Instructor's Manual to Accompany Santrock and Yussen's Child Development: An Introduction,* 4th ed. Dubuque, IA: Wm. C. Brown.

6. Have you heard of **Oscar Kriesen Buros**? Back in the 1930s he began Buros' *Mental Measurement Yearbook,* which describes and evaluates published psychological tests. By 1936, there were already more than 4,000 standardized tests. Buros suggested that 9 out of 10 of these tests were unreliable. In this critique he provided the following examples of poor test items:

   Do you think this school is run as if it were a prison?
   With what person do you spend the most time? (correct answer was supposedly "mother"; there was no adjustment for age of test-taker)

   This institution

   a. is the most beloved of institutions.
   b. is necessary to the very existence of civilization.
   c. gives real help in meeting moral problems.
   d. will destroy civilization if it is not radically changed.
   e. has done more for society than any other institution.

   Do you think that standardized tests are more reliable than they were in the 1930s? Why? Do you think that most classroom tests are reliable? Can you think of examples of unreliable or invalid tests that you have taken?

Source: Gerow, J. 1988. *Time Retrospective: Psychology 1923-1988.* 24.

7. Have the class discuss whether or not child prodigies or geniuses are well-adjusted or maladjusted individuals. Do they have more mental problems? Are they odd? Do they fail to live up to their expectations? In what ways can schools and families help bright youngsters adjust to their circumstances? Contrast the findings of Terman's longitudinal study of **William James Sidis** provided here.

   William James Sidis, the son of Russian immigrants, was taught by his father to read by age 3, type by 4, and read Russian, French, and German at 5 and Hebrew, Greek, and Latin by 6. Before he was 7 he passed out of seventh grade and passed a medical school examination on the human body. By 10 he understood integral calculus.

At 12 he entered Harvard. By adolescence he lost his goals and dropped out of graduate school. He lost a teaching job, was arrested at a radical demonstration, refused to attend his father's funeral, and became a cynical and eccentric person holding clerical jobs. He was poor and unemployed when he died at 46 from a brain hemorrhage. Rumors existed that he committed suicide.

The Sidis example has been given many times as a reason that schools should not have acceleration and enrichment programs. However, more case examples suggest that "burnout" is rare and successes are much more likely.

Have students propose alternative explanations for Sidis' decline. Have them suggest ways to help child geniuses.

Sources: Montour, K. 1977. William James Sidis, the broken twig. *American Psychologist, 32,* 265-279; Townsend, J. K. & Gensley, J. T. 1978. The experts react to stereotyping gifted children. *The Gifted Child Quarterly, 22,* 217-219.

---

8. Genetic and environmental influences on intelligence: Have students describe each of the following kinds of research, and provide the advantages and disadvantages for each:

    a. Experiments with animals
    b. Studies of human families
    c. Twin studies
    d. Adoption studies

9. Inform students how some persons have tried to claim that there are significant racial differences in IQ. Others, however, claim that the difference is basically a socioeconomic status (SES) difference. Have the class brainstorm all sorts of possible research studies that could be done to help decide this issue, including some actual studies such as the work of Sandra Scarr.

    One possibility is to see if there are SES differences in IQ in homogeneous cultures. In one recent study, Polish children from families of low SES had lower average scores on IQ tests than Polish children from higher SES families.

Source: Galkowski, T., Jacunska, M., & Scott, R. 1987. IQ and achievement profiles of disadvantaged children: Polish-American comparisons. *The Mankind Quarterly, 28,* 13-26.

---

10. Here is an activity on fluid and crystallized intelligence:
    1. Compose or adapt standard IQ test items (one source is the Eysenck reference) that measure **fluid intelligence** and **crystallized intelligence.** Develop an "IQ test" of 35-50 items.
    2. Ask your students if they would like to take an IQ test (most will want to do this task). Give them several minutes to work on the test. You can observe how they "take" the test, and your comments should generate discussion.
        A. Most students will have worked *eagerly* on the test; most students take IQs and testing very *seriously.*
        B. Students knew how to take the test even with minimal instructions. When uncertain of an answer, they took a "best guess." In other words, the students are *"test-wise."*
        C. Students *needed* to have and understand the test answers (if the instructor delayed in giving the answers, they *protested*).
        D. Students were *upset* when informed that the test could not determine their actual IQs and when no norms were provided.
    3. Have students discuss what their attitudes about the test and actions during the test say about society's beliefs about intelligence and IQ tests.
    4. Why was the test important to most students? Would a 70-year-old person be as interested in learning his or her IQ? Why not? Would someone their own age but not enrolled in college be as interested? Why or why not?

5. How does being "test-wise" affect performance on an IQ test? How would you have approached the test differently if you had not taken any tests for ten years?
6. Did you prefer crystallized or fluid items? What kinds of items do you think should be featured in an intelligence test?

Source: Eysenck, H. J. 1962. *Know your own IQ.* New York: Penguin.

11. Have half of the class create and develop an educational program based on a genetic interpretation of differences in IQ scores, and the other half create an educational program based on an environmental interpretation of differences in IQ scores. Each group should begin by listing the assumptions it is working with, as well as data presented in the text or during class that is relevant to its position. Students should then consider what forms of treatment might be recommended by the model they are using.

If the view that intelligence is determined largely by genetic considerations were officially adopted, education would be a matter of matching individuals to appropriate skills. Testing aptitude or intelligence testing in particular, would be a very important part of this system. After all, a child would be born with a certain amount of intelligence and that would be all that he or she would ever get. Measure it early and there would be no need to waste money educating those children who have little ability. One might even consider testing the parents to identify intelligent families.

Jensen suggested that individuals with lower intelligence use a different mode of thought or learning than more intelligent individuals. If his concept or a similar concept was true, it could be used to determine teaching styles of knowledge and skills for different children.

If one adopted the position that intelligence is dependent solely on experience, aptitude tests would not make sense. Every child's aptitude would be the same, limited only by the types of experiences available. An educational system based on this idea would provide stimulating environments and experiences and design plans to provide compensatory experiences for children with deficiencies. The view would be that any child could succeed, (regardless of family background or race, etc.), if given the proper experiences.

Source: Adapted from King, M. B. & Clark, D. E. 1989. *Instructor's Manual to Accompany Santrock and Yussen's Child Development: An Introduction,* 4th ed. Dubuque, IA: Wm. C. Brown.

CRITICAL THINKING EXERCISES

Exercise 1

The study of intelligence illustrates many of the issues that define the nature of development as outlined in Chapter 1 of *Child Development.* In fact, all but one of these issues is illustrated in Chapter 9. Which one is omitted or receives the least play in the material on intelligence? **Circle the letter of the best answer, and explain why it is the best answer and why each other answer is not as good.**

A. biological, cognitive, and socioemotional processes
B. periods of development
C. maturation and experience
D. early and later experience
E. continuity and discontinuity

Exercise 2

Robert Sternberg's triarchic theory is more than just an example of a multifactor theory of intelligence. It is also an attempt to reformulate the psychometric approach to intelligence in a fashion that will promote new research and progress in the study of intelligence. Sternberg's new approach was inspired mainly by one of the several perspectives on cognition. Which of the following was it? **Circle the letter of the best answer, and explain why it is the best answer and why each other answer is not as good.**

A. Piagetian/cognitive developmental
B. Vygotsky's theory
C. Learning
D. Cognitive social learning
E. Information processing

Exercise 3

Arthur Jensen is both famous and infamous for his claim that the main causes of individual differences in intelligence are genetic. One of his stronger arguments are based on the positive correlation between degree of genetic relatedness and intelligence (e.g., intelligence is more highly correlated between identical twins than it is between fraternal twins). Which of the following statements is an assumption one must make, rather than in inference or an observation, in order to accept the evidence from studies such as twin studies as evidence for a genetic cause of individual differences in intelligence? **Circle the letter of the best answer, and explain why it is the best answer and why each other answer is not as good.**

A. Identical twins have exactly the same genetic makeup.
B. The environments of all pairs of siblings in the studies that Jensen reviewed are identical.
C. Genetic differences between individuals cause intellectual differences.
D. Modifying environments will have little effect on intelligence.
E. The correlation of IQs averages .82 for identical twins, but .50 for fraternal twins.

ANSWER KEYS FOR CRITICAL THINKING EXERCISES

Exercise 1

A. This is not the best answer. The chapter addresses these issues in a number of places. For example, the issue of biological processes arises in the material on the correlation between habituation in 6-month-old infants and their later measured intelligence at 6 and 9 years of age. Similarly, concerns in the heredity-environment controversy addresses biological and social processes. Social processes are discussed in the section on culture and ethnicity.
B. This is not the best answer. The issue is raised in the early definition of IQ (MA/CA), as well as the discussion of infant intelligence and its relationship to later intelligence, as well as concerns about the stability of intelligence.
C. This is not the best answer. The relative influence of maturation and experience (nature vs. nurture) is directly addressed in the section on the heredity-environment controversy, as well as in the material on culture and ethnicity.
D. This is the best answer. Although there is material on infant intelligence, how well it predicts later intelligence, and on the stability of intelligence, there is no material on the question of whether there are crucial or critical experiences early in life for the development or expression of intelligence later in life. This has been an issue in research on intelligence, but the work does not appear in Chapter 9.
E. This is not the best answer. Although the question is not addressed very extensively, the comparison/contrast of different approaches to intelligence states that the psychometric approach to intelligence views the development of intelligence as continuous. This is also true by implication, because even though the chapter talks about infant intelligence and later intelligence, it does not discuss stages that appear along the way from one to the other.

Exercise 2

A. This is not the best answer. The main reason is that Sternberg makes no use of stages in his theory; stages are the hallmark of cognitive developmental theories. Furthermore, he makes no attempt to modify cognitive developmental concepts to account for individual differences.
B. This is not the best answer. Vygotsky's emphasis is on the nature of teacher/learner interaction in the service of cognitive development. There is a strong emphasis on individual differences in Vygotsky's theory, but Vygotsky emphasized social interaction as the mechanism of cognitive change, and gave less attention to cognitive processes. As indicated in (E) below, Sternberg's theory focuses very much on mental components, which indicates his thinking is more akin to the information processing perspective.
C. This is not the best answer. Simply put, the learning perspective gives the mental mechanisms proposed by Sternberg as the basis of intelligence no play in its account of adolescent learning.
D. This is not the best answer. In contrast to the learning approach, cognitive social learning does invoke mental mechanisms to explain adolescent learning. However, unlike Sternberg's theory, this approach does not use an analysis of mental components.
E. This is the best answer. As indicated in (B) above, Sternberg's theory is essentially a classification of mental components that are involved in individual differences in intelligent behavior. In fact, one part of the theory is componential intelligence, which appears to be made of the basic mental processes information psychologists study. The second level of the theory seems to have much to do with aspects of cognitive monitoring. The third appeals to long-term memory as a factor in intellectual functioning.

Exercise 3

A. This is not the best answer. This statement is an observation, being a statement of "the way things are" for identical twins (assuming no genetic accidents that may have altered one or both twins' genetic makeup).
B. This is the best answer. Jensen does not consider the possibility that one or more genetic-environment interaction creates substantially different environments for fraternal twins from those for identical twins, and hence the possibility for different environmental effects on intelligence. (See Chapter 2 for the discussion of different heredity-environment interactions.)
C. This is not the best answer. The statement is an inference. The work upon which Jensen relied is essentially correlational, and hence it is not direct evidence of a cause-effect relationship. Thus Jensen interprets the facts as such.
D. This is not the best answer. This is an inference, based on Jensen's belief that environment contributes little to individual differences in intelligence.
E. This is not the best answer. It is an observation, being namely the result of examining various studies of the correlations between identical and fraternal twins and averaging their results.

RESEARCH PROJECT 1   REVIEWS OF INTELLIGENCE TESTS

There are many intelligence tests that follow the pattern of the Binet and Wechsler scales, but not all are equally good. For this project you will gather information from Oscar Buros's *Mental Measurement Yearbook* to find out which are the best by the standards outlined in *Child Development*.

Consult the latest edition of the *Mental Measurement Yearbook* available in your college or university library. Locate reviews on as many intelligence tests in the yearbook as you can and systematically record information available in the review on each test's reliability and validity (remember that there are different forms of each of these criteria). For example, you could construct a table in which you list the name of a test, and in associated columns you could list numerical values for tests of reliability and validity.

Once you have collected all the information you can, answer the following questions in a brief write-up of your findings:

Questions

1. Were you able to compare the tests on the same measures?
2. Which test is most reliable? Which test is most valid?
3. What other information besides measures of reliability and validity appear to have been important to reviewers of tests?
4. Which test among those that you found is the best? Justify your answer.

Use in Classroom

In large or small group formats, have students report their findings and state what they each have decided about what the best intelligence test is. Make sure that students give their reasons for their decisions. Keep track of the discussion by listing nominations for best tests on blackboard or overhead (or whatever display you have), with notations about the reasons students give for their decisions. Use the discussion to promote students' awareness of the several issues that may influence decisions about which test to use, how to use test results, and how to improve measures of intelligence.

RESEARCH PROJECT 2   CREATIVITY

This exercise illustrates structured interview methods and a test of creativity. Give a creativity task to two children, one age 10 and the other age 15. In order to test the two children, you will need to clear this through the human subjects review board at your school and get a signed informed consent form from the children's parents.

Evaluate the children's responses with the hypotheses that there may be both age differences and individual differences in creativity. Two tasks are to be presented to each child. Be sure to keep a "straight face" during the child's response period and to treat both children the same. Use the following data sheet and data summary sheet for collecting and summarizing data. Then answer the questions that follow after completing the interviews of the children.

_____

Child 1:   Age _____ Sex _____

_____

Task one: What are some unusual ways to use a spoon?

Task two: How many objects can you name that are red?

_____

Child 2:   Age _____ Sex _____

_____

Task one: What are some unusual ways to use a spoon?

Task two: How many objects can you name that are red?

_____

Data Summary:

1.   Count the number of responses for each child for each task. Enter into the following table.

Task	Child 1	Child 2
1		
2		

2.   Without looking at the data first, create a scale measuring the originality of the responses and score the responses for originality.

Questions

1.   Which child had the larger number of responses for task 1? For task 2?
2.   Which child had more original responses for task 1? For task 2?
3.   Overall, which child seemed to provide more creative responses? To what would you attribute this? How does your finding fit with information on creativity presented in the text? Do you think your particular tasks were appropriate for eliciting creative responding in children? Why or why not?

Use in Classroom

Have the students present their data from the research project. Analyze the data for age and individual differences in number of responses and originality of responses. Is there as much variability within each age as there is between ages? Is there as much variability within the 5-year-old children as there is within the 10-year-old children? Could some of the variability be due to differences between experimenters, rather than due to differences in the children? Did any sex differences appear in the data? How did researchers create the originality scale? What criteria did they use in scoring the responses? How difficult a task was devising the scale? Was the scale objective enough to allow another individual to use it and come up with the same scoring of the responses? What is the possible validity of the measure of creativity they used?

The older children are likely to produce more suggestions for different ways to use a spoon; possibly that may be because the older children know more. The suggestions may not really be unusual. The older children are likely to know more things that are red. This latter question seems to require thinking that is more convergent than divergent.

Experimenters can inadvertently cause differences or variability in the data by not treating each subject the same. Preferential smiling, laughing, or scowling might encourage some and discourage other responses. A standardized procedure is essential.

ESSAY AND CRITICAL THINKING QUESTIONS

Comprehension and Application Essay Questions

We recommend that you provide students with our guidelines for "Answering Essay and Critical Thinking Questions" when you have them respond to these questions. Their answers to these kinds of questions demonstrate an ability to comprehend and apply ideas discussed in this chapter.

1.   Define intelligence and discuss how the idea relates to concepts of cognition developed in earlier chapters.
2.   Outline the development of intelligence tests, and discuss whether or not these tests directly measure intelligence.
3.   What are reliability and validity, and how are they important in the discussion of intelligence? Explain.
4.   Compare and contrast the Stanford-Binet and Wechsler Scales.
5.   Compare and contrast one traditional approach to intelligence (e.g., Binet) with one more modern approach (e.g., Gardner).
6.   Does intelligence appear to be one thing, or many? Defend your answer.
7.   How is infant intelligence measured? Do any infant measures predict childhood intelligence?
8.   Discuss the hereditary-environmental issue of intelligence, and give three examples of environmental influences.
9.   What is a culture-fair test?
10.   Explain why developmentalists attempt to create culture-fair tests, and evaluate their success at doing so to date.
11.   How have intelligence tests been used? Misused? Does the evidence warrant discontinuation of their use, or modifying their use?
12.   Compare and contrast at least three perspectives on adolescent cognitive development. In your answer address the roles of nature versus nurture, stages, individual differences, and cognitive mechanisms in each perspective. Also, discuss the methods each perspective seems to promote in research on adolescent development.
13.   How is mental retardation defined? How is it related to intelligence? Explain.

14. How is giftedness defined? How is it related to intelligence? Does any particular theory of intelligence explain giftedness better than others? Explain.
15. How are intelligence and creativity alike, and how are they different? What are the main characteristics of creativity?

16. Explain how retardation, giftedness, and creativity reflect (or do not reflect) the extremes of intelligence.

Critical Thinking Questions

We recommend that you have students follow our guidelines for "Answering Essay and Critical Thinking Questions" when you ask them to prepare responses to these questions. Their answers to these kinds of questions reflect an ability to apply critical thinking skills to a novel problem or situation that is *not* specifically discussed in the chapter. These items most appropriately may be used as take-home essay questions (e.g., due on exam day) or as homework exercises that can be answered either by individuals or groups. Collaboratively answered questions encourage cooperative learning by students, and reduce the number of papers that must be graded.

1. At the end of Chapter 9 Santrock indicates books that provide practical knowledge about children and lists resources for improving the lives of children. Choose one of these books or resources and read it or learn as much as you can about it. Then write a brief review in which you (a) characterize the book or resource, and (b) explain how the book or resource relates to material in the chapter.
2. Chapter 1 defines the nature of development in terms of biological, cognitive, and social processes, and periods or stages. Indicate your ability to think critically by identifying material in this chapter that illustrates developmental processes and periods. If there is little or no information in this chapter about developmental processes and periods, identify and explain how developmental processes and periods could be used to guide the analysis of any topic in the chapter.
3. According to Chapter 1, three fundamental developmental issues concern: (a) maturation (nature) versus experience (nurture), (b) continuity versus discontinuity, and (c) early versus later experience. Indicate your ability to think critically by identifying material in this chapter that illustrates each of the three fundamental developmental issues. If there is little or no information in this chapter about fundamental developmental issues, identify and explain how these issues could be used to guide the analysis of any topic in the chapter.
4. One aspect of thinking critically is to read, listen, and observe carefully and then ask questions about what is missing from a text, discussion, or situation. For example, the material in previous chapters of *Child Development* has suggested that individual differences in basic mental processes are related to individual differences in intelligence, but there is no more detailed treatment of this topic in chapter 9. Indicate your ability to think critically by (a) listing as many questions as you can about the relationship between individual differences in basic processes and individual differences in intelligence, and (b) speculating why Santrock does not discuss this topic more fully.
5. Santrock sets off several quotations in this chapter. Indicate your ability to think critically by selecting one of the quotes and (a) learning about the author and indicating why this individual is eminently quotable (i.e., what was this individual's contribution to human knowledge and understanding), (b) interpreting and restating the quote in your own terms, and (c) explaining what concept, issue, perspective, or term in this chapter that Santrock intended this quote to illuminate. In other words, about what aspect or issue in development does this quote make you pause and reflect?
6. Chapter 2 indicates that theories help us explain data and make predictions about various aspects of development. Chapter 2 then presents six different theoretical approaches (i.e., Freudian, cognitive, behavioral and social learning, ethological, ecological, and eclectic theory), but notes that no single approach explains the complexity of development. Indicate your ability to think critically by (a) perusing this chapter for topics influenced by at least one of the six theoretical approaches, and (b) explaining which theoretical approach dominated the topic in question. If the presentation is entirely atheoretical, identify and explain how one of the theoretical approaches could be used to guide the analysis of the topic in question.
7. How do children of high, medium, and low intelligence perform on Piagetian or information processing tasks? Apply your knowledge about the scientific method by designing a study to answer this question: (a) What specific problem or question do you want to study? (b) What predictions would you make and test in your study? (c) What measures would you use (i.e., controlled observation in a laboratory, naturalistic observation, interviews and questionnaires, case studies, standardized tests, cross-cultural studies, physiological research, research with animals, or multimeasure, multisource, and multicontext approach) and how would you define each measure clearly and unambiguously? (d) What strategy would you follow--

correlational or experimental, and what would be the time span of your inquiry--cross-sectional or longitudinal? (e) What ethical considerations must be addressed before you conduct your study?

8.   According to Chapter 2, your author wants you to become a wise consumer of information about child development by: (a) being cautious about media reports, (b) distinguishing between nomothetic research and idiographic needs, (c) recognizing how easy it is to overgeneralize from a small or clinical sample, (d) knowing that a single study is usually not the defining word about some aspect of child development, (e) remembering that causal conclusions cannot be made from correlation studies, and (f) always considering the source of the information and evaluating its credibility. Indicate your ability to think critically by, first, selecting an article from either a journal, magazine, or newspaper about any topic regarding Intelligence, and, second, evaluating it in terms of these six objectives. If the information in the article is insufficient to evaluate one of these objectives, then specify what kind of information you would need to evaluate the objective.

10 Language Development

SUGGESTIONS FOR LECTURE TOPICS

1. Autism

Characteristics

About 1 in 2500 individuals have **autism,** first identified in 1943 by Leo Kanner (Caparulo & Cohen, 1982). Four times as many boys as girls are autistic. The main characteristics of autism are the inability to estimate emotional and social relationships, disinterest in playmates, very strong desire to be by oneself, not wanting to be touched or held, not crying for attention, and not cuddling.

Many exhibit **echolalia** (repeating the phrases of others), obsessive counting, repeatedly asking nonsense questions, staring, manipulating objects (e.g., flicking a light switch for hours), unusual motor movements (e.g., rocking, head banging), self-abuse (e.g., biting finger down to the knuckle, keeping scab on scalp open to feel the throbbing, biting a hole the size of a silver dollar in one's shoulder), and resistance to environmental changes (e.g., not adjusting to a change in furniture arrangement) (Lovaas, 1987; Tanguay, 1980).

Causes

Unlike early researchers, today's experts do not blame autism on parental behavior or attachment to the child. The cause is most likely biological, proposed etiologies including genetic explanations (e.g., a by-product of the fragile X syndrome), rubella during pregnancy, metabolic conditions, seizures, and CNS abnormalities (Chance, 1987).

Treatment

Autism has a poor prognosis. About one half of sufferers are classified as mentally retarded, and many live their lives in institutions. However, one two-year behavior modification program (at the cost of $40,000 per child) dramatically changed the odds (Lovaas, 1987). Forty-seven percent of those in the treatment achieved normally (compared to 2 percent of the control group). Of the remaining subjects, 40 percent were mildly retarded and 10 percent remained profoundly retarded (in the control group, 45 percent were mildly retarded and 53 percent were profoundly retarded). (*Sources:* Caparulo, B. K. & Cohen, D. J. 1982. The syndrome of early childhood autism: Natural history, etiology and treatment. In E. F. Zigler, M. E. Lowler, & I. F. Child (Eds.). *Socialization and Personality Development* 2nd ed. New York: Oxford University Press; Chance, P. 1987 (Dec.). Saving grace. *Psychology Today,* 42-44; Lovaas, D. I. 1987. Behavioral treatment and normal education and intellectual functioning in young autistic children. *Journal of Consulting & Clinical Psychology, 55,* 3-9; Tanguay, P. E. 1980. Early infantile autism. In H. J. Grossman & R. L. Stubblefield (Eds.). *The Physician and the Mental Health of the Child,* Monroe, WI: American Medical Association.)

2. Readings to Preschoolers

Children in the play years love to look at picture books and have stories read to them. Psychologists believe that when parents read aloud to their young children it builds good parent-child communication, and helps to prepare necessary skills for learning to read on their own.

The ability to read by oneself is developed not overnight, but in three distinct stages (Gibson & Levin, 1975). When parents make a regular practice of reading stories to their preschoolers, they facilitate their children's movement from one stage to another. In the first stage, preschoolers realize that spoken words can be represented in print, i.e., parents do more than make up a story to the pictures in their books, but take the story itself from markings on the pages. Once preschoolers have made this association, they enter the second stage, in which they learn that those markings represent words. Children in this stage often try to match the spoken word to the page's markings. This attempt can be fraught with many errors, such as a belief that each letter rather than groups of letters is the equivalent of a word (Smith, 1977), but by the time children are in the third and final stage of pre-reading, they have accomplished some basic skills. In the third stage, children are able to recognize letters and some of the sounds that make up words, and some youngsters even try to figure out unfamiliar words by sounding out their components. Children whose parents read to them have more practice at learning reading-readiness skills such as recognizing various letters, understanding letter order, matching and blending sounds, and perceiving differences in how words look (Venezky, 1975). They learn that reading is an enjoyable task to share, and they have parents who model reading and reading enjoyment.

Reading out loud to children is an activity that can be begun in infancy or preschool years and continued through all the school years. In the preschool years, being read to by parents tends to promote children's desire to read. For older children, being read to by parents promotes children's reading skills. Children of all ages enjoy listening to books that are too difficult to be read by themselves, and parents can choose books to read that broaden their children's interests and knowledge (Kimmel & Segel, 1983).

What kinds of books should parents read to their young children? Very young children like books with lots of pictures that they can view while parents read a story. Preschool children seem to like stories that are in verse better than those in prose (Hayes et al., 1982). Nursery rhymes and other rhyming stories may help in building phonological skills, or familiarity with component sounds in words. Research findings suggest that a strong relationship exists between knowledge of nursery rhymes and acquisition of phonological skills; knowledge of nursery rhymes at 3 years predicted rhyme detection skills at 4 years old (MacLean et al., 1987). On the other hand, young children can remember more about stories told in prose than those in rhyme (Hayes et al., 1982). To build attention span and memory abilities and to build phonological skills, parents would do well to read a variety of rhyming and prose stories to their children.

Parents might wish to consider the gender-role stereotypes presented in books. In research with preschool children, children who were read gender-stereotypic children's books usually played with gender-typed toys after the story. However, children who were read nonstereotypic children's books more often chose nonstereotypic toys (Ashton, 1983). Some book publishers have tried to reduce sexism in books by making more storybook characters of indeterminate gender. However, when mothers read stories to their preschoolers, the mothers used masculine pronouns 95 percent of the time when referring to these indeterminate gender characters (DeLoache et al., 1987). Since preschoolers are very interested in what boys and girls are able and allowed to do, this behavior by parents may lead children to have limited expectations for girls' behaviors. Parents may wish to be careful about how they refer to gender.

In addition to reading books that their children find enjoyable and have picked out for themselves, parents may wish to locate award-winning children's books to assure high quality. Librarians are also excellent references for choosing good children's books. Once children can read for themselves, they tend to prefer to read books that were once read to them than to choose other books (McCormick, 1977).

Once a storybook is chosen, parents can make the storytime more enjoyable by improving their reading-aloud skills, such as taking some time to create a good, warm atmosphere and comfortable physical setting. Many parents find that young children especially like to be read to each night just before bedtime. Storytelling occasions are times in which parents can become "hams" and create a mood by reading dramatically, modifying volume and pace of speech to fit the story's action, and changing voice for the various characters (Kimmel & Segel, 1983). When reading aloud to children, adults should throw out their inhibitions and self-consciousness and read for their children's entertainment and joy.

Parents can also help children relate printed words with meanings by making use of printed words found in the environment (McGee, 1986). Many parents of preschoolers have been surprised to see their children call out letters on the TV screen during "Sesame Street" or hear their children call out "McDonalds" while pointing to the appropriate sign at the restaurant. Young children may correctly point out the letter M on a package of "M&Ms" or be able to differentiate the M and the S on the cover of "Ms" Magazine. One study found that 3- to 6-year-olds could recognize more words on food labels than they did from books (Jones & Hendrickson, 1970). More than half of youngsters from 4 to 6 years old correctly identified some of the words contained in photographs of natural settings (Ylisto, 1967). This recognition of letters and words in the environment can help young children learn the correspondence between printed and spoken words (Hiebert, 1978).

Parents can help children prepare for reading acquisition by using words that naturally occur in the environment. While preparing lunch, parents could casually point out the word soup on a soup can or milk on the milk carton. When children express interest in printed words on food labels or in magazines, parents can tell their children what the words are while pointing to each word as spoken. Parents and preschool teachers can encourage youngsters to find words in their environment and incorporate these words into play/learning. Even youngsters who are not very interested in words in books often are quite interested to discover what the words in their environment mean (McGee, 1986).

In a more active strategy, parents can create play kits that include print materials. A restaurant play kit can include play dishes, play food, order pads, play money, and menus. In this way, young children get to interact with print materials in meaningful situations (McGee, 1983). Another suggested activity is to use food packages and coupons to encourage preschool children to find two identical food packages, to match the correct coupon to the food item, and to find particular letters on the different food items (Tompkins, 1984). These types of activities provide reading variety, encourage children to explore words in their environment, and build reading interest during play.

Reading to children is beneficial for all preschoolers toward increasing language development. After daily book-reading for a three-month period, both 2- and 3-year-olds scored higher than children in control groups on listening vocabularies, speaking vocabularies, and average sentence length (Burroughs, 1972; McCormick, 1977). Studies done several years apart found a positive relationship between being read to and success in first-grade reading (Almy, 1949; Durkin, 1966). (*Sources:* Almy, M. 1949. *Children's experiences prior to first grade and success in beginning reading.* Contributions to Education, No. 954. New York: Bureau of Publications, Teachers College, Columbia; Ashton, E. 1983. Measures of play behavior: The influence of sex-role stereotyped children's books. *Sex Roles, 9,* 43-47; Burroughs, M. 1970. *The stimulation of verbal behavior in culturally disadvantaged three-year-olds.* Doctoral dissertation. Michigan State University; DeLoache, J. S., Cassidy, D. J., & Carpenter, C. J. 1987. The three bears are all boys: Mothers' gender labeling of neutral picture book characters. *Sex Roles, 17,* 163-178; Durkin, D. 1966. *Children who read early.* New York: Teachers' College Press, Columbia University; Gibson, E. & Levin, H. 1975. *The psychology of reading.* Cambridge, MA: MIT Press; Hiebert, E. H. 1978. Preschool children's understanding of written language. *Child Development, 49,* 1231-1234; Jones, M. A. & Hendrickson, N. J. 1970. Recognition by preschool children. *Journal of Home Economics, 62,* 263-267; Kimmel, M. M. & Segel, E. 1983. *For reading out loud!* New York: Delacorte Press; Maclean, M., Bryant, P., & Bradley, L. 1987. Rhymes, nursery rhymes, and reading in early childhood. *Merrill-Palmer Quarterly, 33,* 255-281; McCormick, S. 1977. Should you read aloud to your children? *Language Arts, 54,* 139-143; McGee, L. M. 1983. May I take your order? *First Teacher, 4,* 13; McGee, L. M. 1986. Young children's environmental print reading. *Childhood Education,* December, 118-125; Smith, F. 1977. Making sense of reading—and of reading instruction. *Harvard Educational Review, 47,* 386-395; Tompkins, G. E. 1984. Use product packaging to teach skills. *Early Years, 15,* 36-37; Venezky, R. L. 1975. Prereading skills: Theoretical foundations and practical applications. In T. A. Brigham, R. Hawkins, J. W. Scott, & T. F. McLaughlin (Eds.). *Behavior analysis in education: Self-control and reading.* Dubuque, IA: Kendall/Hunt; Ylisto, I. 1967. *An empirical investigation of early reading responses of young children.* Unpublished doctoral dissertation, University of Michigan, Ann Arbor.)

3. Gilles de la Tourette Syndrome

The **Gilles de la Tourette Syndrome** (or Tourette syndrome), which affects 100,000 Americans, involves learning problems (e.g., short attention span, hyperactivity, school disruption, obsessions, and compulsions), tics, blinking eyelids, twitching, spasmodic movements, grimacing, and jawdropping. In time, joint-snapping, head jerks, and other convulsive movements develop. Finally, those with Tourette syndrome make uncontrollable noises (e.g., snorting, hissing, grunting, clicking, barking, gurgling), and obscene eruptions of words. Some patients experience compulsive vomiting. One tick pattern may last for months or years and then suddenly be replaced by a different pattern.

Most sufferers start to have symptoms between the ages of 2 and 18. The disorder starts with a simple tic (one fourth of all children have transient tics) sometime by the age of 11 (95 percent of the time). Then body twitches and vocal tics are added. The vocal tics often include obscene words because these words use "basic" high probability sounds which the patient cannot censor. For most victims, it is a lifelong syndrome.

Historically, a variety of treatments have been employed. Most of them were useless and cruel, because most assumed the sufferer was possessed by the devil; even recently some families of Tourette patients request rites of exorcism. Patients were subjected to exorcism, asylums, insulin therapy, prolonged sipping of water (under the misconception that Tourette is similar to hiccups), lobotomy, and electroshock.

In modern times, self-treatment has often been alcohol, which seemed to lessen the symptoms. Others use a **"storing up" method** in which they can temporarily stop the behaviors and then "explode" in a safer situation. Now, two medications have shown some success although not without serious side effects including feeling dull, apathetic, and non-energetic: halopcridol and clonidine. **Haloperidol,** often prescribed for schizophrenia, helps three fourths of Tourette patients. **Cogentin** is usually co-prescribed to alleviate some of the side effects. **Clonidine,** an antihypertensive, works in a similar area of the brain. In 1989, an experimental drug called **Prozac,** an antidepressant, was being tried out. This medication increases the level of serotonin in the brain.

Because of these medicines and because of new data from PET scans and EEGs, researchers are now narrowing in on the etiology of Tourette syndrome. Researchers suspect that Tourettes is genetic, because 90 percent of sufferers have other family members with Tourette, and four times more males than females suffer from it. PET scans reveal that these patients have different **basal ganglia** activity than do others. This area of the brain is involved in physical coordination and in relaying signals from the cerebral cortex to the brain stem. Haloperidol and clonidine decrease dopamine in this area. By combining PET and EEG data, research suggests that the specific area involved in Tourettes seems to be the **cingulate cortex,** the emotional language circuit.

Tourette syndrome is probably genetically transmitted. In one study, 385 members of a Canadian family were evaluated; 41 definitely had Tourette syndrome and another 38 were possible diagnoses. (*Sources:* Policoff, S. P. 1990 (June). Diseases your doctor may miss. *Ladies' Home Journal*, 104-109; Simons, J. A., Irwin, D. B., & Drinnin, B. A. 1987. *Instructor's Manual to Accompany Psychology, the Search for Understanding*, St. Paul: West Publishing.)

4.   Bilingualism and Math Ability

Not only do children in Asian countries learn more math than American children, but Asian-American children outperform Hispanic-American, African-American, and European-American children enrolled in the same schools. Is the best explanation genetic? Effort put into studying?

These explanations might seem adequate until you look at subgroups of Asian-American children. Asian-American children who are bilingual and whose homes prefer their Chinese, Japanese, or Korean language show superior performance in math, but third- or fourth-generation Asian-American children who speak English at home do about the same as other cultural groups. Something about the Asian languages was suspected as important, because children who were bilingual in both Spanish and English performed below the national average in math achievement.

Chinese, Japanese, and Korean languages all use the same number system. Unlike the English-speaking (or other Western languages) system in which children have to learn an irregular pattern of number names (up to 20) that gives no clue to the base-10 structure of the number system, the spoken forms in Asian language provide these clues.

Twelve is not "twelve" in Asian languages but a spoken equivalent of "ten-two." "Twenty" (20) is "two-tens." Do you remember your confusion as a young child trying to figure out the differences between "sixteen" and "sixty"? Asian languages would be "ten-six" and "six-tens"—both terms convey the concept of place values in a natural way.

Some researchers believe that this difference in spoken language helps Asian children achieve an earlier and a stronger grasp of the base-10 system. This grasp helps them to understand concepts such as carrying, borrowing, and decimals.

One study that revealed these differences was done with blocks. Some blocks were ten-blocks which equaled ten unit-blocks. Japanese children and American children were told to use these blocks to depict the number 42. Most Japanese children used four 10-blocks and two unit-blocks. Most American children used 42 unit-blocks. The majority of American children were unable to come up with the alternative way to depict 42. (*Source:* Miura, I. T. & Okamoto, Y. 1989. Comparisons of U. S. and Japanese first graders' cognitive representation of number and understanding of place value. *Journal of Educational Psychology, 81,* 109-113.)

5.   Television and Vocabulary Building

Television plays a big role in preschoolers' lives; by age 3 the average American child is watching in excess of two and a half hours of television daily. Not only this, but when the television is on in the home, 3-year-olds are viewing 67 percent of the time and 5-year-olds 70 percent of the time. As covered in the text, television viewing can be shown to influence children's aggression and prosocial behaviors, as well as their concepts on gender and age roles. Can television also educate and build language skills?

During the preschool years, children learn to understand over 14,000 words, or more than nine new words a day. They do this without explicit word-by-word tutoring, but by learning from conversational interactions, and from activities such as storybook sharing. The process of learning new words in this informal way involves **"fast mapping''**—a quick, initial partial understanding of a word's meaning on the basis of even a single exposure. Children can learn about an unfamiliar word when it is surrounded by known vocabulary and familiar context.

Informally, educators and parents respond to the idea that television can build vocabularies; after all, parents rely on "Sesame Street" to teach their preschoolers. How can research look at television's ability to serve as a vocabulary enhancer?

In one study, two six-minute animated programs were used to introduce preschoolers in an experimental group to 20 novel words, and those in a control group to 20 familiar words. Each targeted word was used five times during each program. The two vocabulary lists are provided here. As you can see, the experimental list does not include words that parents would ordinarily use in conversing with their preschoolers.

	Experimental	*Control*
Objects		
	Gramophone	Record Player
	Cleaver	Knife
	Vessels	Bowls
	Artisans	Carpenter
	Viola	Violin
Actions		
	Surge	Blow
	Sever	Cut
	Waft	Fall
	Trudge	Walk
	Fabricate	Make
Attributes		
	Makeshift	Pretend
	Malicious	Bad
	Withered	Sick
	Radiant	Pretty
	Nurturant	Kind
Affective state		
	Altruism	Helpful
	Dejection	Sad
	Contentment	Feeling good
	Jubilation	Happy
	Smug	Proud

The study found that both 3- and 5-year-olds can learn new words from brief exposure to television. The older preschoolers learned more words (4.87) than did the younger preschoolers (1.56), suggesting possible influences of accumulated language knowledge or more efficient television viewing. The words that were easiest to learn were: gramophone (94 percent), nurturant (83 percent), viola (71 percent), makeshift (69 percent), malicious (66 percent), artisan (57 percent), and fabricating (46 percent). (*Source:* Rice, M. L. & Woodsmall, L. 1988. Lessons from television: Children's word learning when viewing. *Child Development, 59,* 4200429. [Including Table 1])

6. Language in the Home

What is the language of the United States? While it is English for the majority of Americans, for about one in seven Americans the primary language spoken at home is something other than English. There is an increase in other languages because of the rise of immigration from Latin America and Asia. In 1990, 14 percent of U.S. residents spoke a language other than English at home, a raise from 11 percent in 1980. There are many regional differences— in New Mexico more than one in three (36 percent) and in California nearly one in three (32 percent) spoke a non-English language. About one in four use a different language in Texas, Hawaii, and New York. In twenty-one states, the proportion of people who didn't speak English at home was six percent or less.

The second most common language in the United States is Spanish, which is spoken by more than half of the 31.8 million United States residents who don't routinely speak in English. In descending order, French (1,702,176), German (1,547,099), Italian (1,308,648), Chinese (1,249,213), and Tagalog (from the Philippines) (843,251) are next most common. Compared to 1980, the 1990 census showed that fewer Americans spoke German, Italian, Polish, Greek, and Yiddish at home. Languages with the biggest increases during the 1980s were Spanish, Chinese, Tagalog, Korean, and Vietnamese.

Many immigrants know or are learning English, and 79 percent of those who speak another language other than English say that they can speak English well. Indeed, today's immigrants, just like in previous waves of immigration, realize that those who can speak English earn more than others. However, multiple languages pose important questions about how to conduct education and governmental business. How well do school districts teach children with little English proficiency? And, school districts which can manage to teach bilingually in a couple of languages may find that they have students who know twenty or more different languages. (*Source:* Green, C. (April 28, 1993). For 1 in 7, English not main tongue. *Des Moines Register.* pp. 1-2. Based on 1990 U.S. Census.)

BROWN & BENCHMARK'S HUMAN DEVELOPMENT TRANSPARENCIES (2ND ED.)

Transparency Number and Title

The transparency set, a supplement to *Child Development,* is accompanied by an annotated manual that describes each of the 141 transparencies. The annotated manual also offers suggestions about how to use the transparencies to engage your students in active learning that will stimulate critical thinking and evaluative skills. The following transparencies are appropriate and useful with Chapter 10: Language Development

Transparency Number and Title

55 Language's Rule Systems
56 Brown's Stages of Language Development
57 An Examination of MLU in Three Children
58 Strategies Adults Use to Enhance Language Acquisition
75 An Interactionist View of Language

CLASSROOM ACTIVITIES OR DEMONSTRATIONS

1. Discuss the critical thinking exercises. The intent of Exercise 1 is to apply students' understanding of the five rule systems of language, and to help them to discover what the chapter implies about the timetable of development for these systems. This exercise is straightforward, but the section on middle to late childhood does not refer to each rule system by label the way earlier subsections did, so you may want to discuss with students what topics to look for in preparation for the exercise. For example, you could have the class generate ideas about what would be studied within each topic during middle to late childhood.

    Exercise 2 revisits the "nature of development," this time in a less directive way than in previous chapters. You may want to review the issues presented in Chapter 1 again, but this time give students an opportunity to define and illustrate these on their own. A good idea would be to ask them how each issue would be applied to the study of language development without directly referring to material in the text. For example, have them guess what a discontinuous change in language development would be, and what sort of evidence would demonstrate a sensitive period in language acquisition. The second part of the question is important for two reasons. First, students may have forgotten what a sensitive period is. Second, the text creates a problem for students by asking whether there is a *critical period* for language development. The information presented actually suggests that this is a sensitive period. Students have a great deal of trouble resolving this apparent inconsistency; you will want to discuss with them how to distinguish between these similar concepts.

Exercise 3 is based on material that was presented in a special box in the second edition of *Children*. It is very similar to the treatment of language in animals in the third edition, but differs in a few ways. In any case, notice that the assumption in this exercise is different from that in others: It is the definition of language that seems to rule in the debate. You may wish to discuss how definitions become assumptions, and how questioning or reformulating definitions can reshape argument and lead to new discoveries. For example, questioning the assumption that language had to be oral produced new insights into the essential nature of language and kept alive the hope that chimpanzees could learn a language.

2. Discuss the students' research projects as suggested below.
3. Have students present a debate on language development among a behaviorist, a nativist, and a cognitive theorist. The students who participate in the debate should be ready to explain the basis of language development that their theoretical perspective assumes and the evidence that supports that view.

Source: King, M. B. & Clark, D. E. 1990. *Instructor's Manual to accompany Children.* Dubuque: Wm. C. Brown Publishers.

---

4. Videotape one or more infants between the ages of 9 and 18 months so that students can observe communication patterns of preverbal children. Provide examples of cooing, babbling, intonation patterns, and pseudo-communication patterns. Have students discuss their observations, e.g.:

> What sounds did the infants produce? Were all of their sounds part of their native language? What babbling patterns were used? Did the infants have the same intonation patterns as their parents' native language? Did it seem as if the infant was practicing a conversation format?

Source: Adapted from King, M. B. & Clark, D. E. (1989). *Instructor's Manual to Accompany Santrock and Yussen's Child Development: An Introduction,* 4th ed. Dubuque, IA: Wm. C. Brown.

---

5. Santrock describes the development of language in infants in sufficient detail to allow for a demonstration of the fallibility of human memory. Have students ask their parents to indicate how old they were when

1. the parents could tell the difference between the cry communicating hunger and the cry communicating wet diapers.
2. they spoke their first word (indicate what the word was).
3. they first put two words together.
4. they created their first sentence.

Have all the students bring this data in and then summarize the data and compare it to that provided in the text.

Once the comparison is made, have students indicate why the differences exist and then break them into groups and ask them to design a study that would determine when each of the initial stages of language development occurred. After sufficient time has passed, bring them back together and have them describe their studies and the difficulties they had in designing them. You may want to assign each group a different methodology and force them to use only that methodology to answer their questions.

Source: Temple, Lori L. 1992. *Instructor's Manual to accompany Life-span Development,* Fourth Edition by John W. Santrock, William C. Brown Communications, Dubuque, Iowa

6. In olden times, the deaf were considered to be "dumb" both in hearing and in mental incompetence. In the mid-eighteenth century, however, French priest **Abbe de l'Epe** was the first hearing person to learn the sign language of the deaf, and taught some deaf persons to read using his hand language. It was the beginning of education for the deaf and communication with the hearing world.

   Sacks describes **Sign** as a true language that is complete, complex, and rich, capable of expressing every emotion and idea as effectively and grammatically as speech. Yet, most colleges do not offer college-credit for Sign and do not let it fulfill a second-language requirement for students. Do you feel colleges should offer credit classes in Sign? How do you think colleges should accommodate deaf students (e.g., provide interpreters, closed-captioned educational television, encourage staff members to learn Sign)? What obstacles do deaf people face in the world of the hearing?

Source: Sacks, O. 1989. *Seeing voices: A journey into the world of the deaf.* Berkeley: University of California Press.

7. You should begin this discussion by describing research studies such as **Washoe** (the first ape to be taught sign language) and **Koko** the gorilla. Here is some information about **Gua,** who was the first chimpanzee whom psychologists raised as if human.

   In 1933, **Winthrop Niles Kellogg,** his wife, and their son Donald (10 months old) engaged in an experiment in which Donald was raised with a chimpanzee. **Robert Yerkes,** Yale's ape expert arranged for the loan of Gua, a 7-1/2-month-old female chimpanzee. For 9 months, the Kelloggs and Gua lived in a bungalow near Yale Anthropoid Experiment State in Florida. Both Donald and Gua were cuddled, fed, dressed, and tested.

   Their report in *The Ape and the Child* (published by Whittlesey-House) said that Gua learned to walk upright more quickly than did Donald. Gua liked to pull at hangings, like curtains, tablecloths, skirts. Gua also recognized people better than Donald, by the smell of their chests and armpits, and did better recognizing by clothes than by faces. Donald, on the other hand recognized faces.

   Although Donald liked perfume, Gua did not. Both reacted the same to sweet, salty, and bitter substances, except that Gua was more likely to enjoy sour things.

   Gua recognized herself in a mirror before Donald did, and she was also the first to become interested in picture books. However, Gua did not learn to speak human words.

   At the end of the study the Kelloggs concluded that when Gua was treated as a human child she behaved like a human child in all ways that her body and brain structure allowed. Donald and his parents went on to Indiana University; Gua was returned to Yerkes, where she lived in a cage and was part of experiments.

   What is your opinion of the value of language learning studies with primates or dolphins? Do you have any ethical concerns? How should this type of research be conducted?

Source: Gerow, J. 1988. *Time Retrospective: Psychology* 1923-1988. 16-17.

8. Play a tape of a speech sample of a 2- to 3-year old child. After listening to the speech sample, give the class a transcription of the speech. Have them use the transcript to calculate an MLU for the child. In calculating an MLU, each morpheme is counted. For example, in the utterance "I walked home," the utterance has a length of 4. *I, walk,* the past tense *-ed* and *home* each count as one morpheme.

Source: King, M. B. & Clark, D. E. 1990. *Instructor's Manual to accompany Children.* Dubuque, Wm. C. Brown Publishers.

9. Play a tape of a conversation between a parent and a 2- to 3-year-old child, and provide a transcript of the conversation. Break the students into small groups and have them score, from the transcript, the number of times the mother used each of the following processes; recasting, echoing, and expansions. Have the students refer to the definitions of the terms in their text if necessary. Have them note what the child's responses are to the three different processes used by the parent. Each group should then present the frequencies with which each process is used. Disagreements among groups can be discussed as a reliability issue in their definitions.

Source: Adapted from King, M. B. & Clark, D. E. 1989. *Instructor's Manual to Accompany Santrock & Yussen's Child Development: An Introduction,* 4th ed., Dubuque, IA: Wm. C. Brown.

CRITICAL THINKING EXERCISES

Exercise 1

At the beginning of Chapter 10 Santrock indicates that languages have five rule systems. Later in the chapter he outlines language development in infancy, early childhood, and later childhood. Information about language development seems to be limited to only one system. Which is it? Overall, what is the implication of these omissions? **Circle the letter of the best answer, and explain why it is the best answer and why each other answer is not as good.**

A. phonology
B. morphology
C. syntax
D. semantics
E. pragmatics

Exercise 2

Santrock's treatment of early language development uses many of the organizing concerns and questions that developmentalists employ to study other aspects of human development. Which one of the following developmental concepts, issues, or themes receives the *least* coverage during Santrock's discussion of early language development? **Circle the letter of the best answer, and explain why it is the best answer and why each other answer is not as good.**

A. development as a product of biological, cognitive, and social processes
B. nature versus nurture issue
C. continuity versus discontinuity issue
D. issue of early versus late experience
E. concept of sensitive periods

Exercise 3

Read the following passage ("Ape Talk - From Gua to Nim Chimpsky") outlining the history of attempts to teach apes to talk and sketching the controversy resulting from these attempts. Which of the following statements represents an assumption shared by individuals on each side of the argument, rather than an inference or an observation? **Circle the letter of the best answer, and explain why it is the best answer and why each other answer is not as good.**

A. Communication cannot be called language unless it has phonology, morphology, syntax, semantics, and pragmatics.
B. Washoe put signs together in ways that her trainer had not taught her.
C. Apes do not understand language; rather, they learn to imitate their trainers.
D. Sarah used a symbol that meant "same as" when she asked whether "banana is yellow" was the same as "yellow color of bananas."
E. Chimps use signs to communicate meaning.

It is the early 1930s. A 7-month-old chimpanzee named Gua has been adopted by humans (Kellogg & Kellogg, 1933). Gua's adopters want to rear her alongside their 10-month-old son, Donald. Gua was treated much the way we rear human infants today -her adopters dressed her, talked with her, and played with her. Nine months after she was adopted, the project was discontinued because the parents feared that Gua was slowing down Donald's progress.

About 20 years later, another chimpanzee was adopted by human beings (Hayes & Hayes, 1951). Viki, as the chimp was called, was only a few days old at the time. The goal was straightforward: Teach Viki to speak. Eventually she was taught to say "Mama," but only with painstaking effort. Day after day, week after week, the parents sat with Viki and shaped her mouth to make the desired sounds. She ultimately learned three other words— Papa, cup, and up—but she never learned the meanings of these words and her speech was not clear.

Approximately 20 years later, another chimpanzee named Washoe was adopted when she was about 10 months old (Gardner & Gardner, 1971). Recognizing that the earlier experiments with chimps had not demonstrated that apes have language, the trainers tried to teach Washoe the American sign language, which is the sign language of the deaf. Daily routine events, such as meals and washing, household chores, play with toys, and car rides to interesting places provided many opportunities for the use of sign language. In two years Washoe learned 38 different signs and by the age of 5 she had a vocabulary of 160 signs. Washoe learned how to put signs together in novel ways, such as "you drink" and "you me tickle."

Yet another way to teach language to chimpanzees exists. The Premacks (Premack & Premack, 1972) constructed a set of plastic shapes that symbolized different objects and were able to teach the meanings of the shapes to a 6-year-old chimpanzee, Sarah. Sarah was able to respond correctly using such abstract symbols as "same as" or "different from." For example, she could tell you that "banana is yellow" is the same as "yellow color of banana." Sarah eventually was able to "name" objects, respond "yes," "no," "same as," and "different from" and tell you about certain events by using symbols (such as putting a banana on a tray). Did Sarah learn a generative language capable of productivity? Did the signs Washoe learned have an underlying system of language rules?

Herbert Terrace (1979) doubts that these apes have been taught language. Terrace was part of a research project designed to teach language to an ape by the name of Nim Chimpsky (named after famous linguist Noam Chomsky) (Figure 6.B). Initially, Terrace was optimistic about Nim's ability to use language as human beings use it, but after further evaluation he concluded that Nim really did not have language in the sense that human beings do. Terrace says that apes do not spontaneously expand on a trainer's statements as people do; instead, the apes just imitate their trainer. Terrace also believes that apes do not understand what they are saying when they speak; rather they are responding to cues from the trainer that they are not aware of.

The Gardners take exception to Terrace's conclusions (Gardner & Gardner, 1986). They point out that chimpanzees use inflections in sign language to refer to various actions, people, and places. They also cite recent evidence that the infant chimp Louis learned over 50 signs from his adopted mother Washoe and other chimpanzees who used sign language.

The ape language controversy goes on. It does seem that chimpanzees can learn to use signs to communicate meanings, which has been the boundary for language. Whether the language of chimpanzees possesses all of the characteristics of human language such as phonology, morphology, syntax, semantics, and pragmatics is still being argued (Maratsos, 1983; Rumbaugh, 1988).

ANSWER KEYS FOR CRITICAL THINKING EXERCISES

Exercise 1

A. This is not the best answer. There is no information about sound production, perception, or comprehension during this period of development.
B. This is not the best answer. Nothing is added to the discussion of mean length of utterance of learning of morphology, topics that were discussed for the previous age periods.
C. This is not the best answer. Although there is small discussion of grammar, grammar is not syntax. In any case, the main focus of the discussion is cognitive development's impact on a child's understanding of the finer points of grammar.
D. This is the best answer. The section begins with a discussion of the qualitative changes that begin to occur in a child's understanding of the meanings of words.
E. This is not the best answer. Again, the social uses of language that were discussed in earlier subsections are not discussed in this one.

Implication: The implication is that most or all of development in the four omitted systems typically has taken place by middle to late childhood.

Exercise 2

A. This is not the best answer. The chapter discusses the biological bases of language and the behavioral and environmental views. Language itself is dependent on cognitive processes (e.g., symbolic function). One cognitive characteristic of language is that it is rule-based and generative. Another cognitive feature of language is deep structure.
B. This is not the best answer. The chapter explicitly talks about biological and environmental influences on language, which is one way of talking about nature-nurture issues. The chapter also touches on the classic nature view (that language acquisition is the product of a language acquisition device) and the definitive nurture view (that language is learned in the same way as any other behavior through processes of reinforcement).
C. This is the best answer. This is not because there is nothing relevant in the chapter, but rather because this issue receives least attention. For example, it is not clear whether changes described in the chapter are relatively continuous or abrupt. Likewise, nothing is said about whether individual language styles or abilities persist into later life (the stability/change issue).
D. This is not the best answer. Santrock deals with the issue in the subsection called "Is There a Critical Period for Learning Language?", in which he discusses the importance of exposure to language during roughly the first 12 years of life.
E. This is not the best answer. The idea appears in the chapter under "Is There a Critical Period for Language Learning?" Although this is labeled "critical period," the time frame for language learning is about 12 years, which more nearly fits the definition of sensitive period given in Chapter 1.

Exercise 3

A. This is the assumption shared by both sides. The criterion used to determine whether a communication system qualifies as a language is the presence of one or more rule systems that govern features of the communication system. Individuals on both sides of the debate appear to accept this as a rule for the debate, and what they argue about is whether the communications of apes possess this particular language attribute.
B. This is an observation. Researchers noted and recorded that Washoe put together new combinations of the 160 signs that she had learned.
C. This is an inference. It is Herbert Terrace's interpretation of ape behavior that others have called language. He noted that trainers made signs that the apes reproduced and inferred that this meant that the apes were merely imitating their trainers.
D. This is an observation. It is what researchers saw Sarah do in response to the question.
E. This is an inference. It is the conclusion many researchers have reached from attempts to teach language to apes. Herbert Terrace, however, disputes this claim.

RESEARCH PROJECT 1   MOTHER-INFANT LANGUAGE

In this project, you will examine recasting, echoing, and expanding using naturalistic observation. Go to a local shopping mall and observe a mother with an infant 18 to 24 months old. Observe them for 15 minutes. Record three instances of speech by the mother to the infant, and classify each instance as recasting, echoing, or expanding. Note on the data sheet the mother's statements and then the infant's response to each statement. Then answer the questions that follow.

DATA SHEET

Speech   Response of Infant   Age _____ Sex _____

Statement 1

Statement 2

Statement 3

1. What types of techniques did the mother use with the infant you observed?
2. How did the infant respond to the statement made by the mother?
3. From your observations, do you think recasting, echoing, and expanding are effective techniques in aiding infants to learn language? Why or why not? What variables might have affected the quality of data you collected? Might your conclusions have been different if you had observed a different mother-infant pair? How?

Use in Classroom:

Have the student present data in a class from the research project. Do the observations agree with the presentation in the textbook?

RESEARCH PROJECT 2   LANGUAGE ERRORS

This class project exposes you to the kinds of errors that children make when they are acquiring language. Pair up with another student in the class. One of you will act as the experimenter, while the other will act as the observer. Test two different children, one 3 to 4 years of age, the other 7 to 8 years of age. In order to test the two children, you will need to clear this through the human subjects review board at your school and get a signed informed consent form from the children's parents.

The children will receive three different tasks evaluating their understanding and use of the passive construction. Present an act-out task, an imitation task, and a production task. The task and sentence descriptions follow. Use the accompanying data sheets to record observations. Then answer the questions that follow.

1. Act-out task: Have several objects available, a toy car and truck, a toy doll, a toy horse, cow, dog, and cat. Read the sentences below one at a time, and have the child act out the sentences with the toys.
2. Imitation task: Present each of the sentences below to each child, and have the child repeat the sentences back to you.
3. Production Task: Perform the actions in each of the sentences below with the toys for the child. Ask the child to tell you what happened, starting with the first noun in the sentence. For instance, for item "e" roll the car along so that it hits the truck, and then ask the child to tell you what happened beginning with the truck.

a. The car hit the truck.
b. The dog was kicked by the cat.
c. The boy was bitten by the dog.
d. The boy hit the cat.
e. The truck was hit by the car.
f. The cow stepped on the horse.
g. The cat kicked the dog.
h. The cat was hit by the boy.
i. The dog bit the boy.
j. The horse was stepped on by the cow.

(Data sheet begins on next page.)

DATA SHEET

Task	Child 1	Child 2
	Sex___Age___	Sex___Age___

Act-out task

Sentence a
Sentence b
Sentence c
Sentence d
Sentence e
Sentence f
Sentence g
Sentence h
Sentence i
Sentence j

Task	Child 1	Child 2
	Sex___Age___	Sex___Age___

Imitation task

Sentence a
Sentence b
Sentence c
Sentence d
Sentence e
Sentence f
Sentence g
Sentence h
Sentence i
Sentence j

Production task

Sentence a
Sentence b
Sentence c
Sentence d
Sentence e
Sentence f
Sentence g
Sentence h
Sentence i
Sentence j

_____

Questions

1. What did the 3- to 4-year-old child do on the act-out task? The imitation task? The production task? Was performance on one task better than on the others? If so, which? What sorts of errors appeared in the act-out task? What about the imitation task? The production task? Were the errors similar in the various tasks?
2. What did the 7- to 8-year-old child do on the act-out task? The imitation task? The production task? Was performance on one task better than on the others? If so, which? What sorts of errors appeared in the act-out task? What about the imitation task? The production task? Were the errors similar in the various tasks?

Chapter 10

3. Compare the two children. What differences if any did you see on their performances on these three tasks? How would you account for the differences? What is the nature of language learning that seems to be occurring during this time?
4. What criticisms could be leveled at the procedures you used in this demonstration? For example, do you think each task should have had different questions?

Use in Classroom

Have students present the data from the research project in class. What kinds of errors did the younger children make on the tasks? Were there individual differences within age groups present (that is, did some of the younger children perform all tasks well, while other children made errors with all tasks?)? How did the older children perform on these tasks? Were some tasks easier? What do these findings tell us about the development course for understanding active and passive sentences? What strategies did children use when they made errors?

ESSAY AND CRITICAL THINKING QUESTIONS

Comprehension and Application Essay Questions

We recommend that you provide students with our guidelines for "Answering Essay and Critical Thinking Questions" when you have them respond to these questions. Their answers to these kinds of questions demonstrate an ability to comprehend and apply ideas discussed in this chapter.

1. Explain what makes language distinct from other forms of communication.
2. Explain the idea of infinite generativity and the five rule systems of language.
3. What evidence is there that there are biological influences on language acquisition?
4. What evidence is there that there are environmental influences on language development?
5. Explain the interactionist view of language development; give examples of the idea, and discuss why the idea has only recently emerged.
6. What preverbal linguistic behaviors do infants display? Describe each. What difference does deafness make?
7. Characterize the development of language in infants; give examples.
8. For a period of time, infants utter sentences of approximately one word. Explain whether these utterances accurately reflect the level of thinking of a child.
9. What evidence is there that children acquire rules for language use rather than individual responses? Explain.
10. Describe the development of at least one of the five systems of language from infancy through late childhood.
11. Describe the three ways to teach reading, and explain which is most favored today.
12. What is the importance of understanding bilingual behavior and bilingual education? Explain.

Critical Thinking Questions

We recommend that you have students follow our guidelines for "Answering Essay and Critical Thinking Questions" when you ask them to prepare responses to these questions. Their answers to these kinds of questions reflect an ability to apply critical thinking skills to a novel problem or situation that is *not* specifically discussed in the chapter. These items most appropriately may be used as take-home essay questions (e.g., due on exam day) or as homework exercises that can be answered either by individuals or groups. Collaboratively answered questions encourage cooperative learning by students, and reduce the number of papers that must be graded.

1. At the end of Chapter 10 Santrock indicates books that provide practical knowledge about children and lists resources for improving the lives of children. Choose one of these books or resources and read it or learn as much as you can about it. Then write a brief review in which you (a) characterize the book or resource, and (b) explain how the book or resource relates to material in the chapter.
2. Chapter 1 defines the nature of development in terms of biological, cognitive, and social processes, and periods or stages. Indicate your ability to think critically by identifying material in this chapter that illustrates developmental processes and periods. If there is little or no information in this chapter about developmental processes and periods, identify and explain how developmental processes and periods could be used to guide the analysis of any topic in the chapter.
3. According to Chapter 1, three fundamental developmental issues concern: (a) maturation (nature) versus experience (nurture), (b) continuity versus discontinuity, and (c) early versus later experience. Indicate your

ability to think critically by identifying material in this chapter that illustrates each of the three fundamental developmental issues. If there is little or no information in this chapter about fundamental developmental issues, identify and explain how these issues could be used to guide the analysis of any topic in the chapter.

4. One aspect of thinking critically is to read, listen, and observe carefully and then ask questions about what is missing from a text, discussion, or situation. For example, chapter 7 contains very little information about language development in deaf children. Indicate your ability to think critically by (a) asking as many questions as you can about language development in deaf children, and (b) speculating why Santrock does not discuss this topic more fully.

5. Santrock sets off several quotations in this chapter. Indicate your ability to think critically by selecting one of the quotes and (a) learning about the author and indicating why this individual is eminently quotable (i.e., what was this individual's contribution to human knowledge and understanding), (b) interpreting and restating the quote in your own terms, and (c) explaining what concept, issue, perspective, or term in this chapter that Santrock intended this quote to illuminate. In other words, about what aspect or issue in development does this quote make you pause and reflect?

6. Chapter 2 indicates that theories help us explain data and make predictions about various aspects of development. Chapter 2 then presents six different theoretical approaches (i.e., Freudian, cognitive, behavioral and social learning, ethological, ecological, and eclectic theory), but notes that no single approach explains the complexity of development. Indicate your ability to think critically by (a) perusing this chapter for topics influenced by at least one of the six theoretical approaches, and (b) explaining which theoretical approach dominated the topic in question. If the presentation is entirely atheoretical, identify and explain how one of the theoretical approaches could be used to guide the analysis of the topic in question.

7. How does language development proceed when an infant is exposed regularly to two languages? Does the infant learn both languages? Does she learn one better than the other? Apply your knowledge about the scientific method by designing a study to answer this question: (a) What specific problem or question do you want to study? (b) What predictions would you make and test in your study? (c) What measures would you use (i.e., controlled observation in a laboratory, naturalistic observation, interviews and questionnaires, case studies, standardized tests, cross-cultural studies, physiological research, research with animals, or multimeasure, multisource, and multicontext approach) and how would you define each measure clearly and unambiguously? (d) What strategy would you follow--correlational or experimental, and what would be the time span of your inquiry--cross-sectional or longitudinal? (e) What ethical considerations must be addressed before you conduct your study?

8. According to Chapter 2, your author wants you to become a wise consumer of information about child development by: (a) being cautious about media reports, (b) distinguishing between nomothetic research and idiographic needs, (c) recognizing how easy it is to overgeneralize from a small or clinical sample, d) knowing that a single study is usually not the defining word about some aspect of child development, (e) remembering that causal conclusions cannot be made from correlation studies, and (f) always considering the source of the information and evaluating its credibility. Indicate your ability to think critically by, first, selecting an article from either a journal, magazine, or newspaper about any topic regarding Language Development, and, second, evaluating it in terms of these six objectives. If the information in the article is insufficient to evaluate one of these objectives, then specify what kind of information you would need to evaluate the objective.

Socioemotional Development and The Self

11 Attachment, Temperament, and Emotional Development

SUGGESTIONS FOR LECTURE TOPICS

1. Evolution of the Concept of Attachment

A presentation on the evolution of the concept of attachment would be an excellent case study of progress in developmental psychology research. Tracing this evolution is an excellent opportunity to illustrate the nature of scientific process and progress, the value of critical thinking, the importance of both productive controversy generated by alternative points of view and the eclectic melding of points of view.

Begin your lecture with an overview of the classic work on dependency in parent-child relations. Early on, the concept of an emotional bond between parent and child was regarded as highly important (e.g., Freud); however, direct study of the bond was lacking. Early attempts relied on simple, unitary measures that ultimately failed to provide convincing evidence for the claim that dependency was a stable characteristic. At that time some researchers concluded that it was a developmentally useful construct, especially those with a learning orientation.

Meanwhile, researchers with psychoanalytic and ethological orientations (e.g., Bowlby, Ainsworth) began to suggest that the emotional bond between parents and infants should be called an attachment and regarded as an organized system of behavior rather than a simple, unitary trait. This meant that quantitative measures were inappropriate and that qualitative measures were required. The ultimate expression of this trend was to create the "strange situation" as a procedure for identifying attachment quality in infants. Developed from techniques used to study monkeys, this procedure provided a means for making inferences about attachment that were firmly rooted in observational procedures. Today, hundreds of studies have been done on developmental correlates and consequences of qualitative individual differences in attachment at all age levels.

As successful as the construct and the methods used to study it have been, very recent work has become critical of it. You may want to include a summary of these criticisms to cap your presentation, possibly to illustrate that an additional value of the attachment work is that it has revealed what we do not know about the subject.

A very useful summary of some of this work is found in Eleanor Maccoby's (1980) *Social Development*.

2. Comparing Alternative Forms of Infant Care

An important sociocultural concern is the question of how modern trends in infant care are influencing infant development. More and more babies are being cared for in diverse out-of-home settings. A problem is that it becomes very difficult to make generalizations about the effects of these highly variable, "nontraditional" approaches to infant care. The text touches on this issue briefly noting contradictory findings and suggesting that the important variable is infant care quality, not out-of-home care *per se*.

But where is quality infant care likely to be found? Is it best to place an infant in situations that are as much like home as possible? Are grandparents the best caregivers?

Potential answers to these questions are given in a book by Sandra Scarr. Summarize the findings of her review, and relate them to the material presented in the textbook.

A couple of important issues should be expanded upon in this lecture. One is the importance of recognizing that researchers have biases and values. Day care is an economic, social, and political issue as well as a psychological one, and the questions and answers various researchers provide are likely to be driven by the stands they implicitly or explicitly take. Another is the fact that work in this area is entirely correlational, making it difficult to claim that day care is a *cause* of either loss or gain. Other very important variables are associated with variations in the type and quality of day care infants receive, a point that underscores once again the importance of being aware of the values and biases brought to research.

A nice concluding touch would be to draw parallels between the findings of research on out-of-home infant care and of other work on variations in early experience and their effect on infant development. You might want to comment on how well this work informs "good" out-of-home care and, conversely, whether the day-care studies replicate findings from other research.

3. Observing the Social Interactions of Infants

Expand your treatment of observational research on infant development by presenting a lecture on recent studies of infant social interaction. This field is rich in examples of systematic, structured observations and will provide you with many examples of the varieties of observational approaches available. This information can also serve as a vehicle to compare and contrast the strengths and weaknesses of the different approaches. Furthermore, the material is fascinating in its own right.

You may wish to begin with a brief review of your talk about RDS babies (see Chapter 5) or a reprise of work on attachment. Or, you may want to begin with the detailed work of Brazelton, Stern, and others that showed how an infant's and caregiver's behavior can involve a tight interplay of actions and reactions, even when infants are in the earliest stages of motor development (smiling and gazing are early powerful forms of interaction). Discuss indications that this interplay is involved in eventual attachment between infant and caregiver and how it transforms as cognitive and motor capacities enlarge.

Having characterized adult-infant interaction, proceed to present work that demonstrates social interactions between infants and their peers. This topic is neglected in your text, but there is compelling information that infants are capable of interacting with other infants, have individual differences in their ability to do so, and develop relationships with peers that they interact with regularly. The observational work that has supported these conclusions is often complex, but sketching its main features may provide valuable insights to present or potential parents on how to observe their own infants and otherwise expand their recognition of the value of early experience in social as well as cognitive spheres. Indeed, the strongest correlates of day-care attendance cited are variations in the quality of social interactions among children who experience different types of care from an early age.

4. Dealings with Difficulty Children

In the "Blame the Mother" era of the 1950s, Alexander Thomas and Stella Chess took note that their own children had very different personalities in spite of having the same two parents. They also noted that parental characteristics did not predict the problems of the juvenile patients with whom they were working. These observations led to lifelong research on temperament. They came up with several categories of temperament: activity, rhythmicity, approach, withdrawal, adaptability, threshold, intensity of reaction, mood quality, distractibility, and persistence. They condensed these categories to three temperament styles: easy babies, slow-to-warm-up babies, and difficult babies.

About 10 percent of all babies fit the description of difficult babies (some prefer the term challenging babies). They typically have trouble sleeping, eating, and following instructions, and are destructive, negative, and inconsistent. They are a high proportion of the children with behavioral problems, and they have adverse effects on parents.

Parents feel out of control, anxious, angry, guilty, depressed, frustrated, isolated, and vulnerable. They are often inconsistent in handling their difficult offspring—they move from appeasement to severe punishment, in unhealthy cycles. When they are using scolding, yelling, and spanking, they often increase the difficult child's aggression and resistance. When they are overprotective and overpermissive, they increase the child's dependence and manipulation.

Parents of difficult children should rule out other causes (e.g., autism, mental retardation, attention-deficit disorder with hyperactivity, depression). They should decrease their emotional responses to the children. They should increase their use of behavior modification techniques, especially positive reinforcement and 5-10 minute time-out periods, and they should consistently use "yes, but", as in "Yes, I know you want to watch TV, but it is time for bed now." (*Source:* Liptak, G. S. 1990 (April). Dealing with the difficult child. *Resident & Staff Physician*, 41-48.)

5. Choosing Quality Child Care

a. Know your own preferences about type of child-care facility. Choosing family day care or other forms of day care is not as important as the quality of child care itself. Which type of setting appeals to the parent and child? Why? Do you want a setting that is cognitively-oriented? Physical play-oriented?

b. Do consider how many children are at the location and the adult-child ratio. For preschool children, the ratio should be about 1 adult for every 4 children. Ideally, there are no more than 16 children in the entire group.

c. Observe a potential child-care facility for at least two hours. Observe the kinds of play and activity centers provided, and what kinds of equipment are present. Does the physical environment and the variety of activities provided allow the adults to meet young children's individual needs?

d. Watch for how caretakers interact with the children. Do they seem supportive and friendly? Do they reinforce prosocial behaviors among children? Are children gently encouraged to try new activities? Can children receive appropriate physical touching from the adults? Do caretakers seem flexible, confident, competent, and sensitive? Do the children seem happy to be at the center? How does the staff handle accidents, fighting, emotional upsets, and sleepiness?

e. Consider impressions about the center's appearance. Do the physical facilities seem clean, cheerful, and safe? Is there enough light? Enough warmth? Are there annoying smells or a very loud noise level? Is there a quiet area? Is there a well-equipped playground? Is there a space to store a child's personal belongings? Are there enough art supplies and appropriate toys?

f. Try to detect the values and beliefs emphasized by the center. Can the school director describe his or her personal child-care philosophy? Are the caretakers non-sexist and non-racist? Do play materials and books reflect gender and racial stereotypes? Are boys and girls encouraged to play with a wide range of toys?

g. Observe the play patterns. Are there toys that encourage both large and fine motor development? Are there materials for dramatic play, art work, and solitary play? Are the activities mainly structured? Are educational tasks encouraged but not pressured onto the children?

h. Notice how the child-care center interacts with parents. Are parents allowed to drop in as visitors unannounced? Are there parent-caretaker-child conferences? Can parents make suggestions about the center or how to interact with their preschoolers? Are you able to adjust child-care hours as needed?

i. How does your child react during a visit?

(*Sources:* Olds, S. W. 1986. *The working parents' survival guide.* New York: Bantam; Ramey, C. T. 1981. Consequences of infant day care. In B. Weissbound & J. Musick (Eds.). *Infants: Their social environments.* Washington, D.C.: National Association for the Education of Young Children; Scarr, S. 1984. *Mother care/other care.* NY: Basic Books; Brenner, B. 1990 (March 12). Off to a good start. *Education in America: A new look.* New York: Newsweek, Inc., Shell, E. R. 1989 (Dec.). Now, which kind of preschool? *Psychology Today,* 52-57.)

6. Separation Anxiety Disorder

A child who has separation anxiety disorder has anxiety that is specifically attached to separation from important others or from one's familiar environment. The child may experience high levels of panic and distress under these circumstances. Adults will notice that these children experience profound fears about the well-being of parents or themselves, and these fears are often accompanied by fantasies about possible accidents, significant illness, or traumatic events. With age, these fears and fantasies typically become more specific and more developed.

During the separation, these children typically exhibit social withdrawal, apathy, and lack of involvement in play or school activities. Typically they have sleep disturbances and frequent nightmares. Other fears might include that of animals, monsters, burglars, and kidnappers. They exhibit age-inappropriate clinging behaviors and may follow a parent around the house, refuse to sleep at a friend's house, and avoid overnight camp.

When a separation is anticipated or is occurring, many of these children have physical symptoms including nausea and headaches. Some exhibit aggression towards those forcing separation. Other characteristics might include demanding, attention-seeking behaviors, excessive conformity, and depression.

Often children with separation anxiety disorder come from close-knit, caring families. Often, the onset of this disorder comes after a traumatic event, such as moving, illness or death in the family, or the loss of a pet.

The following questions are typical of those asked by an interviewer who is interested in diagnosing this disorder:

a. Does the child unrealistically worry about bad things happening to the family?
b. Does the child display clinging or shadowing behaviors?
c. When separated from parents, does the child complain of nausea or headaches?
d. When parents are about to leave, does the child often cry, panic, or have a temper tantrum?
e. When away from parents, does the child behave in a socially withdrawn, apathetic, sad manner?
f. Are there frequent nightmares about being left alone?
h. Is the child reluctant to sleep alone or refuses to sleep away from home?
i. Does the child show a persistent pattern of school refusal in order to be at home with parents?

(Material adapted from: Samuels, S. K. & Sikorsky, S. (1990). *Clinical evaluations of school-aged children.* Sarasota, FL: Professional Resource Exchange, Inc.)

7.   Covering up Feelings

One of the acceptable "distortions" and "concealments" in society is to disguise the facial expressions of negative feelings. After learning to control negative words and to be verbally polite, children are expected to work on controlling their true feelings in their faces.

In one study, children were asked to describe the facial expression of a child their age on receiving a present of an ugly sweater. First graders said that they thought the child would look disappointed. Half of the fifth graders thought the child would succeed in concealing disappointment.

When asked how successful a child their age would be in pretending to be indifferent when (a) teased or (b) losing a contest and hearing the applause for the winner, even fifth graders thought they would be unable to hide their true feelings.

Sometimes children try not to show the feeling, making the negative feelings go away by distraction or switching to happy thoughts. It is not uncommon for children to suggest that visually distressed adults try these strategies, because they find the adults' displays of negative emotions upsetting. (*Sources:* Gnepp, J. & Hess, D. L. R. 1986. Children's understanding of verbal and facial display rules. *Developmental Psychology, 22,* 103-108; Band, E. B. & Weisz, J. R. 1988. How to feel better when it feels bad: Children's perspectives on coping with everyday stress. *Developmental Psychology, 24,* 247-253.)

8.   Facial Expression and Emotion

Silvan Tomkins, Carroll Izard, and Paul Ekman are important researchers in the field of facial expression and emotion. All found high agreement across members of various Western and Eastern literate cultures in selecting emotional descriptors for various facial expressions. Ekman and Friesen found that a preliterate culture in New Guinea also agreed with the literate societies about which expressions fit with different situations (e.g., death of a child, seeing friends, a fight). Moreover, they found that there was universality in spontaneous expressions. Cultural differences were explained by display rules, or culture-specific rules about who can show which emotion, when, and to whom.

A (non-replicated) research study by Schachter and Singer in the 1960s led many psychologists to the conclusion that all emotions had the same physiological activity, and only the extent of the emotional arousal differed. Emotions were given different labels due to the perceived situation and resulting cognitions. However, current researchers are again examining whether there are emotion-specific physiological changes.

Emotions can be considered as families. For example, there are sixty anger expressions that share core configurational properties that separate them from the family of fear expressions and disgust expressions, for example. The anger family has a wide variation in intensity from annoyance to rage, and it has many forms from resentment with its grievance, indignation, and outrage to vengeance to berserk. (*Source:* Ekman, P. (April 1993). Facial expression and emotion. *American Psychologist,* 384-392. Much additional lecture information is available in this article.)

9.   Biology and Temperament

From the MacArthur Longitudinal Twin Study, involving 200 primarily white, healthy 14-month-old twin pairs, Robert Emde concluded that identical twins' temperaments are more similar than fraternal twins. By their second year, identical twins are about twice as likely to be comparable on measures of emotional reactivity than are fraternal twins. Overall, genes tend to account for about 40 to 50 percent of cognitive skill differences, 30 to 40 percent of temperament differences, and 20 to 30 percent of emotional differences. One aspect of temperament that is significantly influenced by heredity are shyness about anything unfamiliar and activity levels.

Nathan Fox of the University of Maryland reported that EEGs differ widely for adults and children with different temperaments. Less cheerful infants and adults have greater right frontal EEG activation, and happier infants and adults have greater left frontal activation. Four-year-old children who are more likely to initiate social contacts (e.g., asking others to play) and whose are rated as happier by mothers, had greater left frontal activation than right. Anxious, withdrawn, non-involved children had greater right frontal activation than left. When these same children were only four months old, those who were more active and irritable had more activity in their right EEGs; those who are very active and cheerful had more activity in their left EEGs. At fourteen months these individuals who were irritable had higher levels of stranger anxiety and more clinging behaviors. (*Source: APA Monitor,* 1993 (January), and the Biology and Temperament conference held in Bloomington, 1993(Otober).

BROWN & BENCHMARK'S HUMAN DEVELOPMENT TRANSPARENCIES (2ND ED.)

Transparency Number and Title

The transparency set, a supplement to *Child Development*, is accompanied by an annotated manual that describes each of the 141 transparencies. The annotated manual also offers suggestions about how to use the transparencies to engage your students in active learning that will stimulate critical thinking and evaluative skills. The following transparencies are appropriate and useful with Chapter 11: Attachment, Temperament, and Emotional Development.

Transparency Number and Title

13	Erikson's Trust versus Mistrust
24	Bandura's Model of the Reciprocal Influence of B, P, and E
26	Psychoanalytic Theories
28	Ethological Theories
59	Paid Maternity/Paternity Leave Provisions in Various Western Countries
60	Chess and Thomas's Dimensions and the Basic Clusters of Temperament
61	The Developmental Course of Infant Emotions

CLASSROOM ACTIVITIES OR DEMONSTRATIONS

1. Discuss the critical thinking exercises. Exercises 1 and 2 are different from the previous thinking exercises. Exercise 1 requires much more specific evaluation of the evidence presented in the text for the various topics listed in the exercise. Students now are not simply required to decide whether there is any evidence at all, but are asked to evaluate whether the evidence is appropriate. In order to prepare them to do this you will probably want to review rules for interpreting the adequacy of scientific evidence. Students will need to remember, for example, what inferences are permissible from correlational and experimental research. In this discussion you may also want to explore how the type of questions being asked is related to the type of research that is adequate. Descriptive questions need observational research; questions about patterns or associations are answered with correlational research; questions about cause and effect need experimental research. Discuss these points with students, possibly reviewing earlier material with these points in mind.

   Exercise 2 represents the first time since Chapter 2 that students have had to apply the theoretical perspectives. You may want to discuss with them how well they remember these perspectives, and either provide a review or have them review the theories. If you had them analyze parenting practices or the things different theorists would notice in observation of parents when they studied Chapter 2, revisiting that material would also be helpful. In any case, either give students a list of the key feature of each perspective, or have them develop such a list as an in-class activity.

   Exercise 3 is a straightforward continuation of the inference, assumption, and observation problems.

2. Discuss the students' research projects as suggested below.

3. Should the care, training, and education of children be based on scientific research and theory rather than intuition, religion, or tradition? What are the advantages and disadvantages of using scientific guidelines? Is enough known to be able to rear children scientifically? What are some examples of scientific suggestions for rearing children? How many students believe that their parents reared them according to scientific guidelines?

Source: Simons, J. A., Irwin, D. B., & Drinnin, B. A. 1987. *Instructor's Manual to Accompany Psychology, The Search for Understanding,* St. Paul: West Publishing.

---

4. B. F. Skinner built a "baby box," an incubator-like apparatus in which he raised his second daughter, Deborah. Henry Hope, head of Indiana University's fine arts department, also used the invention to raise his twin boys Roy and Ray.

   The box had a constant temperature of 88 degrees and humidity of 50 percent. There was a canvas mattress at the bottom stretched over the air filters that regulated the temperature and humidity. The baby box had a picture window and sound-absorbing walls.

None of these three children seemed to have any developmental problems or advantages from this unusual "air crib," but attempts to manufacturer and sell these cribs have not met with success. For a while, rumors existed that Skinner's daughter Deborah had committed suicide, but in reality, she became a successful artist.

What would be the advantages and disadvantages of this "baby box"? Would you raise a baby using this? Why or why not? What kinds of modifications might you propose for other baby apparatuses, such as high chairs, playpens, etc.?

Sources: Skinner, B. F. 1979 (March). My experience with the baby tender. *Psychology Today;* Gerow, J. 1988. *Time Retrospective: Psychology 1923-1988*, 45.

---

5. Erikson thought a child's sense of trust was the cornerstone of all future personality development. Which aspects of parenting lead to this sense of trust? What roles do physical comfort, consistency, lack of fearful situations, and satisfaction of hunger and thirst play? What is the role of parental attentiveness? Do you think that trust is developed more easily by later-born children because their parents are more confident? What aspects of being the first born counterbalance the advantages of having experienced parents?

Source: Maier, H. 1969. *Three Theories of Child Development.* New York: Harper & Row.

---

6. Though most people have grown used to the idea of placing preschool children in day care, there are still those who say that there are too many dangers associated with placing infants into that environment. To help students discover the latest findings on the issue of day care with infants, have each one go to the library and get two articles about the effects of day care. Be sure they get one showing the positive effects and one showing the negative effects.

During the class period, break students up into groups of four and have each group summarize their findings. Each group should be able to list at least four pieces of evidence in favor of day care and four against. Have the class create a collective list.

Once the evidence is provided, have the students go back to their groups and put together a list of the characteristics that would be present in a model day-care program for infants and then cumulate the lists and discuss the characteristics.

Source: Temple, Lori L. 1992. *Instructor's Course Planner to accompany Life-span Development,* Fourth Edition by John W. Santrock, William C. Brown Communications, Dubuque, Iowa.

---

7. Have students work in groups of three; one person in the group roleplays a child and the other two roleplay the parents. Provide each group with a slip of paper that tells them three bits of information: (1) child's temperament (easy, difficult, slow-to-warm-up); (2) parental belief about heredity vs. environment (strong heredity, strong environment, interaction model); and (3) specific situation (visit to the doctor's office, child's first day at school, child at bedtime, child in a toystore, child in a grocery store, child in a restaurant). You may put students in groups of 9 or 12 so that one three-person unit roleplays, and the others "feed" suggestions on how to handle the situation.
Example slips:

"Taking a slow-to-warm-up child to the doctor's office; parents believe in the environmental position."
"A difficult child is in the cereal aisle of the grocery story; parents believe in a heredity position."
"An easy child's first day of school; parents believe in the interaction model."
"A difficult child in a restaurant; parents believe in the environment position."

[Note: Difficult and slow-to-warm-up roleplays present more challenge, so you might want to use more of these situations than easy child.]

After roleplays, discuss which characteristics and behaviors students chose to portray for the different temperaments. What kinds of parental responses did the three temperaments elicit?

Source: Simons, J. A. 1987. Dealing with temperaments: A role-play exercise. Ankeny, IA: Des Moines Area Community College.

8.   Are individual differences due to differences in characteristic mood states? Tellegen (1985) stated that people inherited a tendency toward positive affectivity (which influences sociability), negative affectivity (which influences adjustment and constraint), and constraint (which influences conscientiousness). Bluss and Plomin (1984) propose sociability, emotionality (adjustment), and activity (consciousness, ambition). Do you believe that people are born with different potentials for various personality traits? Do you think that genetic screening for prenatal testing will someday evaluate potential personality? Should educational programs differ for individuals with varying mood states/temperaments?

Sources: Bluss, A. H. & Plomin, R. 1984. *Temperament: Early developing personality traits.* Hillsdale, New Jersey: Erlbaum; Tellegen, A. 1985. Structures of mood and personality and their relevance to assessing anxiety, with an emphasis on self-report. In A. H. Turner & J. D. Masger (Eds.). *Anxiety and the Anxiety Disorders.* Hillsdale, NJ: Erlbaum.

CRITICAL THINKING EXERCISES

Exercise 1

In Chapter 8 Santrock describes many claims about social development during infancy. The quality of the evidence that supports each claim is quite varied. Which of the following claims is *least* supported? That is, which evidence is least convincing according to scientific criteria? **Circle the letter of the best answer, and explain why it is the best answer and why each other answer is not as good.**

A.   Secure attachment is related to social competence.
B.   Under stress, infants show stronger attachment to their mothers than their fathers.
C.   Extensive day care during the first year of an infant's life is associated with negative outcomes later in life.
D.   The expression of emotions by infants follows a predictable developmental course.
E.   John Bowlby believes that insecure attachment leads to a negative cognitive schema.

Exercise 2

In previous chapters of *Children* there has been little opportunity to apply the various theories of development that were outlined in Chapter 2. Chapter 8, however, presents research and theorizing motivated by several of these theories. Santrock directly identifies some of these, but does not do so for all topics. Listed below are topics from Chapter 8 paired with theoretical perspectives. Decide which of these pairs is accurate. **Circle the letter of the best answer, and explain why it is the best answer and why each other answer is not as good.**

A.   reciprocal socialization: psychoanalytic theory
B.   attachment: cognitive theory
C.   temperament: ethological theory
D.   the father's role: behavioral theory
E.   day care: ecological theory

Exercise 3

Attachment is a major topic in the study of infant social development. One reason why it is given emphasis is because attachment represents a centerpiece for several different theoretical accounts of early social relationships. Which of the following statements best represents an assumption by attachment researchers, rather than an inference or an observation? **Circle the letter of the best answer, and explain why it is the best answer and why each other answer is not as good.**

A. An infant cries when separated from its mother because she is attached to her mother.
B. The most important relationship in an infant's life involves attachment to a primary caretaker.
C. Eighteen-month-old infants who are insecurely attached to their mothers exhibit more frustration behavior than securely attached infants.
D. Providing an infant with a comfortable, safe environment creates an attachment bond between an infant and caretaker.
E. Some babies do not look at their mothers or try to be near them.

ANSWER KEYS FOR CRITICAL THINKING EXERCISES

Exercise 1

A. This statement requires at least correlational, longitudinal evidence for support. Sroufe's research reported in the text provides it.
B. Lamb's study reported in the text is an experimental test of this hypothesis that confirms it. Tired infants exposed to a strange situation sought their mothers instead of their fathers.
C. The evidence is mixed, but there is research that documents the association between day care early in infants' lives and later negative outcomes. The contradictions in the research seem to be satisfactorily resolved by the claim that later outcomes are a function of the quality of day care delivered to infants in the first year of their lives.
D. Izard's research represents years of observational study and the development of a meticulous system for classifying infant facial expressions. Furthermore, longitudinal work has documented the developmental course of emotional expressions, as indicated in the table presented in the text.
E. No evidence is presented to support this claim. The claim is stated as an interesting idea about the origins of childhood and adolescent depression.

Exercise 2

A. This is not an accurate pair. While psychoanalytic theory does stress the importance of early relationships to personality and social development, it does not treat extensively the influence of an infant's behavior on an adult caretaker's behavior. In fact, the theory seems to imply a unidirectional analysis, focusing on how adult behavior determines personality outcomes in interaction with the developmental stage of the infant. The detailed analysis of adult-infant interaction as a system of mutually regulated and synchronized behaviors, intensively studied through observational techniques, is better paired with behavioral or ethological theories.
B. This is not an accurate pair. Missing is any account of a mental or perceptual basis of the phenomena of attachment. Attachment theory, however, focuses on a system of behavior between caretakers and infants and posits the existence of a bond between them. Parallels between human and animal attachments and the survival value of the system are stressed. These are ethological notions.
C. This is the most accurate pair. Key ideas are the claim that temperament has a biological basis and survival value. An interest in individual differences is also a mark of the biological heritage of ethological theory.
D. This is not an accurate pair. If behavioral theory had motivated research in this area, there would be an analysis of the rewards and punishments currently operating in families or societies to encourage or discourage fathers from taking part in child rearing. However, the focus is a more observational study of what fathers are doing. It is not particularly clear that the material in the chapter derives from any specific theoretical perspective, but the use of animal research to answer the question of whether fathers can parent adequately on their own suggests an ethological influence. Perhaps this material is best described as eclectic or without theoretical basis.
E. This is not an accurate pair. As was the case with item "D," it is not clear that a specific theoretical approach has motivated research on day care. The stimulus appears to be more pragmatic and empirical, namely, the simple need to analyze and evaluate a major change in the early social life of infants that has occurred over the past three decades. Interestingly, the ecological perspective could be used to organize and discuss information in this area, but that has not been done explicitly in this chapter. Also, Belsky, who views families as subsystems of individuals, is a researcher in this area, suggesting that he has done some systems analysis of day care and its effects on children.

Exercise 3

A. This is an inference. It is an explanation offered to account for the observation that infants often cry when they are separated from their mothers.

B. This is the assumption. One indication is Kagan's challenge that attachment is not as important as other researchers think it is. Another is that this point is taken for granted in the text, without justification or evidence. A third is that if researchers did not believe this, so much work would probably not have been invested in studying it.

C. This is a summary of data collected by Sroufe and others in their studies of the correlates of securely and insecurely attached infants. Simply stated, infants who were classified as insecurely attached were later seen to be more likely to fuss, cry, or be angry if they were challenged with a problem or difficult task.

D. This inference is the conclusion of a variety of studies of the causes of attachment in humans and monkeys. Researchers have tested hypotheses about the causes of attachment in experimental and correlational studies. They have concluded from this work that comfort and safety are primary determinants of attachment.

E. This is something seen in both systematic and casual observations of infants. It is one way that researchers and caregivers have seen babies behave in the presence of their mothers.

RESEARCH PROJECT 1: ATTACHMENT BEHAVIORS

In this exercise you will examine attachment behavior using naturalistic observation. Go to a local shopping mall and observe a mother with an infant 12 to 18 months old. Observe for a period of 15 minutes. Describe the behaviors you witness, using the following data sheet. Then answer the questions that follow:

Behaviors   Child Age _____ Sex _____

Talking
Laughing
Tickling
Clinging
Crying
Escaping
Retrieving
Mutual gaze
Hitting
Smiling
Yelling
Generally positive interaction
Generally negative interaction

Questions

1. What kinds of behaviors did your mother-infant couple engage in? Did the infant use the mother as the base for exploration? What was the infant allowed to explore?
2. According to the categories secure and insecure, how did this pair seem? Were interactions generally positive or negative? Did the relationship seem warm and affectionate, or hostile?
3. What kind of parenting style seemed to characterize this pair: authoritarian, authoritative, permissive-indulgent, or permissive-indifferent? Do you think the style is partially determined by the age of the infant? How?

Use in Classroom

Discuss the research project. Have students pool their data. How many of the infants were rated as securely attached? What behaviors led to that classification? How many infants were rated as insecurely attached? What behaviors led to that classification? What parenting styles were represented in this population? What contributed to the classification or parenting styles? Would those be likely to change with the age of the child?

Possible observed behaviors are: protesting a separation when a mother walks around the shopping cart to get something from the shelf, and resistance or ambivalence when the mother picks the child up after paying for the groceries.

The students should be able to observe authoritarian, permissive, and authoritative parenting styles. A mother might be very controlling and slap a hand for reaching for an item on a shelf, she might simply let the child run wild, or she might constantly talk to the child, explaining why taking things is not good. The older the child, the more likely the mother is to use language as a means of controlling the child's behavior, or to include language in the interchange.

RESEARCH PROJECT 2   INFANT TEMPERAMENT

Observe three infants in whatever settings or circumstances are most readily available to you. Record as much of their behavior as you can, but your goal is to classify each infant according to (a) the three types of children identified by Chess and Thomas which are summarized in Chapter 11 of *Child Development*, and (b) the three different dimensions of temperament suggested by Plomin. Therefore, be sure to study these classification systems thoroughly; if you think it is necessary, consult the original sources for each system from the references listed in the back of *Child Development*.

You may use any sort of data sheet that you or your instructor choose, but for each child you should record your observations and decisions in a format like the following:

Infant 1   Sex_____   Age_____

Observations:

Chess and Thomas Classification:	Easy	Difficult	Slow-to-warm-up
Plomin Dimensions:	Low	Medium	High
Emotionality			
Sociability			
Activity Level			

Questions

1. How easy or difficult was it for you to observe relevant infant behavior? Why?
2. Were you able to make the classifications? Why or why not?
3. What did you find out?
4. How would you improve the method you used to do your observations?
5. What would you like to find out about infant temperament using observational methods like these?

Use in the Classroom

Pool the student data in an appropriate table on a blackboard or an overhead. Determine (a) whether one type of infant is more prevalent than the other two; and (b) whether one intensity of temperament dimension is more frequently encountered than others. Lead students in a discussion both of their findings and of the methods they used to collect the data. What concerns them? What would they like to control? How would they like to improve the procedure? Make appropriate suggestions or your own in the discussion.

ESSAY AND CRITICAL THINKING QUESTIONS

Comprehension and Application Essay Questions

We recommend that you provide students with our guidelines for "Answering Essay and Critical Thinking Questions" when you have them respond to these questions. Their answers to these kinds of questions demonstrate an ability to comprehend and apply ideas discussed in this chapter.

1. Define attachment, and compare and contrast the psychoanalytic and ethological theories of attachment.
2. Indicate and explain the individual differences in attachment, and the relationship of early attachment to latter social interactions.
3. Compare and contrast fathers' and mothers' ability to care for infants, and each parent's typical caregiving practices.
4. If your were a parent who could stay home with your children or place them in day care, what factors would you consider in making this decision?
5. Describe the differences among easy babies, difficult babies, and slow-to-warm-up babies.
6. What do the researchers believe about the stability of temperament throughout childhood?
7. Analyze your own temperament. Indicate whether your temperament is better explained by the Chess and Thomas or the Buss and Plomin approach. Also indicate how stable your temperament has been over the course of your development and what factors may have contributed to this stability or lack of stability.
8. Explain how developmentalists have studied emotions in infants.
9. Summarize findings about infant emotions.
10. Describe the three types of infant cries.
11. Describe the typical order of emotional development.
12. Compare and contrast the views of Bowlby, Beck, and Seligman on depression.
13. What is cognitive appraisal, and what is the difference between primary and secondary appraisal?

Critical Thinking Questions

We recommend that you have students follow our guidelines for "Answering Essay and Critical Thinking Questions" when you ask them to prepare responses to these questions. Their answers to these kinds of questions reflect an ability to apply critical thinking skills to a novel problem or situation that is *not* specifically discussed in the chapter. These items most appropriately may be used as take-home essay questions (e.g., due on exam day) or as homework exercises that can be answered either by individuals or groups. Collaboratively answered questions encourage cooperative learning by students, and reduce the number of papers that must be graded.

1. At the end of Chapter 11 Santrock indicates books that provide practical knowledge about children and lists resources for improving the lives of children. Choose one of these books or resources and read it or learn as much as you can about it. Then write a brief review in which you (a) characterize the book or resource, and (b) explain how the book or resource relates to material in the chapter.
2. Chapter 1 defines the nature of development in terms of biological, cognitive, and social processes, and periods or stages. Indicate your ability to think critically by identifying material in this chapter that illustrates developmental processes and periods. If there is little or no information in this chapter about developmental processes and periods, identify and explain how developmental processes and periods could be used to guide the analysis of any topic in the chapter.
3. According to Chapter 1, three fundamental developmental issues concern: (a) maturation (nature) versus experience (nurture), (b) continuity versus discontinuity, and (c) early versus later experience. Indicate your ability to think critically by identifying material in this chapter that illustrates each of the three fundamental developmental issues. If there is little or no information in this chapter about fundamental developmental issues, identify and explain how these issues could be used to guide the analysis of any topic in the chapter.
4. One aspect of thinking critically is to read, listen, and observe carefully and then ask questions about what is missing from a text, discussion, or situation. Indicate your ability to think critically by (a) speculating about why Santrock's discussion about the development of attachment does not include behavioral, ecological, and eclectic accounts, and (b) presenting your own behavioral, ecological, and eclectic accounts for the development of attachment.
5. Santrock sets off several quotations in this chapter. Indicate your ability to think critically by selecting one of the quotes and (a) learning about the author and indicating why this individual is eminently quotable (i.e., what was this individual's contribution to human knowledge and understanding), (b) interpreting and

restating the quote in your own terms, and (c) explaining what concept, issue, perspective, or term in this chapter that Santrock intended this quote to illuminate. In other words, about what aspect or issue in development does this quote make you pause and reflect?

6. Chapter 2 indicates that theories help us explain data and make predictions about various aspects of development. Chapter 2 then presents six different theoretical approaches (i.e., Freudian, cognitive, behavioral and social learning, ethological, ecological, and eclectic theory), but notes that no single approach explains the complexity of development. Indicate your ability to think critically by (a) perusing this chapter for topics influenced by at least one of the six theoretical approaches, and (b) explaining which theoretical approach dominated the topic in question. If the presentation is entirely atheoretical, identify and explain how one of the theoretical approaches could be used to guide the analysis of the topic in question.

7. In this chapter Santrock briefly discusses how policies regarding maternity/paternity leave differ throughout the world. Apply your knowledge about the scientific method by designing a study to determine whether paid maternity/paternity leaves affect childrens' development: (a) What specific problem or question do you want to study? (b) What predictions would you make and test in your study? (c) What measures would you use (i.e., controlled observation in a laboratory, naturalistic observation, interviews and questionnaires, case studies, standardized tests, cross-cultural studies, physiological research, research with animals, or multimeasure, multisource, and multicontext approach) and how would you define each measure clearly and unambiguously? (d) What strategy would you follow--correlational or experimental, and what would be the time span of your inquiry--cross-sectional or longitudinal? (e) What ethical considerations must be addressed before you conduct your study?

8. According to Chapter 2, your author wants you to become a wise consumer of information about child development by: (a) being cautious about media reports, (b) distinguishing between nomothetic research and idiographic needs, (c) recognizing how easy it is to overgeneralize from a small or clinical sample, (d) knowing that a single study is usually not the defining word about some aspect of child development, (e) remembering that causal conclusions cannot be made from correlation studies, and (f) always considering the source of the information and evaluating its credibility. Indicate your ability to think critically by, first, selecting an article from either a journal, magazine, or newspaper about any topic regarding Attachment, Temperament, and Emotional Development, and, second, evaluating it in terms of these six objectives. If the information in the article is insufficient to evaluate one of these objectives, then specify what kind of information you would need to evaluate the objective.

12   The Self and Identity

SUGGESTIONS FOR LECTURE TOPICS

1.   Self concept

A discussion of the development of self-concept could center around Coopersmith's (1967) work with 10- and 12-year-old boys. He identified four factors that contribute to self concept:

   a. significance—how much is a person loved and approved of by others.
   b. competence—how well does a person perform tasks he or she considers to be important.
   c. virtue—to what extent does a person feel he or she has attained the expected moral standards of their culture.
   d. power—how well and to what extent can a person control himself or herself and his or her influence on others.

Coopersmith found that those who believe they possess these qualities had higher self-esteems than those who did not.
   After defining the term and discussing the factors, students may want to know what they can do to ensure that their children develop a strong sense of self. Coopersmith suggests that to foster self-esteem, parents can do the following:

   a.   try to keep their own esteems high
   b.   communicate concern and interest to their child
   c.   encourage interaction with the child
   d.   engage in joint activities
   e.   use reinforcement rather than punishment to reinforce rules
   f.   encourage self-reliance and independent behavior tempered with protection from too much pressure

2.   Erikson's identity struggle

Erik Erikson's own identity struggle provides an interesting example of identity crisis. One can begin Erikson's story of his own identity struggle at its resolution. Erikson's identity was confirmed when he named himself—Erik, son of Erik. Erikson's father abandoned Erik and his young mother shortly after Erik's birth. He was raised by his Jewish stepfather (Dr. Homburger) and grew up as a Jew in the public school system and as a goy (blond hair and blue eyes) in Hebrew school. Erikson did not find out until high school that he was adopted and that his father had abandoned him. As a young man Erikson wandered around Europe as an artist, searching for himself and his work. Through a connection with a high school friend, Erikson landed a job as a teacher in a school set up for children in therapy and children of parents in therapy or in training to be therapists with Sigmund and/or Anna Freud. While working at this school Erikson became a certified Montessori school teacher and a psychoanalyst. With the approach of a Nazi army, Erikson and his new wife Joan left for the United States. On entering the United States, after finding himself as a teacher and a therapist, he took the final step in claiming his identity—he named himself, Erik Homburger Erikson.

3.   Research on Identity: Erikson to Marcia

Erik Erikson's ideas about identity development during adolescence are the standard concepts used to organize and integrate diverse aspects of adolescent social development. They form a complex conceptual network that Erikson himself admits is not transparent. However, textbook treatments are necessarily brief and often distort or misrepresent the concepts. Although Santrock's treatment is accurate, it is brief, and a more detailed presentation may help clarify and deepen students' understanding of the theory.
   Give a lecture that is directly based on Erikson's writings collected in *Identity: Youth and Crisis* (1986). You will find that the first two or three essays give a full treatment of Erikson's ideas about identity. Quote them liberally as you characterize the richness, complexity, and ambiguity of Erikson's ideas. Notice how Erikson actually refuses to define the concept in a compact way, and explore his reasons for doing so. Notice also that he offers several pithy characterizations of identity. Other interesting observations include his original idea that the identity

crisis was entirely an unconscious process, but that modern fascination with the idea has almost mandated that it be excruciatingly conscious.

As rich as Erikson's ideas are, the problem with them is that they are not operationalized in ways that appeal to researchers. With publication of his doctoral thesis in 1966, James Marcia changed things. Marcia proposed and demonstrated that a valid and reliable interview could yield a four-way classification of identity status derived from Erikson's theory. The textbook mentions Marcia, but links the importance of Marcia's work to the continued influence of Erikson's theory. Flesh out your lecture with a sampling of quotes from Marcia's research report. You may also wish to informally explore your students' identity statuses as part of the in-class activity suggested below.

Marcia's work has been criticized. If you have time, explore some of the modifications by Hal Grotevant and others.

4.   Alfred Adlers' Disability Compensation and Depression

According to psychoanalytic theorist Alfred Adler, depressed persons suffer from **disability compensation,** i.e., they try to lean on others by exaggerating their own inadequacies. Depressed persons exaggerate the hazards of living while striving for unrealistic lofty goals. When they fail to reach these unreachable goals, the depressed persons blame others and their life circumstances for the failures. In other words, the depressed individuals express anger at not getting their own way and also express contempt for others. By choosing grandiose aspirations that can rarely be achieved, depressed individuals are doomed to failure. Then, they deal with failure by using alibis, evasions, and self-bemoaning, and by extorting sympathy and sacrifices from others. Depressed persons go to great lengths to prove to others how sick and disabled they are and, therefore, manage to escape many social obligations, and do not fairly reciprocate friendships. (*Sources:* Adler, K. A. 1961. Depression in the light of individual psychology. *Journal of Individual Psychology, 17,* 56-67; Ansbacher, H. L. & Ansbacher, R. R. 1956. *The Individual Psychology of Alfred Adler.* New York: Harper.)

5.   Having or Being

In his last book, *To Have or To Be,* Erich Fromm (1976) wrote "As long as everybody wants to have more, there must be formations of classes, there must be class war, and in global terms, there must be international war. *Greed and peace preclude each other."* (p. 6)

Modern society provides people with the expectation that unlimited production and unlimited consumption are possible and even desirable. Most people believe having more things will lead to higher self-esteem, more self-satisfaction, and increased happiness. In contrast, Fromm concluded:

a.   Unrestricted possessions do not make people feel well or happy or meaningful. Radical hedonism, the pursuit of maximum pleasure, does not satisfy human nature and tends to alienate people from harmony and peace.

b.   Rather than gaining freedom and independence through possessions, many individuals feel lost in the work environments necessary to obtain those possessions.

c.   Ideas and preferences are manipulated by mass communication, industry, and government.

d.   Rich nations are able to acquire more and more while poor nations become poorer and poorer.

e.   The processes involved in making things and building things create environmental dangers, and these processes are bringing such rapid change that people are continually stressed.

(*Source:* Fromm, R. 1976. *To have or to be?* New York: Harper & Row.

BROWN & BENCHMARK'S HUMAN DEVELOPMENT TRANSPARENCIES (2ND ED.)

Transparency Number and Title

The transparency set, a supplement to *Child Development*, is accompanied by an annotated manual that describes each of the 141 transparencies. The annotated manual also offers suggestions about how to use the transparencies to engage your students in active learning that will stimulate critical thinking and evaluative skills. The following transparencies are appropriate and useful with Chapter 12: The Self and Identity.

CLASSROOM ACTIVITIES OR DEMONSTRATIONS

1.   Discuss the critical thinking exercises. The point of Exercise 1 is to have students attend to the methodological pitfalls of research on identity and self-concept, especially because of the emphasis on intervention that follows in the wake of these topics. For example, even Santrock appears to fall into traps here, because right after he issues a warning about correlational research in understanding the relationship between parenting characteristics, he appears to give a causal interpretation to research on correlations between peer support and self-esteem that he discusses in the next chapter!

    In any event, you will probably want to review the earmarks of the various types of research. Students quickly seem to forget these if they do not rehearse them. One way to teach them would be to help them determine which types of research generated some of the findings in the chapter.

    Just as exercise 1 stimulates a review of important concepts from chapter 2, so also does exercise 2 promote a review of material in chapter 1. Erikson's theory provides an excellent opportunity to illustrate developmental concepts. You may want to review the five developmental issues with your students prior to assigning this exercise.

    Exercise 3 is another exercise in identifying givens in theorizing that may establish important limits on hypotheses researchers entertain. For example, self-esteem could be an expression of temperament. Extreme cases of low self-esteem may be caused by a biologically based depression. If you are feeling generous, suggest to students that they are looking for a belief that appears to limit the sorts of hypotheses researchers are entertaining about the causes of low or high self-esteem.

2.   Discuss the students' research projects as suggested below.

3.   Have students write down their ideas about the physical characteristics of the ideal male and female, including height, weight, hair color and length, eye color, physical proportions, and amount of body hair. (Some classes initially protest this exercise and yet when they go along with the instructor they have as many definite ideas about the ideals as do other classes).

    Now ask students to rate themselves from 0 to 10, with 10 the ideal, on how closely they match the ideal for their own sex. Collect the responses and have a few students summarize the results (e.g., calculate average heights and weights and provide frequency distributions for the various physical characteristics). Have these students present the results to the class.

    Do people tend to rate themselves high or low? Why? How do the physical ideals compare with the statistics of average physical characteristics in this country (e.g., taller, weigh less)? How does physical attractiveness affect the way we interpret another's behavior (e.g., "beautiful is good" hypothesis)? How does physical attractiveness affect our interpersonal attraction levels? How have physical ideals affected our lives and our self-evaluations? How have physical ideals changed over the years?

Source: Simons, J. A., Irwin, D. B., & Drinnin, B. A. 1989. *Instructor's Manual to Accompany Psychology, the Search for Understanding.* St. Paul: West Publishing.

---

4.   The subjective self can be described as our global impressions of ourselves, and the objective self can be defined as how others see us. This exercise requires students to list their self-characteristics and to identify

those that have been revealed to other class members. Students are also asked to list the observed characteristics of other class members. The instructor then collects all the feedback sheets and reads them aloud anonymously, while the students try to guess who is being described. The students' comparisons between their subjective selves and their objective selves can provide an excellent opportunity for insight.

Walraven, M. G. 1993. *Instructor's Course Planner* to accompany John Santrock's *Adolescence*, 5th ed. Dubuque, Ia: Brown and Benchmark, Publishers

5. The Q-sort method of self-concept assessment is another classroom activity that you can use to distinguish between the real and the ideal self-concept. Using this method you hand out fifty cards containing adjectives to each student and instruct them to sort the cards into piles describing themselves as they are today (e.g., pile 1 = very characteristic of me; pile 2 = very uncharacteristic of me). Then you ask them to sort the cards as they would like to be. The two sortings are then compared. You can point out to students that this technique can be used to evaluate the stability of self-concept and to evaluate the efficacy of therapeutic outcomes.

Walraven, M. G. 1993. *Instructor's Course Planner* to accompany John Santrock's *Adolescence*, 5th ed. Dubuque, Ia: Brown and Benchmark, Publishers

6. Here is an activity in which students can compare their real and ideal selves:

    1. Using complete sentences, write a list of your limitations and faults (e.g., "I smoke cigarettes," "I'm 20 pounds overweight," "I procrastinate on written assignments," "My nose is too large.").
    2. Rewrite the statements in terms of ideal self and real self (e.g., "My ideal self is a nonsmoker," "My ideal self weighs 20 pounds less," "My ideal self does written assignments promptly rather than at the last minute," "My ideal self has a smaller nose.").
    3. Look at this second group of statements. Are your ideals realistic? Which ones now seem most important? What can you do to move toward your ideal self descriptions? Do you wish to modify your behaviors or your attitudes toward yourself?

Source: Frager, R. & Fadiman, J. 1984. *Personality and personal growth.* 2nd edition. New York: Harper & Row.

7. Santrock discusses the developmental precursors of positive self-concept and self-esteem in children and adolescents. An activity dealing with this topic is asking students to write a one-paragraph sketch of the low self-esteem child, and then providing them with the following clinically and empirically derived portrait:

distrusts others	responds inappropriately to criticism or
feels like a loser	flattery
feels rejected and mistreated	negative about competition
blames others for her problems	hypercritical of others
tries to appear big in others' eyes (fronting)	poor self-discloser
bluffs and cons people	won't try new things

Walraven, M. G. 1993. *Instructor's Course Planner* to accompany John Santrock's *Adolescence*, 5th ed. Dubuque, Ia: Brown and Benchmark, Publishers

8. Many individuals fail to distinguish between self-acceptance and self-esteem. **Self-acceptance** is the unconditional acceptance of self regardless of behavior or others' approval. **Self-esteem** is the valuing of

self because of competent, correct, or intelligent behavior. Many individuals focus on self-esteem and label themselves either good or bad. Individuals may be better off to focus on self-acceptance.

Some therapists believe that a primary goal of the counseling process is client self-acceptance. Individuals who do not value themselves develop a variety of other problems: overfocusing on faults, inefficient problem-solving, exaggeration of faults, living to get approval from others, self-destructive behaviors, suicidal ideation, avoidance behaviors, psychosomatic disorders, sabotaging of self-improvement attempts, immersion in a fantasy world, obsession with comparing self with others, great guilt, living for short-term pleasures rather than long-term goals, lack of self-discipline, severe depression, hostility, achieving only to achieve status, and exaggeration of self-role behaviors.

Is self-acceptance the most important life goal? Is self-acceptance more important than self-esteem? Why do you believe your position? Do you think that self-acceptance will lead to thinking, feeling, and behaving better? How might counseling from different theoretical perspectives help clients accept themselves?

Sources: Ellis, A. 1977. Psychotherapy and the value of a human being. In A. Ellis & R. Grieger (Eds.). *Handbook of Rational-Emotive Therapy.* New York: Springer; Rogers, C. 1961. *On becoming a person.* Boston: Houghton Mifflin.

---

9. Have students in small groups recall their personalities at age 8 to 9 (3rd or 4th grade), and describe their personalities at age 13 to 14 (8th or 9th grade). If they have difficulty doing this, ask them how they responded in certain situations in 4th grade: for example, going to a birthday party, going out to dinner with their families, buying something from a salesclerk in a store, asking their teachers questions, or playing on the playground with other children. Thinking about their behaviors in certain situations may allow them to generate descriptions of themselves at that age. Have them think about situations during junior high school to generate a second description. How did they change? What remained the same? Were there changes in personality from middle elementary school to junior high that are common to many or all students? What are these? What influences in their lives might have promoted change?

Source: Adapted from King, M. B. & Clark, D. E. (1989). *Instructor's Manual to Accompany Santrock and Yussen's Child Development: An Introduction,* 4th ed. Dubuque, IA: Wm. C. Brown.

---

10. Marcia (1980) expanded on Erikson's description of the conflicts encountered at the identity versus identity confusion stage. Four types of resolution are described: identity diffusion, identity foreclosure, identity moratorium, and identity achievement. The resolutions vary on two dimensions, the presence or absence of a crisis and the presence or absence of a sense of commitment to an identity. After describing each type of resolution, students should be able to give examples of people experiencing the different resolutions. To test their ability to do so, you may want to give them some examples and ask them to identify the status of the adolescent in the scenario.

   a. Marsha is a 14-year-old who, when asked what she wants to do when she graduates from high school, replies, "Maybe I will get married and have some children, or maybe I will be a neurosurgeon, or a fashion designer." (identity moratorium)

   b. Seventeen-year-old Suzanne is questioning the tenets of the religion in which she was brought up. She is, for the first time, examining her beliefs and considering other belief systems. At the end of the period, she chooses to follow the same religion as her parents. (identity achievement)

   c. Lorraine is 16 years old, and when asked what she wants to do when she graduates from high school, replies, "I never really thought about it. I guess I will decide when the time comes." (identity diffusion)

   d. After Bill graduates from high school, he plans to go into his father's business. He has been talking this over with his parents since he was a preschooler and is eager to fulfill his parents' expectations. (identity foreclosure)

   e. Richard was asked to debate issues concerning premarital sex in his health class. His parents always taught him that premarital sex was wrong and that they would be very disappointed if they discovered that he had participated. After thoroughly investigating the consequences of premarital sex, Richard came out against it. (identity achievement)

Source: Temple, Lori L. 1992. *Instructor's Course Planner to accompany Life-span Development,* Fourth Edition by John W. Santrock, William C. Brown Communications, Dubuque, Iowa

11.   Do people have one self or many selves? One identity or many identities? The answer for most of the history of mainstream American psychology as been "One" to both questions. Indeed, when the answer is "Two or more" the predominant view is that such an individual is mentally ill or under extreme stress. Nevertheless, there is a growing movement that suggests that people's selves are not necessarily composed of one integrated entity, but rather that people may in fact be whole collections of several relatively unintegrated selves. Try this idea out on your students as a counter to Erikson's ideas. Have them discuss it; have them share experiences that have suggested to them that they are less integrated than they thought they were supposed to be. You can flesh your own understanding of the idea out and develop a more formal lecture on the topic by consulting the following sources: Cushman, P. (1990). Why the self is empty: towards a historically situated psychology. *American Psychologist, 45,* 599-611; Gergen, K. J. (1991). *The Saturated Self.* New York: Basic Books; Sampson, E. E. (1990). The decentralization o f identity. *American Psychologist, 45,* 1203-1211.

CRITICAL THINKING EXERCISES

Exercise 1

An important theme of chapter 12 is that it is possible to intervene in the lives of children in ways that will help teenagers form integrated self-concepts, acquire positive self-esteem, and develop clear senses of identity. An important step toward justifying this claim is evaluating the kinds of research that support such a claim. Which type of research appears to define the bulk of research reviewed in chapter 12? **Circle the letter of the best answer and explain why it is the best answer and why each other answer is not as good.**

A. case studies
B. observational studies
C. correlational research
D. experimental research
E. It is not possible to tell from the text.

Exercise 2

Erikson's theory of identity development is a *tour de force* of developmental thinking. It illustrates virtually all of the developmental issues outlined in chapter 1 of *Child Development* under the topic of "The Nature of Development" Which of the following statements represents Erikson's position on these issues least well? (You may wish to review relevant material in chapter 2 to do this exercise.) **Circle the letter of the best answer and explain why it is the best answer and why each other answer is not as good.**

A. Biological, cognitive, and socioemotional processes contribute to identity development.
B. There are stages in the development of identity.
C. Identity development results from both maturation and experience.
D. The development of identity is continuous.
E. Early experience plays a role in identity development.

Exercise 3

Chapter 12 describes several of the causes and correlates of self-esteem in adolescents. Which of the following appears to be an assumption most researchers in this area make, as opposed to an inference or an observation? **Circle the letter of the best answer and explain why it is the best answer and why each other answer is not as good.**

A. High self-esteem is associated with parental expression of affection.
B. Peer support influences self-esteem in adolescents than it does in children.

C. Some youth with low self-esteem come from conflicted families.
D. Intervention must occur at the level of causes of self-esteem.
E. The causes of self-esteem are experiential rather than genetic or maturational.

ANSWER KEYS FOR CRITICAL THINKING EXERCISES

Exercise 1

A. This is not the best answer. Santrock does rely on a few case studies to illustrate the material. For example, Erikson's analysis of Hitler, Luther, and Ghandi is a series of case studies; and the discussion of identity development among Native American youth relies on a case study. But the majority of work appears to come from systematic assessment of large numbers of youths in comparative or experimental research.
B. This is not the best answer. The only indication that observational research figures in the study of the self and identity is Figure 12.3, which lists behavioral indicators of self-esteem. The rest of the chapter describes questionnaire and interview measures of this and other constructs.
C. This is the best answer. Most of the work described in the chapter describes comparisons of the self-concept, self-esteem, or identity of adolescents who inhabit different situations (e.g., families, peer relations) or have different other characteristics (e.g., achievement, gender, ethnicity). This work is essentially correlational.
D. This is not the best answer. No experimental work seems to be cited in chapter 12.
E. This is not the best answer, though one might make an argument that it is the second best answer. The phrase (or words of similar meaning) "research shows" appears often in this chapter. That is, findings are summarized with too little information to indicate what type of research generated the results. Nevertheless, over the whole chapter, there is enough information to suggest that correlational research is the dominant type in the study of self and identity.

Exercise 2

A. This is not the best answer. (Remember, we are looking for the least accurate statement!) Erikson specified genetic bases of identity development, which is based on an active cognitive processing of socioemotional experience.
B. This is not the best answer. The development of identity begins at birth, even though it is not the focus of personality development until adolescence according to Erikson's theory.
C. This is not the best answer. As indicated in (A) above, nature and nurture both have a role in Erikson's theory.
D. This is the best answer. Erikson's account, do be distinguished from research findings such as the Watermans' work, indicates that identity has precursors in earlier developmental stages, but that these precursors are different in kind, complexity, and organization. For example, prior to adolescence a child's sense of self is a mix of identifications with other people in the child's life. The formation of an identity results in a sense of self that is not simply the final quantitative refinement of these previous identifications, but a new integration and organization of them.
E. This is not the best answer. As indicated above, the nature of an individual's identity depends on resolutions of all of the previous four crises in the life cycle of an individual.

Exercise 3

A. This is not the best answer. This statement expresses the finding of a correlation between parenting characteristics and adolescents' self-esteem, which is an observation.
B. This is not the best answer. This is an inference about the presumed reason that peer support is more highly correlated with self-esteem in adolescents than it is with self-esteem in children.
C. This is not the best answer. This is an observation: researchers have noted this fact in assessments of children from conflicted families.
D. This is not the best answer. This is Susan Harter's conclusion based on research concerned with attempts to improve self-esteem, and hence it is an inference.
E. This is the best answer. Nowhere in chapter 12 does the possibility that biological factors play a role in self-esteem arise, and it seems that researchers do not look for biological factors as possible causes. For example, when Susan Harter looks for causes of self-esteem, she looks for them in the areas that adolescents themselves regard as most important to their senses of self. Thus she and other researchers appear to assume that biological factors are irrelevant. (A possible exception to this is the importance   of appearance to self-esteem among

adolescents. But the Harter, at least, refers to this as "perceived" appearance, which appears to emphasis the subjective rather than the objective evaluation of this dimension.)

RESEARCH PROJECT 1   DEVELOPMENT OF SELF IN INFANTS

This project examines the development of the self in infants. You will test an 8-month-old infant and an 18-month-old infant with a mirror recognition task. Two tasks will test for mirror recognition of the self and of an object near the infant. Then answer the questions about your observations. The task descriptions, worksheet, and questions follow.

Task 1:   Have the mother stand behind the infant and hold an attractive toy above and slightly behind the infant's head, so that the infant can see the toy in the mirror but cannot see the toy itself. Record whether the infant reaches for the reflection of the toy in the mirror or turns around and reaches for the toy itself.

Task 2:   For one minute, count the number of times the infant touches his or her nose while looking in the mirror. Then have the mother put a dab of rouge on the infant's nose, and turn the infant back toward the mirror. For the next minute count the number of times the infant touches its nose and the number of times it touches the reflection of its nose. Use the following worksheet for your data.

DATA SHEET

	Child 1	*Child 2*
	Sex _____ Age _____	Sex _____ Age _____

Task 1

    Reaches to mirror

    Reaches to toy

Task 2

    Touches mirror

    Touches nose

Questions

1. Does the 8-month-old infant reach for the object? Does the 18-month old reach for the object? Does either infant reach for the reflection of the toy in the mirror? If so, which infant?
2. How does the 8-month-old infant react to his or her image in the mirror with the rouge on his or her nose? How does the 18-month-old infant react to the image in the mirror with the rouge on the nose? Do the infants of different ages react differently? Explain this difference.
3. Is there a difference in the development of the ability to recognize the self and the ability to recognize an object in a mirror? If so, why would this be?

Use in Classroom

Have students present the data from the research project. Divide the data by age and sex of the subjects. Evaluate the data for age and sex differences. Do the infants solve both tasks at the same age? If so, what age? If not, which task is solved first? What would account for the age differences in behavior? What is developing? What cognitive, social, and biological factors might account for the developmental change?

The younger child will probably be oriented to the mirror for both tasks. That is, he or she will attend to the spot on the nose of the reflection and the reflection of the toy behind. Both the rouge spot on the nose and the real toy are likely to be ignored or discovered accidentally. The older child is likely to be oriented to the self for the rouge and to the toy behind him or her. He or she is likely to touch the spot on his or her nose and turn around to look at the real toy. Sex differences are unlikely to emerge.

Maturation of the nervous system and visual system, the appearance of mental representation and symbolic abilities, and experience with mirrors might all be factors in this development.

RESEARCH PROJECT 2 MARCIA'S STATUSES OF IDENTITY

This project examines Marcia's statuses of identities in college students (18 to 20 years old). Interview ten college students (if you are 18 to 20, you may be a subject), and have them identify their current identity status. Then answer the questions that follow.

Subjects:

1.   Choose which of the statements here best reflects you currently:
   A.   "I believe that I have made commitments to my future career and life. A while back, however, I had a rough time deciding what I wanted to do with my life."
   B.   "I really don't know what I want to do with my life, but I am trying to make up my mind about my options. I guess I'm having an identity crisis."
   C.   "I know what commitments I am going to make in my life. Seems like I always have known where I'm heading. I can't remember it being very difficult to decide."
   D.   "I really don't know what I want to do with my life, but I'm not losing any sleep over it. Sometime I'll decide what I want to do, but not right now."

DATA SHEET

Subject Choice	Sex	Age	Statement
1	F/M	18/19/20	A/B/C/D
2	F/M	18/19/20	A/B/C/D
3	F/M	18/19/20	A/B/C/D
4	F/M	18/19/20	A/B/C/D
5	F/M	18/19/20	A/B/C/D
6	F/M	18/19/20	A/B/C/D
7	F/M	18/19/20	A/B/C/D
8	F/M	18/19/20	A/B/C/D
9	F/M	18/19/20	A/B/C/D
10	F/M	18/19/20	A/B/C/D

Questions

1.   How did your ten students break down by identity achievement (A), identity moratorium (B), identity foreclosure (C), and identity diffusion (D)?
2.   Do female and male subjects tend to give the same responses?

3.   Do you think you would get similar answers if you used 18- to 20-year-old subjects who were not enrolled in college? Married young adults? Parents?

Use in Classroom

Have students pool their data. What is the most typical identity status? Least typical? Are there any sex differences? What identity statuses do your class members remember going through? How did different identity statuses affect emotions? Self-confidence? Self-esteem?

ESSAY AND CRITICAL THINKING QUESTIONS

Comprehension and Application Essay Questions

We recommend that you provide students with our guidelines for "Answering Essay and Critical Thinking Questions" when you have them respond to these questions. Their answers to these kinds of questions demonstrate an ability to comprehend and apply ideas discussed in this chapter.

1.   Compare and contrast the ideas of self-understanding and self-recognition. Illustrate your answer with examples.
2.   Summarize the development of self-understanding from early childhood through adolescence, giving examples of the changes.
3.   Lay out your personal self-understanding, and demonstrate to what extent your own self-understanding illustrates the seven dimensions of self-understanding detailed by Santrock in chapter 10 of *Adolescence*.
4.   Explain the role of perspective-taking in self-understanding.
5.   Describe the variety of ways developmentalists measure self-esteem, and indicate how one might use them in research on self-esteem.
6.   Describe factors that are related to self-esteem, and evaluate the idea that research has shown these factors to be causal influences on self-esteem.
7.   What are the basic concepts of Erikson's theory about identity development? Explain why Erikson's ideas about identity are complex.
8.   Define Marcia's idea of identity status and explain how it differs from Erikson's concept of identity.
9.   Describe how identity changes in terms of the identity statuses from high school through college.
10. Explain how families are thought to influence identity formation.
11. Compare and contrast identity development in ethnic minority youth versus White American youth.
12. Compare and contrast identity development in males versus females.

Critical Thinking Questions

We recommend that you have students follow our guidelines for "Answering Essay and Critical Thinking Questions" when you ask them to prepare responses to these questions. Their answers to these kinds of questions reflect an ability to apply critical thinking skills to a novel problem or situation that is *not* specifically discussed in the chapter. These items most appropriately may be used as take-home essay questions (e.g., due on exam day) or as homework exercises that can be answered either by individuals or groups. Collaboratively answered questions encourage cooperative learning by students, and reduce the number of papers that must be graded.

1.   At the end of Chapter 12 Santrock indicates books that provide practical knowledge about children and lists resources for improving the lives of children. Choose one of these books or resources and read it or learn as much as you can about it. Then write a brief review in which you (a) characterize the book or resource, and (b) explain how the book or resource relates to material in the chapter.
2.   Chapter 1 defines the nature of development in terms of biological, cognitive, and social processes, and periods or stages. Indicate your ability to think critically by identifying material in this chapter that illustrates developmental processes and periods. If there is little or no information in this chapter about developmental processes and periods, identify and explain how developmental processes and periods could be used to guide the analysis of any topic in the chapter.
3.   According to Chapter 1, three fundamental developmental issues concern: (a) maturation (nature) versus experience (nurture), (b) continuity versus discontinuity, and (c) early versus later experience. Indicate your ability to think critically by identifying material in this chapter that illustrates each of the three fundamental

developmental issues. If there is little or no information in this chapter about fundamental developmental issues, identify and explain how these issues could be used to guide the analysis of any topic in the chapter.

4.   One aspect of thinking critically is to read, listen, and observe carefully and then ask questions about what is missing from a text, discussion, or situation. For example, self-concept and identity appear to be highly cognitive in nature, such that it would seem that their development would be related to the development of formal operations. But no there is no information about this in chapter 12. Indicate your ability to think critically by (a) listing as many questions as you can about possible relationships between cognitive development and the development of self-concept and identity, and (b) speculating why Santrock does not discuss this topic more fully.

5.   Santrock sets off several quotations in this chapter. Indicate your ability to think critically by selecting one of the quotes and (a) learning about the author and indicating why this individual is eminently quotable (i.e., what was this individual's contribution to human knowledge and understanding), (b) interpreting and restating the quote in your own terms, and (c) explaining what concept, issue, perspective, or term in this chapter that Santrock intended this quote to illuminate. In other words, about what aspect or issue in development does this quote make you pause and reflect?

6.   Chapter 2 indicates that theories help us explain data and make predictions about various aspects of development. Chapter 2 then presents six different theoretical approaches (i.e., Freudian, cognitive, behavioral and social learning, ethological, ecological, and eclectic theory), but notes that no single approach explains the complexity of development. Indicate your ability to think critically by (a) perusing this chapter for topics influenced by at least one of the six theoretical approaches, and (b) explaining which theoretical approach dominated the topic in question. If the presentation is entirely atheoretical, identify and explain how one of the theoretical approaches could be used to guide the analysis of the topic in question.

7.   Question 4 above suggest that there may be a relationship between cognitive development and the development of identity. Apply your knowledge about the scientific method by designing a study that will determine whether and what this relationship is: (a) What specific problem or question do you want to study? (b) What predictions would you make and test in your study? (c) What measures would you use (i.e., controlled observation in a laboratory, naturalistic observation, interviews and questionnaires, case studies, standardized tests, cross-cultural studies, physiological research, research with animals, or multimeasure, multisource, and multicontext approach) and how would you define each measure clearly and unambiguously? (d) What strategy would you follow--correlational or experimental, and what would be the time span of your inquiry--cross-sectional or longitudinal? (e) What ethical considerations must be addressed before you conduct your study?

8.   According to Chapter 2, your author wants you to become a wise consumer of information about child development by: (a) being cautious about media reports, (b) distinguishing between nomothetic research and idiographic needs, (c) recognizing how easy it is to overgeneralize from a small or clinical sample, (d) knowing that a single study is usually not the defining word about some aspect of child development, (e) remembering that causal conclusions cannot be made from correlation studies, and (f) always considering the source of the information and evaluating its credibility. Indicate your ability to think critically by, first, selecting an article from either a journal, magazine, or newspaper about any topic regarding The Self and Identity, and, second, evaluating it in terms of these six objectives. If the information in the article is insufficient to evaluate one of these objectives, then specify what kind of information you would need to evaluate the objective.

13 Gender

SUGGESTIONS FOR LECTURE TOPICS

1. Researching Gender Roles

When they study gender roles, psychologists have tended to emphasize gender differences. Scientific observations start with the assumption that males are reason-oriented and females are emotion-oriented. In doing this, psychologists have followed prevailing cultural beliefs that male and female are opposites, that women are the vassals of nonmasculine traits, and that gender differences are based on biological differences (Hare-Mustin & Marecek, 1986). Yet, which would be a longer list: a list of how females and males are different or a list of how females and males are similar?

On the other hand, when not directly observing gender roles, psychologists have sometimes ignored gender differences. Prior to the 1970s, many research studies used male subjects and generalized the results to all people. Since the male norms were most valued within the society, all human behavior was measured on the basis of the male norm. Psychology needs to develop research that neither overestimates gender differences (called an **alpha bias**) nor underestimates gender differences (called a **beta bias**). "Paradoxes arise, because every representation conceals at the same time it reveals. For example, focusing on gender differences marginalizes and obscures the interrelatedness of women and men, as well as the restricted opportunities of both. It also obscures institutional sexism and the extent of male authority . . . [On the other hand, the beta bias attempt at denying differences reaffirms male behavior as the standard against which all behavior is judged.]" (Hare-Mustin & Marecek, 1988, p. 462). Both psychology and society are in the process of learning how to think more constructively about gender roles. (*Source:* Hare-Mustin, R. T. & Marecek, M. 1988. The meaning of difference: Gender theory, postmodernism, and psychology. *American Psychologist, 43,* 455-464.)

2. Measuring Gender-Role Orientation

A review and analysis of attempts to create developmental measures of gender-role orientation over the past 40 years is an excellent vehicle for teaching about the foibles and successes associated with psychologists' attempts to develop measures of complex characteristics and traits. Present a lecture in which you discuss the evolution of contemporary ideas about gender-role orientation and associated measurement techniques. Your aim is to explore and clarify difficulties researchers have had in developing clear, reliable, and valid measures of the construct. You may also want to comment on such issues as the stability of gender roles in development, multiple perspectives on gender-role development, and how different theoretical orientations produce different measures.

You may wish to begin with a brief class discussion about how researchers or practitioners can identify children's gender-role orientations. Your class should be able to generate some of the ideas that have been tried, and you may enjoy working with them to develop these into possible measures.

Having done that, trace some of the main approaches. Begin with the classic It Scale, an attractively simple device, but one plagued with interpretive difficulties. Discuss procedures rooted in the social learning and cognitive traditions.

A useful source for additional ideas is the second edition of *Children* (see Chapter 13, pages 434-439). Santrock outlines several developmental, conceptual, and methodological issues that are important to understanding measures of gender-role orientation.

3. The Four Rules of Male Gender-Role

Both boys and girls believe that male gender-role deviations are more serious than female gender-role deviations (Smetana, 1986). Traditionally, males are taught four strong rules about their gender-role (David & Brannon, 1976):

a. "No sissy stuff." This rule encourages boys to be as different from girls as possible (e.g., "Don't be a baby and don't be a girl.").
b. "Be a big wheel." This rule encourages boys to be superior to others and to compete rather than to cooperate (e.g., "Winning is everything.").
c. "Be a sturdy oak." This rule encourages male independence and self-reliance, but may also keep boys from asking for help when they need help and from feeling comfortable with their emotions (e.g., "Big boys don't cry.").

d.   "Give 'em hell." This rule encourages boys to be power-oriented, aggressive, ruthless and even violent (e.g., "My dad can whip your dad.").

(*Sources:* David, D. S. & Brannon, R. 1976. *The forty-nine percent majority: The male sex role.* Reading, MA: Addison-Wesley; Smetana, J. G. 1986. Preschool children's conceptions of sex-role transgressions. *Child Development, 57,* 862-871.)

4.   A Sociobiology Viewpoint on the Gender Differences in Sexuality

According to Symons (1979), humans, like other species, inherit characteristics that maximize their personal transmission of genes to the next generation. For women, who can only pass on their genes in a small number of children, investing in the survival of their children is crucial. Men, however, can father many children. Therefore, the following gender differences are "wired-in":

a.   Men desire many sex partners; women do not.
b.   Men's nature is polygamous; women are more inflexible.
c.   Men are sexually jealous; women want security more than fidelity.
d.   Men are sexually aroused by women's appearance; women are not as sexually aroused by men's appearance.
e.   Men are biologically programmed to pursue many women to be able to impregnate many; women are biologically programmed to be hesitant and coy so they can assess the male's genetic risk, nurturance, and willingness to protect.
f.   Men are more competitive, and competitiveness over women is the number-one cause of violence.
g.   Men are programmed to think youth and beauty are sexually attractive; women think political and economic power is sexy.

Do students like this theory? Do they believe that gender differences in sexuality are biologically based? Why or why not? Can they think of alternative explanations for these gender differences? If the sociobiological position is correct, would it be possible to reduce these gender differences? How? Would changes be made differently if these gender differences were not learned? (*Source:* Symons, D. 1979. *The evolution of human sexuality.* New York: Oxford Press.)

5.   Gender Differences as Social Interactions

Sex differences seem to be minimal when looked at in terms of individual differences, but increase when researchers look at social interactions between pairs of small children. Several studies show that preschool children have higher levels of social behavior when playing with a same-sex partner than when playing with an opposite-sex partner. Moreover, passive behavior is greatly increased for a small girl when she plays with a boy than when she plays with another girl. In fact, in girl-girl pairs passive behavior seldom occurs—less than occurs in boy-boy pairs (Maccoby, 1990).

By 4-1/2 years, children show a definite preference for same-sex playmates. This preference is stronger at 6-1/2, when children spend eleven times as much time with same-sex as opposite sex partners (Maccoby & Jacklin, 1987). Gender segregation is found cross-culturally and in a variety of settings. This preference resists change from adults.

Children choose same-sex playmates spontaneously in situations without adult pressure. This gender segregation, however, is not closely linked to engaging in sex-typed activities. Segregation occurs even during gender neutral play. This same-sex preference is also unrelated to how children score on measures of masculinity or femininity.

Maccoby (1990) suggests two main reasons for this sex-segregation: (1) boys are more oriented toward rough-and-tumble play, competition, and dominance and many girls find this aversive, and (2) girls have difficulty influencing boys. Girls try to influence others almost entirely by making polite suggestions to others; boys, however, influence others by direct demands. Boys become less responsive to polite suggestions, and therefore are barely influenced by girls (Serbin et al., 1984). Girls may simply not want to interact with boys who are unresponsive to their requests and they initiate boy partners first (Maccoby, 1990).

Who stays closer to the teacher—girls or boys? The correct answer is: It depends. In same-sex groups, all-girl groups actually stayed farther from the adult than did all-boy groups. But, when the groups were mixed, girls tended to stay closer to the adult than did the boys. Why? When boys demand concessions from girls, adults tend to keep it fair.

Although it's hard to determine the causes of preschool boy and girl differences in influencing others, these differences create more sex-segregation and allow differences in play styles, friendship patterns, and negotiation to grow throughout the school years (see Maccoby, 1990). (*Sources:* Maccoby, E. E. 1990 (April). Gender and relationships: A developmental account. *American Psychologist,* 513-520; Maccoby, E. E. & Jacklin, C. N. 1987. Gender segregation in childhood. In H. W. Reese (Ed.). *Advances in child development and behavior.* (Vol. 20, pp. 239-288). New York: Academic Press; Serbin, L. A., Sprafkin, C., Elman, M., & Doyle, A. 1984. The early development of sex-differentiated patterns of social influence. *Canadian Journal of Social Science, 14,* 350-363.)

6.   A Sociobiological Explanation for Male Spatial Skills Superiority

If you are not a sociobiologist, you might suggest that males average higher in spatial skills because as boys they had more opportunities to watch and help their fathers build and fix things. Girls who were interested in spatial skills were not reinforced for their interests and learned to adapt their interests in other areas.

But a sociobiologist would suggest that this sex difference is rooted in biological differences. Research by Steven Gaulin has found that spatial skills superiority is not just limited to the human species. For example, male rats typically run through mazes more quickly than female rats. Gaulin suggests that in many species males have good navigational skills because it helps them find more mates.

To test this sociobiological explanation, Gaulin did research with voles, burrowing rodents that look like furry mice. He compared the maze-running abilities of the polygynous meadow voles with the monogamous prairie voles. Because of their mating and territorial habits, meadow voles cover a large territory in which numerous females have small territories, and Gaulin thought male meadow voles would need to be good at processing spatial information. However, the monogamous male prairie voles live with their mates within a small territory, and excellent spatial abilities would not be as important for survival.

Gaulin found that male meadow voles outperform female meadow voles on seven different mazes, but that no sex difference was found for the prairie voles. For male meadow voles, the voles with the best spatial abilities had the most mates and passed their genes down through the generations, improving this ability. (*Source:* Gadsby, P. 1990 (April). Wanderlust. *Discover,* 24.)

7.   Researching Gender Roles

When they study gender roles, psychologists have tended to emphasize gender differences. Scientific observations start with the assumption that males are reason-oriented and females are emotion-oriented. In doing this, psychologists have followed prevailing cultural beliefs that male and female are opposites, that women are the vassals of nonmasculine traits, and that gender differences are based on biological differences (Hare-Mustin & Marecek, 1986). Yet, which would be a longer list: a list of how females and males are different or a list of how females and males are similar?

On the other hand, when not directly observing gender roles, psychologists have sometimes ignored gender differences. Prior to the 1970s, many research studies used male subjects and generalized the results to all people. Since the male norms were most valued within the society, all human behavior was measured on the basis of the male norm. Psychology needs to develop research that neither overestimates gender differences (called an **alpha bias**) nor underestimates gender differences (called a **beta bias**). "Paradoxes arise, because every representation conceals at the same time it reveals. For example, focusing on gender differences marginalizes and obscures the interrelatedness of women and men, as well as the restricted opportunities of both. It also obscures institutional sexism and the extent of male authority . . . [On the other hand, the beta bias] attempt at denying differences reaffirms male behavior as the standard against which all behavior is judged." (Hare-Mustin & Marecek, 1988, p. 462). Both psychology and society are in the process of learning how to think more constructively about gender roles. (*Source:* Hare-Mustin, R. T. & Marecek, M. 1988. The meaning of difference: Gender theory, postmodernism, and psychology. *American Psychologist, 43,* 455-464.)

8.   The Lower Expectations of Female Students

A study of 265 fourth- and fifth-graders by Myrna Whigham had findings consistent with others in that it found that girls rate themselves lower than do boys and give themselves less credit for their achievements. When asked why they do well in science and math, girls are apt to say it is due to cooperative work with other students while boys are more likely to credit themselves and their ability. Fathers are more likely to think that their sons are better in math (and more likely to get an A) while girls are more likely to be good in reading.

A study of 3000 freshmen entering Iowa State University found that male students rated themselves higher than females in academic ability, originality, emotional health, physical health, popularity, and self confidence in social skills. Male students only rate themselves lower than females in writing ability. Moreover, 70 percent of male freshmen but only 55 percent of female freshmen rated their intelligence as above average. (*Source:* Carter, K. (January 30, 1993). Female pupils lack confidence. *Des Moines Register.* p. 1.)

BROWN & BENCHMARK'S HUMAN DEVELOPMENT TRANSPARENCIES (2ND ED.)

Transparency Number and Title

The transparency set, a supplement to *Child Development*, is accompanied by an annotated manual that describes each of the 141 transparencies. The annotated manual also offers suggestions about how to use the transparencies to engage your students in active learning that will stimulate critical thinking and evaluative skills. The following transparencies are appropriate and useful with Chapter 13: Gender.

Transparency Number and Title

10	Biological, Cognitive, and Socioemotional Processes in Life-Span Development
24	Bandura's Model of the Reciprocal Influence of B, P, and E
25	Bronfenbrenner's Ecological Model
26	Psychoanalytic Theories
27	Cognitive Theories
28	Ethological Theories
29	Ecological Theories
35	The Genetic Difference between Males and Females
36	Genotypes and Environments
95	Comparing Cognitive Development and Gender Schema Theories of Gender Development
96	Visuospatial Abilities of Males and Females
97	Gender Role Classification

CLASSROOM ACTIVITIES OR DEMONSTRATIONS

1. Discuss the critical thinking exercises. Exercise 1 is the first exercise that requires students to use the guidelines for being a wise consumer of information about adolescent development, and they may be surprized that they should apply these guidelines to textbook material. You may thus want to introduce the exercise with (a) a review of the guidelines, and (b) a discussion about the fact that the guidelines need to be applied to any information students encounter about adolescent development. You might also point out that previous discussions and exercises have identified occasional shortcomings in the text, and that it behooves them to be on their guard and think critically about everything that they learn.

   Exercise 2 is another in a series of exercises that have asked students to integrate material across sections of chapters. We recommend simply that you be sure that students understand the concepts relevant to carrying out the exercise.

   Exercise 3 represents a combination of the types of assumption, observation, and inference exercises that students have encountered in previous chapters. This exercise points up that a theoretical assumption has practical consequences in terms of instruments that researchers create to measure theoretical constructs. You might point out to students that that is what they are looking for, a theoretical bias that has influenced how researchers measure gender role orientations or classifications. This exercise could dovetail nicely with the lectured suggested on the same topic.

2. Discuss the students' research projects as suggested below.

3. This classroom activity involves a procedure used in Inga Broverman's research (see Broverman, I., et al (1972). Sex-role stereotypes: a current appraisal. *Journal of Social Issues, 28,* 59-78). Divide the class randomly into thirds, asking one-third to describe a competent women, one-third to describe a competent man, and one-third to describe a competent adult. Each group is then given bipolar adjective scales (e.g., gentle-rough, tactful-blunt) to formulate their descriptions. The class then analyzes the result. Are competent adults described in masculine terms?

   Broverman found that most of her competency or instrumentality items were masculine-oriented, while most of the warmth-expressive items were feminine oriented. You can emphasize some of Santrock's comments about androgeny and competence, and you might point out certain dilemmas associated with traditional sex roles. For example, traditional males are often "unsexed" by failure, while traditional females are "unsexed" by success. Patterns of dominance and dependency may lead to problematic heterosexual relationships as well. A good way to conclude your comments could be to read the Berkely Men's Center Manifesto from the *Journal of Social Issues, 34,* 110.

Walraven, M. G. 1993. *Instructor's Course Planner* to accompany John Santrock's *Adolescence,* 5th ed. Dubuque, Ia: Brown and Benchmark, Publishers.

---

4. Divide the class into small groups and have the groups plan a preschool that would maximize the development of varied sex roles in adolescents. What factors need to be taken into account? What data presented in the book are relevant?

5. For years there has been a tremendous amount of debate over gender differences in development. To facilitate the students' understanding of the difficulty in determining which traits provide consistent sex differences and which ones do not, assign them a trait and send them off in search of the evidence. Students should be paired up and each pair assigned one trait. They should come back with evidence for and against sex differences, and they should be asked to evaluate the evidence and indicate whether or not they think there are differences.

   Some possible traits might include motor development (i.e., gross and fine motor skills), verbal abilities, spatial abilities, mathematical abilities, school performance, achievement motivation, emotional expression, compliance, dependency, activity level, and aggression.

6. Have students discuss how parents reward and punish boys and girls differently and thereby contribute to gender differences in behaviors, beliefs, and so forth. Have them provide specific examples.

   Parents, especially mothers, act fairly consistently toward boys and girls, but the subtle differences contribute to gender-typed behavior. For example, parents are more favorably responsive to girls talking about emotions and feelings than they are toward boys. In fact, they may give negative responses to boys who act or talk about being sad.

   Parents are also more negative toward sons who act dependent than to daughters who act dependent.

   Parents are more likely to punish sons for misbehavior. They also allow sons to be more independent and expect less compliance.

Sources: Russell, G. & Russell, A. 1987. Mother-child and father-child relationships in middle childhood. *Child Development, 58,* 1573-1585; Fuchs, D. & Thelen, M. H. 1988. Children's expected interpersonal consequences of communicating their affective state and reported likelihood of expression. *Child Development, 59,* 1314-1322.

---

7. Have students pair up and do a role-taking task, with males playing the female role and females playing the male role. This activity can allow each sex to try to understand the feelings of the other in certain situations. Have them roleplay situations like the following:

   a. A male is drunk at a party. He wants to drive home, but his sober girlfriend wants to drive instead.
   b. A girl becomes pregnant and tells her boyfriend.
   c. A female is transferred from her job to another city and tells her husband.
   d. A male is transferred from his job to another city and tells his wife.
   e. A woman wants to go to work but her husband is against it, and they are trying to settle the conflict.
   f. A girl asks a guy out. Or, a guy asks a girl out.
   g. A husband loses his job and tells his wife. Or, a wife loses her job and tells her husband.
   h. A boss makes advances on a worker.
   i. A husband wants another child but his wife does not.
   j. A boy wants to live with a girl but the girl wants marriage. Or, a girl wants to live with a boy but the boy wants marriage.
   k. A girl picks up a boy in a bar. Or, a boy picks up a girl in a bar.

These tasks, if done well, allow the students to empathize with the opposite sex. It is expected that the roleplaying will most likely be stereotyped, with males portrayed as dominant and independent and females as emotional and dependent. It is also predicted that in the worker scenes, the male's job situation will take priority over the female's. Students may attempt to simplify these situations by having the female stay home and have a family.

Source: Adapted from King, M. B. & Clark, D. E. 1989. *Instructor's Manual to accompany Santrock and Yussen's Child Development: An Introduction,* 4th ed. Dubuque, IA: Wm. C. Brown.

---

8. A number of theorists have suggested that intimacy is the goal of young adulthood. Some feminist psychologists have talked about this in terms of connections and webs of relationships. Carol Gilligan and a groups of researchers at the Harvard Center for the Study of Gender and Development see finding oneself and valuing oneself within the context of connectedness as a growing edge of women. (A growing edge is a personal frontier of knowledge.) With this theoretical perspective in mind, and with the individuation index and the interview schedule from *Women's Ways of Knowing* as guides, here is a connectedness index: Have students respond to the following questions:

    a. List several relationships that have been important to you over the past several years.
    b. How have these relationships helped to shape who you are?
    c. How have you helped to shape these persons who helped to shape you?
    d. List two situations in which you solved a problem that took your own needs into consideration along with the needs of the other people involved in the problem.

Source: Morehouse, R. E. & Vestal, L. B. 1994. *Instructor's Manual with Test Item File to accompany Human Development*, Second Edition, by John Dacey and John Travers. Dubuque, William C. Brown Communications, Inc.

---

9. Changing gender-typed behaviors have occurred in two directions. One trend has been to free children (and adults) from rigid gender-typed patterns, thereby allowing them more androgynous choices. The other trend has been to train **gender-deviant** children, mostly boys, to exhibit more appropriate gender-typed behaviors. Gender-deviant boys are boys who both prefer traditionally feminine activities and avoid traditionally masculine activities (Huston, 1983). Obviously, such strategies are controversial. What do you think is appropriate?

Source: Huston, A. C. 1983. Sex-typing. In P. E. Mussen (Ed.). *Handbook of child psychology.* 4th ed., Vol. 4. New York: Wiley.

---

10. Have students state their opinions about whether "traditional" mother-wife women, career women, or **superwomen** who combine aspects of both lifestyles are mentally healthiest. Why do they choose their positions?
     Here are some conclusions of research studies done in the 1980s that can be added into the discussion:

     • Women experience substantially more change than men in the transition to parenthood.
     • The transition to parenthood is particularly stressful for working-class women and working mothers who are rearing difficult infants or infants with continuing health problems.
     • Mothers tend to blame themselves for anything that goes wrong in their children's lives.
     • Role strain is decreased when husbands approve of and support their wives' choices.
     • Role strain is increased when women are dissatisfied with child-care arrangements.
     • Most couples do not reassign household responsibilities such as shopping, cleaning, cooking, and ironing with equity when both partners have outside employment.
     • Mental health seems to be more affected by marital satisfaction than by job satisfaction.

- For women, work often buffers marital stress but parenthood exacerbates occupational stress.
- Coping is associated with high income, high job satisfaction, not marrying early, and being able to arrange time for family activities.
- Multiple roles are associated with superior health, an autonomous sense of self, and self-rating one's lifestyle positively.
- Problems can accumulate across roles, but just as likely participation in multiple roles can cancel some of the negative events generated by a specific role.
- When the additional role of caring for elderly parents in one's home is added, the result is often a hampered career, emotional stress, financial hardship, strained personal relationships, and decline in physical health.

By 1990, articles were suggesting that "working mothers" and "stay-at-home mothers" were battling with each other over who was better off, doing better for their kids, having more fulfilling lives. Mixed messages to women about their "proper roles" and "supermom expectations" lets this mommy conflict be laden with frustration, insecurity, jealousy, and guilt. The Darton (1990) article provides lots of examples and quotations for discussion. In the discussion, note how our language is devoid of terms like "superdad" and "working daddy vs. stay-at-home daddy." Do you think, perhaps, that women focus on other women when they ought to be dealing with how to share and complement roles with the fathers?

Sources: McBride, A. B. 1990 (March). Mental health effects of women's multiple roles. *American Psychologist, 45,* 381-384; Darton, N. 1990 (June 4). Mommy vs. Mommy. *Newsweek,* 64-67.

---

11. Use this chart to begin discussion about students attitudes about women's careers.

	1972	*1985* (Male, Female)
No work after marriage	12%	2% (2%, 0%)
Interrupted work option (to have children)	40%	48% (48%, 54%)
Minimal career involvement after children	38%	9% (9%, 1%)
Continuous career involvement	4%	33% (33%, 32%)
No marriage option	____	7% (7%, 3%)

Source: Phillips, S. D. & Jonston, S. L. 1985. Attitudes toward work roles for women. *Journal of College Student Personnel, 26,* 334-338.

---

12. Have students discuss what they know about the history of sex discrimination in this country (e.g., when women couldn't vote, the origin of the saying "a thumb's rule" had to do with the size of a stick with which husbands could beat women, differences in salaries) and how much progress the country has made in the twentieth century. See if students think that progress is being made.

Use this quote by former Supreme Court Justice Brennan: "There can be no doubt that our Nation has had a long and unfortunate history of sex discrimination. Traditionally, such discrimination was rationalized by an attitude of `romantic paternalism' which, in practical effect, put women not on a pedestal, but in a cage." (Frontiero vs. Richardson, 1973). Did former laws put women in a cage, or was it on a pedestal?

Source: Magnuson, E. 1990 (July 30). Right turn ahead? *Time,* 16-18.

---

13. Most Americans have multiple roles—work, family, schooling, and so on. How do males and females cope with having a variety of goals? Have class members provide examples.

Introduce the ideas of Eccles (1987), who claims that women worry about reconciling their career and personal goals while men tend to compartmentalize their goals. What about their socialization leads to this gender difference? How is it exhibited, for example, by behaviors within the family (e.g., men don't say, "I'm not sure if I want to have children because it will interfere with my career.")?

Source: Eccles, J. S. 1987. Gender roles and women's achievement-related decisions. *Psychology of Women's Quarterly, 11,* 135-172.

14.   Ask students about their preferences for daughters or sons, and the reasons for their preferences. Are there differences in preferences between (1) parents and non-parents; (2) young, middle, or older adults; (3) females and males; (4) different ethnic or racial groups? If differences do exist, how might they be explained?

    Enhance the discussion with examples of gender preferences in other cultures. For example, Bumiller (1990) writes about the Indian blessing "May you be the mother of a hundred sons." India is a culture that puts much pressure on women to produce sons instead of daughters. Daughters represent huge financial problems for families, as there will be a need to go into debt for a dowry. Girls receive less education, less medical care, and less food than do boys. Women's work includes field work, housework, cooking, tending cows, making cow-dung cakes for fuel, and hauling water. Girls are often married before their adolescence, and beatings are a fairly routine aspect of marriage.

Source: Bumiller, E. 1990. *May you be the mother of a hundred sons.* New York: Random House; Shapiro, L. 1990 (June 25). Millions of daughters. *Newsweek,* 57.

CRITICAL THINKING EXERCISES

Exercise 1

At the end of Chapter 2 of *Child Development* Santrock presents some guidelines for being a wise consumer of information about adolescent development. Study the pairings of guidelines and research findings presented in Chapter 11 below, and decide which pair is most apt (that is, which pair represents an appropriate criticism of the information presented in the chapter). **Circle the letter of the best answer, and explain why it is the best answer and why each other answer is not as good.**

A. A single study is usually not the defining word: the psychological and behavioral differences between boys and girls become greater during early adolescence.

B. Causal conclusions cannot be made from correlational data: In a study of 4th, 6th, and 8th grade boys and girls in schools, boys were involved in more interactions with their teachers than were girls.

C. It is easy to overgeneralize from small or clinical sample: American citizens believe that the federal government should promote programs that reduce unequal educational opportunities for females.

D. Distinguish between nomothetic research and idiographic needs: About 70 percent of prime-time characters on television were males during the 1970s.

E. Consider the source of information and evaluate its credibility: The claims of Robert Bly.

Exercise 2

In Chapter 13 Santrock presents evidence that an intensification of gender differences between boys and girls occurs during early adolescence. This is an example of a concept discussed elsewhere in the chapter. Which is it? **Circle the letter of the best answer, and explain why it is the best answer and why each other answer is not as good.**

A. biological influences
B. gender-role stereotyping
C. developmental windows of gender opportunity
D. asymmetric gender socialization
E. gender-role transcendence

Exercise 3

In this chapter Santrock describes attempts to define and measure gender roles. Which of the following statements constitutes an assumption made by gender role researchers, rather than an inference or an observation? **Circle the letter of the best answer, and explain why it is the best answer and why each other answer is not as good.**

A. Girls should grow up to be feminine and boys should grow up to be masculine.
B. Gender-role stereotypes are more harmful to females than to males.
C. Femininity and masculinity are separable aspects of personality that have their own unique characteristics.
D. Androgynous individuals are more flexible and mentally healthy than masculine or feminine individuals.
E. Rather than merge gender roles, females and males should transcend gender-role characteristics.

ANSWER KEYS FOR CRITICAL THINKING EXERCISES

Exercise 1

A. This is not the best answer. Santrock cites at least two or three studies that support this claim.
B. This is not the best answer. Santrock does not say that the relationship is causal.
C. This is not the best answer. This information comes from a Gallup Poll, which presumably relies on a large, representative sample of American citizenry.
D. This is not the best answer. The estimate appears to be based on a comprehensive survey of television shows, not on someone's own experience or personal observations of the shows.
E. This is the best answer. Bly's qualifications as a credible informant on men's issues is not established in the text; he is only identified as a literary man. Neither are Bly's claims about the society since the Industrial Revolution buttressed with authoritative sources. Thus we are given no reason to believe that Bly is a credible commentator on men's issues in gender role development.

Exercise 2

A. This is not the best answer. Gender intensification is not said to be brought on by biological changes, but rather by socialization pressures (social processes).
B. This is not the best answer. Although gender intensification results in boys and girls acting out stereotypes, the process itself is not an example of stereotyping. The main point is that it occurs at a specific point in an adolescents' life, which makes (D) the better answer.
C. This is the best answer. Among other things, Santrock cites gender intensification as an example. The idea is that early adolescence is an especially important time for the socialization of gender role behavior.
D. This is not the best answer. The material in the text suggests that boys and girls experience and express gender role intensification equally.
E. This is not the best answer. This concept does not apply at all. Gender role intensification involves an enhanced focus on what it means to be male or female, the exact opposite of the idea of gender-role transcendence.

Exercise 3

A. This is an assumption, but it is not one that is made by gender researchers today. Santrock mentions this point as being an assumption held by previous generations of researchers.
B. This is an inference. It is based on the observation that males enjoy more favorable gender stereotypes, which (logically) suggests that they will be less harmed by them than women. However, the actual claim is not supported in the chapter with direct evidence.
C. This is the assumption. This belief led researchers to develop separate scales for masculinity and femininity. However, the belief itself has not been independently confirmed, and the text does not present either argument or evidence for its validity.
D. This is an observation. The statement is presented as a description of individuals who are classified as androgynous.

E.   This is an inference. It is the conclusion of Pleck's argument that gender-role classifications create false dichotomies or contrasts, and that individuals are actually unique and must resolve gender issues on their own terms.

RESEARCH PROJECT 1   GENDER ROLES AND TELEVISION

In this project, you will be required to evaluate three prime-time television shows for gender role stereotyping. **Pick three shows between 8:00 and 9:00 EST that children might watch.** For each show record the following information: (1) number of male and female main characters; (2) occupations of main male and female characters; (3) thematic connections between males and females (e.g., female in distress and male as rescuer); (4) personality characteristics of one male and one female from the show (use the Bem androgyny scale to determine masculinity, femininity, or androgyny). Use the following data sheet to record information. Then answer the questions that follow.

DATA SHEET

Program _____   Male_____   Female_____

Number

Occupations

Connections

Gender Classification

Questions

1.   In the shows you watched, were more main roles taken by males or females? What kinds of occupations did the males have? What kinds of occupations did the females have? Were there status differences in the occupations of the males and females? What were they?
2.   What kinds of themes connected the males and females in the television programs you watched? Were the themes stereotyped for male-female relationships?
3.   What were the sex-typed categories of the males portrayed on television: (masculine, cross-sexed, androgynous)?
4.   What were the sex-typed categories of the females portrayed on television: (feminine, cross-sexed, androgynous)?
5.   What do you think these models are teaching children about what it means to be a male or a female in our society? Do you think these models are a fair representation of the way women and men act in the real world?

Use in Classroom

Have students present their information from the research project in class. Examine the data overall, looking at: (1) the relative number of males and females in primary roles; (2) the relative status of the males' and females' occupations; (3) the thematic relationships presented between males and females, and the extent to which these tie into sex stereotyping; and (4) the relative presentation of androgynous, cross-sexed, and sex-stereotyped males and females on television. Ask the students to examine specific programs for differences. Are some shows more stereotyped than others? Which ones are less stereotyped? In the stereotyped programs, is one sex portrayed as more advantageous or as better than the other? Which one? How do the class data relate to the data on stereotypes presented in the text? If the programs generally support gender-role stereotypes, how does this affect the developing child? If males are presented as the more interesting and preferred sex, could this account for the tomboyish behavior of girls in middle childhood? How?

It is expected that there are still more males than females represented, and that the males have higher-status occupations. Frequently women are still portrayed as the romantic interest or the damsel in distress who must be rescued by the male. The majority of males and females portrayed on television are sex-typed rather than androgynous, and the data would be expected to show this.

These models present children with an idea of what it is to be a man or a woman in our culture. To the extent that the male role is more valued and interesting, it could provide a model of activities for both females and males, and may contribute to the tomboyish behavior of girls in middle childhood.

RESEARCH PROJECT 2 COLLEGE STUDENT GENDER-ROLE CLASSIFICATIONS

Table 11.1 in *Adolescence* presents items from the Bem Sex Role Inventory (BSRI). For this project you will use this inventory to determine the gender-role classifications most common among students you know on your campus.

Have five women and 5 men whom you know respond to the items of the inventory, following instructions given in Table 11.1, either reading the items from your text or from a duplicate of the inventory that you prepare for them to complete (can you think of problems associated with having participants respond to the items from the text?). When one of your participants completes the inventory you can score it immediately according to instructions in the table and discuss the result. Or you can score the inventory later. In either case, when you have collected data from all of your respondents, assemble them in a table that breaks down scores on the masculinity and femininity items for both males and females. Calculate a mean and a standard deviation for each of the four columns of data that you will have.

Next, again following the instructions in the table, classify the gender roles of each of your subjects. Then create a two by four contingency table that shows the number of men and women who fall into each of the four gender role classifications.

Prepare a brief report which contains your tables and answers to the following questions:

Questions

1. What were your expectations about the masculinity and femininity scores? The gender-role classifications of men and women? Why?
2. Did your results confirm your expectations?
3. How does what you have learned from collecting and analyzing these data compare to information in your text?
4. What are important limitations on your conclusions?
5. Are you satisfied that this is a good way to measure gender-role orientation? Why or why not?

Use in Classroom

If you may want to have students compare each other's findings, have them read each other's reports in small groups and note where they obtained similar and different results. Groups can then report what they learned to the class. Or you can have several students present their findings to the class, and have the class do comparisons among the reports.

You can also tally the data some or all of the individuals collected in appropriate tables on a blackboard or overhead. Present and analyze (or have the class analyze) these pooled results. Find out if everyone's results were the same as the grand result, and discuss deviations from it. Use the student's reports as a basis to discuss issues in the measurement of gender roles, perhaps in the context of lecture suggestion 2 above.

ESSAY AND CRITICAL THINKING QUESTIONS

Comprehension and Application Essay Questions

We recommend that you provide students with our guidelines for "Answering Essay and Critical Thinking Questions" when you have them respond to these questions. Their answers to these kinds of questions demonstrate an ability to comprehend and apply ideas discussed in this chapter.

1. Compare and contrast the various theories of gender role development; cite data, if it is available, that confirms or disconfirms each theory.
2. What evidence is there that nature and nurture influence gender roles? Discuss and evaluate the evidence presented in *Child Development*.
3. Explain the difference between identification and a social learning theory, and cite the major social influences on gender role.
4. Discuss and cite evidence for cognitive influences on gender role development.

5. Define the concept of gender-role stereotype and discuss whether stereotypes influence the development of gender role.
6. Distinguish the ideas of gender role and sex difference, and indicate the nature and causes of sex differences as they are understood today.
7. Explain the idea that opportunities for gender role development are not equal for boys and girls
8. Explain how researchers measure and classify gender roles.
9. Describe and explain developmental trends in gender differentiation during adolescence.
10. Define androgeny and gender role transcendence, and explain why some researchers prefer one or the other concept.
11. Explain why Jean Baker Miller and others have developed a distinct feminist perspective on female gender role development.
12. Compare and contrast women's and men's gender issues.

Critical Thinking Questions

We recommend that you have students follow our guidelines for "Answering Essay and Critical Thinking Questions" when you ask them to prepare responses to these questions. Their answers to these kinds of questions reflect an ability to apply critical thinking skills to a novel problem or situation that is *not* specifically discussed in the chapter. These items most appropriately may be used as take-home essay questions (e.g., due on exam day) or as homework exercises that can be answered either by individuals or groups. Collaboratively answered questions encourage cooperative learning by students, and reduce the number of papers that must be graded.

1. At the end of Chapter 13 Santrock indicates books that provide practical knowledge about children and lists resources for improving the lives of children. Choose one of these books or resources and read it or learn as much as you can about it. Then write a brief review in which you (a) characterize the book or resource, and (b) explain how the book or resource relates to material in the chapter.
2. Chapter 1 defines the nature of development in terms of biological, cognitive, and social processes, and periods or stages. Indicate your ability to think critically by identifying material in this chapter that illustrates developmental processes and periods. If there is little or no information in this chapter about developmental processes and periods, identify and explain how developmental processes and periods could be used to guide the analysis of any topic in the chapter.
3. According to Chapter 1, three fundamental developmental issues concern: (a) maturation (nature) versus experience (nurture), (b) continuity versus discontinuity, and (c) early versus later experience. Indicate your ability to think critically by identifying material in this chapter that illustrates each of the three fundamental developmental issues. If there is little or no information in this chapter about fundamental developmental issues, identify and explain how these issues could be used to guide the analysis of any topic in the chapter.
4. One aspect of thinking critically is to read, listen, and observe carefully and then ask questions about what is missing from a text, discussion, or situation. For example, Chapter 13 presents psychoanalytic, learning, and cognitive accounts of gender role socialization, but omits any explicit ecological or ethological account. Indicate your ability to think critically by (a) formulating an ecological or ethological accounting of influences on gender role development, and (b) speculating why Santrock does not discuss these topics more fully.
5. Santrock sets off several quotations in this chapter. Indicate your ability to think critically by selecting one of the quotes and (a) learning about the author and indicating why this individual is eminently quotable (i.e., what was this individual's contribution to human knowledge and understanding), (b) interpreting and restating the quote in your own terms, and (c) explaining what concept, issue, perspective, or term in this chapter that Santrock intended this quote to illuminate. In other words, about what aspect or issue in development does this quote make you pause and reflect?
6. Chapter 2 indicates that theories help us explain data and make predictions about various aspects of development. Chapter 2 then presents six different theoretical approaches (i.e., Freudian, cognitive, behavioral and social learning, ethological, ecological, and eclectic theory), but notes that no single approach explains the complexity of development. Indicate your ability to think critically by (a) perusing this chapter for topics influenced by at least one of the six theoretical approaches, and (b) explaining which theoretical approach dominated the topic in question. If the presentation is entirely atheoretical, identify and explain how one of the theoretical approaches could be used to guide the analysis of the topic in question.
7. An interesting topic not included in chapter 11 is the gender role development of gay and lesbian adolescents. Apply your knowledge about the scientific method by designing a study that will explore a specific gender issue in a comparison of homosexual and heterosexual teenagers: (a) What specific problem

or question do you want to study? (b) What predictions would you make and test in your study? (c) What measures would you use (i.e., controlled observation in a laboratory, naturalistic observation, interviews and questionnaires, case studies, standardized tests, cross-cultural studies, physiological research, research with animals, or multimeasure, multisource, and multicontext approach) and how would you define each measure clearly and unambiguously? (d) What strategy would you follow--correlational or experimental, and what would be the time span of your inquiry--cross-sectional or longitudinal? (e) What ethical considerations must be addressed before you conduct your study?

8.   According to Chapter 2, your author wants you to become a wise consumer of information about child development by: (a) being cautious about media reports, (b) distinguishing between nomothetic research and idiographic needs, (c) recognizing how easy it is to overgeneralize from a small or clinical sample, (d) knowing that a single study is usually not the defining word about some aspect of child development, (e) remembering that causal conclusions cannot be made from correlation studies, and (f) always considering the source of the information and evaluating its credibility. Indicate your ability to think critically by, first, selecting an article from either a journal, magazine, or newspaper about any topic regarding Gender, and, second, evaluating it in terms of these six objectives. If the information in the article is insufficient to evaluate one of these objectives, then specify what kind of information you would need to evaluate the objective.

14   Moral Development

SUGGESTIONS FOR LECTURE TOPICS

1.   Morality and Politics

Some critics of Kohlberg's theory of moral reasoning have suggested that his insistence on the invariance of the sequence of moral development reflects a liberal political bias. Kohlberg believed that development must go from stage 3 to 4 and then to 5 and to 6, but stage 4 seems to reflect conservative politics to a degree while stage 5 is more aligned with liberal political positions. Therefore, Kohlberg appeared to believe that liberals were more morally advanced than conservatives (Simpson, 1987).

However, another way to conceptualize Kohlberg's theory is that all individuals develop from stage 2 to stage 3, but after stage 3 the other stages represent three alternatives to systematic thinking. Under this model, the first three stages are all prepolitical stages in which there is no systematic vision, and individuals do what is good rather than what is right. The last three stages are political stages in which systematic thinking is done from one of three perspectives (Simpson, 1987).

Stage 4 is called a conservative position and centers around the concepts of "law and order," authority, fixed rules, social order, duty, private property, and preservation of regulations. Stage 4 is the most common adult morality. Stage 5 is called a liberal position in which individuals emphasize recognition of individual rights, promotion of social welfare, and equality of opportunity. Finally, Stage 6 is labeled egalitarian, and in this stage the rights of humanity are emphasized. Stage 6 involves moral principles that center on all people being treated equally and egalitarian conceptions of property (Simpson, 1987).

One study looked at the moral judgment and attitudes of 183 political resisters in the areas of antinuclear politics, draft resisters, and tax resisters. Compared to nonresisters, resisters more strongly rejected political and social authority and believed that individual conscience was a better guide to conduct than were laws. Notice that political resisters espouse views that place them in stage 5 and 6 moral reasoning. In fact, the study found that political resisters measured higher in moral judgment levels (in Kohlberg's framework) than did conservatives (typically stage 4), but not higher than liberals (typically stage 5). Resisters were also more reluctant to have positions that gave them authority over others and were less likely to have conventional religious affiliations (Presley, 1985).

(*Sources:* Presley, S. L. 1985. Moral judgment and attitudes toward authority of political resisters. *Journal of Research in Personality, 19,* 135-151; Simpson, E. 1987. The development of political reasoning. *Human Development, 30,* 268-281.)

2.   Eisenberg's Model of Moral Development

Eisenberg suggests that Kohlberg's model is too rigid; she suggests that children's moral reasoning is not very predictable because children can reason from several different levels rather than using one level and only being able to advance. In Eisenberg's model, the higher levels are found only in older children, but children can use any of the levels for which they are capable. A child who can use high-level abstract reasoning doesn't have to use it.

Eisenberg's model gives equal value to justice-oriented and caring-oriented moral reasoning.
The six levels:

A.   **Self-centered reasoning.** At this level the individual is concerned with consequences to oneself. One may choose to assist or not assist because of (a) personal benefit or loss; (b) the expectation of reciprocity; (c) one needs the other, or likes or dislikes the other. This level is frequently used by preschoolers and early elementary-school children.

B.   **Needs-oriented reasoning.** Concern for the needs is expressed, without role-taking or empathy, even though there may be a conflict with one's own needs. Some preschoolers and many school-age children use this mode of reasoning.

C.   **Stereotyped and/or approval-oriented reasoning.** This level involves stereotyped ideas of good/bad people and good/bad behavior and the desire to win approval. This level is used by some school-aged children and adolescents.

D.   **Empathetic reasoning.** The individual can use some role-taking, empathy, and recognition of the other's humanness. There is awareness of the emotional consequences of helping (feeling good) or not helping (feeling guilty). This is the common level for a few older school-age children and many adolescents.

E. **Partly internalized principles.** Justifications for actions involve internalized values (e.g., concern for others' rights). The ideas are not clearly thought out or strongly stated. This is the common mode for a few adolescents and adults.

F. **Strongly internalized principles.** Justifications for actions are based on strongly-felt internalized values (e.g., wanting to improve society, belief in equality of all). Emotional consequences involve self-respect and living up to one's own values. This form of reasoning is rare.

(*Source:* Eisenberg, N. 1989. The development of prosocial values. In N. Eisenberg, J. Reykowski, & E. Staub (Eds.). *Social and moral values: Individual and social perspectives.* Hillsdale, NJ: Erlbaum.)

3.   Understanding Kid's Lies

Paul Ekman believes that children can invent as many types of lies as grown-ups; children lie to conceal and avoid punishment or to enhance their prestige, and they tell both cruel and kind lies. Unlike Jean Piaget, who believed that children younger than 7 did poorly in distinguishing between fantasy and truth, recent researchers believe that 4-year-olds can tell deliberate lies to get out of trouble. Young children tell lies even though 92 percent of 5-year-olds believe it is always wrong to lie. And although all children tell lies, 28 percent of 11-year-olds still say that they have never told a lie.

Although young children have some concept of lying, children under eight do not always understand that false information may not be lying. If a parent tells a first grader that pictures are being taken at school on Wednesday and the parent is misinformed and the pictures are taken on Thursday, the child thinks the parent has told a lie rather than being confused on dates.

Some children who tell a lot of lies have important psychological problems:

•   They are three times more likely to be treated for psychological problems.
•   In a study done in England, one-third of the chronically lying children ended up being convicted of theft by young adulthood.
•   Children who have the **"machiavellian"** characteristics of being cynical and desiring power often lied to achieve their goals.

On the other hand, children who lied well were often capable of impressing grown-ups more than honest children. Adults rating children from tape recordings rated manipulative children as more honest than less manipulative ones.

Parents who are distressed by their children's lying may try harsh punishment to discourage lying. However, threats of harsh punishment may actually increase the amount of lying. Instead, young children could be read moral stories such as "The Boy Who Cried Wolf," and older children can be engaged in discussions about honesty based on news items. Moreover, parental modeling of honesty can help teach children to tell the truth.

Lies do have some positive value. According to psychologist Michael Hoyt, ". . . the child's first successful lie breaks the tyranny of the parental omniscience . . . the child begins to feel that it has a mind of its own, a private identity unknown to its parents." As teenagers, concealment and misleading peak, partially because adolescents are trying so hard to become independent from their parents. (*Sources:* Ekman, P. 1989. *Why Kids Lie.* Charles Scribner's Sons; Darnton, N. 1989 (October 2). Understanding kids' lies. *Newsweek,* pp. 62-63.)

4.   Violence and Adolescents

The quantity and degree of violence among youth is on the increase (Toufexis, 1989). For example, some youths are voluntarily engaging in "wilding," which involves finding people to torment and hurt for no purpose other than to brutally harm other persons. Nearly 90 percent of Americans think teenage violence is a larger problem today than it was in the past. Do you agree? If so, why? Here's a list of possible causes: genetic factors (among males, testosterone rises rapidly during puberty), family violence (both for modeling violence and for causing neurological damage that may increase violent tendencies), poverty (1 in 5 are raised below the poverty level; perception may be that there are fewer avenues out of poverty now), family neglect (young parents, career parents), failure of education (more than 25 percent of teens drop out of school; even some graduates are functional illiterates), violent television (by age 16, children have seen 33,000 murders and at least 200,000 acts of violence on TV), movies (e.g., increase in sadistic slasher films), recorded music (e.g., heavy metal lyrics which encourage violence including rape and incest), comic books (e.g., bondage, torture, killings), sex in advertising, and lack of positive alternatives. What can help to reduce teenage violence?

One innovative program in Los Angeles has assigned juvenile felons to work with handicapped children as part of probation (Murr, 1990). One hundred five probationers attend classes at the Southeast Community Day Center in Bellflower, where two hours each day are assigned to training, exercising, and feeding 225 disabled children from Pace School. Although 22 failed the program, the more typical result is better school grades and a desire to graduate from high school. (*Sources:* Toufexis, A. 1989 (June 12). Our Violent Kids, *Time,* 52-58; Murr, A. 1990 (May 7). When gangs meet the handicapped. *Newsweek,* 71.)

5.   Excuse Making

When was the last time you used an excuse? If you are typical, it was probably not too long ago. Excuses play a central role in getting along with others and with oneself. Many excuses are lies while others are subjective, biased interpretations of the situation. What purposes do excuses serve? Excuses may be used to help maintain a positive self-image, to keep a good image for oneself, and for the external audience.

Excuses are used in many situations for several reasons. Excuses can be used to disguise an inferior performance or to keep others for reaching negative conclusions about your abilities, skills, or character. Excuses also serve to keep others from objecting that group norms have been violated. Excuses may give people permission to take risks and chances, since they can give an excuse if they fail.

To summarize, two conditions increase the probability that individuals will give an excuse: (1) The probability of giving an excuse increases the more the individual is linked to a bad performance, and (2) The probability of giving an excuse increases the more the performance is seen as negative.

"Anticipatory excuses" are most effective. Excuses that precede poor performance seem more plausible than when the same excuses are used after a poor performance. The student who says "I hope I do all right on this exam—my kids weren't feeling well last night" is seen as more truthful than the student who later says "The reason this score isn't very high is that my kids weren't feeling well last night."

Snyder suggests three forms of excuses. The most elementary type is the "I didn't do it" format. In this type, the excuse-maker is severing causal connection, and the blame is placed on someone else. This form is typical of sports fans who identify with their team when the team wins ("We won!") but not when the team loses ("They lost.")

"It's not so bad" is the second type, and it involves repackaging or reframing maneuvers. This form of excuse usually involves self-deception or things "escaping one's notice." Students may lament, ". . . but I didn't realize it was supposed to be typed, and it is neatly printed." At least three variations of this form exist: (1) The standards may be reworked ("Well, a D isn't so bad on such a hard test," (2) Lower expectations for future performances may be offered ("I may not be able to accomplish as much as I would like in my first political term because my predecessor has left me with such terrible conditions,") and (3) The bad act may be embedded in a larger good context. ("While none of us like economic recession and high unemployment, these unfortunate aspects have put an end to inflation.")

The third type of excuse is the **"Yes, but . . ."** excuse. With this type of excuse, the individual accepts responsibility but weakens the accountability link. The person may claim that others would have done the same or done as poorly ("Well, this isn't a terrible exam score, but did you notice how many Cs the teacher gave out?") Another "Yes, but . . ." excuse is to blame bad luck ("Well, I studied hard for this test, but unfortunately, the teacher asked almost all his questions over the one chapter I had to skim."). "Yes, but . . ." excuses can even include the long-term strategy of presenting oneself as inferior or of little effort ("Well, the reason my score is low is because I just haven't been able to `get into' this semester at all.").

What kinds of excuses do you use? What purpose do these excuses serve? Would the world be a better place if no one used excuses? (*Sources:* Snyder, C. R. 1984 (Sept.). Excuses, excuses. *Psychology Today,* 50-55; Snyder, C. R., Higgins, R. L., & Stucky, R. J. 1983. *Excuses: Masquerades in search of grace.* New York: Wiley.)

6.   Growing Up Worrying about Megadeth

A nuclear holocaust, or **megadeath,** is a twentieth-century concern, and children and adolescents are more concerned about nuclear war than are adults. Nearly one half of young people over 10 believe a nuclear war in their lifetime is probable (Tizard, 1986). Unlike earlier generations, one half worry about nuclear war, and about one fourth have intense anxiety worrying about dying from a nuclear explosion (Tizard, 1986; Hamilton et al., 1987). The effects of this belief are considerable confusion, pessimism, hopelessness, futility, and emphasis on immediate gratification (Yankelovich & Doble, 1984; Escalona, 1982; Abraham, 1983; Schwebel, 1982).

Consider these differences in emotional and cognitive experience from the 1930s until the 1980s. In the 1930s through the 1950s, children's most common fears were personal safety, the dark, thunder and lightning, animals, and supernatural beings. However, from the 1960s on, children's most common fears became political fears, such as war and Communism (Tizard, 1986). Some children worry so much about nuclear war that they often wonder if the plane flying overhead is planning to drop a bomb (Yudkin, 1984). Younger children seem to have more anxiety than older children because they are incapable of understanding the tensions and decisions that would be necessary before nuclear weapons would be used (Tizard, 1986).

However, adolescents, too, are quite concerned about a possible nuclear holocaust. Although many adolescents do not realize that any nuclear weapons were used in World War II, they do seem to understand that survival is unlikely if today's nuclear bombs are used (Tizard, 1986). In a 1982 survey of high school seniors from 130 schools, 35 percent agreed with the statement that "Nuclear or biological annihilation will probably be the future of all mankind within my lifetime." In 1976 only 23 percent of high school seniors had agreed (Bachmann, 1983). The following survey results suggest that nuclear concern among children and teenagers is present in all industrialized countries (Bower, 1985; Tizard, 1986; Yudkin, 1984):

- In a survey of 1,151 students in three large American cities, 40 percent were aware of the possibility of nuclear war by age 12.
- More American (39 percent) than Soviet (12 percent) children think that war will occur in their lifetimes.
- When Finnish teenagers were asked to list their three greatest fears, war finished number one.
- Swedish teenagers were asked to prioritize a list of 14 fears. Nuclear war finished first, ahead of fear of parental death.
- Likewise, a survey in Toronto, Canada found that the number one worry of 37 percent of 12-year-olds was war and peace.

Although nuclear war was a possibility in the 1950s, in that era more children and adults believed that nuclear war was survivable. Schools had **air raid drills** ("Don't forget to duck and cover,") and many families built **bomb shelters,** in which they expected to live in cramped quarters until the environment was once again safe. Today's young and old do not believe that these simple procedures would protect them. The resulting powerlessness over nuclear war may keep some young people from making plans for the future and produce feelings of hopelessness. Some psychologists believe that the increased rate of suicide among teenagers is associated with their belief that war is inevitable.

Children and adolescents of the nuclear age can benefit from attempts to influence the possibility of disarmament and peace. Young people can be encouraged to write letters to the President and other politicians, participate in peace movements, and discuss disturbing political issues with family members (Yudkin, 1984).

A recent study (Hamilton et al., 1987) of 297 college students (average age of 18.7 years; range 17-24 years) and 546 of their parents (average age of 47; range 31-73 years), was conducted concerning views of nuclear war. As expected, the college students were more distressed about nuclear war than were their parents, and they were less likely to believe they could survive a war and less likely to want to be a survivor. On the whole, women were more upset about the nuclear threat than were men. The researchers found nine different orientations about the threat of nuclear war, and these orientations are summarized here:

RM- Romanticist: Human beings are basically good—that is, they are rational, caring, and desire self-preservation for all people. In a nuclear crisis, political leaders will act rationally for the good of all humanity and nuclear war will be prevented.
HD- Hedonist: The best one can do in dealing with the nuclear threat is to concentrate on getting the most pleasure out of life *today*. The focus of attention is best placed on personal pleasure, feeling good, and getting what I want out of life in the time remaining.
ST- Stoic: There is not much anyone can do to prevent a nuclear war or survive it. Yes, there would be casualties and destruction, but some people would survive, eventually rebuild, and life (perhaps even better than it now is) would go on.
DT- Deterrentist: Nuclear war can be prevented through building and maintaining a strong nuclear arsenal. As a result of the balance of power and the recognition that there will be no winners in a nuclear exchange, maintaining our nuclear strength will continue to provide effective deterrents to global conflict.
AF- Altruistic Fatalist: Since I am realistically unable to reduce the threat of nuclear war, why worry about it? The best I can do is to use my available talents and abilities to make the lives of my fellow human beings better and contribute to humanity in the best way that I can.
DA- Disarmist: Nuclear war can be prevented through active, vocal effort on the part of concerned citizens to convince world powers to disarm. There will be no nuclear war if there are no nuclear weapons.

Chapter 14

TH- Theist: Whether or not we have a nuclear war is up to God—I place my full trust in His divine wisdom and guidance. Should nuclear war occur, God will decide what the outcome will be.

EL- Eliminationist: Due to the political stance of the Soviet Union and the fact that the U.S.S.R. cannot be trusted, the best solution is to eliminate the nuclear threat altogether. A prompt, unexpected, first strike by the United States would do away with the Communist menace and preserve life and the democratic ideal throughout the world.

SV- Survivalist: Nuclear war is survivable if appropriate precautions are taken. By investing time, money, and energy into the construction of blast and fallout-proof shelters that will accommodate large groups of people (myself, family, friends) comfortably for several months, we would survive, rebuild, and go on to create a new world.

When the researchers compared the anxiety levels of persons in each of the orientations, they found that some orientations have different outlooks about the future. For example, both **hedonists** and **disarmists** are high in anxiety and are often preoccupied with the nuclear war threat. However, the hedonists are pessimistic about their ability to help reduce the risk of nuclear war, while the disarmists are the most optimistic about their ability to influence a reduction in nuclear war potential. Though both the hedonist and disarmist orientations are typical of females, the women who are disarmists believe their personal influence more than do the hedonists. Although both groups have high anxiety, those who believe they can help prevent nuclear war have a stronger sense of purpose, of a future, and fewer feelings of hopelessness. Males are more likely to be **deterrentists** than are females. Deterrentists believe that nuclear war can be prevented by building nuclear weapon supplies—the "best defense is a strong offense" approach. Persons in this orientation are likely to have lower levels of anxiety than those in the hedonist and disarmist orientations. More research needs to be conducted to understand the strengths and disadvantages of each of these orientations.

[Álso: Use the 1990 *Time* article by Toufexis to discuss problems caused by the meltdown at the **Chernobyl** nuclear plant. This article includes several photographs. The cost of this one accident is $358 billion dollars. Farmers are noting many birth defects among livestock. Humans are experiencing high levels of thyroid disease, anemia, cancer, fatigue, loss of vision, loss of appetite, and a drop in immunity level.]

(*Sources:* Abraham, H. D. 1983. Inching toward Armageddon: A psychiatric view. *The Yale Journal of Biology and Medicine, 56,* 67-78; Bachmann, J. 1983. How American high school seniors view the military. *Armed Forces and Society, 10,* 86-104; Bower, B. 1985. Kids and the bomb: Apocalyptic anxieties? *Science News, 128,* 106-107; Escalona, S. 1982. Growing up with the threat of nuclear war: Some indirect effects on personality development. *American Journal of Orthopsychiatry, 52,* 600-607; Hamilton, S. B., Knox, T. A., Keilin, W. G., & Chavez, E. L. 1987. In the eye of the beholder. Accounting for variability in attitudes and cognitive/affective reactions toward the threat of nuclear war. *Journal of Applied Social Psychology, 17,* 927-952; Tizard, B. 1986. The impact of the nuclear threat on children's development. In M. Richards & P. Light (Eds.). *Children of social worlds: Development in a social context.* Cambridge, MA: Harvard University Press; Toufexis, A. 1990, (April 9). Legacy of a disaster. *Time,* 68-70; Yankelovich, D. & Doble, J. 1984. The public mood: Nuclear weapons and the U.S.S.R. *Foreign Affairs, 63,* 33-46; Yudkin, M. 1984. When kids think the unthinkable. *Psychology Today, 18,* 18-25.)

7. 724 Children

What are "724 children?" They are children who are kept at home, indoors, seven days a week, 24 hours a day due to the widespread violence in the American culture. A look at a few current statistics from a survey of elementary school-aged children show why a growing number of parents are making their children become "724 children." In New Orleans, 90 percent of the children have witnessed violence, 70 percent have observed a weapon being used, and 40 percent have witnessed a corpse. In Los Angeles, nearly one in five children have witnessed a homicide. In a different study done by Boston City Hospital, it was found that one in 10 patients in a pediatric primary care clinic had witnessed a shooting or stabbing before they were six years old. In a study of Seattle public high school students, 34 percent said they had ready access to handguns, 11.4 percent of the male students said they owned a gun, and 6.6 percent of the males had carried a gun to school. In the United States, gunshot wounds are now the second leading cause of death among high school-age children.

Due to the violence, some children are having the symptoms of post-traumatic stress disorder. The symptoms include poor concentration, recurring sleep disturbance, hypervigilance, flashbacks, fatalistic beliefs, and increased risk taking. Many of these children have difficulty dealing with why their parents and other significant adults can not keep them safe.

What are the long-term effects of such pervasive exposure to violence? Of being a "724 child?" Might these children believe that they do not have much of a future, and that there is little reason to becoming educated or to making safe sex choices? For some, might they become lifelong victims (in inner cities, victims have a 4 percent chance of experiencing violence again)? For others, might they try to empower themselves by taking weapons to school (according to a 1990 survey, one in every five high schools studied had carried a weapon to school during the previous month; for one in twenty the weapon had been a gun) or by becoming the aggressor instead of the victim? (*Source:* Will, G. F. (March 22, 1993). "Medicine" for "724 children." *Newsweek.* p. 78; Squirt, squirt you're dead. *Time.* June 22, 1992. p. 35.)

BROWN & BENCHMARK'S HUMAN DEVELOPMENT TRANSPARENCIES (2ND ED.)

Transparency Number and Title

The transparency set, a supplement to *Child Development*, is accompanied by an annotated manual that describes each of the 141 transparencies. The annotated manual also offers suggestions about how to use the transparencies to engage your students in active learning that will stimulate critical thinking and evaluative skills. The following transparencies are appropriate and useful with Chapter 14: Moral Development.

Transparency Number and Title

24	Bandura's Model of the Reciprocal Influences of B, P, and E
26	Psychoanalytic Theories
27	Cognitive Theories
73	Preoperational Thought's Characteristics
85	Characteristics of Concrete Operational Thought
101	Characteristics of Formal Operational Thought
109	Kohlberg's Moral Reasoning Stages

CLASSROOM ACTIVITIES OR DEMONSTRATIONS

1. Discuss the critical thinking exercises. If you are using these exercises systematically both you and your students may be well-practiced in carrying them out. Nevertheless, you may find it helpful to students to at least determine that they are conversant with the dimensions that define the nature of development as presented in Chapter 1, and if they are not, do a brief review. One thing to point out is that attempting to discover the developmental issues that are or are not explored in the chapter is a useful way to discover potential gaps in what we know about moral development, or ideas about new areas of research, as well as a basis for criticizing work that is available.

     The intent of exercise 2 is mainly to help students to appreciate the extent to which Damon's research uses and integrates the range of research on moral development in his approach to moral education. Damon's work is a very good example of what it means to take an eclectic perspective. Doing this exercise will underscore for students the ideas that developmentalists continue to find powerful in their attempt to understand the bases of moral development.

     Exercise 3 simply continues the series of assumption, inference, and observation exercises. In preparing students to do this one you could hint that focussing on what is directly relevant to Kohlberg's assessment of moral development will lead to success. Also, the text indicates directly Rest's criticism of Kohlberg's reliance on a single measure of moral development.
2. Discuss the students' research projects as suggested below.
3. Do we really care about others, what happens to them, how they feel, and whether life is positive for them? Or do we always have ourselves as the target of our concern? Do we help others for their sake, or only for our own? A **terminal value** would be if we value others for their own sake. An **instrumental value** would be if we value others because it is to our advantage to do so. Which is more true of human nature?

     Some psychologists seem to believe that **altruism,** valuing and pursuing another person's welfare as a goal, is a fantasy. These psychologists see humans as **social egoists.** As William James put it in 1890, "We know how little it matters to use whether *some* man, a man taken at large and in the abstract, prove a failure or succeed in life—he may be hanged for aught we care—but we know the utter momentousness and terribleness of the alternative when the man is the one whose name we ourselves bear." Besides William James, Freud's psychoanalytic theory and Skinner's behaviorism make strong social egoist assumptions.

     Social egoism as a dominant psychological philosophy is also exhibited in the amount of research done on such self-emphasizing topics as: self-awareness, self-monitoring, self-presentation, self-handicapping, self-deception, self-evaluation, self-affirmation, self-discrepancy, self-expansion, and self-esteem. Many theories in social psychology assume that people are out for themselves, among them social comparison theory, social exchange theory, and equity theory.

Yet, Batson and his colleagues (see Batson, 1990) did a series of research studies that suggest that there is altruism or true empathy-induced helping. His studies looked at alternatives such as helping (1) to reduce aversive empathic arousal, (2) to avoid social and self-punishments (e.g., shame and guilt), and (3) to seek social and self-rewards, and found that some helping occurs because of altruism.

Batson (1990, p. 344) concludes "All the research . . . suggests that our capacity for altruistic caring is limited to those for whom we feel empathy. In study after study, when empathy for the person in need is low, the pattern of helping suggests underlying egoistic motivation. It is not that we never help people for whom we feel little empathy; we often do . . . We care for them instrumentally rather than terminally." Furthermore, even when we have concern for others, we might not act on it if the cost of helping is painfully high.

Source: Batson, C. D. 1990 (March). How social an animal? The human capacity for caring. *American Psychologist, 45,* 336-346.

---

4. Present the four moral dilemmas and have students respond to them and explain their responses (essentially Kohlberg's tasks). Then have the students break into small groups and analyze their results according to Kohlberg's six stages. Do their reasons fit into his categories? Why or why not? How do their patterns of results support or not support his stage model? Are all their responses in one stage? What kind of mixture or patterning is evident?

Dilemma 1: In Europe, a woman is near death from cancer. There is one drug that the doctors think might save her. It is a form of radium that a druggist in the same town has recently discovered. The drug is expensive to make, but the druggist is charging ten times what the drug cost him to make. He paid $200 for the radium and is charging $2,000 for a small dose of the drug. The sick woman's husband, Heinz, goes to everyone he knows to borrow the money, but he can get together only about $1,000. He tells the druggist his wife is dying and asks him to sell the drug for $1,000 now and the rest later. The druggist says, "No, I discovered the drug and I'm going to make money from it." Heinz is desperate and considers breaking into the man's store to steal the drug for his wife. Should he? Why or why not?

Dilemma 2: John and Mary are taking a class together and are strongly attracted to one another. They want to have sex together, but John is married, although the marriage is having difficulties. Should they sleep together? Why or why not?

Dilemma 3: Dr. Johnson makes decisions about which patients have access to a kidney machine. Patients who do not get access will die. There are far more people who need the machine than can be accommodated by it, so there is a waiting list for those not yet on it. Dr. Johnson's young daughter is injured in a car accident and has kidney damage. She needs access to the machine to live. Should Dr. Johnson take another patient off the machine to put his daughter on? Why or why not?

Dilemma 4: You are shopping with a friend when you notice that your friend is shoplifting. You look around and notice that the store manager is watching you. What should you do? Why?

Source: Adapted from King, M. B. & Clark, D. E. 1989. *Instructor's Manual to Accompany Santrock and Yussen's Child Development: An Introduction,* 4th ed. Dubuque, IA: Wm. C. Brown.

---

5. Most western societies emphasize honesty, and children are taught to "always tell the truth." In contrast, the Japanese have an ethic called **tatemae,** which is the desirable ethical decision to avoid telling the truth to preserve social harmony.

What are the advantages and disadvantages of tatemae? Under what circumstances would you use tatemae? Do you believe children should be taught to "always tell the truth?" Why?

Source: Kagan, J. 1984. *The nature of the child.* New York: Basic Books.

6. Present these survey results from an August 28-29, 1989 poll by Yankelovich Clancy Shulman for TIME/CNN and discuss reactions to these statistics:

   1. Compared with ten years ago, are companies today more loyal or less loyal to their employees?

      More: 25%   Less: 57%

   2. Compared with ten years ago, are employees today more loyal or less loyal to their companies?

      More: 22%   Less: 63%

   3. Do you think it is likely or unlikely you will change jobs within the next five years?

      Likely: 50%   Unlikely: 45%

   4. What do you like most about your job? (choose one)

      What you do at work: 38%
      The people you work with: 30%
      Your salary: 9%
      Your chances of being promoted: 5%
      Your boss or supervisor: 4%

Source: Castro, J. 1989 (Sept. 11). Where did the gung-ho go? *Time,* 52-56.

7. Compare your students' attitudes and interests with the 1992 (27th annual) UCLA survey of 213,630 first year college students at 404 colleges and universities. Discuss the trends and the implications for society. Is the increased interest in social issues partially due to the LA riots of the previous spring?

   * An all-time high of 42 percent (up from 33.7 percent in 1991) agreed that "helping to promote racial understanding" is "essential" or "very important."

   * Six out of seven freshmen (85.1 percent) disagree with the statement that "racial discrimination is no longer a major problem in America."

   * An all-time high of 43.3 percent (39.6 percent in 1991) see "influencing social values" as an "essential" or "very important" goal in life.

   * A nearly record level 20.1 percent (20.6 percent in 1990) want to "influence the political structure."

   * About one in three (30.7 percent) endorsed "becoming a community leader" as "essential" or "very important," compared to 14.9 percent in 1972.

Source: Did LA riots shake up student attitudes? *NEA Higher Education Advocate.* Vol. X, No. 4, February 1993, p. 1; Copies of *The American College Freshman: National Norms for Fall 1992* available for $20 plus $3 shipping from Higher Education Research Institute, UCLA Graduate School of Education, 405 Hilgard Avenue, Los Angeles, CA 90024-1521.

8. There are many ways to describe the behavior of juvenile delinquents. Statistics and data about their characteristics, though important, may not always be learned as efficiently as we would like. One way to help the statistics come to life is to take a field trip to the local juvenile detention center. Most facilities will allow tours if the groups are not too big. If possible, the tour should include a look at the holding tanks, solitary confinement, day rooms, and offices. Staff are usually willing to give a short presentation about the services they provide and the clientele they serve. Before going, prepare students with a lecture on forms of detention and encourage them to form a list of questions to ask the juvenile court staff.

    If a trip to juvenile court is not possible, you may want to focus the classroom activity on how statistics about delinquency are gathered. Break students into groups and have them design a study to determine the frequency of drug use in high school. Be sure you point out some of the problems associated with asking the students directly about their drug usage behavior. Also point out the problems with questionnaires, gaining permission from parents, and the ethical issues involved.

Source: Temple, Lori L. 1992. *Instructor's Course Planner to accompany Life-span Development,* Fourth Edition by John W. Santrock. Dubuque: William C. Brown Communications.

---

9. Do you think that parents should be held responsible for their children's crimes? A Florida law subjects parents to a 5-year prison term and a $5,000 fine if a child uses a gun that was left around the house. A Maryland judge jailed the parents of a 14-year-old chronic truant. A Wisconsin law forces grandparents to support the babies of their teenage children. An Indiana judge ordered parents to pay over $30,000 for their son's incarceration and treatment in a juvenile correctional home because the parents' substance abuse and marital discord had contributed to their son's delinquency. Do you agree with these decisions? Why, or why not?

Source: Kantrowitz, B. 1989 (October 2). Now, parents on trial. *Newsweek,* 54-55.

CRITICAL THINKING EXERCISES

Exercise 1

As we noted concerning Erikson's theory in Chapter 12, the study of moral development is another excellent example of developmental thinking. Yet the various issues receive variable emphasis or are not emphasized at all in Chapter 14. Which issue appears to receive the least attention in this chapter? **Circle the letter of the best answer, and explain why it is the best answer and why each other answer is not as good.**

A. Development results from biological, social, and cognitive processes.
B. There are periods of development.
C. Nature and nurture interact to produce development.
D. Development may be either continuous or discontinuous.
E. Early experience is often important for later development.

Exercise 2

One approach to moral education discussed in *Child Development* is William Damon's Comprehensive Approach. One question to ask is how this approach relates to the various theories and studies about moral development presented previously in the chapter. Which of the following statements accurately represents a way in which Damon's approach applies what we know about moral development? **Circle the letter of the best answer, and explain why it is the best answer and why each other answer is not as good.**

A. Processes of reinforcement and punishment probably play little role in moral education.
B. Damon's approach to moral education stresses moral reasoning over moral behavior and moral feelings.
C. Damon's approach is essentially an application of Kohlberg's theory to moral education.
D. Damon's approach is not different from the values clarification approach.

E.   Psychoanalytic accounts of moral development play no role in Damon's theory.

Exercise 3

James Rest has been a critic of Kohlberg's assessment of moral reasoning. Which of the following is an assumption that Kohlberg made about measuring moral reasoning, rather than an inference or an observation, that Rest criticized? **Circle the letter of the best answer, and explain why it is the best answer and why each other answer is not as good.**

A.   Moral development is based on moral reasoning and unfolds in a series of stages.
B.   In a 20-year longitudinal investigation, the uses of Stages 1 and 3 decreased.
C.   Children's moral orientation unfolds as a consequence of their cognitive development.
D.   Children's moral reasoning advances when children are exposed to more advanced moral reasoning than their own.
E.   The assessment of moral reasoning may rely on a single method that requires individuals to reason about moral dilemmas.

ANSWER KEYS FOR CRITICAL THINKING EXERCISES

Exercise 1

A.   This is not the best answer. Although the chapter does not treat biological processes in moral development, it covers social and cognitive processes extensively.
B.   This is not the best answer. This is clearly treated in the theories of Piaget and Kohlberg, both of which receive research support for their claims.
C.   This is the best answer. There simply is not treatment of this issue in the chapter.
D.   This is not the best answer. The theories of Piaget and Kohlberg, and many theories derivative from them (e.g., Hoffman's., Gilligan's, Damon's) postulate that there are discreet, discontinuous stages of moral development.
E.   This is not the best answer. Although there is limited treatment of this idea, it is there, at least in the discussion of psychoanalytic accounts of the development of moral feeling.

Exercise 2

A.   This is not the best answer. Damon speaks of negative consequences that can result from punishment; but he also speaks of the importance of normal, everyday interactions to moral education. Although Damon does not describe these processes explicitly, they probably come into play in attaching emotions to behavior (e.g., fear) and regulating behavior in social contexts that teach rules and standards.
B.   This is not the best answer. Damon's approach includes reference to feelings like compassion and empathy.as well as fear and guilt. There is a clear affective dimension that motivates moral behavior in his approach.
C.   This is not the best answer. Damon's theory includes some of Kohlberg's ideas about the value of social interaction, exposure to standards, and moral reasoning. But he seems to play down the stage concept, and he plays greater stress on the importance of emotions, parent-adolescent relations, and culture.
D.   This is not the best answer. For one, Damon appears to advocate a more direct approach to moral education. For another, his approach is far more comprehensive, including formal and informal teaching, and emphasizing that life's experiences are important to moral education. Damon also regards the contexts of moral education and relationships between pupil and teacher as important contributors to development, about which values clarification apparently has little to say.
E.   This is the best answer. There is no explicit use of psychoanalytic concepts in the approach, nor does Damon appear to base his ideas on Erikson's claims about stages of moral development. For example, Damon does not claim that moral learning is specific to childhood and ideological concerns specific to adolescence. He seems to be arguing that moral learning takes place throughout childhood and adolescence, and makes no specific reference to ideology.

Exercise 3

A.   This is not the best answer. Santrock indicates that this was Kohlberg's conclusion after 20 years of work. Therefore the statement is an inference, and not an assumption that Kohlberg makes about measuring moral development.

B. This is not the best answer. It is an observation, a statement of results from an investigation. In any event, the statement is irrelevant to measuring moral development.

C. This is not the best answer. This is also a conclusion Kohlberg drew from analyzing the answers children gave to the moral dilemmas he used to measure moral dilemma. (Note: even if students argue that this is an assumption, it is not something that Rest criticized.)

D. This is not the best answer. The is an observation that researchers have generated when they have studied the influence of models on children's moral reasoning.

E. This is the best answer. Kohlberg apparently believed that he need use only one method to measure moral development. Rest pointed out the benefits of using alternative methods as well.

RESEARCH PROJECT 1   MORAL MESSAGES IN ADOLESCENTS' LITERATURE

This project is a preliminary examination of the values that are being emphasized in adolescents' literature. Have students go to a public library and ask the librarian for assistance in locating adolescents' literature that has been excellently reviewed (e.g., has received awards or good critical reviews), and also deals with situations requiring a moral decision. Choose five books. Students should write up a summary of their impressions, including whether books emphasize, minimize, or even ignore the following issues:

> achievement, nurturance, cooperation, competition, endurance, taking chances, doing one's best, kindness, honesty, caring

Does the book emphasize doing right in order to:

> have a good life
> be liked or appreciated
> avoid punishment
> do the right thing
> follow the law

	Book 1	Book 2	Book 3	Book 4	Book 5
Values that are emphasized:					
Reasoning for acting moral:					
Consequences for acting bad:					
Other:					

Questions

1. What values were most evident in the five books you read? What values were largely missing?
2. What reasons are given in the books for acting moral? Which of Kohlberg's stages are emphasized? Is it influenced by children's typical reasoning stages? Is a caring orientation or a justice orientation provided more often?
3. What consequences are given to those who choose to act improperly?

Use in Classroom

You might ask students to bring one or more of their book choices with them. Discuss the patterns that the various books show in values, moral reasoning, and consequences for poor behavior. Discuss whether students like the way the books deal with morality. Also, were there any books that they would not recommend, and why?

RESEARCH PROJECT 2   MORAL DEVELOPMENT QUOTES

This project is a short survey to see if individuals rank moral reasoning similarly to Kohlberg's six stages. Choose one of the following quotes from each of the stages as marked in the parentheses. Write each quote on a file card (do not provide the stage number), and label each quote randomly by an alphabetical letter. Find six college students (three female and three male) who are willing to rank the quotes from highest moral reasoning to lowest moral reasoning. Compare their answers to Kohlberg's. Also ask each subject to pick out the quote that best reflects their own moral beliefs.

Quote Pool:

"The point is to get into heaven by hook or crook." —Denis Diderot (1)

"Every disorder of the soul is its own punishment." —Saint Augustine (1)

"No person in the world ever attempted to wrong another without being injured in return—some way, somehow, sometime." —William George Jordan (1)

"There are two ways of paying, and we have a choice. One is service and the other is suffering." —Isabel M. Hickey (1)

"Too much of a good thing is wonderful!" —Mae West (2)

"'Am I living in a way which is deeply satisfying to me, and which truly expresses me?' This I think is perhaps the most important question for the creative individual." —Carl Rogers (2)

"What is moral is what you feel good after." —Ernest Hemingway (2)

"I have a simple philosophy. Fill what's empty. Empty what's full. And scratch where it itches." —Alice Roosevelt Longworth (2)

"Grant that I may not so much seek to be consoled as to console . . . To be understood as to understand . . . To be loved as to love . . . for it is in giving that we receive . . . it is in pardoning that we are pardoned . . . " —St. Francis of Assisi (3)

"What you do not want others to do to you, do not do to others." —Confucius (3)

"Life is not so short but that there is always time enough for courtesy." —Ralph Waldo Emerson (3)

"Make yourself a blessing to someone." —Carmelia Ellot (3)

"Karmic, cosmic justice will be done. Maybe not in the short run, seemingly, but in the long run, definitely." —Shirley MacLaine (4)

"It may make a difference to all eternity whether we do right or wrong today." —Arthur Clarke (4)

"My country right or wrong." (4)

"This thing must be put bluntly: every man who has more than is necessary for his livelihood and that of his family, and for the normal development of his intelligence, is a thief and a robber. If he has too much, it means that others have too little." —Romain Rolland (5)

"Morality is the observance of the rights of others." —Dagobert D. Runes (5)

"From each according to his abilities, to each according to his needs." —Karl Marx (5)

"Be compassionate. The universality of evil makes human compassion necessary." —Rollo May (5)

"We are all dependent on one another, every soul of us on earth." —George Bernard Shaw (5)

"Treat all men alike. Give them all the same laws. Give them all an even chance to live and grow." —Chief Joseph (6)

"A world at peace will be one where the rights of every human being—dignity, liberty, and the basic rights of education and health care—will be respected." —Kris Kristofferson (6)

"Each time a man stands up for an ideal, or acts to improve the lot of others, or strikes out against injustice, he sends forth a tiny ripple of hope." —Robert F. Kennedy (6)

"We hold these truths to be sacred and undeniable: that all men are created equal and independent." —Thomas Jefferson (6)

"I had to make do with my own truth, not accept from others what I could not attain on my own." —Carl G. Jung (6)

"To cling to the principles of the Judeo-Christian ethic—honesty, integrity, compassion, love, ideas of hope, charity, humility—is an integral part of any person's life no matter what his position in life may be." —Jimmy Carter (6)

"This is what you should do: love the earth and sun and the animals, despise riches, give alms to everyone that asks, stand up for the stupid and crazy, devote your income and labor to others, hate tyrants, argue not concerning God, have patience and indulgence toward the people." —Walt Whitman (6)

"I think we all have moral obligations to obey just laws. On the other hand, I think that we have moral obligations to disobey unjust laws because non-cooperation with evil is just as much a moral obligation as cooperation with good." —Martin Luther King, Jr. (6)

"Sometimes you have to go above the written law." —Fawn Hall (6)

"For the whole law is fulfilled in one word, `You shall love your neighbor as yourself.' " —Galatians 5:14 (6)

Quote Letter:	Kohlberg's Rank:				Subjects' Responses:		
		F #1	F #2	F #3	M #1	M #2	M #3
	1						
	2						
	3						
	4						
	5						
	6						

(Circle the preferred quote choice of each subject.)

Questions

1. Why did you pick the quotes that you did? Do you think your choices influenced the results?
2. How closely did the subjects reflect Kohlberg's hierarchy?
3. Some research findings suggest that Kohlberg's six stages are more typical of male morality than female morality. Did your male subjects reflect Kohlberg's rating more closely than did females?
4. Gilligan's research suggests that females choose caring morality over justice morality, and that males prefer the reverse. Do your subjects' choices reflect this gender difference?
5. Evaluate the use of quotations in moral development research. What are the advantages and disadvantages?

Use in Classroom

Have the students share their quote choices and their research results. Have them discuss possible gender differences in moral development and what they would attribute these differences to. Have them share family quotes/sayings that were morality messages when they were growing up.

ESSAY AND CRITICAL THINKING QUESTIONS

Comprehension and Application Essay Questions

We recommend that you provide students with our guidelines for "Answering Essay and Critical Thinking Questions" when you have them respond to these questions. Their answers to these kinds of questions demonstrate an ability to comprehend and apply ideas discussed in this chapter.

1. Define and give examples of what psychologists mean by the term moral development.

2. Compare and contrast Piaget's and Kohlberg's theories of moral development. Which seems more relevant to the study of adolescence? Why?
3. Can models influence children's moral development? How? Describe relevant evidence.
4. How have critics reacted to Kohlberg's theory? Do they object to it entirely, or do they wish to modify it? What value does the theory have in the face of such criticism?
5. Compare and contrast behavioral and social learning theories of moral development. Which is most compatible with Kohlberg's theory? How?
6. Describe the roles of resistance to temptation and self-control in the social learning theory of moral development. Cite relevant research.
7. What roles do reinforcement, punishment, and imitation play in shaping moral behavior?
8. What role do feelings play in moral behavior? Where do these feelings come from? How do they become *moral* feelings?
9. Define altruism, and discuss the roles that moral thinking and feeling play in expressions of altruism.
10. Compare and contrast any two approaches to moral education.
11. Compare and contrast the definitions of juvenile delinquency and conduct disorder, and discuss why these two definitions are different.
12. Summarize personality and social factors involved in delinquency, and discuss how these may be related.
13. Summarize Joy Dryfoos's seven guidelines for prevention of and intervention with juvenile delinquency, and discuss the nature of the evidence that these are appropriate guidelines.

Critical Thinking Questions

We recommend that you have students follow our guidelines for "Answering Essay and Critical Thinking Questions" when you ask them to prepare responses to these questions. Their answers to these kinds of questions reflect an ability to apply critical thinking skills to a novel problem or situation that is *not* specifically discussed in the chapter. These items most appropriately may be used as take-home essay questions (e.g., due on exam day) or as homework exercises that can be answered either by individuals or groups. Collaboratively answered questions encourage cooperative learning by students, and reduce the number of papers that must be graded.

1. At the end of Chapter 14 Santrock indicates books that provide practical knowledge about children and lists resources for improving the lives of children. Choose one of these books or resources and read it or learn as much as you can about it. Then write a brief review in which you (a) characterize the book or resource, and (b) explain how the book or resource relates to material in the chapter.
2. Chapter 1 defines the nature of development in terms of biological, cognitive, and social processes, and periods or stages. Indicate your ability to think critically by identifying material in this chapter that illustrates developmental processes and periods. If there is little or no information in this chapter about developmental processes and periods, identify and explain how developmental processes and periods could be used to guide the analysis of any topic in the chapter.
3. According to Chapter 1, three fundamental developmental issues concern: (a) maturation (nature) versus experience (nurture), (b) continuity versus discontinuity, and (c) early versus later experience. Indicate your ability to think critically by identifying material in this chapter that illustrates each of the three fundamental developmental issues. If there is little or no information in this chapter about fundamental developmental issues, identify and explain how these issues could be used to guide the analysis of any topic in the chapter.
4. One aspect of thinking critically is to read, listen, and observe carefully and then ask questions about what is missing from a text, discussion, or situation. For example, Santrock presents information about cognitive and social processes involved in moral development and behavior, but he makes no mention of biological processes that may be involved. Indicate your ability to think critically by (a) listing as many questions as you can about possible biological influences and processes on moral development, and (b) speculating why Santrock does not discuss this topic more fully.
5. Santrock sets off several quotations in this chapter. Indicate your ability to think critically by selecting one of the quotes and (a) learning about the author and indicating why this individual is eminently quotable (i.e., what was this individual's contribution to human knowledge and understanding), (b) interpreting and restating the quote in your own terms, and (c) explaining what concept, issue, perspective, or term in this chapter that Santrock intended this quote to illuminate. In other words, about what aspect or issue in development does this quote make you pause and reflect?
6. Chapter 2 indicates that theories help us explain data and make predictions about various aspects of development. Chapter 2 then presents six different theoretical approaches (i.e., Freudian, cognitive, behavioral and social learning, ethological, ecological, and eclectic theory), but notes that no single

approach explains the complexity of development. Indicate your ability to think critically by (a) perusing this chapter for topics influenced by at least one of the six theoretical approaches, and (b) explaining which theoretical approach dominated the topic in question. If the presentation is entirely atheoretical, identify and explain how one of the theoretical approaches could be used to guide the analysis of the topic in question.

7. Is level of moral reasoning related to identity status? For example, does an identity achieved person reason at a higher moral level than an identity diffuse person? Apply your knowledge about the scientific method by designing a study that will answer a question about the relationship between level of moral reasoning and level of identity development: (a) What specific problem or question do you want to study? (b) What predictions would you make and test in your study? (c) What measures would you use (i.e., controlled observation in a laboratory, naturalistic observation, interviews and questionnaires, case studies, standardized tests, cross-cultural studies, physiological research, research with animals, or multimeasure, multisource, and multicontext approach) and how would you define each measure clearly and unambiguously? (d) What strategy would you follow--correlational or experimental, and what would be the time span of your inquiry--cross-sectional or longitudinal? (e) What ethical considerations must be addressed before you conduct your study?

8. According to Chapter 2, your author wants you to become a wise consumer of information about child development by: (a) being cautious about media reports, (b) distinguishing between nomothetic research and idiographic needs, (c) recognizing how easy it is to overgeneralize from a small or clinical sample, (d) knowing that a single study is usually not the defining word about some aspect of child development, (e) remembering that causal conclusions cannot be made from correlation studies, and (f) always considering the source of the information and evaluating its credibility. Indicate your ability to think critically by, first, selecting an article from either a journal, magazine, or newspaper about any topic regarding Moral Development, and, second, evaluating it in terms of these six objectives. If the information in the article is insufficient to evaluate one of these objectives, then specify what kind of information you would need to evaluate the objective.

Social Contexts of Development

---

15 Families

SUGGESTIONS FOR LECTURE TOPICS

1. A Two-Dimensional Framework for Parenting Styles

The discussion of parenting styles can be enhanced by providing a two-dimensional framework adapted from the work of Slater (1962). Where a parent falls on the permissive-restrictive dimension in concert with where they fall on the warm-cold dimension may result in different types of behavior from their children. In a crude approximation to Slater's work, the following two-dimensional description is offered.

Permissiveness

indifferent		democratic
neglectful		permissive
		nonconformist

Cold ————————————————————————————— **Warm**

demanding		indulgent
authoritarian		protective
abusive		authoritative

Restrictive

A description of the four parenting styles defined in the text can come out of Slater's more comprehensive approach. Examples of the type of behaviors parents engage in should be numerous, and an emphasis on the behaviors of the children they parent might help bring the points home.

Disciplinary approaches are tied fairly closely to parenting styles, and could be presented at the same time. Parents using inductive techniques to discipline attempt to reason with their children and most often adopt an authoritative parenting style. This disciplinary style fosters compliance, encourages the development of empathy, and enhances self-control. Parents who use a power-assertive disciplinary style make use of physical rewards and punishment. They are most apt to adopt an authoritative parenting style, and their children are likely to behave when the contingencies are right but may not know how to behave when the reinforcements and punishments are not clear. Parents who use loss of love as a disciplinary style isolate or ignore their children when they misbehave. They are more likely to adopt a permissive-indifferent parenting style. The two styles together produce children who are anxious and uncertain.

2. Stages of Growth for a Stepparent and the Hansel and Gretel Syndrome

Miller has proposed that the development from outsider to parent is a gradual process that varies with each child; Miller proposes that it takes as many years to become the parent as is the child's history with the initial, biological parent. Thus, a 5-year-old will develop a mature, parenting relationship with a stepparent by the age of 10. Miller proposes a three-stage growth for stepparents. Healthy relationships move from **Guest** (Courteous) to **Friend** (Sharing) to **Parent** (Intimacy). Unfortunately, the stepparenting stages can be negative and move from **Intruder** (Resentment) to **Competitor** (Hostilities) to **Enemy** (Hate).

In the first stage, being warm, friendly, and interested helps a new stepparent to be perceived as Guest and be treated courteously. However, negative personality characteristics, breaking "established" family rules, or making rules and disciplining increase the chances of being perceived as an Intruder and being resented.

With time, the stepparent's status moves ahead into either a Friend or a Competitor. A friend is liked and trusted and is someone with whom to share. A "friend" stepparent is listened to with respect but the children may still reserve some affection, keep some possessions private, and not want the stepparent in a lawmaking role. In the third stage of parent or enemy, the parent perceives the stepparent as a policy maker, comforter, disciplinarian, and emotional supporter.

Some stepparent relationships, however, are quite dysfunctional (The Hansel and Gretel Syndrome). Forty-three percent of all **fatal abuse cases** occur in the homes of stepparents. A child living with a stepparent is almost 100 times more likely to be murdered than a child living with two biological parents. Of 508 solved Detroit homicides in 1972, only 6 percent were committed by blood relatives, but 19 percent were committed by people related by marriage (e.g., spouses, stepparents, or in-laws). (*Sources:* Miller, D. M. 1984. A model for stepfamily development. *Family Relations, 33,* 365-372; Pringle, H. 1989 (December). The Hansel and Gretel syndrome. *Omni, 38,* 127.)

3.   Adolescent Identity Crisis versus Parental Midlife Crisis

The text does a good job of describing the difficult balance of achieving independence in the turbulent period of adolescence when attachment to parents and relationships with peers are important. One important consideration in the success of surviving adolescence is the developmental stage the parents are in when their children hit their teenage years.

    The typical teenager's parent is between the ages of 35 and 45. While their children are dealing with issues of identity and independence, parents are dealing with the very first stages of a mid-life transition. The parents may be struggling with career problems, marital problems, the beginning of some health problems, and emotional turmoil associated with reaching the halfway point to the end of their lives. How the parents cope with their concerns may contribute to the success or failure of their adolescent's adjustment.

    Parents in their late forties and early fifties may actually be better prepared for the turmoil caused by the changes in their children. By 50, most parents have put to rest many of the issues surrounding the mid-life transition. The physiological changes in women are beginning to disappear or are becoming part of their identity. The psychological changes men undergo have just about run their course and the troubles associated with the onset of old age have not yet begun to take their toll. Parents may have the time and energy to be open to the needs of their adolescents during this period without having to deal with similar issues of identity and physical changes.

    With more and more people waiting until their mid- to late thirties to have children, more and more people will be having teenagers when they are in their late fifties and even early sixties. While parents are dealing with the difficulties of chronic illness, the ends of their careers, and thoughts of retirement, they may not have the energy to guide their teens through the many changes they are experiencing. Teenagers will also have the added burden of dealing with the aging of their parents before they fully understand what it means to be an adult. The combination can make for a difficult transition; however, with open communication and an understanding of the developmental needs of both the teen and older adults, families can remain attached, and still encourage the development of independence.

4.   Childhood Traumas

Three types of childhood traumas are victimization, loss, and family pathology. Here is a brief introduction to each of these types.

I.   Victimization
    A.   This category includes assault, robbery, rape, incest (which can be put under family pathology), and serious accidents.
    B.   Stages
       1.   Impact
          a.   usually high intensity and short duration
          b.   emotional shock symptoms such as numbness, feelings of vulnerability, and helplessness
          c.   Bodily symptoms might include tight throat, shortness of breath, abdominal distress, physical weakness, sleep disturbances, and loss of appetite.
          d.   might experience shame, guilt, and blame
       2.   Recoil
          a.   periods when they attempt to just go on with their lives
          b.   alternating with periods of obsessively going over the event with fantasies, planning, or phobic reactions
          c.   blaming of oneself, friends, family, or police might also occur

       3.   Reorganization
          a.   a return to psychological equilibrium
          b.   occasional flashbacks or extreme agitation
II.   Loss
    A.   Losses include apparent losses, changes, and unnoticed loss (marriage, achievements, and successes can be loss of an earlier life style). Losses include death, involuntary separation, or injury. It also includes divorce, moving, changing schools, leaving home, weaning, and puberty.

B. Kübler-Ross' stages of loss
   1. denial
   2. anger
   3. bargaining
   4. depression
   5. acceptance
C. Frears and Schneider's stages of loss
   1. initial awareness (e.g., shock, loss of equilibrium, lowered resistance)
   2. strategies to overcome loss (e.g., adaptive defense cycles of holding on and letting go)
   3. awareness of loss (e.g., loneliness, helplessness, exhaustion)
   4. completions (e.g., healing, acceptance, resolution)
   5. empowering the self
   6. transcending the loss
D. Special concerns with children
   1. may not have capacity to recognize, understand, and resolve loss
   2. may develop apathy and withdrawal behaviors because their basic needs are not being met

III. Family pathology
A. Four broad categories of family dysfunction
   1. inadequate families: lack physical or psychological resources for coping with normal stressors
   2. anti-social families: their values might encourage dishonesty or deceit.
   3. discordant and disturbed families: have poor interpersonal contracts and disturbance
   4. disrupted families: inadequate adjustment to loss by death, divorce, or separation
B. Patterns of parental influence in children showing emotional disturbance: rejection, overprotection, unrealistic demands, overpermissiveness, faulty discipline, inadequate and irrational communication, and undesirable parental modeling

(Adapted from: Johnson, K. (1989). *Trauma in the Lives of Children*. Benton Harbor, MI: Hunter House.)

5. Parent Behavior and Mealtimes

What can parents do to build good eating habits and good table manners with preschoolers? The suggestions provided here can build the foundation for years of pleasant and well-rounded eating:

a. Parents can teach manners by example rather than by demanding good manners. Modeling appropriate conversation, use of utensils, and body language will help young children know the appropriate way to act at a dinner table.

b. When children can manage the adjustment, have them share eating arrangements with the rest of the family. Use chairs (higher than is typical, or with a telephone book to give them height) at the table, and provide the child with utensils.

c. Help children learn that mealtime is a special occasion. Do not use mealtimes to bargain, lecture, or reprimand. It is better to send a child from the table than to use the setting as a battle zone.

d. Help youngsters to acquire new tastes by serving a variety of foods to sample. Parents can give their children a small taste of a strange food and let their offspring decide if they would like more, and how much.

e. Prepare foods that minimize dinner mishaps. Children are less likely to spill if their cup is only filled halfway, sandwiches are easier to handle if cut in quarters, and thin soups are more convenient if served in a cup.

f. Help preschoolers get used to foods that are convenient for the parents. For example, when preschoolers like cheese, parents can serve a nutritional and quick meal while traveling of crackers, cheese, and apple.

g. Once children are old enough to understand, provide some "anytime-you're-hungry" nutritional snacks. After all, a 40-pound child needs 1,800 calories (a 135-pound woman needs 2,200). Appropriate snacks that are easy for preschoolers to get for themselves include: small boxes of raisins, apples, bananas, plain crackers, small cups with green peas, small containers of applesauce, cheese, and vegetable sticks. Small children also like to pick out their snacks at the grocery store—picking their own shiny red apple can be as much fun as letting them pick out their own candy bar.

h. It is okay for preschoolers to eat the same food day after day, as long as a variety of nutritious foods are added to this one.

i.   Young children need 30-40 percent of calories from fat, but it is still better to provide unsaturated than saturated fat. Serve margarine instead of butter; baked or broiled instead of fried meat and fish; 2 percent or 1 percent milk instead of whole milk; bagels or English muffins instead of croissants or doughnuts; air-popped popcorn or pretzels instead of potato chips; frozen low-fat yogurt or frozen fruit bars instead of premium ice cream; reduced-fat instead of full-fat cheeses.

(*Sources:* Leach, P. 1982. *Your baby & child from birth to age five.* New York: Alfred A. Knopf; Schuster, C. S. & Ashburn, S. S. 1986. *The process of human development: A holistic life-span approach,* 2nd ed., Boston: Little, Brown; American Dietetic Association, 1989. What makes Johnny Grow?)

6.   Birth Order and Scientific and Religious Revolutions

Frank J. Sulloway suggests that most of the major innovators in science over the last 400 years are *not* firstborns. **Birth order** is the most reliable indicator of whether a scientist is for or against radical innovations. By looking at the birth order of 2,784 scientists who took sides during the 28 major scientific revolutions since the sixteenth century, Sulloway found that 23 of the 28 revolutions were led by laterborns. Moreover, firstborns with younger siblings were the least likely to accept new theories; next came only children; then laterborn eldest sons (those with one or more older sisters and at least one younger brother); and then laterborn only sons. The most radical scientists of all were younger sons with at least one older brother. (The major exception: firstborn Albert Einstein.)

In religion, the Reformation could be interpreted as a conflict between firstborns who typically supported Rome and laterborn Protestants. (The major exception: Martin Luther was a firstborn.) (*Source:* Woodward, K. L. & Denworth, L. 1990 (May 21). The order of innovation. *Newsweek,* 76.)

7.   You- and I-Messages

How parents make requests of their children and how they tell them about their behaviors has a big influence on parent-child communication. When parents (and other persons) give **"you-messages,"** children (and other recipients) may feel "put-down." Examine these "you-messages": "You are naughty." "You are acting like a little brat." "You are giving me a headache." "You know better." "You are doing way too much shouting." "You better stop that." "You are interrupting me." "Why didn't you put your clothes away?" "You-statements" come off as critical, powerful, and accusatory statements.

On the other hand, **"I-messages"** are acceptable ways to simply and honestly talk about unacceptable behavior. Parents who use "I-messages" communicate their feelings, criticize behavior and not the whole person, and allow their children space and responsibility to change the situation. Here's how "I-messages" work: "I would like you to quiet down because I have a headache." "I would like you to stop running in the house." "I would like to finish this statement before you speak." "I get upset when you climb on the furniture." "I would appreciate your cleaning your room this afternoon." Authoritative parents tend to use a lot of "I-messages"; these statements allow parents to model expression of honest feelings, give reasons for requests, and limit criticisms to specific behaviors rather than focusing on *you.* (*Source:* Gordon, T. E. 1975. *P.E.T.—Parent effectiveness training.* New York: Peter H. Wyden, Inc.)

8.   Communicating Caring and Love

Here are five approaches that parents try to use to communicate love but which do not work (Hart, 1987):

a.   *Overpermissiveness.* Children do not learn to love by getting to do anything they want. Children with reasonable limits feel the most love.
b.   *Martyrdom.* Parents who are self-sacrificing for their children often end up themselves feeling depleted, and their children end up feeling guilty or incompetent. Children learn a lot by doing things for themselves.
c.   *Overprotection.* Children need to be protected from danger and harm, but overprotection smothers children not with love but with doubts about their own capabilities.
d.   *Material possessions.* Material possessions can never be a substitute for expressions of love. Children would rather do things with their parents than get things from them (although time from time children may not realize this).
e.   *Quantity time without quality.* Children need parents to be there with them and for them, more than always to be around but uninvolved.

What communicates love? Taking children seriously and valuing their ideas and activities. Taking the time to listen to what they are doing, feeling, and believing. Helping children do things but not doing everything for them. These strategies express love and build self-esteem (Hart, 1987). Working on healthy communication helps children to feel support within the family, and allows them to feel good in their play activities and in their relationships with their peers. (*Source:* Hart, L. 1987. *The winning family: Increasing self-esteem in your children and yourself.* New York: Dodd, Mead & Company.)

9.   The Potter, Gardner, Maestro, and Consultant Parenting Patterns

The **"potter"** has these beliefs: (1) Parents have full responsibility and authority for their children. They must provide carefully structured experiences and answer all their questions; (2) Parents determine what a child becomes. It is important to teach correct principles; (3) Children's mistakes are failures and the result of poor teaching; (4) Parents explain their children's feelings to them; (5) Parents believe constructive activities are important in producing offspring who are successful, productive society members; (6) Parents have a strong sense of duty about family, work, religion, and society; (7) Desirable behavior should be rewarded.

   The **"gardner"** has these beliefs: (1) They believe in the innate goodness of humans. Parents who provide opportunity for growth will have children who become mature, competent adults; (2) Children go through different stages of development, and these parents are aware of these stages; (3) Acceptance of children's uniqueness; (4) Modeling is more important than having lots of rules; (5) Children should be able to explore their own interests; (6) Parents set limits that are needed for health and safety; (7) Children sometimes act childish.

   The **"maestro"** believes: (1) Democracy is important. Everyone is respected and listened to; (2) Pride is experienced toward group achievement; (3) Each family member's personal life is protected; (4) The home environment is carefully designed and structured and children's lives are organized; (5) Children are given responsibilities.

   The **"consultant"** emphasizes: (1) Parents try to understand themselves; (2) Both children and parents are learning and growing; (3) Parents know and accept themselves. They are confident in their abilities and accepting of limitations. This attitude and acceptance is also presented toward their children; (4) Children are related to as peers and also accepted as unique; (5) They don't worry about what other parents think.
(*Source:* Wood, S. J., Bishop, R. S. & Cohen, D. 1978. *Parenting: Four patterns of childrearing.* New York: Hart.)

10.   Family Characteristics Associated with Lower Drug Use

The following family characteristics are associated with *lower* substance usage (Coombs & Lansverk, 1988):

- Warm feelings between parents and teenagers. Although most youths felt closer to their mothers, it was warm relationships with fathers which was most associated with less drug usage.
- Teenagers who emulated their parents and who thought it was important to get along with them were less likely to use substances.
- Teenagers who felt that their parents trusted them were unlikely to use drugs.
- Teenagers who got favorable parental feedback were not likely to use drugs.
- Parents, especially fathers, who helped their teenagers with personal problems and decisions had offspring who did not use many drugs.
- Parents who set clear and consistent limits were more successful in raising drugfree offspring. These parents were not more punitive. Parents who required their teenagers to do homework and who limited television viewing were likely to have teenagers who did not use drugs.

(*Source:* Coombs, R. H. & Lansverk, A. 1988. Parenting styles and substance use during childhood and adolescence. *Journal of Marriage and the Family, 50,* 473-482.)

11.   Parent-Teen Talk

How much do parents and their adolescent offspring talk? One study found that the total daily exchange of communication between parents and teenagers is less than 15 minutes—about 12 minutes to discuss schedules and chores and the remainder for personal exchange. A teen magazine poll of over 1000 teen girls found that fewer than one-third reported turning to their mothers for advice.

Can these statistics be improved? Parents can initiate changes by acknowledging their adolescents' feelings and opinions and valuing their children as unique individuals. They can also try the following basic aspects of true communication: (1) Asking better questions—Don't ask "What's wrong with you?" but something like, "You seem bothered. Can I help in some way?" (2) Listen without interrupting, and give full attention, including eye contact and nodding. (3) Try to hear without judgment, and with a will to learn about the child. (4) Try to understand the child's views, and what circumstances have shaped these views. (5) Respond, but use words like "Are you aware of the consequences?" or "I don't agree with you" rather than with "That is wrong" or "How dare you say that to me?"

In addition to daily oral communication, some families incorporate family meetings, note-writing, and journals. (*Source:* Miller, M. S. 1989 (Oct.). How to talk to your teenager. *Good Housekeeping, 251.*)

12.   Socioeconomic Differences in Parenting

Who's more permissive in parenting—middle-class mothers or working-class mothers? The answer depends on whether you are asking about today or pre-WWII. From 1930 until the end of WWII, working-class mothers tended to be more permissive than middle-class mothers. Since then, however, middle-class mothers have been more permissive than working-class mothers.

Working-class mothers place greater emphasis on conformity in their children than do **middle-class mothers.** Middle-class mothers are more concerned about the development of internal standards of control. Children of middle-class parents are likely to be punished on the basis of their **intentions in the behavior;** children of working-class parents are more likely to be punished on the basis of the **actual behavior.**

In 1980 Maccoby condensed all the research on the relationship between parenting and social class and found the following few **SES** (socioeconomic status) differences:

- Lower-SES parents emphasize obedience, respect, neatness, cleanliness, and staying out of trouble. Higher-SES parents emphasize happiness, independence, creativity, curiosity, ambition, and self-control.
- Lower-SES parents are more power-assertive, authoritarian, and controlling. They use more physical punishment. Higher-SES parents are more democratic and either permissive or authoritative. They often discipline using induction.
- Higher-SES parents talk to their children more, use more reasoning with them, and use more complex language when talking with their children.
- Higher-SES parents show more warmth and affection toward their children.

Maccoby found these social-class differences across race and culture in the United States. However, these SES differences are merely averages, and parents of both lower and higher SES levels exhibit a variety of parenting styles. Moreover, SES differences are diminishing, and not very large at this time. (*Sources:* Kohn, M. 1977. *Social competence, symptoms and underachievement in childhood: A longitudinal perspective.* Washington, D.C.: Winston; Maccoby, E. E. 1980. *Social development: Psychological growth and the parent-child relationship.* New York: Harcourt Brace; Bronfenbrenner, U. 1958. Socialization and social class through time and space. In E. E. Maccoby, T. M. Newcomb, & E. C. Hartley (Eds.). *Readings in social psychology* 3rd ed. New York: Holt, Rinehart and Winston.)

13.   Working Moms, Daycare Alternatives, and Satisfied Lives

The Census Bureau says that 57 percent of all American women with children under the age of six are in the labor force. Twenty-eight percent of these children are cared for in their own homes (fifteen percent by the father, eight percent by a grandparent, two percent by some other relative, and 5 percent by a nonrelative). Thirty-seven percent are cared for in someone else's home (twenty-four percent are in a nonrelative's home and thirteen percent in a relative's home). Twenty-six percent are cared for in an organized child-care facility. Only eight percent are cared for by their mother at work.

As a society that values children, it is interesting how little child-care workers are paid. Here are comparisons of weekly wages for jobs in 1992.

Child-care worker	$154
Cleaning person	$191
Cashier	$219
Waiter/Waitress	$222
Bartender	$251

School teacher	$561
Firefighter	$636
Registered nurse	$662

A study conducted with 1,123 Canadian women by Ethel Roskies of the University of Montreal found that professional women who marry and have children are more content than those that are married professional women without children, who in turn were more satisfied than single career women with no children. The three groups did report equal levels of job satisfaction. The income of lawyers, engineers, and accountants were about the same for all groups but different for physicians. (*Sources:* U.S. Census Bureau, 1988 data. Gates, D. (February 22, 1993). Mary Poppins speaks out. *Newsweek,* 66-67; Study of career women finds children add to satisfied lives, *Des Moines Register,* November 22, 1992.)

BROWN & BENCHMARK'S HUMAN DEVELOPMENT TRANSPARENCIES (2ND ED.)

Transparency Number and Title

The transparency set, a supplement to *Child Development*, is accompanied by an annotated manual that describes each of the 141 transparencies. The annotated manual also offers suggestions about how to use the transparencies to engage your students in active learning that will stimulate critical thinking and evaluative skills. The following transparencies are appropriate and useful with Chapter 15: Families.

Transparency Number and Title

21	Piaget's Stages of Cognitive Development
24	Bandura's Model of the Reciprocal Influence of B, P, and E
25	Bronfenbrenner's Ecological Theory
26	Psychoanalytic Theory
62	A Pyramid of Services to Improve Family Health and Well-Being
64	Family Interactions
78	Classification of Parenting Styles
79	Children under 18 Living with One Parent: 1980 and 1991
106	Old and New Models of Parent-Adolescent Relationships
114	Leaving Home: Single Young Adults
115	The Joining of Families through Marriage: The New Couple
116	Becoming Parents and Families with Children
117	Families with Adolescents
118	Mid-Life Families
119	Families in Later Life

CLASSROOM ACTIVITIES OR DEMONSTRATIONS

1. Discuss the critical thinking exercises. Exercise 1 is an opportunity to review the major theoretical perspectives, as well as a chance to apply them. An important feature of the experience is that it forces students to consider how a theoretical perspective might influence the study of a topic like families, something which Santrock does not do explicitly. You might carry out a discussion of this by having students suggest the kinds of issues and research that proponents of the different perspectives would consider important.

   Exercise 2 aims to have students apply a developmental issue that Santrock does explicitly mention in the chapter, but which he does not use as a means of organizing or integrating subsequent material. Having students perform this exercise could provide a meaningful way to review the chapter, and would support the analysis of issues that they began in Exercise 1.

   Exercise 3 is a change from the previous "observation, assumption, and inference" exercises of the previous two chapters. This exercise requires students to analyze the material on attachment, autonomy, and conflict to identify which statement represents an area not explored in the discussion but which is relevant to it. Suggest to students that they look for the statement that Santrock does not directly address, and to test how changing the statement would change their view of the advice Santrock appears to give about letting adolescents make some of their own decisions.

2. Discuss the students' research projects as suggested below.

3. Should the care, training, and education of children be based on scientific research and theory rather than intuition, religion, or tradition? What are the advantages and disadvantages of using scientific guidelines? Is enough known to be able to rear children scientifically? What are some examples of scientific suggestions for rearing children? How many students believe that their parents reared them according to scientific guidelines?

Source: Simons, J. A., Irwin, D. B., & Drinnin, B. A. 1987. *Instructor's Manual to Accompany Psychology, the Search for Understanding,* St. Paul: West Publishing.

4. Have students describe their relationships with a parent at 6 years of age and currently. How has the relationship changed? What factors in development might account for the changes? How would the different theories - psychoanalytic, behavioral, cognitive, and biological - account for the differences?

Source: King, M. B. & Clark, D. E. 1990. *Instructor's Manual to accompany Children.* Dubuque, Wm. C. Brown Publishers.

5. Have students think about a conflict they had with their parents at 15 or 16. What was the conflict about? How did they and their parents deal with it? How did it get resolved? How might various theorists interpret the conflict and conflict resolution?

Source: King, M. B. & Clark, D. E. 1990. *Instructor's Manual to accompany Children.* Dubuque, Wm. C. Brown Publishers.

6. Parent-child relationships and relationships with peers may include sentences that "shoot the other person down." In parent-child relationships, these sentences can add fuel to bickering situations. Take a few minutes to share these statement with students, and discuss whether they have ever used or heard these kinds of statements. Discuss the manifest and latent meanings of these statements and generate healthier statements.

    I don't understand why you do these things.
    How could you do such a thing?
    I've never heard of such a thing.
    How could someone with your brains and your background do such a thing?
    I'm stumped, you really have confused me.
    You are going too fast. Please go over it one more time so I'll understand.
    You should know how I'm suffering.
    I cannot believe you are going to do that now, when . . .
    I do not understand how one little _____ is going to hurt you.
    You never tell me what you're thinking.
    Do it for me.
    You've offended me.
    I demand an apology.

Source: Dyer, W. 1978. *Pulling Your Own Strings.* New York: Thomas Y. Crowell Co.

7. Divide the class into groups of three to six students and have them wrestle with common parenting situations. Have group members present individual views and reasons, and then try to reach a consensus. Here are some problems to give to groups. You may give each group different situations and have them present their finalized position to the larger class; or, each group can resolve the same situations in order to save time to let students discover whether each group used similar solutions.

- Your 13-year-old and your 15-year-old want to play Nintendo all the time.
- The seventh-grade math teacher sends a note home saying that your child rarely does his homework and is easily distracted in class.
- Your 13-year-old daughter wants to know why you won't let her wear makeup, nylons, and earrings. She says all her friends do.
- You find out that your sixth grader has removed a couple of cans of beer from your refrigerator.
- Your eighth-grader and peers seem to delight in sprinkling their conversation with an assortment of swear words.
- Your tenth-grader starts to insist that she will only wear certain expensive brands of jeans, shoes, and tops; and they are so expensive that your budget could not afford very much.
- Your seventh-grader thinks she is old enough to date and is interested in a ninth-grade guy.

A variation is to have students resolve these problems using a particular parenting style, such as, authoritarian, permissive-indulgent, authoritative.

Source: Adapted from Simons, J. A. (1987). *How Would You Handle It?: A Classroom Activity.* Ankeny, IA: Des Moines Area Community College.

---

8. By writing down your responses to the following questions about your family, you can begin to analyze your own family constellation. Your impressions about parents and siblings are more influential than what the actual situation really is. Remember that your family makeup and atmosphere did not force you to become who you are today, but these factors did help to shape your decisions and personality.

1. List your parents (and other primary caretakers, e.g., stepparents, grandparents). For each, answer the following questions:

    Current age?
    Occupation?
    Description?
    Favorite child? Why?
    Ambitions and goals for children?
    Relationships to children?
    Sibling most like this person? Why?
    Relationship with other adult(s)?
    Attitude toward life?
    Birth order in their childhood family?

2. Write the name and age of each sibling (including self) according to birth order. Include stepsiblings and other persons that acted as family members. Briefly describe each person on your list, then answer the following questions:
    Which one was most different from you? How?
    Which one was most like you? How?
    Who fought and argued?
    Who played together?
    Who took care of whom?
    Did any have to deal with prolonged illness or handicaps?

    For each of the following adjectives, decide which sibling it best describes and least describes: intelligent, hard-working, conforming, rebellious, pleaser, critical, considerate, selfish, humorous, materialistic, spoiled, punished, spontaneous, attractive, strongest, idealistic, sensitive, obstinate, helping.

3. What are the subfamilies (i.e., siblings separated by five or more years) in your family?
4. What were the most important family values?
5. What saying could be your family motto?
6. What are your early recollections? Describe these memories and your feelings about these memories. What themes do these memories represent?

7.   What kinds of patterns are revealed by these data? What factors have been most significant in your lifestyle? How does your childhood influence your life now?

Source: Material is selected from Eckstein, D., Baruth, L., & Mahrer, D. (1982). *Life Style: What It Is and How to Do It.* Dubuque, IA: Kendall/Hunt.

9.   Answer the following questions about siblings, family size, and only children. How is your sibling-IQ?

1.   About what percentage of children have no siblings?
A. 25   B. 15   C. 10   D. 5   E. 1
2.   What percentage of young and middle-aged adults have at least one living sibling?
A. 95   B. 88   C. 72   D. 63   E. 51
3.   The majority of adult siblings contact each other several times a year.
A. True   B. False
4.   Generally, siblings grow farther apart during adolescence than they were during the school-aged years.
A. True   B. False
5.   Which pair is most likely to experience intense sibling rivalry?
A. Sister-Sister   B. Sister-Brother   C. Brother-Brother
6.   "Intense sibling loyalties" are more likely to develop when siblings suffer parental losses, and yet get to grow up together in emotionally trying conditions.
A. True   B. False
7.   Which parenting response tends to decrease sibling-sibling aggression?
A. Physical punishment   B. Laissez-faire
8.   The _____ child in the family was more often the favorite of the mother and the _____ child was least often a parental favorite.
A. oldest; youngest   B. oldest; middle   C. middle; oldest
D. middle; youngest   E. youngest; oldest   F. youngest; middle
9.   Aggression between two siblings is more common when their ages are
A. more than five years apart.   B. three or four years apart.
C. less than three years apart.
10.   Physically active individuals are more likely to have _____.
A. an older brother   B. a younger brother   C. an older sister
D. a younger sister   E. no siblings

Answers: 1. C; 2. B; 3. A; 4. B; 5. C; 6. A; 7. B; 8. F; 9. C; 10. A.

Sources: Cicirelli, V. G. (1982). Sibling influence throughout the lifespan. In M. E. Lamb & B. Sutton-Smith (Eds.). *Sibling Relationships: Their Nature and Significance across the Lifespan.* Hillsdale, NJ: Lawrence Erlbaum; Bank, S. & Kahn, M. D. (1982). Intense sibling loyalties. In M. E. Lamb & B. Sutton-Smith (Eds.). *Sibling Relationships: Their Nature and Significance across the Lifespan.* Hillsdale, NJ: Lawrence Erlbaum; Felson, R. B. & Russo, N. (1988). Parental punishment and sibling aggression. *Social Psychology Quarterly, 51,* 11-18; Longstreth, L. E., Longstreth, G. V., Ramirez, C., & Fernandez, G. (1975). The ubiquity of Big Brother. *Child Development, 46,* 769-772; Harris, I. D. & Howard, K. I. (1984). Correlates of perceived parental favoritism. *The Journal of Genetic Psychology, 146,* 45-56; Simons, J. A. (1988). *A Sibling Quiz: Classroom Activity.* Ankeny, IA: Des Moines Area Community College.

10.   Most people believe that previous generations had numerous extended families and today we have isolated nuclear families. Actually, at the beginning of the twentieth century, shorter lifespans meant that the majority of families were one-generation families while, today, three- to five-generation families are more typical.

Today's statistics include:

- Three-fourths of people over 65 are grandparents; three-fourths of them see their grandchildren every week or every other week; one-half see them almost daily.
- Middle-aged women are often caretakers of young adult children, grandchildren, and aging relatives.
- In the typical family, daughters and daughters-in-law hold families together. The women call parents (and parents-in-law), remember and plan for special occasions, and visit sick relatives.
- How does this information differ from our stereotypes of modern families? How have longer lifespans changed the responsibilities of family members? Why have most of these responsibilities fallen to women? What are the advantages and disadvantages of longer lifespans? What adaptations in society would better fit today's longer lives?

Sources: Schlossberg, N. K. 1984. Exploring the adult years. In A. M. Rogers & C. J. Scheirer (Eds.). *The G. Stanley Hall Lecture Series, Vol. 4.* Washington, D.C.: American Psychological Association.

11. The course is basically structured around families—kids being reared by one or two parents. Yet many kids are growing up in situations much different from the norms. Have students discuss the half million children a year that are in various substitute care situations. You may want to contrast today's problems and solutions with ones tried in previous years (e.g., in 1854 the Children's Aid Society sponsored "orphan trains" that shipped over 100 thousand children out west). Today, for example, there are more than 276,000 children in foster homes. Some babies are known as boarder babies, because they are born addicted and their addict mothers leave the hospital without signing away parental rights. Thousands more are with one or both parents but are homeless.

Source: Stinson, D. L. 1990 (Spring). Nobody's children. *Life,* 80-85.

12. When the term **empty nest syndrome** was first used, it was used to describe the negative experience of the mother when her children were grown and left home—the women had to grieve the loss of their mothering role. As middle-aged women saw options to have careers, the empty nest syndrome began to be viewed as an experience to anticipate joyfully (**upswing hypothesis**). Some psychologists also thought that fathers who missed out on active fathering when the children were young and then got "into" being father might now have the most negative empty nest syndrome. Obviously, there are many possible reactions for the experience of offspring leaving the home—for the mother, for the father, and for the offspring. In your classroom, have students discuss aspects of this experience in their own families.

You might want to compare birth-order effects or gender effects. In how many families did children leave in the order of their age? Did boys and girls leave in the same way? Were parents reluctant to have you leave, or did they want you to leave before you were ready? Did anyone have the experience of leaving and then having to temporarily move back? How does going away to college modify the empty nest syndrome? Was leaving a different experience for those who entered the military, went off to college, got married, or left for employment?

Source: Simons, J. A. 1987. Empty nest syndrome discussion notes. Ankeny, IA: Des Moines Area Community College.

13. As family structures have changed due to increases in divorces and single parenting, grandparents' roles have also changed. As a result, more decisions about grandparents' visitation rights are being made by courts and state legislatures. Since the mid-1970s, all 50 states have passed laws granting grandparents the right to petition the courts for legally-enforced visitations privileges. Before this time period, grandparents had no rights to their grandchildren except by consent of the children's parents.

Early court decisions (e.g., Odell vs. Lutz, 1947) emphasized parental autonomy and ruled that grandparent visitation rights would undermine parental authority. In fact, grandparent visitation rights could subject children to intergenerational conflict (e.g., Noll vs. Noll, 1950). These rulings also went along with the long tradition that the legal system should only intervene in the family in extreme circumstances. Early granting of grandparents visitation rights (e.g., Benner vs. Benner, 1952) came in cases in which the grandchildren had lived with the grandparents for extended periods, or in cases in which the parents were deemed "unfit" and the grandparents were given custody.

Recent rulings are more likely to view grandparent visitation as a way of preserving the child's continued contact with a family line and as a way of providing an alternative source for family support. These decisions are most likely made when children have experienced the death of a parent, or long-term separation from one parent due to divorce. Even then, courts make the determination of grandparent visitation rights based on the children's "best interests." Thus, to some degree, courts are recognizing the importance of the extended family, the possible psychological support of the older generation to children, and, in general, the political clout of older Americans.

Have students discuss the pros and cons of regulated and enforced grandparent visitation rights. Part of the discussion can involve the roles that grandparents play in grandchildren's lives (e.g., alternative caregivers, playmates, family historians and transmitters of family values and traditions, advice givers to parents). Part of the discussion should deal with how to resolve intergenerational conflict, how to determine the "children's best interests," the consequences of grandparent visitation rights on family functioning, and how to resolve the grandparent policy.

Source: Thompson, R. A., Tinsley, B. R., Scalora, M. J., & Parke, R. D. 1989. Grandparents' visitation rights: Legalizing the ties that bind. *American Psychologist, 44,* 1217-1222.

---

14.   Why have children? Ask class members to list reasons why couples have children; for example, what value do children serve? Compare their suggestions to those offered by Hoffman and Hoffman:

1.   adult social status and identity.
2.   expansion of the self, tie to a larger entity, sense of immortality.
3.   morality, religion, good of the group, altruism, normality.
4.   primary group ties, affiliation.
5.   stimulation, novelty, fun.
6.   creativity, accomplishment, competence.
7.   power, effectiveness, influence.
8.   social comparison, competition.
9.   economic utility.

Source: Hoffman, L. W. & Hoffman, M. L. 1973. The value of children to parents. In J. T. Fawcett (Ed.), *Psychological perspectives on population* (pp. 19-76). New York: Basic Books.

CRITICAL THINKING EXERCISES

Exercise 1

Chapter 2 of *Child Development* lays out five different theories that have been proposed as a means of organizing and integrating what we know about adolescence. Interestingly, Chapter 6 makes no direct reference to any one of them. Nevertheless, it is possible that one of these theories is more influential than others in contemporary research on families. Based on what *Child Development* teaches about theories and about families, which theory appears to have been most influential on the sorts of research and thinking presented in the chapter on families? **Circle the letter of the best answer, and explain why it is the best answer and why each other answer is not as good.**

A.   Psychoanalytic theories
B.   Cognitive theories
C.   Behavioral and social learning theories
D.   Ecological theories

E. Ethological Theories

Exercise 2

Chapter 15 of *Child Development* presents a discussion of the "developmental construction of relationships," in which two views are outlined, the continuity view and the discontinuity view. Although there is no subsequent direct reference to these views later in the chapter, subsequent material can be construed as bearing on these views. Below are section headings for some of the material. Review each of the sections and decide which best supports the continuity view of the developmental construction of relationships. **Circle the letter of the best answer, and explain why it is the best answer and why each other answer is not as good.** (*Hint:* There is more than one "best" answer.)

A. The Family Life Cycle (pp. 475-479)
B. Parenting Styles (pp. 480-481)
C. Autonomy and Attachment (pp. 485-486)
D. Sibling Interaction and Socialization (484)
E. Models of Divorce Effects (487-488)

Exercise 3

Contrary to what was previously believed, needs for autonomy and attachment appear to be complementary influences on adolescent social development. Needs for autonomy push adolescents to discover their strengths and limitations, whereas needs for attachment keep them connected to adults who nurture and support their explorations. It is therefore appropriate to allow adolescents to have control over some aspects of their lives. Which of the following is an assumption, rather than an inference or an observation, that underlies advice based on these conclusions? **Circle the letter of the best answer, and explain why it is the best answer and why each other answer is not as good.**

A. The key limitation on adolescents' ability to make good decisions is lack of knowledge.
B. Attachment to parents contributes to social adjustment.
C. Adolescents who are securely attached to their parents experience little depression.
D. Attachment to parents promotes positive relationships with peers.
E. Parents who recognize the attachment-autonomy connection will not experience conflict with their teenage children.

ANSWER KEYS FOR CRITICAL THINKING EXERCISES

Exercise 1

A. This is not the best answer. One reason is that nowhere is Freud or Erikson directly cited in the text. The work of two psychoanalysts is cited, however, (Blos and Mahler), but these only briefly and only in a discussion of attachment and autonomy. But psychoanalytic theories do not play a role elsewhere in the chapter. No reference is made to the classic issues (e.g., Oedipal conflict).
B. This is not the best answer. While cognitive factors are cited as influencing such things as parent-adolescent conflict, no cognitive or cognitive developmental analysis of, say, adolescents' ideas about families, appears in the chapter. For example, one might expect something along the lines of Selman's theory of perspective taking, or Dodge's analysis of stages of information processing about interpersonal conflict, but these types of theories and analyses do not receive play.
C. This is not the best answer. Although there is a long tradition of citing learning and imitation processes in characterizing the influences of parents on children, nowhere in this chapter does Santrock cite learning or social learning processes in parent-adolescent relationships.
D. This is the best answer. From the start of the chapter there is an emphasis on systems of interacting individuals. Persistent chapter themes include how individuals' experiences in one sphere of life influence their experience in others. For example, families themselves are described of systems of mutually interacting individuals, and the contexts (life period, sociocultural, and historical) of families and the resulting differences of family influence on children are treated.

E. This is not the best answer. Missing is any discussion of evolutionary significance of families and family characteristics, or any other biological contribution to family structure and function. There is also no discussion of critical periods in family development, or in family contributions to child development.

Exercise 2

A. This is not a best answer. This section explicitly focuses on stages in family life and on the different issues that parents face concerning their own relationship and their relationships with their children.
B. This is not a best answer. The main reason is that this section is not about the developmental construction of relationships. It does not treat how early experience of the different styles of parenting relate to later social adjustment. (Note: Baumrind's actual work could be construed as relevant to this issue. Students may be aware of this, in which case (B) is an acceptable best answer. Our point is that Santrock's treatment does not cast her findings in a developmental light.)
C. This is a best answer. This section explicitly establishes relationships between the quality of early parent-child attachments and later child-peer attachments.
D. This is not a best answer. This section emphasizes ways in which sibling relationships differ from parent-child relationships.
E. This is a best answer. The two models discussed indicate that there are relationships between the nature of a family and the effects of divorce, the nature of family functioning prior to and after divorce, and other within and across time connections that are consistent with a continuity model view of the developmental construction of relationships.

Exercise 3

A. This is the assumption. The specific advice is to allow teenagers to make decisions when they have enough knowledge about the choices they have, that is, to relinquish control over these decisions. This appears to assume that knowledge is the main factor determining the quality of decisions because it does not mention that other factors could influence decision making. However, Chapters 4 and 5 describe several other factors (e.g., logical thinking, specific limitations on adolescents' decision-making capacities associated with age) that probably have a strong influence on adolescent decision making and probably should be included in decisions about granting autonomy.
B. This is an inference. It is one interpretation of the correlational data which have established a connection between quality of attachment and quality of social adjustment.
C. This is an observation. Research has documented this association.
D. This is an inference, for the same reason that *B* is: The supporting evidence is correlational.
E. This is an inference. It is an extension of information presented in the text about optimal ways to parent adolescents, a hypothesis about the effects of recommended parenting practices. It is also an incorrect extension of the information because work done to date appears to suggest that some degree of conflict is probably both necessary and desirable. For example, some kinds of conflict appear to promote identity development.

RESEARCH PROJECT 1   COMPARING PARENTING GUIDES

Acquire two recent parenting guides from a library or bookstore. The guides should (1) be directed toward the same age group (e.g., infancy, preschool, school-aged, adolescent) and (2) address at least one common issue in parenting. Your task is to compare the ideas in the book and critique the worth of the two guides. Include specific examples from the books, discuss the theoretical positions of the authors, and address the ways in which the authors define parenting and parent-child relationships. Write a critique of the two books in which you choose one book as better than the other and provide reasons for your choices. Within the context of your critique, address the following questions:

Questions

1. What kinds of parents would benefit from each of the two books? Who is the targeted audience?
2. What kinds of parenting issues do the books cover? Are the books comprehensive in approach or do they focus on just a couple of parenting concerns?
3. What is the theoretical persuasion of the authors? For example, do they use behavioristic or psychoanalytic terminology? Moreover, what is the tone of each book: sympathizing, encouraging, preaching?
4. Is each book practical? Is either book too idealistic?

5. Do the books use actual research findings to back the authors' positions? Do the authors provide useful case study examples? Do the books include practical exercises or activities for parents or for parents and children?
6. Are the books structured in a way that makes it easy for parents to use the books?
7. Which book did you prefer? Why? Are there things in either book that you view as inaccurate or poor advice? What was the best advice or concept that you came across?

Use in Classroom

One variation of this project is to assign specific books to students so that you receive a variety of critiques. You might want to duplicate all reports so that students can have a collection for future reference. Or, you could have students present oral reports on their books. Another variation would be to have students choose parenting books from different eras—how does a current selection compare with one published in the 1950s?

RESEARCH PROJECT 2   INTERVIEWING TEENS ABOUT THEIR PARENTS

This is a project that you will especially want to clear with your IRB, so if you decide to use it, be sure to have it reviewed before your school term begins! On the face of it innocuous, asking children about their parents has perhaps a larger potential to reveal troubling information than in times past.

Students should locate three children, a preteen, an early adolescent, and a late adolescent. The basic task is to do a brief interview with each, getting answers to the following basic questions:

1. What do you like most about your parents?
2. What do you like least about your parents?
3. What do you fight about most with your parents?
4. What do you fight about least with your parents?
5. Could you "make it" without your parents? Why or why not?

If possible, students should tape-record their respondents answers for later transcription. If this is not possible, perhaps they could work in pairs, one person doing the interview and the other recording the answers. Once they have a written copy of the interview, students should answer the following questions:

Questions

1. How do the answers from the three respondents compare? How were they similar, how different?
2. Given what you know about styles of parenting, how would you classify each respondents parenting style (from your respondents' perspectives)?
3. How do your respondents answers compare to information given in your text? Do they confirm or disconfirm information there?
4. How confident are you that your respondents answered truthfully? Was there any evidence that they had difficulty answering? Or deliberately mislead you?
5. How do you feel about research on parenting that relies on interviews, now that you've had a small experience of it yourself?

Use in Classroom

You can use students answers to all or just some of the above questions in classroom discussion about parenting. Some things that would be interesting to do: (a) Do a comparison and contrast of the experience of the three age groups based on the students' data. Then compare their findings to information in *Adolescence* . (b) Count the frequencies of each parenting style, broken down by age group. If there are interesting age trends, discuss what they might mean. For example, it is possible that younger adolescents will perceive their parents as more authoritarian. If that is true, what does it mean? If it is false, how do we interpret it? (c) Use the answers to questions 4 and 5 to fuel a discussion of research methodology. Students should have acquired all sorts of insights into problems and pitfalls of interviews, as well as an appreciation of the compelling and rich wealth of information this technique can produce.

ESSAY AND CRITICAL THINKING QUESTIONS

Comprehension and Application Essay Questions

We recommend that you provide students with our guidelines for "Answering Essay and Critical Thinking Questions" when you have them respond to these questions. Their answers to these kinds of questions demonstrate an ability to comprehend and apply ideas discussed in this chapter.

1. How are the concepts of reciprocal socialization and the family as a system related to each other? How are they different?
2. Compare and contrast the continuity and the discontinuity view of the developmental construction of relationships.
3. How can parents adapt their childrearing practices to the developmental status of their children? Give examples.
4. What are the main parenting issues during the family life cycle?
5. Sketch the sociocultural and historical changes that define the context of parenting today.
6. Define the four parenting styles, and describe the personalities of children who experience them.
7. Distinguish between child abuse and maltreatment, summarize the factors that contribute to it, and discuss how to intervene in cases of abuse and maltreatment.
8. Compare and contrast the influence of siblings, peers, and parents on adolescents.
9. Indicate and explain the relationship between attachment and autonomy, and evaluate the claim that secure attachment promoters personal adjustment.
10. Describe some of the factors that contribute to the escalation of parent-adolescent conflict that typically occurs during early adolescence. In your view, do these lead you to favor a continuity or a discontinuity view of the developmental construction of relationships? Why?
11. Describe the effects of divorce and remarriage on adolescents. In view of these, would it be better for parents to avoid divorce "for the sake of the children?" Why or why not?
12. Using information from your text, evaluate the idea that mothers should not work because doing so harms their children's development.
13. What is a latchkey child, and how does being one affect the developing self?
14. Compare and contrast the families of White Americans, African Americans, and Latino Americans.

Critical Thinking Questions

We recommend that you have students follow our guidelines for "Answering Essay and Critical Thinking Questions" when you ask them to prepare responses to these questions. Their answers to these kinds of questions reflect an ability to apply critical thinking skills to a novel problem or situation that is *not* specifically discussed in the chapter. These items most appropriately may be used as take-home essay questions (e.g., due on exam day) or as homework exercises that can be answered either by individuals or groups. Collaboratively answered questions encourage cooperative learning by students, and reduce the number of papers that must be graded.

1. At the end of Chapter 15 Santrock indicates books that provide practical knowledge about children and lists resources for improving the lives of children. Choose one of these books or resources and read it or learn as much as you can about it. Then write a brief review in which you (a) characterize the book or resource, and (b) explain how the book or resource relates to material in the chapter.
2. Chapter 1 defines the nature of development in terms of biological, cognitive, and social processes, and periods or stages. Indicate your ability to think critically by identifying material in this chapter that illustrates developmental processes and periods. If there is little or no information in this chapter about developmental processes and periods, identify and explain how developmental processes and periods could be used to guide the analysis of any topic in the chapter.
3. According to Chapter 1, three fundamental developmental issues concern: (a) maturation (nature) versus experience (nurture), (b) continuity versus discontinuity, and (c) early versus later experience. Indicate your ability to think critically by identifying material in this chapter that illustrates each of the three fundamental developmental issues. If there is little or no information in this chapter about fundamental developmental issues, identify and explain how these issues could be used to guide the analysis of any topic in the chapter.
4. One aspect of thinking critically is to read, listen, and observe carefully and then ask questions about what is missing from a text, discussion, or situation. For example, we might expect from earlier treatments in *Child Development* that the ideas of Freud and Erikson would have played a large role in our understanding

of family influences on adolescence. Yet neither theorist makes an appearance in this chapter. Indicate your ability to think critically by (a) listing as many questions as you can about how Freudian concepts relate to family influences on adolescence, and (b) speculating why Santrock does not discuss this topic more fully.

5. Santrock sets off several quotations in this chapter. Indicate your ability to think critically by selecting one of the quotes and (a) learning about the author and indicating why this individual is eminently quotable (i.e., what was this individual's contribution to human knowledge and understanding), (b) interpreting and restating the quote in your own terms, and (c) explaining what concept, issue, perspective, or term in this chapter that Santrock intended this quote to illuminate. In other words, about what aspect or issue in development does this quote make you pause and reflect?

6. Chapter 2 indicates that theories help us explain data and make predictions about various aspects of development. Chapter 2 then presents six different theoretical approaches (i.e., Freudian, cognitive, behavioral and social learning, ethological, ecological, and eclectic theory), but notes that no single approach explains the complexity of development. Indicate your ability to think critically by (a) perusing this chapter for topics influenced by at least one of the six theoretical approaches, and (b) explaining which theoretical approach dominated the topic in question. If the presentation is entirely atheoretical, identify and explain how one of the theoretical approaches could be used to guide the analysis of the topic in question.

7. This chapter discusses the relationship between parenting style and personality development. Apply your knowledge about the scientific method by designing a study to determine the relationship between parenting styles and children's present or future personalities: (a) What specific problem or question do you want to study? (b) What predictions would you make and test in your study? (c) What measures would you use (i.e., controlled observation in a laboratory, naturalistic observation, interviews and questionnaires, case studies, standardized tests, cross-cultural studies, physiological research, research with animals, or multimeasure, multisource, and multicontext approach) and how would you define each measure clearly and unambiguously? (d) What strategy would you follow--correlational or experimental, and what would be the time span of your inquiry--cross-sectional or longitudinal? (e) What ethical considerations must be addressed before you conduct your study?

8. According to Chapter 2, your author wants you to become a wise consumer of information about child development by: (a) being cautious about media reports, (b) distinguishing between nomothetic research and idiographic needs, (c) recognizing how easy it is to overgeneralize from a small or clinical sample, (d) knowing that a single study is usually not the defining word about some aspect of child development, (e) remembering that causal conclusions cannot be made from correlation studies, and (f) always considering the source of the information and evaluating its credibility. Indicate your ability to think critically by, first, selecting an article from either a journal, magazine, or newspaper about any topic regarding Families, and, second, evaluating it in terms of these six objectives. If the information in the article is insufficient to evaluate one of these objectives, then specify what kind of information you would need to evaluate the objective.

16   Peers, Play, and the Media

SUGGESTIONS FOR LECTURE TOPICS

1. Parents versus peers

A common stereotype of peer influence on adolescents is that peer influence inevitably places adolescents in conflict with their parents. An older term in the literature for this conflict is cross-pressure. Interestingly, research has never been particularly supportive of this notion, but the stereotype persists and is commonly cited as a reason that parenting teenagers is so difficult.

Santrock addresses this issue in *Adolescence* in a couple of different ways, but you can add to it in a lecture on the nature of parent versus peer influence. A good way to do so would be to consider in detail the classic work of Clay Brittain (Brittain, C.V. 1963 Adolescent choices and parent-peer cross pressures. *American Sociological Review, 28,* 358-391). Brittain, a sociologist, presented teenagers with a series of hypothetical dilemmas in which an adolescent receives conflicting advice from parents and peers. In his research he had participants decide which advice the adolescent followed. A clever feature of Brittain's research was that he presented subjects with the same dilemmas two weeks later, but reversed the advice parents and peers were giving in them, and again had his participants decide which advice the adolescent followed. If his respondents shifted their decisions in either the new peer or parent endorsed alternative, Brittain had a measure of parent or peer orientation. If his respondents continued to endorse the same solution despite the change in who endorsed it, Brittain had a measure of independence from parent or peer influence.

Get a copy of Brittain's research report. Read a sample dilemma to the class, and discuss with your students whether or not the dilemmas seem compelling to them as problems about which peer and parent advice might clash. Review Brittain's research design and strategy, and discuss its strengths and weaknesses. Finally, review his findings, and relate them to more contemporary research. You will be able to show that research on this issue has been very consistent over the years: Parent and teen influences are as likely to complement each other as they are to contradict each other.

This lecture is a good point of departure for later lectures and discussions on conditions and factors that genuinely do put peer influences in opposition to parents' influences on their teenage children.

2. Cognitive Interventions with Socially Dysfunctional Youth

Proponents of theories of social cognition claim that immature or poorly functioning thought about social relationships and processes is a fundamental cause of antisocial or disordered social behavior. There are both Piagetian and information processing variants of this theme. That is, some have attempted to show that socially dysfunctional youth lag behind peers in their stage of social cognitive thought (e.g., Robert Selman), whereas others attempt to show that problems lie in the steps or processes of social cognition (e.g., Kenneth Dodge).

Compare and contrast these points of view. Outline each, and show how it translates into intervention strategies. Robert Selman and Kenneth Dodge have both published work on these efforts.

Evaluate each approach in terms of the other. Which is easier to adopt? Which translates most clearly into intervention strategies or techniques? Which is better supported by evaluative data?

This material is useful as an illustration of the practical value of research on social cognition. It is also an opportunity to review the structural, functional, and information processing approaches to cognitive development and to illustrate how these approaches have branched into other research areas.

3. Observations of Adolescents

One theme of the several "observation" lecture sections in this manual is that observations become more important and useful the more they can be focused and structured. However, the initial steps toward making focused and structured observations often involve relatively free and unstructured observations.

A peculiarity of our knowledge about adolescent social life is that there is little sound observational data. For example, to this day, Dexter Dunphy's intensive study of Australian youth and the patterns of cliques and crowds that they form is a unique reference. Explore how Dunphy obtained the data that led him to characterize the development of adolescent groups. Present these techniques without comment to your class, and allow them the chance to react with appropriate criticisms.

A second, more modern attempt to fill the gaps in our knowledge of adolescents' daily life is Csikszentmihalyi's "beeper studies" that form the basis of his book *Being Adolescent* (1984). Discuss the strengths and weaknesses of this work, and compare it directly to Dunphy's earlier research. Also compare the research on adolescents to work with younger age groups; speculate on the likelihood that it is possible to gather comprehensive observational information on adolescents' daily social lives.

4.   Changes in Friendship during the Elementary School Years

a.   Before the age of 8, friendships are very short-lived, partly because young children do not acknowledge people having stable psychological characteristics. By fourth grade, friendships last as long as they do in later grades. More than two-thirds of friends in the fall are still friends at the end of the school year.
b.   At 7, friendships are based on superficial factors; by 9, compatible personalities are more important. For example, in one study children were told that Robby was their age; half of the children were told Robby was "real nice" and half were told he "had a new Lego game." Seven-year-olds were more likely to want to play if Robby had been described as nice.
c.   As children get older, they engage in more self-disclosure with their friends. However, they tell less to acquaintances.

(*Sources:* Berndt, T. J., Hawkins, J. A., & Hoyle, S. G. 1986. Changes in friendship during a school year: Effects on children's and adolescents' impressions of friendship and sharing with friends. *Child Development, 57,* 1284-1297; Boggiano, A. K., Klinger, C. A., & Main, D. S. 1986. Enhancing interest in peer interaction: A developmental analysis. *Child Development, 57,* 852-861; Rotenberg, K. J. & Sliz, D. 1988. Children's restrictive disclosure to friends. *Merrill-Palmer Quarterly, 34,* 203-215.)

5.   Parental Guidelines for Preschoolers' TV Watching

Parents of preschoolers should try to make television viewing a fun and educational experience. Here are a few suggestions for increasing the positive benefits of television for children:

a   Cut back on total viewing time. By decreasing viewing time, parents can expect that their children will shift away from an impulsive intellectual style to one more reflective. Spending more time with art, books, and play increases children's nonverbal IQ scores (Gadbery & Schneider, 1978). Four-year-olds who frequently watched television had less self-restraint than others their age, and six years later they were more aggressive and restless than their peers (Singer et al., 1984).
b.   Children learn more from television programs if parents or other adults view the shows with them and provide guiding commentaries to the shows (Corder-Bolz & O'Bryant, 1978). Parents should discuss with their children the television commercials that they see and explore toy manufacturers' claims about the products (Adams & Fuchs, 1986).
c.   Parents should consider reducing both aggressive television programs and the number of aggressive toys that small children possess (Adams & Fuchs, 1986).
d.   Try not to use the television as an easy babysitter. Encourage children to watch shows that promote healthy values, increase knowledge, and teach children about different cultures and diversity of peoples, such as Sesame Street, Mister Rogers' Neighborhood, and Big Marble (Greenfield, 1984). (*Sources:* Adams, D. M. & Fuchs, M. 1986 (November). The video media and cultural misunderstanding. *USA Today,* 79-81; Corder-Bolz, C. R. & O'Bryant, S. L. 1978. Can people affect television? Teacher vs. program. *Journal of Communication, 28,* 97-103; Gadbery, S. & Schneider, H. 1978. Effects of parental restrictions on TV viewing. Paper presented to the American Psychological Association; Greenfield, P. M. 1984. *Mind and media: The effects of television, video games, and computers.* Cambridge, MA: Harvard University Press; Singer, J. L., Singer, D. G., & Rapaczynski, W. S. 1984. Family patterns and television viewing as predictors of children's beliefs and aggression. *Journal of Communication, 34,* 73-89.)

6.   Combining Play Types

Young children combine the types of play. For example, they may use their constructions in dramatic play. They may build a structure that is then turned into a grocery store or castle or school in which to continue pretend play. Some children tend to be **dramatists,** who do more dramatic play and use constructive materials to aid in interaction with others. A big and small block are turned into a mommy and baby going shopping. Or blocks are turned into cookies that are passed out to others. Other children are **patterners,** who make configurations out of play materials, tend to build designs with blocks, and exhibit curiosity about how their objects work. Patterners do more than the average amount of constructive play. (*Source:* Christie, J. F. & Johnsen, E. P. 1987. Reconceptualizing constructive play: A review of the empirical literature. *Merrill-Palmer Quarterly, 33,* 439-452.)

7.   Leaders and Followers in Preschool Play

The roles played by preschool children in play have been compared to the roles within a medieval kingdom, complete with kings, lords, bishops, vassals, and serfs (Adcock & Segal, 1983; Segal et al., 1987). **Kings,** not very common in either medieval kingdoms or in children's play, are leaders who like to engage in play fighting. Kings are rather outgoing, fun-loving, self-confident, and independent.

A more common leader role is the **lords.** Lords are boys and girls who prefer dramatic (pretend) play and whose personal style is often bossy, assertive, and idea-oriented. Lords tend to lead a small but stable group of followers and do much of the direction and control of play.

The third type of leader is the **bishops,** who have flexible, nurturant, verbal, instructing, and reasonable personalities. Bishops often prefer dyadic play and are successful mediators of quarrels and quite creative in problem-solving.

The two follower styles are vassals and serfs. **Vassals** try to be the favored playmate of either a lord or a king. To reach this goal, vassals tend to do the bidding of their leader and try to keep others in the group from taking over this favored position. **Serfs** have the least power and tend to follow their leaders and accept any roles assigned to them. They are peripheral group members. Other serfs wander from group to group, spend much of the time observing groups at play, or are rejected from all groups. Serfs use more fantasy play than other types, probably to enhance the quality of their play potential.

When conflict arises, kings, lords, and vassals use force, rules, and adult intervention to resolve conflicts. Bishops use distraction to try to settle disagreement, and they sometimes use crying in conflict resolution. Serfs tend to have only force as a tool in conflict resolution.

Since vassals may become aggressive when they are unable to develop a very close relationship with a strong leader and serfs may become aggressive as a way of protesting their low social status, researchers have tried pairing unsuccessful serfs and vassals with bishop-type children to try to build harmonious dyadic relationships. Once these children were paired with adopting bishops, their acts of aggression went down over time (Segal et al., 1987). (*Sources:* Adcock, D. & Segal, M. 1983. *Making friends.* Englewood Cliffs, NJ: Prentice-Hall; Segal, M., Peck, J., Vega-Lahr, N. & Field, T. 1987. A medieval kingdom: Leader-follower styles of preschool play. *Journal of Applied Developmental Psychology, 8,* p. 92.)

8.   Dungeons and Dragons

Many preadolescents become fans of Dungeons & Dragons, a medieval adventure game first developed in 1974 by Gary Geigex. The game's creator believes his game enhances imagination, provides a symbolic representation of adult challenges, and encourages cooperation among players. In this game, players who cooperate and join their complementary spiritual, physical, and magical powers together increase their rewards and lessen their chances of misfortune. However, some critics believe that the game has been the cause of some adolescent suicides; they believe that adolescents can get lost in a fantasy world and end their lives. Yet in its first 10 years of existence (during which more than two million copies of the basic game were sold) only two avid players committed suicide. (*Source:* Fisher, K. 1984. Game helps youths pass from magic to maturity. *APA Monitor,* Dec. 14.)

9.   Television Shows that Sell Toys

Children often become interested in specific toys by seeing television commercials about these products. Sometimes the children's shows themselves are used to market toy products. By the late 1970s, Hanna-Barbera cartoon characters were marketed on more than 4,500 products. In 1980 and 1981, cartoon characters Strawberry Shortcake and the Smurfs were introduced, and each has sold over a billion dollars worth of related merchandise. In 1984, the FCC dropped all limitations of ads per show ratio, and both program-advertising and number of actual commercials increased. In that year alone, He-Man and the Masters of the Universe sold seventy million action figures (Engelhardt, 1986). In 1989, Teenage Mutant Ninja Turtles became a popular show with turtles selling movies, videos, clothes, sheets, toy objects, cereal, and many other items. Many people believe that children cannot resist the appeal of this programming, and that they cannot make accurate judgments about the accuracy of the advertising.

The average child watches four hours of action-packed television each day, and these shows are sponsored by the manufacturers of action-packed toys. In the 1980s, the sales of war toys increased more than 200 percent, and now exceed $1 billion annually. Children copy the television shows in playing with these war toys—both increasing violent play and decreasing creative play. Oftentimes children do not realize that they may hurt their playmates when they imitate aggressive behavior of a cartoon figure. Also, when they do hurt someone else while imitating a cartoon character, they often blame the cartoon character.

Parents can: (1) limit children's exposure to action shows and related toys; (2) encourage children to make imaginative props from cardboard boxes and tubes, Legos, Play-Doh, and other available materials, rather than just copy a show's plot; (3) engage their children in conversation about the characters. (*Sources:* Engelhardt, T. 1986. Saturday morning fever. The hard-sell takeover of kids' TV. *Mother Jones,* Sept. 39-48, 54; Ludtke, M. 1990 (March 26). How to neutralize G. I. Joe. *Time,* 84-86; Carlsson-Paige, N. & Levin, D. 1990. *Who's calling the shots?: How to respond effectively to children's fascination with war play and war toys.* New Society Publishers.)

10.   The Purposes of Peer Relations

Peer relationships serve several important functions, including play participants, emotional security, norm setting, instruction and modeling, and life adjustment.

During the middle childhood years, children often engage in dramatic play that allows them to practice roles and interactions. Also during the school years, children need other participants to be able to play games. Young and schoolaged children are more comfortable in a strange situation when there is another child present. The presence of a familiar child is more comforting to most children than is the presence of a familiar adult. Children learn both norms and skills from their peers. Most of the norms endorsed by schoolaged children are consistent with those expected by parents and other adults. Children also teach each other how to get along in the world. Sometimes oral child-to-child teachings involve many misconceptions, such as many of the ideas passed around about human sexuality.

Having good peer relations in childhood is a predictor of good adult personality and social relations. Although many children without effective peer relationships become effective, socially adept adults, some socially isolated and withdrawn children become schizoid or engage in aggressive and antisocial activities, and some antisocial, aggressive children become antisocial adults. (*Sources:* Asher, S. R. 1978. Children's peer relations. In M. E. Lamb (Ed.). *Social and Personality Development,* NY: Holt, Rinehart & Winston; Leventhal, B. L. & Dawson, K. 1984. Middle childhood: Normality as integration and interaction. In D. Offer & M. Sabshin (Eds.). *Normality and the Life Cycle: A Critical Integration,* NY: Basic Books.)

11.   Dating May Be Easier than It Looks

In one research study by Russell Clark and Elaine Hatfield, "slightly unattractive" to "moderately attractive" male and female college students were asked to approach an attractive person of the opposite sex and say, "I have been noticing you around campus and I find you to be very attractive." Depending on their experimental condition, this statement was followed by:

   a.   "Would you go out with me tonight?"
   b.   "Would you come over to my apartment tonight?"
   c.   "Would you go to bed with me tonight?"

The results:

   a.   Half of the men (50 percent) and more than half the women (56 percent) agreed to go out with a stranger.
   b.   Most women (94 percent) refused to go to the apartment, and none agreed to go to bed that night.
   c.   Most men would go to the woman's apartment (69 percent), and to bed that night (75 percent).

Are these results surprising or expected by students? What expectations do they give for the striking gender differences that were found? (*Source:* Hatfield, E. & Sprecher, S. 1986. *Mirror, mirror . . . The importance of looks in everyday life.* Albany, New York: State University of New York Press.)

BROWN & BENCHMARK'S HUMAN DEVELOPMENT TRANSPARENCIES (2ND ED.)

Transparency Number and Title

The transparency set, a supplement to *Child Development*, is accompanied by an annotated manual that describes each of the 141 transparencies. The annotated manual also offers suggestions about how to use the transparencies to engage your students in active learning that will stimulate critical thinking and evaluative skills. The following transparencies are appropriate and useful with Chapter 16: Peers, Play, and the Media.

Transparency Number and Title

24   Bandura's Model of the Reciprocal Influence of B, P, and E
25   Bronfenbrenner's Ecological Model
80   Peer Aggression
81   Types of Social Play
82   Five Types of Children's Play
92   The Functions of Friendship
102   Where Adolescents Spend their Time
103   What Adolescents Spend their Time Doing
104   People With Whom Adolescents Spend their Time
107   Dunphy's Progression of Peer Group Relations in Adolescence
113   Sternberg's Triangle of Love

CLASSROOM ACTIVITIES OR DEMONSTRATIONS

1. Discuss the critical thinking exercises. Like Exercise 1 for Chapter 6, Exercise 1 for Chapter 7 requires students to be aware of the perspectives that motivate and inform research presented in the chapter. You may want to repeat a review of the distinguishing features of the perspectives in order to prepare them for the exercise. However, in this chapter the influence of the perspectives is more clearly signaled in language and reference than in the previous chapter.

    Exercise 2 is designed to promote students' attention to the kinds of research that form the basis of conclusions in the chapter. But it is different from previous exercises in that it requires students to draw a conclusion about the whole chapter. The main thing to do is advise students to heed the instruction to keep track of the kinds of research reported in the chapter. You may want to discuss with them an appropriate means (e.g., a table) to do that. You may also want to review the earmarks of the different types of research.

    Exercise 3 mainly forces students to consider the basis of the various statements contained in it. You could mention that the assumption in this exercise is the least well supported claim, one that Santrock seems to want us to accept *a forteriori*.

2. Discuss the students' research projects as suggested below.

3. Demonstrate the power of groups by reenacting the Asch conformity experiment. This is easily done, but you have to take care in recruiting class members to be your confederates. Use this experience to discuss the nature and influence of real conformity pressures in adolescents lives.

4. Bradford Brown has documented the existence of different peer crowds in high schools (see Brown, B.B., Lohr, M.J. & Trujillo, C. (1990), Multiple crowds and multiple life styles: adolescents' perceptions of peer-group stereotypes. In R.E. Muus (Ed.), *Adolescent behavior and society: a book of readings.* New York: McGraw-Hill Publishing Company). You should find that your students can attest to this as well. Have your students list the major high school crowds that they can remember. Urge them to use the names that identified these crowds, and to write brief descriptions of the individuals who belonged to each.

    Next, collect the lists of crowds from some or all of your students, or have them read their lists to the class. In either case, write the names down on blackboard or overhead. Attempt to note where students from different high schools report the same type of crowd, and keep track of the number of crowds students report.

    In the end, you should be able to show that the number types of crowds are fairly similar from high school to high school. For example, there should be athletic crowds, academic crowds (though Brown's work suggests they will be small), rebellious crowds, out-of-it crowds, political crowds. Whatever you find, relate the classes reports to material in *Adolescence* on the nature, significance, impact, and functioning of adolescent crowds.

5. Adolescent musical preferences may be analyzed to determine whether adolescents are making political or value-oriented statements that separate them from adults. You can engage the class in a very interesting activity by playing tapes or CDs of songs from the 1960s, 1970s, 1980s, and 1990s and having students analyze these songs in terms of (a) sexual themes; (b) conflict with or rebellion against adults; and (c) adolescent preoccupations (e.g., love, cars, sex). You can also mention some of the early accusations against rock music (e.g., being communist-inspired, or an immoral influence on youth). Michael Walraven, who made this suggestion for a class activity in the instructor's course planner for the fifth edition of *Adolescence*, recommend these songs:

> Queen, "I'm in Love with My Car"
> Jackson Brown, "Cocaine" and "Daddy's Tune"
> Joni Mitchell, "Big Yellow Taxi"
> Stevie Nicks, "Stop Dragging My Heart Around"
> Crosby, Stills, Nash, and Young, "Teach Your Children Well"
> Bob Dylan, "The Times, They are a-Changing"
> Cat Stevens, "Peace Train", "Father and Son", Where Do the Children Play?"
> Bob Seger, "Night Moves"

Walraven, M. G. 1993. *Instructor's Course Planner* to accompany John Santrock's *Adolescence*, 5th ed. Dubuque: Brown and Benchmark, Publishers.

6. Ask students to describe the first friendship they can remember and a more recent friendship. What did they do with their first friend? What did they know about that friend? What about their recent friend? How does the intimacy in the two friendships differ? How does this difference confirm or deny the developmental data presented in the text? Are there general characteristics for earlier or later friendships for the groups?

Early friendships are generally based on proximity and similarity. Friendships later in life involve more intimacy than friendships early in life. Younger friendships might be expected to focus on play activities; friendships of older individuals might focus more on conversation and sharing ideas and feelings.

Students are likely to remember more details about their friends in junior high school and high school relative to their memories of specific activities. Because of the more intimate nature of friendships in the later years of school, they probably learned more about these people at the time. There is also a time compound to explain the difference.

Source: Adapted from King, M. B., & Clark, D. E. 1989. *Instructors' Manual to Accompany Santrock and Yussen's Child Development: An Introduction,* 4th ed. Dubuque: Wm. C. Brown Publishers.

7. Have your students develop psychometric techniques to identify individuals who are popular, socially accepted, and have high status. You can suggest naturalistic observations of adolescent groups, and encourage students to define operationally behaviors that reflect the underlying construct (e.g., number of times a person complies with someone else's suggestions, time spent talking, seating arrangements). This exercise can be used to introduce the sociogram, or students could develop a paper-and-pencil measure of popularity. Whatever approach you encourage or students take, have students think of ways to validate their instruments and to compare them with measures described in the literature.

Walraven, M. G. 1993. *Instructor's Course Planner* to accompany John Santrock's *Adolescence*, 5th ed. Dubuque, Ia: Brown and Benchmark, Publishers.

8. S. S. Hendrick and C. Hendrick have created, validated, and done considerable research with an instrument called "The Love Attitude Scale". This is a device for determining which of seven different types of love predominates in the a respondents love relationships. If you can, get a copy of the scale from the Hendrick's book, *Liking, Loving, and Relating* and administer it to your class. Have your students score

their responses. Depending on how shy and responsive your class is, you can collect the data as a basis for discussing the prevalence of different types of love among their cohort, among younger adolescent cohorts, and among adult cohorts. The experience may also be the springboard for a discussion of methodological issues in the study of love (can you really use questionnaires to study it?), or the controversy about whether love and romance is a fit topic for research.

9.   Many school-aged children dial 900 telephone numbers to hear recorded messages from teen idols, listen to Santa Claus or super-heroes, or to get tips on video games. These 900 calls typically cost $2.00 for the first minute and $0.45 for each additional minute. The numbers are advertised on television during after-school hours, and many children make these phone calls without asking parental permission. What should be done about this expensive situation?

   After soliciting class suggestions be certain to mention that telephone companies who receive complaints from a parent will get a refund—*one* time. The phone company can also put a 900 block on one's phone.

Source: Littell, M. A. 1989 (Nov.). Mother & child: The high cost of 900 numbers. *Good Housekeeping,* 80.

---

10.   Do adolescents have the right to determine what music they wish to hear? Or, should parents, politicians, and religious leaders restrict teenagers from music that is violent and/or sexually explicit? If you think it should be restricted, who should determine the restrictions? What restrictions do you think are appropriate?

   Here are results of The Newsweek Poll done by the Gallup Organization in a national telephone survey of 604 adults on June 13-14, 1990:

   A judge in Florida has ruled that some lyrics of the rap group 2 Live Crew are so violent and sexually explicit as to be obscene. Those who sell or perform this music now face prosecution. In your own community, do you think such music should be:

5%	Available to any buyer
38%	Available only to adult buyers
22%	Available to any buyer but with a warning label
32%	Not available

   How do these survey results compare to the class' opinion?

Sources: Salholz, E., Clift, E., McDaniel, A. & Reiss, S. 1990 (June 25). Value judgments. *Newsweek,* 16-18; Lacayo, R. 1990 (June 25). The rap against a rap group. *Time,* 18.

---

11.   Take this seven-item quiz about television. The correct answers are listed below.

   1.   Daytime shows for children have more commercials than evening shows for adults.
       A. True   B. False
   2.   A child has spent 11,000 hours in school by the time of high school. How many hours has the child spent watching television?
       A. 2,000 hours B. 10,000 hours   C. 15,000 hours
   3.   Is there a relationship between violence on TV and aggression in children?
       A. Yes   B. No
   4.   What are the two most common advertised products during children's programs?
       A. Toys   B. Diapers   C. Food/snacks   D. Toothpaste
       E. Soda pop
   5.   On Saturday, what percentage of network TV programs for children are cartoons?
       A. 25   B. 50   C. 75   D. 95
   6.   During children's TV programs, cartoon characters and program hosts are not permitted to talk about any commercials.
       A. True   B. False

7. There are government regulations for all advertising that children might see.
   A. True   B. False

Answers: 1. A; 2. C; 3. A; 4. A & C; 5. D; 6. A; 7. B.

Source: Mohler, M. (1987, April). Test your TV I.Q. *Ladies' Home Journal,* 60.

CRITICAL THINKING EXERCISES

Exercise 1

In the first thinking exercise of the previous chapter you attempted to determine which of the five theoretical orientations Santrock outlined in Chapter 2 of *Adolescence* was most influential in the chapter. Do the same again for Chapter 7: Which theoretical orientation seems to be most dominant in this chapter? **Circle the letter of the best answer, and explain why it is the best answer and why each other answer is not as good.**

A. Psychoanalytic theories
B. Cognitive theories
C. Behavioral and social learning theories
D. Ecological theories
E. An eclectic theoretical orientation

Exercise 2

As you read Chapter 16, keep track (when description is detailed enough) of the types of research that appear to be the basis of our knowledge of peers, play, and the media. When you have completed the chapter, tally up the type that seems to be predominant. Then decide which of the following statements seems to be best supported by your finding. **Circle the letter of the best answer, and explain why it is the best answer and why each other answer is not as good.**

A. Our knowledge of peers, play, and the media is speculative. There are relatively few data, and we must rely on the casual observations of trained developmentalists.
B. Research on peers, play, and the media has produced detailed descriptions, but as yet we lack knowledge of patterns of development and correlates of individual differences in peer relations.
C. We have achieved a fairly comprehensive knowledge of developmental patterns and correlates of individual differences in the peer relations of children and adolescence.
D. Extensive longitudinal and experimental work has given us a firm basis upon which to develop effective intervention programs to counteract poor peer relations and negative influences of the media.
E. Not only do we have adequate knowledge of causal relationships in peer relations, but we also have an extensive evaluation literature in which interventions have been thoroughly evaluated.

Exercise 3

The medium that draws the largest treatment in *Child Development* is television. Which of the following statements represents an assumption, rather than in inference or an observation, that is probably responsible for this focus? **Circle the letter of the best answer, and explain why it is the best answer and why each other answer is not as good.**

A. Television has a greater influence on children's behavior than any other medium.
B. Television can have negative and positive influences on children's behavior.
C. There are 25 violent acts per hour on Saturday morning cartoon shows.
D. Males who watched relatively large amounts of aggressive television are more likely to commit violent crimes later in life.
E. Television causes children to be less creative.

ANSWER KEYS FOR CRITICAL THINKING EXERCISES

Exercise 1

A. This is not the best answer. Psychoanalytic thinking importantly influences the material on friendship, but makes no contribution to the other topics in the chapter. Interestingly, this is true even of the material on romantic relationships.

B. This is not the best answer. Cognitive theories are particularly important in the discussion of popularity, social knowledge, and social information processing; they also seem to contribute to strategies for improving adolescents' social skills. Dating scripts are also examples of cognitive constructs used to understand adolescent peer relations. However, cognitive theories are noticeably absent in discussions of most other aspects of peer relations.

C. This is not the best answer. Behavioral and social learning theories play a role in the analysis of popularity and social strategies for improving adolescents' social skills. There is also the implication that learning and social learning processes play a role in friendship and group formation. But other theoretical orientations seem to have shaped the questions and research methods of most other topics in the chapter.

D. This is not the best answer. Interestingly, in contrast to the analysis of families, the analysis of peer relations involves considerably less attention to interactions between social systems. In fact this perspective appears to get the least play in Chapter 7. The orientation's most obvious influence is the material on ethnic minority adolescents' peer relations, and the consideration of family-peer linkages discussed early in the chapter.

E. This is the best answer. The foregoing arguments make the case for this alternative. All of the perspectives make a contribution to Chapter 7, with none dominant.

Exercise 2

A. This is not the best answer. Santrock cites many studies of the influence of peers, play, and the media on children.

B. This is not the best answer. It is true that research has produced detailed descriptions. For example, there are observational studies of adolescent groups in formation and of children's play groups and activities. But there are also many correlational studies that have tested hypotheses about the cognitive and social correlates of individual differences in the quality of peer relations, variations in children's groups, and the nature of contact with the media.

C. This is the best answer. There are a couple of longitudinal studies cited in the chapter, as well as cross-sectional work that has characterized, for example, age changes in the nature of peer relations and friendship. Further, as indicated in (B), there are many studies of psychological and social correlates of variations in peer relations.

D. This is not the best answer. Very little of the work reported in Chapter 16 is experimental. Correlational work has given us many leads about causes of undesirable developmental outcomes associated with peers, play, and the media, but has not established beyond doubt and controversy the precise mechanisms that explain these correlations.

E. This is not the best answer. Although Chapter 16 mentions an applied literature on training children unskilled in peer relations at different points (e.g., the perspective on parenting and education), the results of evaluations of these programs are not reported in the chapter.

Exercise 3

A. This is the best answer. Santrock makes this statement without argument or appropriate evidence. No comparisons are made.

B. This is not the best answer. The statement is an inference, based on an inventory on the presumably negative and positive things that are portrayed on television.

C. This is not the best answer. The statement is an observation based on systematic studies of Saturday morning cartoons.

D. This is not the best answer. This is an observation (a correlation) that has been generated in longitudinal studies.

E. This is not the best answer. It is an inference about the basis of a correlation negative correlation between amount of television watched and children's creativity.

RESEARCH PROJECT 1   CONFORMITY IN ADOLESCENTS' CLOTHING CHOICES

This research project was suggested to us by a student of ours, Robert Losby, who performed it for a project in developmental psychology. It is a simple way to test the hypothesis that conformity in clothing choice is higher among early adolescents than either among children or among late adolescents.

Your basic task is to observe what brand name of jeans students at an elementary school, junior high school, and high school wear. Find a way to unobtrusively observe students as they enter or leave school. Record the brand names of jeans being worn by students who are wearing jeans. To do this you may need to do some background work on the kinds of jeans available in your community and what they look like from a distance! You will also save yourself some effort if you can prepare a data sheet that has spaces designated for the types of jeans you expect to see.

Prepare a table that shows how many students at each school wore each brand name of jeans. If you know how, computer a chi-square statistic to test for an association between age level and brand of jeans worn. Then answer the following questions.

Questions

1. How many different types of jeans were worn by students at each age level?
2. Was there an association between age levels and brands of jeans worn. (Was the association significant?)
3. What problems did you encounter in doing your observations?
4. Do your data justify a claim that students of one age level are more likely to conform to their peers than students at another age level? Why or why not?
5. How does the information you have collected compare to what you have learned in textbook and lecture?

Use in Classroom:

Collate data from all your students. If you have time and the facilities, compute a chi-square. Have students interpret the findings. Discuss methodological problems in collecting the data and limitations on interpreting the data. Relate your classes results to other material on conformity and peer influences that you have presented or discussed.

RESEARCH PROJECT 2   INTERVIEWING FRIENDS ABOUT DATING

Use the structured interview format presented on the data sheet to interview two friends - one male and one female - about the reasons they date. Record each subject's answers on the data sheet and then answer the questions.

DATA SHEET

Question	Subject 1 Age___Sex___	Subject 2 Age___Sex___
1. What is the most important reason you go on a date?		
2. What are two other reasons you date?		
3. How do you decide whom to date?		
4. What do you do if you are interested in someone you would like to date?		

Questions

1. What was the male's most important reason for dating? How did that differ from his other reasons for dating?
2. What was the female's most important reason for dating? How did that differ from her other reasons for dating?
3. Did the reasons for dating differ for the male and female you interviewed? Did the way they go about getting dates differ? Did they seem to follow traditional male-female roles, or were they nontraditional? How did their reasons for dating compare to the four functions of dating reported in the text?

Use in Classroom

Have students report the categories of reasons males and females gave for dating. Keep track of these on blackboard or overhead. Then create a contingency table in which you record reasons given by male versus females; use this table to assess whether the sexes tend to give different types of reasons for dating. Finally, discuss the extent observed differences (if any) parallel traditional gender roles.

ESSAY AND CRITICAL THINKING QUESTIONS

Comprehension and Application Essay Questions

We recommend that you provide students with our guidelines for "Answering Essay and Critical Thinking Questions" when you have them respond to these questions. Their answers to these kinds of questions demonstrate an ability to comprehend and apply ideas discussed in this chapter.

1. Define the term *peers* and summarize peer group functions.
2. What are the similarities and differences between peer relationships and parent-child relationships?
3. Describe the developmental course of peer relations, and discuss how and why some children experience poor peer relations.
4. Discuss cognitive developmental factors involved in peer relations.
5. List the functions of friendship and discuss whether and how Sullivan incorporates these functions in his developmental model of friendship.
6. Discuss the importance of similarity and intimacy to friendship.
7. Distinguish between children's and adolescents' groups, and compare and contrast the characteristics and functions of adolescent crowds and cliques.
8. Describe Parten's classifications of play.
9. Compare and contrast sensorimotor/practice play and constructive play.
10. How are games different from other play types?
11. List three advantages and three disadvantages of children's television watching.
12. Summarize the research findings on the effects of television aggression on children.
13. List three potential positive and three potential negative effects of computers on children's development.

Critical Thinking Questions

We recommend that you have students follow our guidelines for "Answering Essay and Critical Thinking Questions" when you ask them to prepare responses to these questions. Their answers to these kinds of questions reflect an ability to apply critical thinking skills to a novel problem or situation that is *not* specifically discussed in the chapter. These items most appropriately may be used as take-home essay questions (e.g., due on exam day) or as homework exercises that can be answered either by individuals or groups. Collaboratively answered questions encourage cooperative learning by students, and reduce the number of papers that must be graded.

1. At the end of Chapter 16 Santrock indicates books that provide practical knowledge about children and lists resources for improving the lives of children. Choose one of these books or resources and read it or learn as much as you can about it. Then write a brief review in which you (a) characterize the book or resource, and (b) explain how the book or resource relates to material in the chapter.
2. Chapter 1 defines the nature of development in terms of biological, cognitive, and social processes, and periods or stages. Indicate your ability to think critically by identifying material in this chapter that illustrates developmental processes and periods. If there is little or no information in this chapter about

developmental processes and periods, identify and explain how developmental processes and periods could be used to guide the analysis of any topic in the chapter.

3. According to Chapter 1, three fundamental developmental issues concern: (a) maturation (nature) versus experience (nurture), (b) continuity versus discontinuity, and (c) early versus later experience. Indicate your ability to think critically by identifying material in this chapter that illustrates each of the three fundamental developmental issues. If there is little or no information in this chapter about fundamental developmental issues, identify and explain how these issues could be used to guide the analysis of any topic in the chapter.

4. One aspect of thinking critically is to read, listen, and observe carefully and then ask questions about what is missing from a text, discussion, or situation. For example, a topic that might have been included in this chapter is adolescent gangs. Indicate your ability to think critically by (a) listing as many questions as you can about the nature of peer relations among adolescents in gangs, and (b) speculating why Santrock does not discuss this topic more fully.

5. Santrock sets off several quotations in this chapter. Indicate your ability to think critically by selecting one of the quotes and (a) learning about the author and indicating why this individual is eminently quotable (i.e., what was this individual's contribution to human knowledge and understanding), (b) interpreting and restating the quote in your own terms, and (c) explaining what concept, issue, perspective, or term in this chapter that Santrock intended this quote to illuminate. In other words, about what aspect or issue in development does this quote make you pause and reflect?

6. Chapter 2 indicates that theories help us explain data and make predictions about various aspects of development. Chapter 2 then presents six different theoretical approaches (i.e., Freudian, cognitive, behavioral and social learning, ethological, ecological, and eclectic theory), but notes that no single approach explains the complexity of development. Indicate your ability to think critically by (a) perusing this chapter for topics influenced by at least one of the six theoretical approaches, and (b) explaining which theoretical approach dominated the topic in question. If the presentation is entirely atheoretical, identify and explain how one of the theoretical approaches could be used to guide the analysis of the topic in question.

7. In chapter 13 (p. 409) of *Child Development* Santrock asks an number of questions about the MTV show "Beavis and Butt-Head": What age group are Beavis and Butt-Head most likely to appeal to? Why? Are some adolescents more likely to be attracted to them than others? Apply your knowledge about the scientific method by designing a study that will answer these questions:about "Beavis and Butt-head": (a) What specific problem or question do you want to study? (b) What predictions would you make and test in your study? (c) What measures would you use (i.e., controlled observation in a laboratory, naturalistic observation, interviews and questionnaires, case studies, standardized tests, cross-cultural studies, physiological research, research with animals, or multimeasure, multisource, and multicontext approach) and how would you define each measure clearly and unambiguously? (d) What strategy would you follow-- correlational or experimental, and what would be the time span of your inquiry--cross-sectional or longitudinal? (e) What ethical considerations must be addressed before you conduct your study?

8. According to Chapter 2, your author wants you to become a wise consumer of information about child development by: (a) being cautious about media reports, (b) distinguishing between nomothetic research and idiographic needs, (c) recognizing how easy it is to overgeneralize from a small or clinical sample, (d) knowing that a single study is usually not the defining word about some aspect of child development, (e) remembering that causal conclusions cannot be made from correlation studies, and (f) always considering the source of the information and evaluating its credibility. Indicate your ability to think critically by, first, selecting an article from either a journal, magazine, or newspaper about any topic regarding Peers, Play, and the Media, and, second, evaluating it in terms of these six objectives. If the information in the article is insufficient to evaluate one of these objectives, then specify what kind of information you would need to evaluate the objective.

17 Schools and Achievement

SUGGESTIONS FOR LECTURE TOPICS

1. School Readiness

For preschoolers, **school readiness,** the development of appropriate skills for first grade, should be more important than intelligence measures. Parents might work with their older preschoolers to learn some of the following academic skills (Schuster & Auburn, 1986):

a. Familiarity with the alphabet. Can learn the sequence of the alphabet, recognize the alphabet, and be able to print some letters and identify some of the sounds.
b. Recognizing own name in print and perhaps to be able to print it.
c. Be able to count to at least ten and recognize the different numbers. Can identify number of objects, e.g., three dimes, four pens.
d. Understand the concept of "less" and "more." Can also identify the largest, smallest, longest, and shortest objects.
e. Can name the basic colors.
f. Can tell right from left. Also understands position words, e.g., above, below, under, over, inside, outside, on, and beside.
g. Has some success with telling which items are alike and which are different, in matching rhyming words and objects with similar functions.
h. Can do fundamental self-care—feeding themselves, going to the bathroom alone, washing own hands, and putting on clothes and shoes.
i. Physically can do tasks such as skipping, hopping, and jumping.
j. Can hold a pencil correctly and turn pages of a book. Has rudimentary skills with scissors.

Children who can accomplish these tasks at the beginning of first grade have a definite advantage over other children.

Not all five-year-olds, however, are ready for kindergarten. "Developmentally young" children can benefit from being "redshirted" for a year and starting school the following year. Some school districts have DK (developmental kindergarten), which allows these youngsters to have two years of kindergarten-type atmosphere. Experts vary from believing that 1 percent to 30 percent of five-year-olds could benefit from a one-year delay in the school system. (*Sources:* Schuster, C. S. & Ashburn, S. S. 1986. *The process of human development: A holistic life-span approach,* 2nd Ed., Boston: Little Brown; Elson, J. 1989 (Nov. 13). The redshirt solution. *Time,* 102.)

2. Classroom Control and Motivation

Edward Deci has been investigating intrinsic motivation in the classroom for some time. His research suggests a surprising result: recent emphasis on stiffer graduation requirements, higher achievement standards, and systems to reward teacher excellence may actually produce the opposite result intended. Before explaining how this may occur, open the class up for discussion. Start with Deci's conclusion and ask this question: How is it that demands for higher achievement standards might lead to lower performance by students? Discuss this for a few minutes. Ask for a show of hands of how many agree with Deci. How is it that financial rewards to teachers based on student performance may actually interfere with students' performances outside of class? Discuss this for a few minutes more. Ask students if they agree with Deci that such rewards could be a negative factor in education.

If students haven't mentioned it, remind them about the distinction between intrinsic and extrinsic motivation. Ask if the distinction sheds any light on the questions you have asked them.

Deci's research has shown that giving teachers even very modest reminders about standards and goals of accountability can have disastrous effects on students' performance outside of class. Here's how the study was done: 40 people were instructed to "help" a group of students solve puzzles. Half of the "teachers" were told. "It is your responsibility as a teacher to be sure your students perform up to high standards," a very modest reminder indeed. Certainly it was not as powerful as a monetary reward. The other half of the "teachers" were simply told to help the students. Recordings were made of the 20-minute training sessions. Analysis of these sessions revealed that the teachers given the "responsibility" for "higher standards" pushed their students to perform. For example, they talked three times as much as the other teachers, were more directive, evaluated performance more often, and were much more critical. It is true that the students in these conditions assembled twice as many puzzles as those of the less controlling teachers. Deci argues that this is not the important result. We are not trying to produce classroom performers but persons who perform on their own. The students in both groups were then given the opportunity to solve puzzles without the supervision of their teachers. The students of the "high standards" groups suddenly solved only 20 percent of the number of puzzles as the students who were less controlled did.

Deci argues that excellence in education is a wise aim but not with these controlling methods. He believes that we should encourage teachers who build support systems, teachers who promote self-determination in their students, and those who promote innovation in their teaching and their students. He further argues that procedures for standardized curricula and more competency testing will certainly lead to excellence within the classroom, but will lead to mediocrity outside the classroom.

Discuss with your class how you feel about this issue. It may be appropriate to critique Deci's work. Integrate these findings with material reported in *Adolescence* (or have your students do so as an assignment). Explain how you try to motivate them! (*Source:* Deci, E. L. (1985, March). *Psychology Today*, 52-53.)

3.   Mothers and their Powerful Sons

McCullough has proposed an interesting explanation for the cause of learning to want achievement and power: Mother. McCullough examined the lives of many male leaders and found their mother and her behavior to be a common thread among these men.

Douglas MacArthur's mother Pinky accompanied Douglas to West Point. She set up residence in a hotel across the street from campus for his full four-year tenure there. Franklin D. Roosevelt's mother, Sara, moved to Boston while Franklin attended Harvard. Frank Lloyd Wright's mother, Anna, decided before Frank's birth that he would be an architect. She hung engravings of cathedrals in his nursery. The mothers of Presidents Harry Truman and Lyndon B. Johnson taught them to read before age 5. In these, and many other cases, McCullough pointed out that these mothers made their sons the center of their lives. McCullough also pointed out that in all cases, the mothers had weak or uninspiring husbands and dominant fathers who provided possible models for their grandsons. McCullough believed that sons became these women's vehicles to success. McCullough offers insight from Freud: "A man who has been the indisputable favorite of his mother keeps for life the feeling of a conqueror."

You should point out to your students that these men grew up with only the best education and resources. They were given the opportunities, support, and models to become all that they could. Ask the class to supply additional examples (President Clinton? Newt Gingrich?). Also ask the class to apply the idea to high-achieving women. Finally, be sure to engage the class in a critique of McCullough's method, and entertain a thorough analysis of the limitations of his proof.
(*Source:* McCullough, D. (1980, March). Mama's boys. *Psychology Today*, pp. 32-38.

4.   The Rise and Fall of Fear of Success

Matina Horner achieved wide spread recognition for initiating investigation of a phenomenon that many believed was a powerful explanation of achievement differences between men and women: Fear of success. Horner noted that up until the time of her work, women's achievement motivation had been substantially ignored. In her attempt to develop norms on a projective measure for achievement, Horner found that women were much more likely to express motives to avoid success than to achieve it. The work was instantly influential, even though (perhaps predictably), subsequent criticism blunted its long-term impact.

Nevertheless, a lecture on the rise and fall of Horner's work is a useful way to teach about one way achievement motives are assessed, historical gender biases in the study of achievement motivation, and progress that has been made in comparing male and female achievement motives as a consequence of Horner's work. A way to begin your lecture could be to introduce one of the incomplete stories that Horner used to measure motivation: "At the end of first-term finals, Anne (John) finds herself at the top of her (his) medical school class." Have your students write their own versions of how this story turned out, which they can then compare to Horner's and others' findings.

Give examples of Horner's findings. (see the source below): 66% of women's story completions expressed fear of success in terms of fear of social rejection, worries about womanhood, or denial that the success had actually occured; only 8% of males told similar stories about John (presumably, really themselves). Horner argued that such an achievement avoidance complex would go a long way toward explaining why women achieve less than men.

But her work did not go unchallenged. It was flawed, for example, on methodological grounds. Men only wrote stories about a man, women stories about a woman. What would happen if they wrote stories about the opposite sex? Such a manipulation is necessary because subjects' answers in Horner's study may not have been true projections of their own motivations, but rather stereotypes about success. For example, if men wrote stories about women similar to women's stories, there would be an alternative explanation for such stories.

Subsequent work also challenged the claim that men rarely show fear of success themes in their stories. In one case, Lois Hoffman, in a better controlled study at the same university as Horner did her work, found a proportion of fear of success stories among men that was actually larger than the one for women.

Consult the sources listed below for more details about this work. Also, you can use your students answers for an instant comparison to the findings that you have been discussing.
(*Sources:* Hoffman, L.W. (1974). Fear of success in males and females: 1965 and 1971. *Journal of consulting and clinical psychology, 42,* 353-358; Horner, M.S. (1969). Fail: bright women. *Psychology Today, 2,* 36-38, 62.)

5.   Teaching at the Appropriate Cognitive Level

Is it developmentally appropriate to assume that adolescents are capable of abstract reasoning and formal logic when designing teaching materials and strategies for junior high (middle) school, high school, and college students? One researcher, John Renner, says definitely not - and provides solid data to document the actual incidence of formal operations and to demonstrate the influence of courses that have assumed those abilities on the part of adolescents.

Although the text presents Renner's ideas, you may profitably do so again in class. Get a copy of the book by Renner and his associates, *Research, Teaching, and Learning with the Piaget Model,* and abstract the data about the incidence of formal operations. Summarize, from the text, strategies used in introductory physical science classrooms that assume students are formal operational versus those that assume students are concrete operational. Also in Renner's book is information documenting the changes in the incidence of formal operations associated with learning in each type of class.

Combine with your presentation of Renner's research any additional information you can get about the success of science teaching in America today - now widely regarded as unsuccessful. Is Renner's proposal the answer? If so, why are other nations so successful at teaching science to their teenagers? Determine, if you can, whether science teaching in other countries conforms to Renner's suggestions.

6.   Tracing the Causes of Attention Deficit Disorder

If you have given a lecture on attention and reaction time as was suggested for Chapter 9, you can build on that material by presenting a lecture about the attention deficit disorder. If you have not, a treatment of this subject provides an excellent opportunity to illustrate how specific developmental outcomes are the product of multiple factors in the biological, social, and cognitive realms.

A good place to start is simply to have the class discuss what they know about the disorder. In particular, focus on what they believe causes it. The syndrome is sufficiently well known that most should have ideas about it, and some of them should have had some direct experience with the disorder. Draw out the varieties of interpretations that will be raised such as the minimal brain dysfunction view and the learning view. Keep track of these points because you will want to speak to them when you make a more formal presentation on the subject.

After you close the discussion, begin your lecture with the point that the attention deficit disorder is not a completely understood phenomenon. This is a good opportunity to present a variety of points of view about it. In addition to the biological and learning views, you should be able to find both material that suggests an origin in early family experience and an information processing analyses of the disorder.

When you finish your review of these positions, speculate on a way to integrate them all. For example, consider the possibility that a biological predisposition interacts with family experiences to produce characteristic problems in attention and attentional strategies manifested in the disorder. Evaluate how well current evidence supports this point of view.

7.   Observational Issues Identifying Children with ADHD

There are several issues concerning the need for systematic observation in order to accurately diagnose a child with ADHD and to correctly characterize the syndrome. A discussion of these issues provides additional lessons about the use of observation in both practical and scientific applications.

First, discuss the reasons that ADHD typically is not identified until children are in the first or second grade. A basic point is that the normal, everyday behavior of preschool children is so "hyperactive" in its own right that the behavior does not necessarily draw attention to children who have the disorder. Another way of stating this is that we do not have a sufficient observational basis for identifying ADHD early on. Furthermore, identification of this "abnormality" depends heavily on careful identification of normal behavioral patterns among children.

Second, consider the possibility that hyperactivity is less a problem of too much behavior and more a problem of too much disorganized behavior. In the 1970s researchers made systematic, comparative observations of normal children, hyperactive children, and hyperactive children being treated with Ritalin. They found that those receiving Ritalin did not "slow down," but rather became more organized in their play. This finding called into question the notion that Ritalin (a stimulant) has a truly paradoxical effect (tranquilizing), and gave more support to the idea that the drug acts on brain processes that monitor and organize behavior.

Thus, casual observation of ADHD is inadequate to characterize the disorder. One needs careful descriptions of both "normal" children and those who have the syndrome, as well as detailed, systematic observations of the behavior of the children in question.

8. Science Education

Many experts believe that the state of science education in American schools is pathetic. American students are turned off by the science classes and most adults know a minimum of scientific information. By third grade, half of students do not want to take science. By eighth grade, four-fifths do not want to take science classes. Fewer than half of high school students take any math or science after tenth grade. Only 1 percent of American high school students take calculus (compared to 12 percent in Japan). Only 0.7 percent of American college students major in engineering (4 percent in Japan).

Comparing American students to students in other countries shows that other countries are doing better. Thirteen-year-old Koreans do twice as well as Americans in solving two-step mathematical problems. The average Japanese senior outperforms the top 5 percent of American seniors in mathematics. On a chemistry achievement test, American high-school students scored eleventh of thirteen countries; Hong Kong, England, and Singapore did the best. In physics, American students were ninth and in biology, thirteenth.

Some educators believe that science classes must move away from lecture, textbook, and memorization and use more observation, measurement, collection, categorizing, recording, and interpreting of data. Classes should teach what is interesting and the rest will follow. (*Sources:* Begley, S., Springen, K., Hager, M., Barrett, T., & Joseph, N. 1990 (April 9). Rx for learning. *Newsweek,* 55-64. Cowley, G., Springen, K., Barrett, T., & Hager, M. 1990 (April 9). Not just for nerds. *Newsweek,* 52-54.)

9. High School Dropout Patterns

You hear a lot about high school dropouts these days. It may make you think that there are more dropouts than ever before. Yet, the proportion who drop out of school has stabilized at about 15-16 percent. In 1940, only 38 percent of individuals in their late twenties had a high school degree. The difference is that the high school degree is no longer a luxury.

Who drops out of school? Overall, slightly more males than females make up the dropout population. However, the gender difference increases among African-Americans. Although black females are as likely to graduate high school as are White females, black males have a dropout rate of about 20 percent. The Hispanic dropout rate is larger than the black dropout rate—more than one fourth of female and male Hispanic youths do not finish school.

What are some of the factors that influence dropping out?

    a. The specific school. Impersonal, large inner-city schools tend to have high dropout rates. Dropping out may be contagious within schools, too—as one's friends drop out, one is more likely to consider dropping out.

    b. Not viewing the diploma as a career asset. The unemployment rate for young black men and women who *have* graduated from high school is over fifty percent. Among Hispanics, two fifths of the dropouts are unemployed and over one third of the graduates are also unemployed. Only among the White youth is there a dramatic difference in the unemployment rates of those who have graduated versus those who have not graduated.

    c. Being behind academically. After several years of doing poorly, and perhaps not being able to accomplish work expected of a fourth-grader, some students decide to drop out. In fact, this is the number-one reason why students stop going to school. Preschool enrichment programs change the figures by about 10 percent, but lack of follow-through programs keep the dropout rates high for those who are academically disadvantaged.

    d. Poor English skills. Youth whose native language is not English are more likely to quit school. The dropout rate can be influenced by well-run bilingual school programs. One study found that the Chicago public school dropout rate for Native Americans was 95 percent, but it was only 11 percent at one Chicago high school that ran a bicultural, bilingual program.

    e.   Personal situations. For females, personal situations are the number-one reason for dropping out. Pregnancy and marriage are two common situations.

(*Sources:* Rumberger, R. 1987. High school dropouts: A review of issues and evidence. *Review of Education Research, 57,* 101-121; Barber, L. W. & McClellan, M. C. 1987 (Dec.). Looking at America's dropouts: Who are they? *Phi Delta Kappan,* 264-267.)

BROWN & BENCHMARK'S HUMAN DEVELOPMENT TRANSPARENCIES (2ND ED.)

Transparency Number and Title

The transparency set, a supplement to *Child Development*, is accompanied by an annotated manual that describes each of the 141 transparencies. The annotated manual also offers suggestions about how to use the transparencies to engage your students in active learning that will stimulate critical thinking and evaluative skills. The following transparencies are appropriate and useful with Chapter 17: Schools and Achievement.

Transparency Number and Title

76   Developmentally Appropriate and Inappropriate Practice: I
77   Developmentally Appropriate and Inappropriate Practice: II
83   Percentage and Number of Handicapped Children in the United States

CLASSROOM ACTIVITIES OR DEMONSTRATIONS

1.   Discuss the critical thinking exercises. Exercise 1 focuses on a concept that seems to be a theme of Chapter 8 and important in contemporary educational reform. The main issue here is to make students more sensitive to to the concept of interaction as it relates both to understanding mechanisms of development and to applications of our understanding of those mechanisms. You may wish to discuss with them the more general issue of developmental interactions, how the concept relates to the idea of developmentally appropriate practice, and whether it is yet possible to plan and effect our understanding in our secondary schools.

        If you are using these exercises as assignments or class activities you have probably established a clear and effective routine for preparing students to use them. On exercises like Exercise 2 you are probably reviewing the characteristics of each approach and the kinds of constructs they employ in theory and research. We hope that your students are becoming adroit at identifying these.

        Exercise 3 continues the theme of sensitizing students to the assumptions scientists make in their research. While the particular assumption highlighted in this exercise is significant to basic research, it also figures importantly in the contemporary debate about school assessment. This fact alone buttresses the argument for learning to identify assumptions. You may use these points to teach about these issues as well as to promote the critical thinking skill of differentiating assumptions, inferences, and observations.

2.   Discuss the students' research projects as suggested below.

3.   Ask groups of four to six students to design a curriculum for promoting formal operational reasoning in concrete operational children. During the first part of the discussion, the students should specify what changes normally take place between those two stages. After the initial discussion, the students should identify what activities might promote those changes.

Source: King, M. B. & Clark, D. E. 1990. *Instructor's Manual to accompany Children.* Dubuque, Wm. C. Brown Publishers.

4.   Ask class members for personal experiences with school tracking. How did students figure out which reading level group they were in? What are the advantages of tracking? Disadvantages? How were standardized tests (e.g., Iowa Basic Skills Test) used by school system? How might tracking "water-down" education? Could remedial classes be established in "healthy" ways?

        Use ideas in the article listed below to help you guide the discussion.

Source: Tobias, S. 1989 (Sept). Tracked to fail. *Psychology Today,* 54-60.

5. In 1981, sixth graders (mostly Hispanic) of P.S. 121 in East Harlem were addressed by 71-year-old **Eugene Lang,** a self-made millionaire. On impulse he told them, "If you can somehow manage to graduate from high school, I'll pay your college tuition." In 1990, 34 of 61 students were enrolled at least part-time in colleges, with about one third of them completing their junior year. Another nine of the students had Lang help them find jobs after graduating from high school. When Lang decided to "adopt" this class, he met with them regularly, giving them support, encouragement, and advice.

    Since then, other individuals have adopted classes, and the I Have A Dream Foundation in New York City helps successful business people adopt a class for $300,000. What do you think of such programs? What are the advantages and disadvantages? How might you accomplish the same level of enthusiasm and success with a program that would do more that "hit and miss" certain sixth grade classes?

Source: Marsa, L. 1990 (May). Hands-on education. *Omni, 26,* 77.

6. Should high schools be able to have and enforce dress codes? What restrictions in clothing are reasonable? Would public schools be better off requiring uniforms? What are your personal experiences with school dress codes? How does clothing affect behavioral and academic performance in the schools? Who should establish the dress code?

    In the 1970s and 80s, dozens of federal judges have had to make rulings on whether the constitutional guarantees of privacy and free speech apply to the length of skirts and boots, and to other aspects of clothing such as designer clothes. There is no consensus among these rulings. How would you rule?

    Take the discussion in the direction of other rights or non-rights of high school students. Do high school students have rights to free speech? They used to. In 1943, the Supreme Court (Barnette vs. West Virginia) ruled that it was within a student's right to refuse to salute the flag. In 1969, the Supreme Court (Tinker vs. Des Moines Independent Community School District) ruled that students have constitutional rights to freedom of speech and expression in their schools, when it agreed that students could not be suspended for wearing black armbands to protest the Vietnam War.

    But in 1990, in about 25 states, school athletes must allow mandatory urine testing for cocaine, steroids, marijuana, and alcohol. In Arkansas, school administrators are allowed to use breathalyzer tests, blood tests, and polygraph tests on students. In Arkansas, drug-sniffing dogs are used in schools. According to a 1985 Supreme Court decision (New Jersey vs. TLO), regardless of the Fourth Amendment, students' lockers, gym bags, and purses are subject to spot searches. In a January 1988 ruling (Hazelwood vs. Missouri), the Supreme Court even ruled that administrators have the right to censor school newspapers. Justice Byron R. White wrote, "A school need not tolerate student speech that is inconsistent with its basic educational mission even though the government could not censor similar speech outside the school."

    Do students need their freedoms limited in order to protect them from the dangers of current times? How do issues of confidentiality, privacy, consent, and autonomy relate to teenagers? Why is society growing less tolerant of minors' free speech and more willing to assault their privacy (e.g., 67 percent support mandatory drug testing for all high-school students)? If teenagers would benefit from limited freedom, is the same true for adults?

Sources: Leslie, C. 1989 (Nov. 27). Hey, hairball! You're gone! *Newsweek,* 79; Bentayou, F. 1990 (April). Children, behave. *Omni,* 33.

7. Barker and Gump found differences in school experiences for students, depending on the size of their high schools. The major advantages for attending smaller schools include the greater ability to participate in extracurricular activities (about twice as high), a greater sense of belongingness, and a greater likelihood of achieving one's high school degree.

Have students discuss the advantages and disadvantages of the different size of high schools they attended. Ask if they considered size when they chose a college. What structures develop to compensate for the negative aspects of both small and large schools?

Source: Barker, R. & Gump, P. 1964. *Big school, small school.* Stanford, CA: Stanford University Press.

8. College students often have vivid memories of high school, and you should be able to use these to fuel interesting and productive discussions about many educational issues. Here is a list of questions suggested by Michael Walraven that you could use to start these discussions or introduce lectures:
    1. Should schools stress affective education as much as cognitive education?
    2. Should vocational readiness be emphasized?
    3. Should the school be involved in teaching (instilling) traditional Judeo-Christian values and moral virtues (e.g., respect for authority)?
    4. Should the schools emphasize how to live in a pluralistic society?
    5. Should the schools cater to the beliefs of a minority?
    6. Should bilingual education and other techniques be used to meet the needs of students who do not speak English, especially Asians and Central and South Americans who have been traumatized by was and other stresses?
    7. Should specific patriotic values be instilled?
    8. Should adolescents be encouraged to improve and change society or to conform and preserve traditions?

Walraven, M. G. 1993. *Instructor's Course Planner* to accompany John Santrock's *Adolescence,* 5th ed. Dubuque: Brown and Benchmark, Publishers.

9. Ask students (1) Who is responsible for improving schools? (2) What ideas do they have for improving education? and (3) How well are the public schools doing? Use the following data from a PTA/Newsweek National Education Survey (1993) of 1148 respondents to expand the discussion.

    a. Responsibility for improving schools
        Principals 90 percent
        Parents 90 percent
        Teachers 89 percent
        School boards 86 percent
        Students 81 percent
        Political leaders 75 percent
        The public 70 percent
        Local businesses 53 percent
        Local religious institutions 48 percent

    b. Proposals for improving education
        Combine academics & job training for high school students not going to college 84 percent
        Require national tests 58 percent
        Shift decision making from a central board to individual schools 53 percent
        Allow public school choice 52 percent
        Establish year-round schools 38 percent
        Increase the number of school days from 180 to 220 or more 37 percent

    c. Rating the school system
        Nearly half of all adults (46 percent) give public schools a "C" grade or lower
        Many adults (42 percent) believe the schools will improve over the next five years while 21 percent think the quality will decline
        Most parents (90 percent) feel comfortable when they visit their child's school

Chapter 17

About two-thirds (63 percent) consider their own children "above average"
Most parents (95 percent) say they talk to their children about their classes, about 45 percent say they help children with homework, and 47 percent say they read daily to their children.

Source: Finney, P. B. 1993. The PTA/Newsweek National Education Survey, Education in America, *Newsweek.*

10. You could begin this activity on school prayer by getting students to anonymously answer the few questions listed below from a Parents Poll (1989). Collate the answers, and provide them along with the national public opinion poll findings provided here.

No prayer should be said aloud, but there should be a moment of silence each day so students could pray, meditate or do nothing: 68 percent
A prayer should be said and students should be required to participate: 17 percent
There should be no prayer or moment of silence in public schools: 12 percent

What do the findings of the national poll/class suggest? What values have led to these results (respect for religious diversity/majority rules/respect for Supreme Court decisions, etc.)? Who should decide whether or not schools include prayers (e.g., national government, state governments, local governments, parents)? What are the effects of having or not having prayers in public schools?

Source: Poll results are from Groller, I. 1989 (Sept.). School prayer. *Parents,* p. 28.

11. To each of several small groups of students, assign a goal and have them design a behavioristic environment that would help them reach the goal. Possible goals:

a. Increase individual competition.
b. Decrease racial prejudice.
c. Increase self-esteem.
d. Increase intrinsic interest in learning.
e. Decrease creativity and individuality.
f. Increase respect for authority.
g. Increase creativity and individuality.
h. Increase conformity.
i. Increase cooperation among students.

Have groups present a summary of their best ideas. Also, ask which groups liked the goal they were to work towards. Did groups find they also used techniques other than behavioristic ones.

Source: Simons, J. A., Irwin, D. B., & Drinnin, B. A. 1987. *Instructor's Manual to Accompany Psychology, the Search for Understanding,* St. Paul: West Publishing.

12. Children may have a **performance-goal orientation** (PGO) or a **learning-goal orientation** (LGO). Children with PGO are motivated by grades and praise; it is important to them that others think well of their abilities. Children with LGO are motivated to become more competent and to master the understanding of challenging subjects; it is important to them that they perceive that they are getting better at something. In reality, of course, all children can display either orientation depending on the situation.
Have students discuss: What are the advantages and disadvantages of each orientation? What factors do you think contributed to whether a child is more performance- or learning-oriented? Which orientation should school teachers try to increase, and how might this be accomplished? How do other characteristics affect the orientation?

Information to include during the discussion:

1. The key belief of LGO children is that ability is mainly a matter of how hard you work. PGO children believe that ability is fixed. You could include the concept of locus of control in your discussion.
2. When PGO children are given a new task, they work hard on it if they have confidence in their ability, but give up if their confidence is low. LGO children tend to persist regardless of confidence level.

13. From reading about achievement you may be able to estimate your own achievement need (nAch) level. The three main styles of expressing achievement (and each of these has three substyles) are the direct style, the instrumental style, and the relational style. In the direct achievement style, individuals confront tasks directly and want to achieve tasks through their own efforts. In the instrumental achievement style, individuals achieve by promoting themselves or others. In the relational achievement style, individuals achieve by contributing to the accomplishments of others (Lipman-Blumen et al., 1983).

Your preferences for different achievement styles developed throughout childhood and adolescence, although they can be modified during the adult years. Gender roles are one significant influence on achievement style preferences. More males are socialized to have a direct achievement style and more females are socialized to have a relational achievement style. Family members, friends, and cultural messages further shape and differentiate your achievement choices.

Rate each of the substyles for how typical they are of your own achievement patterns (adapted from Lipman-Blumen et al., 1983). Use a 0 if the style is very atypical of you, a 1 if you occasionally use the style, a 2 if you believe you are average in this pattern, and a 3 if you think that you often use the particular style. After rating the substyles, go back and rank the three major styles from 1 (most typical for you) to 3 (least typical for you).

Rank _____ *Direct style* - I am an individual who likes to achieve and accomplish tasks by my own efforts. I confront tasks directly.

_____ Intrinsic substyle - I tend to compare myself to some standard of performance excellence. For example: I am satisfied with A's and B's and would like to make the dean's list. I like to see "well written" on a paper I have done. I try to do work that meets the high standards set by my boss.

_____ Competitive substyle - I tend to express achievement by trying to do better than others do. For example: I like to get grades that are higher than other students in the class. It is as important to win an athletic competition as it is to do well. I like to hear that my ideas are better than others.

_____ Power substyle - I like to be in charge of and have control over others in order to accomplish achievement goals. For example: I would like to organize and lead a study group in order to improve my grades. I would like to be chairperson of a student organization. I would like a career in management or other area in which I am in charge of other personnel.

_____ Instrumental style - I tend to use myself and others as a way to meet my achievement goals.

_____ Personal substyle - I often achieve by making use of my status, influence, reputation, and personal characteristics. For example: I try to dress for success in order to make a good impression on the people with whom I work. I would like to earn a doctorate degree because I think I would be better able to meet my goals if I could sign Ph.D. after my name. I would like to be on the dean's list or an officer in state organizations because this would help me achieve more.

_____ Social substyle - I tend to use networking to achieve my goals. For example: I plan to join a fraternity or sorority because other members can provide lifelong social and career connections. I think it is important to belong to lots of organizations because you meet people who are able to help you get things accomplished. I try to associate socially with people I admire and with whom I hope to work.

_____ Reliant substyle - I tend to achieve by depending on others for direction. For example: Before studying or writing papers I usually ask instructors and classmates what I should do and how I should do it. I think it's important to get lots of input and feedback from others in order to know how to work on a task correctly. I often get advice on what to do from others rather than deciding goals by myself.

_____ Relational style - I tend to achieve by contributing to the accomplishments of other persons.

_____ Collaborative substyle - I tend to achieve through group effort that includes the sharing of both responsibility and credit. For example: I prefer classes in which projects are done in small groups with shared responsibilities and a common grade. I would rather co-author a paper than write alone. I like working on issues with a group of peers.

_____ Contributory substyle - I tend to play a secondary role of helping others to achieve. For example: I would be willing to work and financially support a spouse while he or she went to college. I like to offer suggestions in committees, but I would not enjoy being the chairperson of the committee. I would enjoy playing supportive roles in arenas such as politics and charitable organizations.

_____ Vicarious substyle - I tend to satisfy my own achievement needs by identifying with the success of other persons who are important to me. For example: I get a lot of school pride when our athletic teams win. I would just as soon help my offspring to accomplish something important than to achieve that accomplishment myself. It is very satisfying to see a co-worker have a great success - I feel like I can identify with the co-worker's achievements.

When you are finished with your rankings, evaluate how you feel about your individual pattern. Are you able to work on achievement in ways that are satisfying to you? How would you change school, work, and family situations to better fit your needs? Have you chosen career goals that will enable you to achieve in ways that fit your pattern? What kinds of changes would you like to make in your achievement styles? What kinds of changes have occurred over your life so far? Regardless of your current achievement styles, which substyle do you wish was your most prominent style? Can you identify achievement styles of your family members? Among your friends? Do you have similar or dissimilar styles to family and friends? How do you think cultural and worldwide influences affect the prominence of different types of achievement styles from generation to generation?

Source: Lipman-Blumen, J., Handley-Isakin, A., & Leavitt, H. J. (1983). Achieving styles in men and women: A model, an instrument, and some findings. In J. T. Spence (ed.) Achievement and Achievement Motives: Psychological and Sociological Approaches. San Francisco: W. H. Freeman.

CRITICAL THINKING EXERCISES

Exercise 1

An important though challenging concept presented in this chapter is aptitude-treatment interaction. Santrock treats this idea in a section of its own, but material elsewhere in the chapter illustrates it. Listed below are several other topics contained in Chapter 8. Which one of them best illustrates the idea of aptitude-treament interaction? **Circle the letter of the best answer and explain why it is the best answer and why each other answer is not as good.**

A. education for disadvantaged children
B. nonsexist childhood education
C. effective schools for young adolescents
D. small classroom size
E. social class

Exercise 2

There are a variety of approaches to understanding motivation, but in terms of the perspectives outline in Chapter 2 of *Child Development*, one general perspective seems to have generated more theories than any other Which is it? **Circle the letter of the best answer, and explain why it is the best answer and why each other answer is not as good.**

A. psychoanalytic
B. cognitive
C. learning
D. ecological
E. eclectic

Exercise 3

On page 262 Santrock discusses the effects of school and classroom size on the affective and cognitive education of adolescents. In order to accept the findings, we must assume that one of the following statements is true. Which one of them is the crucial assumption, as opposed to an inference or an observation? **Circle the letter of the best answer and explain why it is the best answer and why each other answer is not as good.**

A. Standardized tests are valid measures of student achievement.
B. Large schools might not provide a personalized climate for students.
C. Low-responsive schools had higher crime rates than high-responsive schools
D. A pupil who score at about the 63rd percentile on a national test if taught individually would score at the 37th percentile if taught in a class of 40 students.
E. Large class size is associated with lower achievement.

ANSWER KEYS FOR CRITICAL THINKING EXERCISES

Exercise 1

A. This is not the best answer. Programs like Project Head Start aim to provide children with the skills they will need to succeed in school. Therefore their focus is on preparing learners to deal with the school environment, rather than on preparing school environments to deal with individual differences among students.
B. This is not the best answer. The activities suggested for a nonsexist early childhood education are aimed at all children, not being tailored to meet the particular needs of individuals. As such they are not an example of the idea of aptitude-treatment interaction.
C. This is the best answer. A direct quote says it all: "The most striking feature was their willingness and ability to adapt all school practices to the individual differences in physical, cognitive, and social development of their students." (p. 255).
D. This is not the best answer. It is a possible second best, because the material in the text hints that small classes could best achieve aptitude-treatment interactions. But the material focuses mainly on achievement contrasts between students learning in small and large classrooms, and has little to say about actual mechanisms related to learning or adjustment.
E. This is not the best answer. The material in this section is mainly oriented to the fact that social class and race are two student characteristics that schools have not adapted to well.

Exercise 2

A. This is not the best answer. Only one approach, the achievement motivation approach, resembles a psychoanalytic approach, in that it focuses on achievement motivation as a personality construct. But the bases of these approaches are the ideas of Murray and McClelland, and their debt to the psychoanalytic approach seems remote.
B. This is the best answer. The majority of the theories seem to have a cognitive basis. Attribution theories are about causes people attribute to their behavior, intrinsic/extrinsic motivational constructs refer to desires to be competent and how they interact with reward, and the mastery/helpless distinction refers again to attributions people make about their ability to succeed.
C. This is not the best answer. Learning concepts appear to play a role in the analysis of intrinsic versus extrinsic motivation, but other ideas and theories draw on either personality or cognitive constructs.
D. This is not the best answer. None of the theories involve an analysis of the social systems adolescents inhabit and how the interactions of these systems influences achievement motivation.
E. This is not the best answer. The main reason for not choosing this alternative is that one perspective seems to have generated more theories (in Santrock's treatment) than the others. One could certainly describe the area as eclectic, however.

Exercise 3

A. This is the best answer. This is a point one must accept in order to accept the comparisons Santrock cites. There is no discussion of this point. But it is, in fact, a very controversial one that pops up in most school comparisons and discussions of assessment.
B. This is not the best answer. This is an inference, offered as a possible explanation of the fact that less antisocial and more prosocial behavior appear to occur in small versus large schools.
C. This is not the best answer. This an observation. This point has been demonstrated statistically in comparisons of low- and high-responsive schools.
D. This is not the best answer. This is an inference, a deduction based on comparisons of achievement among students in small versus large classrooms.
E. This is not the best answer. This is an observation, a statement of the correlation that exists between class size and achievement.

RESEARCH PROJECT 1   CHILDREN'S ATTITUDES   TOWARD SCHOOL

After acquiring parental approval and a signed informed consent form, ask three students (one in fifth or sixth grade, one in seventh or eighth grade, one ninth or tenth grade, or one in eleventh or twelfth) about their attitudes towards school. Then answer the questions that follow.

DATA SHEET

Questions	Child 1 Grade___ Sex___Age___	Child 2 Grade___ Sex___Age___	Child 3 Grade___ Sex___Age__
Do you like school?	Y/N	Y/N	Y/N
Do you like your teachers?	Y/N	Y/N	Y/N
Do you like the other students?	Y/N	Y/N	Y/N
Compared to other students, how well do you do in school? (better, average, worse)	B/A/W	B/A/W	B/A/W
How do you do in each of the following subjects? (Good, Fair, Poor)			
Math	G/F/P	G/F/P	G/F/P

Questions	Child 1	Child 2	Child 3
History	G/F/P	G/F/P	G/F/P
Art	G/F/P	G/F/P	G/F/P
Physical education	G/F/P	G/F/P	G/F/P
Science	G/F/P	G/F/P	G/F/P
Music	G/F/P	G/F/P	G/F/P
English	G/F/P	G/F/P	G/F/P
Foreign Language	G/F/P	G/F/P	G/F/P

What do you like best about school?

What do you like least about school?

Do you expect to go to college or other school after you get out of high school?

Questions

1.   In general, what are the attitudes toward school? Do students view themselves as successful students?
2.   Do attitudes change as students get older?
3.   What subjects are rated highest?

Use in Classroom

Have students discuss the results of their interviews. What trends appear across subjects? Is there an age trend? Were most students positive or negative toward school? What things were liked or disliked?

RESEARCH PROJECT 2   MOTIVATION - THE VALUES OF ADOLESCENTS

The following project involves taking a survey of values using adolescent subjects. You need to make copies of the questionnaire and get six volunteer subjects to rank the values from 1 (most important) to 16 (least important) in terms of their own personal life goals. You should get two subjects (one female and one male) from each of three age groups: 11 to 13 years old, 14 to 16 years old, and 17 to 19 years old. After collecting the data, answer the questions about your six subjects. Later, in class discussion (or by handout summary of the data), come to some conclusions about adolescent values based on the subject responses of the whole class.

To the subject: I would like you to volunteer to fill out this questionnaire on your life goals. Your responses will be kept confidential, and the only identifying data you need to provide is your age and gender. Please take a few moments to rank the following life goals from most important (1) to least important (16). You may have most of the following as life goals or hardly any as life goals. You are only indicating the relative order of their importance, not rating the importance of each goal. Put your ranking for each of the life goals in the blank provided.

(Data Sheet begins on the next page.)

DATA SHEET

_____ Achievement
_____ Comfort
_____ Contribution
_____ Excellence
_____ Fulfillment
_____ Growth
_____ Knowledge
_____ Love
_____ Peace
_____ Power
_____ Relationships
_____ Security
_____ Self-acceptance
_____ Status
_____ Truth
_____ Wealth

Gender: _____

Age: _____ years
Do you view yourself as more:
_____ idea-centered
_____ person-centered

Do you view your beliefs as:
_____ fairly stable
_____ fairly changeable

Do you think your views are typical of others your age?
_____ Yes
_____ No

Questions

1. What values were ranked most highly by adolescents? What values were least important? Were there many differences across subjects?
2. Do your subjects see themselves as person-centered or idea-centered? Do they see themselves as stable or changeable? Do they see themselves as typical?
3. Do you get a sense of whether there might be an age or gender difference in values? Develop some hypotheses that you can explore after you learn about the results gathered by all class members.

Use in Classroom

Have students present their data from the research project in class. It would be best to gather their surveys ahead of class time and have the data collated and summarized on a handout or transparency. Have students discuss which values are most and least important to adolescents. Have them examine the data for possible age and gender differences. They should also discuss whether teenagers see themselves as person- or idea-centered, stable or changing, and typical or atypical. Discuss the shortcomings of this survey and what future research could be done on this topic.

ESSAY AND CRITICAL THINKING QUESTIONS

Comprehension and Application Essay Questions

We recommend that you provide students with our guidelines for "Answering Essay and Critical Thinking Questions" when you have them respond to these questions. Their answers to these kinds of questions demonstrate an ability to comprehend and apply ideas discussed in this chapter.

1. Compare and contrast the back-to-basics movement and the open education system.
2. Describe a child-centered kindergarten. What is meant by developmentally appropriate practices?
3. Evaluate the importance of preschool experiences to subsequent performance in school. Be sure to cite relevant data.
4. Compare and contrast an academically-oriented American preschool and the typical Japanese preschool.
5. Has Project Head Start been effective? Support your position with research findings.
6. Define school readiness and explain its role in education.
7. Compare and contrast the first transition to school and the transition from elementary school to middle or junior high school.

8. Summarize the characteristics of effective schools for young adolescents, and evaluate your own experience in middle or junior high school using them.
9. List the major reasons for dropping out of high school, and discuss how and whether recommendations about how to reduce the dropout rate speak to those reasons.
10. Compare and contrast secondary schools in the United States, Germany, Japan, Russia, and Brazil.
11. Discuss whether school size and various class characteristics have an important impact on educational outcomes.
12. Define the idea of aptitude-treatment interaction, and give examples of application of the concept.
13. How does social class and ethnicity affect school performance and teacher expectations?
14. Describe the impact of Public Law 94-142 and mainstreaming.
15. Describe attention-deficit hyperactivity disorder and list five possible causes.
16. Compare and contrast any two approaches to understanding motivation. How are these approaches used to understand achievement among adolescents?
17. Should children be rewarded for their achievements? Why or why not? Or when, when not?
18. What do studies of ethnic minorities in the United States and adolescents in other cultures suggest about cultural influences on achievement motivation?

Critical Thinking Questions

We recommend that you have students follow our guidelines for "Answering Essay and Critical Thinking Questions" when you ask them to prepare responses to these questions. Their answers to these kinds of questions reflect an ability to apply critical thinking skills to a novel problem or situation that is *not* specifically discussed in the chapter. These items most appropriately may be used as take-home essay questions (e.g., due on exam day) or as homework exercises that can be answered either by individuals or groups. Collaboratively answered questions encourage cooperative learning by students, and reduce the number of papers that must be graded.

1. At the end of Chapter 17 Santrock indicates books that provide practical knowledge about children and lists resources for improving the lives of children. Choose one of these books or resources and read it or learn as much as you can about it. Then write a brief review in which you (a) characterize the book or resource, and (b) explain how the book or resource relates to material in the chapter.
2. Chapter 1 defines the nature of development in terms of biological, cognitive, and social processes, and periods or stages. Indicate your ability to think critically by identifying material in this chapter that illustrates developmental processes and periods. If there is little or no information in this chapter about developmental processes and periods, identify and explain how developmental processes and periods could be used to guide the analysis of any topic in the chapter.
3. According to Chapter 1, three fundamental developmental issues concern: (a) maturation (nature) versus experience (nurture), (b) continuity versus discontinuity, and (c) early versus later experience. Indicate your ability to think critically by identifying material in this chapter that illustrates each of the three fundamental developmental issues. If there is little or no information in this chapter about fundamental developmental issues, identify and explain how these issues could be used to guide the analysis of any topic in the chapter.
4. One aspect of thinking critically is to read, listen, and observe carefully and then ask questions about what is missing from a text, discussion, or situation. For example, chapter 8 presents information about transitions to elementary school, and from elementary school to middle or junior high school and from high school to college, but does not address the transition from middle school or junior high school to high school. Indicate your ability to think critically by (a) listing as many questions as you can about the transition, and (b) speculating why Santrock does not discuss this topic more fully.
5. Santrock sets off several quotations in this chapter. Indicate your ability to think critically by selecting one of the quotes and (a) learning about the author and indicating why this individual is eminently quotable (i.e., what was this individual's contribution to human knowledge and understanding), (b) interpreting and restating the quote in your own terms, and (c) explaining what concept, issue, perspective, or term in this chapter that Santrock intended this quote to illuminate. In other words, about what aspect or issue in development does this quote make you pause and reflect?
6. Chapter 2 indicates that theories help us explain data and make predictions about various aspects of development. Chapter 2 then presents six different theoretical approaches (i.e., Freudian, cognitive, behavioral and social learning, ethological, ecological, and eclectic theory), but notes that no single approach explains the complexity of development. Indicate your ability to think critically by (a) perusing this chapter for topics influenced by at least one of the six theoretical approaches, and (b) explaining which

theoretical approach dominated the topic in question. If the presentation is entirely atheoretical, identify and explain how one of the theoretical approaches could be used to guide the analysis of the topic in question.

7. Given the fact that commitment to a career is one of the attributes of identity achievement, one would think that a person's identity status would be related to that person's achievement motivation. Apply your knowledge about the scientific method by designing a study that will answer a question about relationships between identity status and achievement motivation: (a) What specific problem or question do you want to study? (b) What predictions would you make and test in your study? (c) What measures would you use (i.e., controlled observation in a laboratory, naturalistic observation, interviews and questionnaires, case studies, standardized tests, cross-cultural studies, physiological research, research with animals, or multimeasure, multisource, and multicontext approach) and how would you define each measure clearly and unambiguously? (d) What strategy would you follow--correlational or experimental, and what would be the time span of your inquiry--cross-sectional or longitudinal? (e) What ethical considerations must be addressed before you conduct your study?

8. According to Chapter 2, your author wants you to become a wise consumer of information about child development by: (a) being cautious about media reports, (b) distinguishing between nomothetic research and idiographic needs, (c) recognizing how easy it is to overgeneralize from a small or clinical sample, (d) knowing that a single study is usually not the defining word about some aspect of child development, (e) remembering that causal conclusions cannot be made from correlation studies, and (f) always considering the source of the information and evaluating its credibility. Indicate your ability to think critically by, first, selecting an article from either a journal, magazine, or newspaper about any topic regarding Schools and Achievement, and, second, evaluating it in terms of these six objectives. If the information in the article is insufficient to evaluate one of these objectives, then specify what kind of information you would need to evaluate the objective.

18 Culture, Poverty, and Ethnicity

SUGGESTIONS FOR LECTURE TOPICS

1.   The Development of Culture and Adolescent Development

In 1970 anthropologist Margaret Mead published a book (*Culture and Commitment: A Study of the Generation Gap.* New York: Doubleday) aimed at trying to explain whether or not their was a generation gap between adolescents and adults in the United States. You probably will not want to lecture on the whole book, but you may find it useful to talk about Mead's idea that the degree of conflict between generations may depend on the state of flux or transition typical of a culture. Mead's ideas may also be a way to show how cultural values may be involved in decisions researchers make about the optimal conditions of development, desirable developmental outcomes, and so on.

Mead proposed that there are three cultural states: postfigurative, cofigurative, and prefigurative. You will want to consult her book for a full account of these, but very briefly, postfigurative cultures are very traditional cultures that have not changed for many generations (e.g., the Amish); cofigurative cultures are those in competition with another, dominating culture, and losing (e.g., immigrant cultures); and prefigurative cultures are those in which indigenous change is the rule rather than maintenance of any sort of cultural status quo (e.g., modern United States). Mead's notion was that generation gaps were most likely to be prevalent in the latter two cultural types.

You can explore several issues against the backdrop of Mead's idea, aside from the generation gap issue. For example, what light does this analysis shed on the predicament of ethnic minorities? On relations between generations? On preparing adolescents for future worlds of work? On the nature of optimal parenting strategies? On the nature of optimal identity outcomes? Use this material as a platform from which to reexamine both issues you have already covered in the course from a cultural perspective, and to preview material you have yet to cover.

2.   Psychosocial Maturity

Some years ago Ellen Greenberger and A. Sorenson published a paper (Greenberger, E. & Sorenson, A.N. 1974. Toward a concept of psychosocial maturity. *Journal of youth and adolescence, 3,* 329-558) on the concept of psychosocial maturity that ties in nicely with many themes of Santrock's treatment of culture. The material is too vast for a single lecture, but you may wish to present the specific aspects of psychosocial maturity that Greenberger and Sorenson identified, and discuss this vis-a-vis the motivation to study cultural influences on adolescence as well the details of those cultural influences. Ellenberger and Sorenson's model is also a good framework within which to discuss the idea of adolescence and what it means to achieve adulthood. In any event, here are the three areas of psychosocial maturity the authors suggest. Consider making a handout of these for your students, and discussing with them how each of these areas relates to what they have already learned in the course about adolescent development, and what they are not learning in the course about cultural influences on adolescent development:

Individual Adequacy
   Self-reliance
      absence of excessive need for social validation
      sense of control
      initiative
   Identity
      clarity of self-concept
      consideration of life goals
      self-esteem
      internalized values
   Work orientation
      standards of competence
      pleasure in work
      general work skills
Interpersonal Adequacy
   Communication skills
      ability to encode messages
      ability to decode messages

empathy
Enlightened trust
    rational dependence
    rejection of simplistic view of human nature
    awareness of constraints on trustworthiness
Knowledge of major roles
    role-appropriate behavior
    management of role conflict
Social Adequacy
Social Commitment
    feelings of community
    willingness to work for social goals
    readiness to form alliances
    interest in long-term social goals

Openness to sociopolitical change
    general openness to change
    recognition of costs of status quo
    recognition of costs of change
Tolerance of individual and cultural differences
    willingness to interact with people who differ from the norm
    sensitivity to the rights of people who differ from the norm
    awareness of costs and benefits of tolerance

3.   A Note on Qualitative Research

Many studies of culture rely on qualitative research methods; indeed, material in Chapter 18 and the lecture suggestions above was based on these. Now is a good time to clarify the differences between qualitative and quantitative research studies. Not having the time or space to do an extensive comparison, this lecture suggestion focuses on a few points: purpose, method, and reporting style.

Purpose

Qualitative studies are intended to describe a given phenomenon in all its complexity. Quantitative studies, specifically experimental studies, are designed to show a cause and effect relationship between a limited number of variables. An elegant experimental design would control all but one or two key variables, and demonstrate a clear cause and effect relationship. An elegant qualitative study would present a multidimensional description of a complex activity or process.

Method

Qualitative methods include in-depth interviews, participant observation, and unobtrusive measures. Researchers are very much a part of the study, and their task is to develop their skills as a human instrument of data collection and analysis. Because the data collected is primarily people's words and actions, the data are extensive and the number of subjects studied is usually small. Experimental studies are the archtypal quantitative study. An experimental study contains one group of subjects who receive a treatment (experimental group), while a like group of subjects receive no treatment (control group). The data collected is specific and can often be translated into numbers. The power of a quantitative study is often dependent on a large number of subjects.

Reporting

Qualitative research projects are reported in a case study of similar method that has "thick descriptions" as its central tenet. Quantitative studies are reported in a technical and highly consistent manner, with statistical levels of significance as an essential part of the study.
    There is a debate as to the compatibility of qualitative and quantitative studies. Each addresses topics in different ways. One way to understand whether a topic for research might be studied by qualitative or quantitative methods is to make two statements: "I would like to understand more about..." versus I would like to prove that..."

If you want to understand more about something, a qualitative study might be the approach to take. If you want prove something, look to a quantitative study.

For fuller discussion of this and related questions, see *Qualitative Approaches to Evaluation in Education,* edited by David Fetterman (1988).

4.   American vs. Japanese Schools

Imagine a country in which nearly everyone is able to read and in which 94 percent of adolescents graduate from high school and 34 percent go on to earn college degrees (Chance, 1987). You really do not have to create such a country in your head; these statistics are from Japan. In fact, the Japanese school system produces students who know as much math at 7 years as British and American students know at 11 (New Scientist, 1986). How do the Japanese achieve such high educational standards?

First, the Japanese place more importance on education in the homes. Many Japanese mothers devote their entire lives to assisting their children with their schoolwork. Japanese mothers play educational games with their children, read to them for hours, and lavish praise on their children as they build skills mastery (Chance, 1987a).

Second, formal education begins early for most Japanese children. Preschool environments in Japan are more controlled, formal, and skill-oriented than preschools in America. Japanese preschoolers learn three alphabets, learn to cooperatively manage daily living tasks, and are introduced to the foundations of traditional school curriculum. The young Japanese children engage in very little unstructured free play.

Third, schoolage Japanese children themselves show greater inner discipline over their school behaviors than do American schoolchildren. Not only do they spend more hours and more days each year in school, but many children attend a **juku,** where they receive private lessons after school. Then they go home and do a few hours of homework for their regular school (Chance, 1987).

Finally, by high school, serious Japanese students do little but study and attend school. They dedicate their lives to studying for extensive comprehensive college entrance exams which will determine their educational and career futures. Their educational obsession may pay off with acceptance into Tokyo or Kyoto universities, the most prestigious Japanese colleges. The first nine years of education are compulsory public schooling. After that, many Japanese children attend a **yobiko,** which are sophisticated private high schools. A yobiko holds classes 5-1/2 days a week, 210 days a year (Walsh, 1987).

Should Americans adopt many of the features of the Japanese school system? Your first reaction might be that the stress of so much schooling would lead to violence or depression! Yet, there are more assaults on teachers in New York City schools than in all of Japan, and the suicide rate among teenagers is higher in the United States than it is in Japan (Chance, 1987).

Yet, adoption of the Japanese system in the United States would probably be unsuccessful for several reasons. First, Americans are accustomed to local control of school systems and seem to value diversity from one school system to the next. The Japanese model features excessive centralization and lack of diversity. Even the Japanese believe that this aspect of their system needs to be changed (Walsh, 1987).

Next, to imitate the Japanese educational system, American mothers would have to be willing to sacrifice their careers to thoroughly supervise and tutor their children (Chance, 1987). Few American women would want to make this choice; however, if they did abandon their careers, business and industry would be shaken by the loss of strong, effective workers. Also, there would not be an efficient tradeoff in quitting jobs that service many people to work exclusively with one or two offspring.

In addition, Japanese parents must spend thousands of dollars on their children's elementary and secondary school education to make them competitive for college (Walsh, 1987). To do this in the American culture would increase the differences in the education of the middle and upper classes and the education of the lower classes. A basic American tenet is to make educational opportunities available for all. In fact, not all Japanese families can afford good education for their children. About 29 percent of Japanese high school graduates go on to undergraduate college programs (another 12 percent enter special training schools); in America, about 55 percent of high school graduates go on to 2- and 4-year colleges. About 3 percent of Japanese college enrollment is in graduate college programs; in America it is about 11 percent (Walsh, 1987).

One other shortcoming of Japanese education is that the college years are as lax as the earlier schooling was intense and competitive. Many Japanese college students spend much of their college years cutting classes, partying, getting drunk, and doing club activities (Walsh, 1987). Most American students study little through high school and then study much harder in college; Japanese students study very hard through high school and then do little studying in college. While the average Japanese high school student knows more than the average American high school student, Japanese college students do little research and may achieve less creative thinking than their American counterparts (Walsh, 1987; Chance, 1987).

What aspects of the American school system would be beneficial additions to the Japanese school system? Should American children attend juku? What aspects of the Japanese school system would be good to adapt to the American school system? Would yobiko be better than the average public high school? Should the school year be lengthened to 210 days? Should school be held on Saturday mornings? Should the American college system be more lenient on issues such as cutting classes and partying?
(*Sources:* Walsh, J. 1987. U.S.-Japan study aim is education reform. *Science, 235,* 274-275; Chance, P. 1987. Asian studies. *Psychology Today,* July, 80.)

5.   The Teen Look in Japan

American teens pay a lot of attention to the latest clothing fads and fashions. So do Japanese youth, where fads are called **bumu.** Over the last few years Japanese youth have gone from one bumu to another. In 1988, **retro bumu** featured the bulky look of the 1950s. Other movements then included a Hell's Angels mode with leather jackets and vests, and an Italian casual mode with Bennetton fashions.

In 1989, bumus included **praddo-bumu,** what the Japanese call upscale preppie, with designers like Ralph Lauren, California influence, and American sportswear. The University of California, Los Angeles sells $16 million worth of T-shirts, warm-up suits, and sweats each year in Japan. The teen style with the longest endurance has been **Amerikaji,** or American casual. (*Source:* Hillenbrand, B. 1989 (Nov. 13). American casual seizes Japan. *Time,* 106.)

6.   Egalitarian motive

In some societies, such as Filipino peasants, the central cultural orientation is an **egalitarian motive** and the belief that all people should be equal. For the Filipinos, society provides a stable central government, sufficient agricultural and natural resources, over 50 percent literacy in English, and yet poor health, malnutrition, and much disease exist. The peasants live in a subsistence economy, do not plan ahead, do not allow government programs to improve agriculture and business, and deliberately avoid individual accomplishments. Americans view this pattern as irresponsible, illogical, and lazy. But from the Filipino perspective, happiness is based on social approval rather than personal prestige and material possessions. The peasants are guided by these aspects of the egalitarian motive:

(1) **Pakiksama.** More importance is placed on good feelings among people than on personal achievements.
(2) **Desirability of just meeting one's needs.** The prevailing attitude is that it is sufficient to just meet the day's needs.
(3) **Leveling.** Any attempts at personal improvement are discouraged by negative results such as teasing, threats, attacks, and gossip.
(4) **"All have a right to live" belief.** While advancement is discouraged, the peasants do help anyone who is having great difficulty in meeting their everyday existence needs.
(5) **Hiya.** Failure to succeed would lead to feelings of embarrassment and inferiority called hiya.

Do the cultural effects of the egalitarian motive surprise you? Are there other effects of the egalitarian motive surprise you? Are there other effects of this motive on a culture? Would it be possible to combine the typical American motives and the egalitarian motive? What do you think the result would be? Could you change some aspects of the egalitarian motive to make it a healthier motive? (*Sources:* Guthrie, G. M. 1970. *The psychology of modernization in the rural Philippines.* I.P.C. Paper No. 8 Quezon City: Ateneo de Manila University Press; Madigan, F. C. (Ed.)., 1967. *Human factors in Philippine rural development.* Cagayan de Oro City: Xavier University Press.)

7.   Rites of Passage: O-Kee-Pa, a Torture Ritual

In American culture, the passage of adulthood comes in bits and pieces—confirmation, getting a driver's license, first shave, first nylons, first date, first time to vote, and so on. In some cultures there is a specific ritual of passage to mark one's introduction to the full adult role. In some cultures, the rite of passage is severe and painful. One such culture was the **Mandan tribe,** a Missouri plains hunting tribe. The ritual was recorded by American artist George Catlin. In the 1840s, smallpox nearly destroyed this tribe.

In the Mandan culture, braves had to endure the **o-kee-pa** to become a warrior. At the onset of this procedure, the initiates went four days and nights without food, water, and sleep.

Next, the chief medicine man cut slices from the chest and shoulders and placed wooden skewers through the muscles. Leather straps were attached to these skewers and secured to the hut's rafters. Initiates were hoisted from the floor, had heavy weights attached to the legs, and were twirled about until unconscious.

Upon recovery, the initiate was to use a hatchet to chop off the little finger of his left hand. Finally, ropes were tied to his wrists and he had to run in a circle until he dropped unconscious from exhaustion. Survivors became full-fledged warriors. (*Source: Strange Stories, Amazing Facts.* 1976. Pleasantville, New York: The Reader's Digest Association, Inc. p. 311.)

8. Cultures and Learning Settings

Cultural upbringing can affect the settings in which we prefer to learn. Asian-Americans and European-Americans seem to have the backgrounds that fit the learning environment found in schools. Other cultures may be practices that put children at disadvantages in the typical school setting.

Children from Native Hawaiian families are used to doing things in cooperative groups. They learn much more when classes are divided into small groups and the teacher moves from group to group for intense instructional spurts, and learn much less in rowed classrooms in which a teacher lectures and asks individuals questions.

On the other hand, Navajo children are reared to be self-sufficient. Their culture emphasizes individuality, and efforts to be controlled feel like a manipulative violation. In classrooms, Navajo children withdraw if teachers become forceful in controlling behavior.

Another Navajo value is wholeness; Navajo children are not inclined to take things apart and examine the parts. This value shows up during storytelling and discussion. These children want the entire story read before the discussion begins.

Teachers willing to learn how their students feel comfortable learning can achieve higher levels of learning in their students. (*Source:* Tharp, R. G. 1989. Psychocultural variables and constants: Effects of teaching and learning in schools. *American Psychologist, 44,* 349-359.)

BROWN & BENCHMARK'S HUMAN DEVELOPMENT TRANSPARENCIES (2ND ED.)

Transparency Number and Title

The transparency set, a supplement to *Child Development,* is accompanied by an annotated manual that describes each of the 100 transparencies. The annotated manual also offers suggestions about how to use the transparencies to engage your students in active learning that will stimulate critical thinking and evaluative skills. The following transparencies are appropriate and useful with Chapter 18: Culture, Poverty, and Ethnicity.

Transparency Number and Title

1	A Garden's Diversity
2	Changes in Ethnic Populations in the United States
3	Daily Statistics
25	Bronfenbrenners' Ecological Theory
102	Where Adolescents Spend their Time
103	What Adolescents Spend their Time Doing
104	People With Whom Adolescents Spend their Time

CLASSROOM ACTIVITIES OR DEMONSTRATIONS

1. Discuss the critical thinking exercises. Exercise 1 sets the occasion for a review of Bronfenbrenner's ecological theory, which you may find useful in its own right as a means of demonstrating the theory's relevance and usefulness to the study of child psychology in particular, and culture in general. In any case, we have found that students find it difficult to differentiate mesosystems from exosystems, macrosystems from chronosystems, and that they benefit from reviewing several specific examples of each before trying to do exercises of this sort.

Exercise 2 is an opportunity to review some of the main schools of thought at the end of the course, and to relate them to the study of ethnicity and culture which is now receiving renewed emphasis in child psychology. Suggest to students that they review relevant material in *Child Development* concerning the theories of the theorists mentioned. You may also want to have them discuss the importance of culture as a unit of analysis in each of the theories, looking for examples in the text or other course materials.

Exercise 3 is simply the final assignment of the series of assumption, inference, and observation exercises that we have provided for each chapter. You may wish to use the exercise as an occasion to review with students the variety of propositions that serve as assumptions in arguments. For example, the assumption here has been a widely shared bias among researchers; elsewhere, assumptions have been definitions, arbitrarily imposed conditions on the interpretation of results, statements of principle, or beliefs about the nature of instruments and methods. Discuss with students whether they believe that they have become adept at identifying assumptions, and whether they recommend that you use these and other critical thinking exercises in future classes.

2. Discuss the students' research projects as suggested below.
3. A way to illustrate how researchers have studied cultural differences in achievement motivation and cooperative versus competitive behavior is to expose your students to an apparatus and procedure Madsen used to study these attributes in Mexican village children and American children. The apparatus is easy to assemble. Tape a sheet of paper to a rectangular board. Screw an eyebolt into each corner of the board and put a piece of string through each eyebolt. Attach all four pieces of string to an empty sewing thread spool, and insert a sharp pencil through the spool.

Four students participate in the experiment, each holding one of the pieces of string. Write each student's name within separate circles on the piece of paper on the board. In the cooperation condition, all students receive a quarter if each student puts a pencil mark in each circle on the paper. In the competition condition, the student who places the most pencil marks in the circle with his or her name in it receives the quarter.

How will your students perform? Find out. Then tell them that Mexican children showed more cooperation in the competition condition of the experiment than did American children. Discuss the students' experience, both in the class and in their lives, and relate that to results from the Mexican children. If you happen to have students from other cultures in your class, be sure to get their input in the discussion. You may also want to include material from Urie Bronfenbrenner's *Two Worlds of Childhood: U.S. and U.S.S.R* about cooperation and competition among children, and the social structures and circumstances that either promote or inhibit cooperation and competition, in these countries.

Walraven, M. G. 1993. *Instructor's Course Planner* to accompany John Santrock's *Adolescence*, 5th ed. Dubuque: Brown and Benchmark, Publishers.

---

4. Invite a representative of a minority ethnic group among students or faculty in the university community, or in the larger community surrounding your institution, to address your class on their individual and collective experience as ethnic minority individuals in the United States. Make sure your students prepare for the talk by reading appropriate material in Chapter 9 and any other relevant sources you can make available to them (your speaker may have suggestions). On the class after this presentation, schedule time to discuss with your students their reactions to the presentation.
5. This activity was created by Amy Zaun, one of our teaching assistants in a section of Adolescent Psychology. The basic idea is to locate students on your campus from other cultures and arrange for them to hold a panel discussion before your class. Have them prepare answers to a series of common questions that they can address in whatever format you find most comfortable. Some of the questions Ms. Zaun used are:

  1. What are the types of food popular in your country?
  2. What do teens typically do on the weekends and in the summer?
  3. Why did you choose to come to the United States? If you have a chance to come back after you leave, will you? Why or why not?
  4. What was your image of the United States before you came? How has it changed?
  5. What part of the American culture can you relate to best? What is the biggest difference between the United States and your country?
  6. What are differences in social conventions of your country and those of the United States?

You may also want to include questions about family life, peer relations, politics, education or any other topic typically studied in adolescent psychology. Ms. Zaun also addressed specific questions to each panel member about their own country, couched in terms of current events there or things for which that country was famous. You may also want to invite students to ask their own questions. Throughout, try to maintain a moderator's role, being as little intrusive as possible, to allow maximum interaction between your students and their guests.

6. Movies are an excellent way to vivify ethnic and cultural differences, and there are numerous ones available. You should browse among those available in your local video stores, but one movie you might consider using is *El Norte*, a story about a Guatemalan boy and his sister who flee to California to escape political repression in their own country. Another, one that has proven compelling to our students, is Spike Lee's *Boyz "N the Hood*. Of course, you may not be able to show an entire movie in a class period, but you could use segments of it to illustrate points you want to make, or you could assign a movie as a class assignment and then discuss it in a subsequent class.

7. Rites of passage are still a popular topic in material on culture and its influence on adolescents. Define the concept for your class and give some examples from the anthropological literature that generated it. Then ask your class whether they think rites of passage exist in American culture. Some students may suggest the possibilities listed in *Child Development*; challenge them to think of others, and to discuss whether Santrock's and their own examples fit the definition of rites of passage. If your class concludes that there really is nothing like a universal American rite of passage, discuss the meaning of significance of its absence in American adolescents' lives.

8. Introduce Ruth Benedict's classic concept of cultural continuity versus cultural discontinuity (Benedict, R. 1938. Continuities and discontinuities in cultural conditioning. *Psychiatry, 1*, 161-167). Then ask the class to discuss whether children experience a continuous or discontinuous transition to adolescence and later to adulthood in the contemporary United States. Include in your discussion the possibility of social class, gender, and ethnic variations in the degree to which the transition is continuous or discontinuous.

9. Adolescence is a recently added developmental stage (a word coined by G. Stanley Hall at the beginning of the twentieth century). Ask students to "brainstorm" the societal changes and influences that produced the need for an adolescence stage. How did the industrial revolution create a need for an adolescence stage? What effects did the need for more education have on the teenage years? Could modern society exist without an adolescence stage? How might society change if teenagers were allowed to compete as equals with adults in the workforce? What are the advantages and disadvantages of adolescence? Why does society hurry individuals through childhood and then suspend them in a prolonged period of adolescence?

Source: Simons, J. A., Irwin, D. B., & Drinnin, B. A. 1987. *Instructor's Manual to Accompany Psychology, the Search for Understanding,* St. Paul: West Publishing.

---

10. One of the **rites of passages** in American society is the senior prom, and nowadays high school proms are expensive. Some retailers estimate that males must spend at least $300 for a prom (tux rental, prom tickets, corsage, dinner, and limousine), with costs often going towards $800. Females can easily spend $400 to $600. Some schools charge as much as $200 per couple for the prom. Some prom couples also go away for the weekend after the prom.
How can proms be so expensive? How do prom-goers afford this rite of passage?

   a. The average 16- to 19-year-old gets $1,250 in allowance each year.
   b. Seventy-five percent of teens have two working parents and fewer siblings, so there is more expendable income.
   c. Fifty-six point four percent of all teenagers have jobs. Teens who work 35 hours or more each week have weekly median earnings of $204; those with part-time jobs average $75 a paycheck.

Opinions:

"Initiation rituals—this business of going from childhood to adulthood—embody and dramatize, and therefore teach the dominant values of the society. In this case it would seem that the dominant value has to do with conspicuous consumption."—G. Whitney Azoy
"Nothing crystallizes a kid's feelings of not belonging better than not having someone to go with to the prom. I've talked to kids who were convinced they were losers because no one had asked them."—Robert Sack

Source: Hodgin, D. 1990 (May 14). Reaching deep to put on the prom. *Insight,* 40-41.

11. Initiate a discussion of cultures and the VCR, microwave, and cable shopping with: "How has the VCR influenced your life?" Students should offer a variety of responses, e.g., greater variety of movies to watch at home, home-made videos for kids' activities, VCR used in hospital delivery rooms, changes in college courses (media in classroom and home-based options), no longer watching 8mm home movies, exercise with Jane Fonda. Off-shoots include "How have VCRs improved the quality of life? What disadvantages have come along with VCRs? What kinds of regulations should be placed on videos?"

Then ask, "How has the VCR influenced other cultures, especially cultures that are not Westernized, or have unstable governments?" Students may not be aware of these factors, which include influencing great cultural and political changes. Although authoritarian governments can control the content of radio and TV programs, they have difficulty in controlling "bootlegged" tapes. It means greater access to the entertainment and educational videos of other countries—which may be an advantage, or may lead to loss of cultural identity. It can be used by revolutionary movements; e.g., rebel soldiers have recorded instances of brutality or fighting to rally support or to inform foreign news organizations. Researchers are also able to record tribal customs for posterity. In January 1989, the Kayapo Indians in the Amazon used videotape to record and publicize the effects of hydroelectric dams on the Brazilian rain forest; they have been successful in putting a proposed dam project on hold.

You can expand the discussion by talking about how all corners of the world now must deal with the results of human progress. Bernie Krause has said, "Even the most remote corners of the world have human noise pollution. In the far reaches of the Amazon basin, you can hear chain saws cutting down the rain forest, bulldozers clearing roads, and motorboats hauling timber down the river—from twenty miles away." Krause managed to record 200 hours of gorillas' vocalizations; all but 15 minutes had human sounds on the tape—airplanes, children, etc.

Another television revolution is shopping by cable television. In 1990, three shopping channels (J. C. Penney, QVC, and Home Shopping Network) did about $1.5 billion in business (in 1985 it was only $1 million). By 1993, it is expected to be a $3 billion business. About 20 percent of viewers with access to a shopping channel make purchases. How does cable shopping affect family patterns of shopping? What are the pros and cons?

You can expand this class discussion again, by focusing in on the effects of the microwave on culture. By the end of the eighties, over 79 percent of U. S. households owned a microwave oven. This meant: (1) ready-made meals could be made in less than 10 minutes (compared to the more than 30 minutes needed for the "earlier revolution"—the TV dinner); (2) school-aged children were old enough to prepare their own hot meals. How has the microwave changed the typical families eating patterns, both food-wise and togetherness-wise? Does the microwave affect gender roles? What is the effect of "zapping" and "nuking" foods versus carefully preparing them? Does the microwave fit our times, or make our times?

Sources: Zoglin, R. 1989 (September 11). Subversion by cassette. *Time,* 80; Smith, E. 1989 (December); Pet shop boy. *Omni,* 20; Visser, M. 1989 (December). A meditation on the microwave. *Psychology Today,* 38-42; Cosin, E. M. 1990 (May 7). From the mall to catalogs to cable. *Insight,* 51; Zimmer, C. 1990. (August). Tech in the jungle. *Discover,* 42-45; Turner, T. 1990 (Spring). Visual media, cultural politics, and anthropological practice: Some implications of recent uses of film and video among the Kayapo of Brazil. *Commission on Visual Anthropology Review.*

12. Each student, or small groups of research, can be assigned a culture to research for aspects that influence development in the culture. Oral reports to the class can be dispersed throughout the semester and should be kept short and rather informal. Other students may wish to add comments when their own cultural ancestry is being covered. You may suggest that groups be picked by finding feature articles in popular magazines (e.g., *Insight, Time, Newsweek, National Geographic*) and then building upon the information in this article.

Chapter 18

Source: Simons, J. A. 1987. Cross-cultural reports: Class project, Ankeny, IA: Des Moines Area Community College.

13. How will America change as Caucasians become a minority group? In the twenty-first century (around 2056 by current estimates), racial and ethnic groups in the United States will outnumber whites for the first time. How will this new pattern influence politics? Education? Culture? Values? Industry?

In 1990, 1 in 4 Americans is Hispanic or nonwhite. By the end of the twentieth century, the Hispanic-American population will increase another 21 percent, the Asian-American populations will increase 22 percent, the African-American population will increase 12 percent and Anglo-American population will increase 2 percent.

Let the class vote on which of the following is likely to occur:

a. America either will become more tolerant of bilinguilism or will continue to use English as its only official language.
b. History textbooks either will continue to feature European history or will become more integrated with diverse cultures' history.
c. Affirmative action programs will increase or decrease.
d. Racial tensions will decrease or increase.
e. Multi-ethnic, multi-racial families will increase or decrease in numbers.
f. Segregation will grow or integration will grow.
g. Either television programming and advertising will become less oriented toward white America, or they will continue to be oriented toward white America.

Sources: Mehta, N. S., Monroe, S., & Winbush, D. 1990 (April 9). Beyond the melting pot. *Time,* 28-31; Salholz, E., Padgett, T., Gonzalez, D. L., & De LaPena, N. 1990 (April 9). The push for power. *Newsweek,* 18-20.

CRITICAL THINKING EXERCISES

Exercise 1

Bronfenbrenner's ecological theory is an an excellent model for analyzing cultural influences on adolescence. However, practice is needed to identify examples of the different systems specified by the theory accurately. Which of the following accurately represents a system paired with a specific claim or finding from studies of culture's influence on adolescence? **Circle the letter of the best answer and explain why it is the best answer and why each other answer is not as good.**

A. Chronosystem: According to Margaret Mead, adolescents in Samoa did not experience as much "storm and stress" as did their American counterparts during the 1920s.
B. Macrosystem: Ethnic minority students learn in schools that are predominantly white and middle class in orientation.
C. Exosystem: Students who have mothers who graduated from college spend more time reading than students whose mothers did not graduate from college.
D. Mesosystem: Erratic discipline is one of the factors that mediate the effects of poverty on delinquent behavior.
E. Mesosystem: America is a nation of blended cultures.

Exercise 2

Chapter 18 is a new addition to *Child Development.* Previous editions of the book did not contain this chapter. Although arguments for the importance of studying culture's influence on child development have come from people doing that research themselves, which of the following developmentalists is most likely to have had the biggest influence on Santrock's decision to include a chapter on culture? **Circle the letter of the best answer and explain why it is the best answer and why each other answer is not as good.**

A. Sigmund Freud
B. Jean Piaget
C. Lev Vygotsky
D. B. F. Skinner
E. Konrad Lorenz

Exercise 3

In the section of Chapter 18 called "Differences and Diversity" Santrock discusses changes in the way contemporary researchers think about the nature of differences between ethnic groups. One of these differences in a changed assumption rather than a changed finding or conclusion. Which of the following statements represents the new assumption? **Circle the letter of the best answer and explain why it is the best answer and why each other answer is not as good.**

A. The extended families of many ethnic minority groups are important factors in coping.
B. Ethnic differences may have either a positive or a negative effect on children's development.
C. Research on the positive aspects ethnic minority status is needed.
D. Ethnic minority groups are not homogeneous.
E. Failure to recognize diversity and individual variations results in stereotyping of ethnic minority groups.

ANSWER KEYS FOR CRITICAL THINKING EXERCISES

Exercise 1

A. This is not the best answer. Margaret Mead was comparing to cultures in order to test ideas about the universality of the adolescent experience. Thus she was examining macrosystems.
B. This is not the best answer. This finding describes a situation in which minority individuals in one microsystem, the school, are influenced by decisions taken by individuals influenced by settings in which the minority individual does not participate (e.g, the microsystems of the majority white culture). Thus this is an exosystem rather than a macrosystem.
C. This is not the best answer. This fact appears best described as a chronosystem, because mothers' attendance or nonattendance at college ocurred well before adolescents became involved in reading. If the information concerned mothers' attending college during their children's adolescence, it would be an exosystem (with respect to the adolescents).
D. This is the best answer. The statement describes a feature of one microsystem associated with the behavior of individuals who inhabit that microsystem in other microsystems of their lives (i.e., the places in which they are delinquent).
E. This is not the best answer. The statement characterizes the nature of American culture overall, and hence it refers to a macrosystem.

Exercise 2

A. This is not the best answer. Freud's theory focused primarily on what Freud regarded as the universal characteristics of development. In that light cultural variations are less interesting. In fact, early on cross-cultural tests of Freud's ideas were undertaken by individuals unfriendly to Freud's theory.
B. This is not the best answer. Like Freud, Piaget was interested mainly in universal aspects of development. Like Freud's theory, Piaget's theory has tended to suffer criticism resulting from cross-cultural comparisons, and has been motivated by researchers who hold a different theoretical perspective.
C. This is the best answer. Vygotsky more than any of the other theorists mentioned here stressed culture's role in children's acquisition of cognitive and linguistic skills. In fact, his work has stimulated a renewed interest in examining cross-cultural differences in the way children approach, for example, memory tasks (e.g., the work of Barbara Rogoff).
D. This is not the best answer. Although Skinner was clearly interested in environmental influences on learning, he focused on a very specific contextual analysis of behavior and its consequences rather than a broad, macroscopic study of cultural variation.
E. This is not the best answer. Lorenz studied biological sources of individual differences and patterns of behavior in animals. The resulting school of ethology has been more interesting in universal aspects of human

development (e.g., the facial expression or emotion) or principles of human diversity rather than an analysis of culture as an influence in its own right.

Exercise 3

A. This is not the best answer. Santrock offers this statement as a generalization of results from research, in which sense it is an inference.
B. This is the best answer. Santrock indicated that previous research proceeded from the assumption that differences between any ethnic minority group and Whites were deficits. That is, there was a bias in the interpretation of these differences.
C. This is not the best answer. This is a conclusion or inference that follows from denying the idea that ethnic differences are deficits.
D. This is not the best answer. This is an observation about the diversity of ethnic groups and their various characteristics.
E. This is not the best answer. This cause-and-effect statement represents an inference about influence of failing to recognize the internal diversity of ethnic groups.

RESEARCH PROJECT 1   RATING TELEVISION DRAMAS FOR REALISM

How realistically do television dramas portray problem-solving solutions for adolescent viewers? This research project will capitalize on a leisure activity to generate data to answer the question.

Watch five prime time television dramas and answer each of the questions suggested below about the program. Rather than simply giving short answers to each question, provide explanations of your answers. Also, be sure to note the information indicated at the beginning of the data sheet you use to rate each show:

DATA SHEET

Date_____   Time_____   Name of Show_____

1.   How realistic is the portrayal of the main character?

2.   How realistic is the portrayal of other characters?

3.   Do you think people in similar situations as the main and other characters of the show would have the same resources for dealing with their problems?

4.   What was the problem that had to be solved in the show? Is this problem typical of problems faced by people in real life?

5.   How realistic are the problem solutions in the show?

6.   Are villains realistically portrayed?

7.   Is violence the main theme of the show?

Summarize your observations of the five shows that you watched. For example, make a statement about how realistically the show portrayed people solving problems, whether the problems portrayed were like problems "real" people face, and so on. Support you answers with appropriate summaries of your ratings across the five shows that you watched.

Use in the Classroom

Have students individually or in groups report their summaries. Tabulate the quantitative aspects of their reports (e.g., whether or not the problems portrayed in shows were realistic). Because students will probably have watched the same episodes of the same shows, you have an opportunity to test agreements among their ratings and to discuss the methodology of the project. Collect data from the majority or all of your students, and use it to arrive at a conclusion about how realistically television drama portray people solving problems.

RESEARCH PROJECT 2   CHILDREN IN MAGAZINE ADVERTISEMENTS

This project explores depictions of children in magazine advertisements. You are to look at one widely circulated magazine and evaluate how ads depict children in infancy, early childhood, middle to late childhood, and adolescence. Evaluate physical appearance, personality, and behaviors. Use this chart to help organize your impressions (use a separate one for each age level), and then answer the questions that follow it.

DATA SHEET

Magazine Title_____   Issue date_____   Number of Ads_____

CHARACTERISTIC:	MALES	FEMALES
physical appearance:		
body message:		
clothes:		
facial expressions:		
personality:		
intelligence:		
activities:		
verbal comments:		
sexuality:		
other:		

Tally the number of each characteristic depicted in the advertisements broken down by males and females.

Questions

1. Are the sexes equally represented in the advertisements?
2. Are the characteristics represented equally for each sex?
3. Compare the various groups in terms of the characteristics you observed portrayed for each in the advertisements. What generalizations about each age group and gender do these portrayals convey?
4. Compare your findings to those obtained by someone who looked at a different magazine. Are your findings similar or different? What do you conclude if they are similar? Different? If they are different, do the differences sensibly relate to differences in the apparent purpose or style of the magazines?

Use in Classroom

You might want to assign specific magazines to students so that you can explore the effects of type of magazine on adolescent images (e.g., *Sports Illustrated* vs. *Ladies' Home Journal*) or gender images (e.g., *Seventeen* vs. *Sassy*). Another variation is to have students evaluate two issues of the same magazine (a current issue and one more than twenty years old) to explore changes in images over the years.

Class discussion will be enhanced if you include some examples of actual ads and have students evaluate them. Class members will want to discuss their favorite examples of stereotyping from the magazines they check out.

ESSAY AND CRITICAL THINKING QUESTIONS

Comprehension and Application Essay Questions

We recommend that you provide students with our guidelines for "Answering Essay and Critical Thinking Questions" when you have them respond to these questions. Their answers to these kinds of questions demonstrate an ability to comprehend and apply ideas discussed in this chapter.

1. Explain why it is useful to study culture as an influence on child development.
2. Explain what cross-cultural comparisons have taught us about the nature of adolescence, achievement, and rites of passage.
3. Compare and contrast the multicultural and fusion models of cultural change in terms of the concepts of assimilation, acculturation, and alternation.
4. Define social class, and explain how it relates to adolescents' families, schools, and neighborhoods.
5. What is the nature and scope of poverty in the United States?
6. Explain the idea that poverty has been feminized in the United States.
7. Explain the idea that social class confounds ethnicity in attempts to use ethnic diversity as explanations of features of adolescent development.
8. What does it mean to say that the idea of diversity applies to ethnic groups individually as well as collectively? Illustrate your answer with examples.
9. Define and distinguish among the concepts of prejudice, discrimination, and bias.
10. Explain the concepts of assimilation and pluralism, and discuss the role these ideas play in value conflicts.

Critical Thinking Questions

We recommend that you have students follow our guidelines for "Answering Essay and Critical Thinking Questions" when you ask them to prepare responses to these questions. Their answers to these kinds of questions reflect an ability to apply critical thinking skills to a novel problem or situation that is *not* specifically discussed in the chapter. These items most appropriately may be used as take-home essay questions (e.g., due on exam day) or as homework exercises that can be answered either by individuals or groups. Collaboratively answered questions encourage cooperative learning by students, and reduce the number of papers that must be graded.

1. At the end of Chapter 18 Santrock indicates books that provide practical knowledge about children and lists resources for improving the lives of children. Choose one of these books or resources and read it or learn as much as you can about it. Then write a brief review in which you (a) characterize the book or resource, and (b) explain how the book or resource relates to material in the chapter.
2. Chapter 1 defines the nature of development in terms of biological, cognitive, and social processes, and periods or stages. Indicate your ability to think critically by identifying material in this chapter that illustrates developmental processes and periods. If there is little or no information in this chapter about developmental processes and periods, identify and explain how developmental processes and periods could be used to guide the analysis of any topic in the chapter.
3. According to Chapter 1, three fundamental developmental issues concern: (a) maturation (nature) versus experience (nurture), (b) continuity versus discontinuity, and (c) early versus later experience. Indicate your ability to think critically by identifying material in this chapter that illustrates each of the three fundamental developmental issues. If there is little or no information in this chapter about fundamental developmental issues, identify and explain how these issues could be used to guide the analysis of any topic in the chapter.
4. One aspect of thinking critically is to read, listen, and observe carefully and then ask questions about what is missing from a text, discussion, or situation. For example, a topic that might have been included in this

chapter is how growing up in different political systems influences any of a number of aspects of children's development. Indicate your ability to think critically by (a) listing as many questions as you can about how growing up under the influence of different political systems influences various aspects of child development, and (b) speculating why Santrock does not discuss this topic more fully.

5. Santrock sets off several quotations in this chapter. Indicate your ability to think critically by selecting one of the quotes and (a) learning about the author and indicating why this individual is eminently quotable (i.e., what was this individual's contribution to human knowledge and understanding), (b) interpreting and restating the quote in your own terms, and (c) explaining what concept, issue, perspective, or term in this chapter that Santrock intended this quote to illuminate. In other words, about what aspect or issue in development does this quote make you pause and reflect?

6. Chapter 2 indicates that theories help us explain data and make predictions about various aspects of development. Chapter 2 then presents six different theoretical approaches (i.e., Freudian, cognitive, behavioral and social learning, ethological, ecological, and eclectic theory), but notes that no single approach explains the complexity of development. Indicate your ability to think critically by (a) perusing this chapter for topics influenced by at least one of the six theoretical approaches, and (b) explaining which theoretical approach dominated the topic in question. If the presentation is entirely atheoretical, identify and explain how one of the theoretical approaches could be used to guide the analysis of the topic in question.

7. Does involvement in religion play a role in child development? If so, how are variations in type of religion and intensity of involvement in religion related to what developmental outcomes? Apply your knowledge about the scientific method by designing a study to answer these questions: (a) What specific problem or question do you want to study? (b) What predictions would you make and test in your study? (c) What measures would you use (i.e., controlled observation in a laboratory, naturalistic observation, interviews and questionnaires, case studies, standardized tests, cross-cultural studies, physiological research, research with animals, or multimeasure, multisource, and multicontext approach) and how would you define each measure clearly and unambiguously? (d) What strategy would you follow--correlational or experimental, and what would be the time span of your inquiry--cross-sectional or longitudinal? (e) What ethical considerations must be addressed before you conduct your study?

8. According to Chapter 2, your author wants you to become a wise consumer of information about child development by: (a) being cautious about media reports, (b) distinguishing between nomothetic research and idiographic needs, (c) recognizing how easy it is to overgeneralize from a small or clinical sample, (d) knowing that a single study is usually not the defining word about some aspect of child development, (e) remembering that causal conclusions cannot be made from correlation studies, and (f) always considering the source of the information and evaluating its credibility. Indicate your ability to think critically by, first, selecting an article from either a journal, magazine, or newspaper about any topic regarding Culture, Poverty, and Ethnicity, and, second, evaluating it in terms of these six objectives. If the information in the article is insufficient to evaluate one of these objectives, then specify what kind of information you would need to evaluate the objective.

Teaching Resources

VIDEO LISTING

Several current videos are listed by age group. At the end of each selection, one or more chapters are suggested as appropriate for the video. When known, the information given includes video title, distributor (abbreviated; see list of addresses and phone numbers provided after the videotapes), number of minutes, (specific number and cost to buy), and brief description.

Order your media well in advance of the beginning of the semester. Follow specific college procedures, and ask your media resource personnel about college-owned videotapes and local sources of tapes.

Although an extensive list is provided, other excellent videotapes are available. We suggest you write to companies listed in this course planner and receive their catalogues.

DEVELOPMENTAL THEORIES

B. F. Skinner and Behavior Change: Research, Practice, and Promise. RP. 45 min. (1510; $495). Skinner and others address the issues and controversies generated by behavioral psychology. **ch. 2**

B. F. Skinner on Behaviorism. RMI. 28 min. (PSY-06; $90). or IM (PH41; $129). Skinner on behavior modification, behavioral technology, and the use of positive reinforcement in shaping human behavior. **ch. 2**

Child Development. RMI. 30 min. (C25-01; $99). Explores the concept of development, introduces theories of development, and presents methods by which we study children. **ch. 2**

Cognitive Development. RMI. 30 min. (C24-16; $90). Looks at the stages of Jean Piaget, his research contributions, and subsequent research that modifies his ideas. **ch. 2**

Contexts of Development. RMI. 30 min. (C25-02; $99). Looks at the interaction among social, economic, and cultural contexts on one's biological and developmental process. **ch. 1, 2 & 18**

Culture, Time, and Place. GPN. 30 min. (Module 6; $80). Language, schooling, and everyday interactions as vehicles of acculturation that communicate values, beliefs, attitudes, and expectations to children. Uses a traditional Japanese religious festival as an example. **ch. 2, 18**

Development and Diversity. GPN. 30 min. (Module 1: $80). Explores the historical, cultural, and individual diversity of childhood; what development is and how it occurs; and the significance of the prolonged period of human infancy and childhood. **ch. 1, 18**

Discovering Childhood. RMI. 60 min. (WLU-201; $90). or IM (TH 252; $129). Looks at historical attitudes toward children and theoretical perspectives including Erikson, Hull, Piaget, Skinner, Havinghurst, and Levin. Also introduces research methodology. **ch. 1 & 2**

The Ecology of Development. GPN. 30 min. (Module 2; $80). Introduces the factors of biological inheritance, temperament, caregiving, family, peers, schooling, culture, and history. Looks at the microsystem, mesosystem, exosystem, and macrosystem. **ch. 2, 18**

Eco-Psychology. TA. 90 min. (WO12-$50). Roszak suggests that a complete psychological theory must examine ecological relationships. His position is that consciousness is not separate from nature, but deeply embedded within it. **ch. 2**

Erik H. Erikson: A Life's Work. DAV. 30 min. ($250). Combines biographical information about Erikson with his theoretical proposals. **ch. 2**

Freud: The Hidden Nature of Man. IM. 29 min. (PH305; $149). Examines Freud's ideas about the id, ego, and superego, the Oedipus complex, the unconscious, and infantile sexuality. **ch. 2**

How Does the Mind Grow? RMI. 60 min. Looks at both stage and information processing theories of cognitive development. Focuses heavily on Piaget's research. **ch. 2**

Observation. MAG. 20-30 min. (Module 4; $35). Reasons for observing children; common errors; techniques; basic components in objective observation; rules for naturalistic observation. **ch. 2**

Piaget's Developmental Theory: An Overview. DAV. 30 min. ($250). Using footage of Piaget and of Elkind interviewing children, presents an overview of Piaget's developmental theory. **ch. 2**

Study of the Child: History and Trends. MAG. 20-30 min. (Module 1; $35). Philosophies of the church, Locke, and Rousseau; contributions of Darwin, Hall, Freud, Binet, Watson, and Gesell; developmental principles; methods of study; modern theories of development. **ch. 1**

Theories of Development. MAG. 20-30 min. (Module 2; $35). Landmarks of development; crisis of development; individual characteristics and influence of heredity and environment; interrelatedness of development. **ch. 1**

The Torch Is Passed. FML. 30 min. ($295). Shows the importance of context by looking at the student movement at Berkeley in the 1960s and then looking at what the members went on to do. **ch. 1**

CULTURE, RACE, AND ETHNICITY

Are We Different? FML. 27 min. ($295). Deals with issues of race, racism, and race relations. **ch. 1, 3, & 18**

The Asianization of America. FHS. 26 min. (HI-1912; $149). Examines the role of Asian Americans half a century after the repeal of the Chinese Exclusion Act. **ch. 1, 3, & 18**

Biculturalism and Acculturation Among Latinos. FHS. 28 min. (IL-3202; $149). Latinos' pressures to reclaim and reaffirm their heritage while assimilating into the dominant American culture. **ch. 1, 3, & 18**

A Confucian Life in America with Tu Wei-ming. PBS. 30 min. (WIWM-225; $40). Looks at the relevance of Confucian philosophy to modern American society. **ch. 1 & 18**

Culture and Personality. IM. 30 min. (SJ07; $119). Looks at Margaret Mead's studies of child-rearing cultures, including Samoa. Looks at personality traits in the United States', Japan's, and China's culture as it relates to their history, environment, and subsistence patterns. **ch. 1 & 18**

Japan: Customs and Manners. IM. 35 min. (SH163; $119). A look at the customs and manners of Japanese society including the bowing, the tea ceremony, and business styles. **ch. 1 & 18**

Just Black? Multi-Racial Identity. FML. 58 min. ($445). Looks at individuals whose parents come from different racial heritages. **ch. 1, 3, & 18**

The Kawelka. IM. 52 min. (SJ253; $239). In Papua New Guinea, status is earned by giving things away, rather than by acquiring them. In the Moka ceremony, people give gifts to other tribes, and the larger the gift the greater the victory over the recipient. **ch. 1 & 18**

The Kumekucha: Women of Tanzania. FHS. 28 min. (IL-3085; $149). The women discuss their multi-role dilemmas in a culture in which men have little work. **ch. 1, 13, & 18**

A Legacy of Lifestyles. CPB. 60 min. (AFRSV; $30). Looks at what constitutes "family" in African Culture including matrilineal, patrilineal, and polygamous traditions. **ch. 1, 15, & 18**

A Matter of Choices. PBS. 60 min. (WINC-102; $60). Looks at the Hopi Indian culture in modern America. **ch. 1 & 18**

The Nature of Culture. IM. 30 min. (SJ02; $119). Examines the learning and sharing of behavior, beliefs, and attitudes in different cultures including the United States, !Kung hunters of Africa, Txukarrame Indians of the Amazon, and Boran of Kenya. **ch. 1 & 18**

Other Voices, Other Songs: The Armenians. FML. 30 min. ($195). Celebrates the survival of a people who have often been persecuted. Looks at the history and cultural background of a half-a-million Armenians. **ch. 1 & 18**

Other Voices, Other Songs: The Greeks. FML. 30 min. ($195). Looks at both European Greeks and American Greeks, including a Greek festival and several Greek-American musical companies. **ch. 1 & 18**

Race and Ethnicity. IM. 30 min. (SH41; $139). Defines minority and explains the significance of race, racism, and ethnicity. **ch. 1, 3, & 18**

Race, Hatred, and Violence: Searching for Solutions. IM. 22 min. (SH81; $159). Explores the problems of racism in American society. **ch. 1, 3, & 18**

PRENATAL DEVELOPMENT

Adoption and Assisted Reproduction: A Look at the Children. FHS. 26 min. (IL-1923; $149). Looks at various examples and discusses possible effects on the offspring. **ch. 3**

The Beginning of Life. BF. 29 min. Describes vividly and accurately the stages of prenatal development. **ch. 3 & 4**

Birth of a Brain. CRM. 33 min. Good photography showing the development of the brain, beginning with the 20-day embryo. **ch. 3 & 4**

Blueprint for Life. RMI. 30 min. (C25-03; $99). Looks at the developing fetus, genes and heredity, and teratogens. **ch. 3 & 4**

Conception and Heredity. MAG. 20-30 min. (Module 5; $35). Beginning of life; cell division; sex determination; function of chromosomes, DNA, and genes; inherited traits; influences of heredity and environment. **ch. 3**

Decoding the Book of Life. MTI. 58 min. (DB-6173C; $350). The genome project including James Watson's views. **ch. 3**

DES: The Timebomb Drug. FML. 27 min. Highlights the effects of teratogens by showing the long-term effects of DES use as a drug to lower miscarriage risks. **ch. 3 & 4**

Everyday Miracle—Birth. FI. 30 min. Shows the moment of conception and scenes up to birth. **ch. 4**

Fetal Alcohol Syndrome and Other Drug Use During Pregnancy. FHS. 19 min. (IL-3134; $149). Profiles a young Apache Indian boy born with FAS, and discusses the common characteristics of these children. **ch. 4**

The Gap Between the Sexes. MTI. 28 min. (DB-6011M; $80). Among other sex difference issues, this program deals with biological differences prior to birth. **ch. 4 & 13**

Having Babies After 30. MTI. 30 min. (DB-5822M; $80). Looks at decision-making among those who have postponed parenthood. **ch. 4**

Heredity and Environment. IM. 30 min. Includes Mendel's work, mitosis, fertilization, the structure of DNA and chromosomes, and nature-nurture controversy. **ch. 3**

How Babies Get Made. MTI. 58 min. (DB-5130C; $99). Genetic differentiation, and how a "master" set of genes is responsible for all genetic duplication. **ch. 3**

How Life Begins. CRM. 22 min. In this third edition, youngsters answer the question "How are babies born?" Animation and color photographs of reproduction processes, fertilization, and prenatal development. **ch. 3 & 4**

Nature & Nurture. FHS. 52 min. Looks at identical twins separated at birth and their similarities as adults. **ch. 3**

Nature's Child: Biological Growth. RMI. 60 min. (WLU-202; $90). The biological processes that occur prior to birth are discussed, including genetics and genetic abnormalities. **ch. 3**

Pregnancy and Substance Abuse. FHS. 28 min. (IL-2882; $149). Looks at the risks of smoking and alcohol during pregnancy, and Michael Dorris (wrote *The Broken Cord*) discusses raising an adopted son with fetal alcohol syndrome. **ch. 4**

Prenatal Development. CRM. 23 min. Illustrates the formation and development of the human fetus. **ch. 4**

Prenatal Development. MAG. 20-30 min. (Module 6, $35). Stages; critical periods; placenta and amniotic sac; environmental factors. **ch. 4**

Prenatal Development and the Birth Process. GPN. 30 min. (Module 3; $80). Examines research on the prenatal period and neonate. Looks at alternative birth processes in Brazil, Russia, and the United States. **ch. 4**

Prenatal Diagnosis: To Be or Not to Be. FML. 45 min. Looks at techniques such as amniocentesis, fetoscopy, and ultrasound which allow detection of more than 80 biochemical abnormalities in utero. Challenging bioethical questions are raised. **ch. 3**

Reproductive System (Second Edition). MTI. (DB-3964; $250). Diagrammatic animation illustrates how hormones from the pituitary gland control the maturation and the function of the reproductive organs. **ch. 3**

So You're Going to Be a Parent. RP. 30 min. (4321; $95). Helps to develop an awareness of the responsibilities, demands, and joy involved in being a first-time parent. **ch. 15**

Understanding Pregnancy. MAG. 20-30 min. (Module 7; $35). Health care supervision; diagnosing pregnancy; physical and psychological changes; prenatal care. **ch. 4**

Web of Life. PBS. 60 min. (SMIW-404; $50). Looks at attempts to understand and control the genetic basis of life. **ch. 3**

Well-Conceived. MTI. 30 min. (DB-5234M; $80). Looks at the importance of prenatal care. **ch. 3**

CHILDBIRTH AND NEONATAL PERIOD

After the Baby Comes Home. FHS. 19 min. (IL-1399; $90). Deals with a variety of issues including postpartum depression, marital stress, sleeping difficulties, sibling reactions, and physical exhaustion. **ch. 4 & 15**

First Adaptations. RMI. 30 min. (C25-05; $99). Looks at the learning capabilities of newborns and experts discuss the growth of the infant brain. **ch. 4 & 5**

Birth at Home. FML. 14 min. Shows a home birth in Australia, including the midwife who uses massage and herbal medicine. **ch. 4**

Five Women, Five Births. DAV. 29 min. Shows five women making birth decisions and then their actual childbearing experiences. **ch. 4**

Great Expectations. RMI. 30 min. (C25-04; $99). Focuses on birth techniques, including vaginal and caesarean births, on Lamaze class, on parental expectations, and premature births. **ch. 4**

Infant Development. IM. 45 min. (TH191; $89). Explores the unique physical, cognitive, and emotional development of the newborn. Includes developmental norms and sequences, what infants know at birth, how language and motor skills develop, and parent/child bonding. **ch. 5, 7, 10**

Life with Baby: How Do Parents Feel? FML. 27 min. ($295). Three families are shown trying to adjust to the real life demands of parenthood. **ch. 15**

Life's First Feelings. MTI. 58 min. (DB-4938C; $99). Looks at the neonate's emotional capabilities and emotional development in infancy. **ch. 11**

Natural Childbirth. MIL. 10 min. A subjective account of the experience of natural childbirth including preparation and delivery. **ch. 4**

The Neonate. MAG. 20-30 min. (Module 8, $35). Alternatives of childbirth care; humanizing hospitals; Apgar Scale; birth trauma; neonatal reflexive behaviors; neonatal sensory capabilities; breast vs. bottle-feeding. **ch. 3, 4, 5**

Newborn: Ready for Life. FML. 28 min. A comprehensive examination of the capabilities of the newborn with demonstrations by Brazelton, Lipsett, and Sanders. **ch. 4**

Our Birth Film—The Human Drama of a Woman and a Man in the Delivery Room. MIL. 26 min. A very personal childbirth film showing a young couple and the birth of their second child. **ch. 4**

Prenatal Development and the Birth Process. GPN. 30 min. (Module 3; $80). Examines research on the prenatal period and neonate. Looks at alternative birth processes in Brazil, Russia, and the United States. **ch. 4**

INFANCY

And Baby Makes Three: Balancing Everyone's Needs. FML. 27 min. ($295). Looks at two couples who have 10-month-old babies. **ch. 15**

Baby Talk. IM. 60 min. (TH244; $89). Examines the stages of language acquisitions beginning with infant cries. Interviews with Noam Chomsky and J. S. Bruner. **ch. 10**

Better Babies. Raising Intellectual "Super Stars." FML. 28 min. ($295). Looks at programs designed to stimulate intellectual ability in infants. **ch. 9**

Birth to One Year. IM. 12 min. (TH176; $99). Focuses on physical and emotional development. **ch. 5 & 11**

Developing Language Skills. IM. 30 min. (TH80; $119). Discusses the relationship between language and thought and contrasts the theories of Piaget and Vygotsky. **ch. 7 & 10**

The Discovery Year. FHS. 52 min. (IL-1626; $149). Looks at a variety of aspects of the first year of life. **ch. 5, 7, 10, 11**

The Emerging Personality. IM. 30 min. Discusses Freud's psychoanalytic theory, Erikson's psychosocial theory, social learning theory, and Mahler's separation-individuation theory. **ch. 12**

First Adaptations. IM. 30 min. (TH320; $139). This program shows how infants' sleeping patterns contribute to mental organization and illustrates how the brain develops. Recreates classic developmental experiments including the visual cliff. **ch. 5**

First Feelings. RMI. 30 min. (C25-07; $99). or IM (TH278; $139). Looks at the role of the infant's relationship with its primary caregiver and at the role of temperament on an infant's personality. **ch. 11**

The First Year. RMI. 30 min. (C25-08; $99). Documents the first year of life of one child from pre-birth and first parental reactions through the first year. **ch. 5, 10, 11, 15**

The First Year of Life. FHS. 28 min. (IL-1413; $149). Examines how the newborn infant sees and hears, when it is first able to perceive a total image of its mother, and how its individuality is developed. **ch. 5 & 12**

Habits of the Heart: Early Relationships. RMI. 60 min. (WLU-207; $90). Looks at infants' relationships in terms of attachment and bonding. **ch. 11**

I, Toddler. RMI. 30 min. (C25-10; $99). or IM (TH280; $139). How toddlers deal with dependence, autonomy, and sense of self. **ch. 12**

Infancy and Early Childhood. CPB. 60 min. (SOLSV; $30). Shows the early effects of the biological and social clocks, including how children develop their unique view of the world. **ch. 5, 8, 12**

Infancy: Beginnings in Cognition and Language. MAG. 20-30 min. (Module 10; $35). Sense and perception; cognitive and language development; parent role in language learning. **ch. 5, 7, 8, 10**

Infancy: Early Relationships. MAG. 20-30 min. (Module 11; $35). Development of trust; mutuality; bonding and attachment; stranger anxiety and separation anxiety. **ch. 11**

Infancy: Landmarks of Development. MAG. 20-30 min. (Module 9; $35). Physical and motor development; principles of development; factors which influence development; regulation of basic processes. **ch. 5**

Infancy: Self and Social World. MAG. 20-30 min. (Module 12; $35). Development of emotions; symbiosis and separation; social awareness; cultural effects on development. **ch. 12 & 18**

Infant Development. IM. 45 min. (TH191; $89). Explores the unique physical, cognitive, and emotional development of the newborn. Includes developmental norms and sequences, what infants know at birth, how language and motor skills develop, and parent/child bonding. **ch. 5, 7, 10, 11**

The Infant Mind. RMI. 30 min. (C25-06; $99). or IM (TH277; $139). This program shows evidence that babies can remember, form concepts, understand cause and effect, and comprehend the world far earlier than was once assumed. **ch. 7 & 8**

Infants Have Feelings Too. MTI. 29 min. (DB-5962M; $80). Looks at the first three years of emotional development. **ch. 11**

Infants in Training: Mastering Early Skills. Looks at perceptual capabilities, habituation, classical conditioning, and operant conditioning. **ch. 5 & 8**

Language and Thinking. RMI. 30 min. (C25-09; $99). or IM (TH279; $139). Observing toddlers in research, experts present theories about the brain and its role in facilitating and processing language during toddlerhood. **ch. 7, 8, 10**

Learning to Communicate: Doing What Comes Naturally. Compares human language and animal communication, discusses the stages of language development, and the effects of deafness. Covers various theories of language development. **ch. 10**

Living the Life of the Toddler. IM. 25 min. (TH188; $139). The camera becomes the eye of the toddler. **ch. 5, 7, 10, 11, 12**

Mastering Early Skills. 60 min. (TH254; $129). Relates physical changes to the development of perceptual capabilities, dealing with habituation, classical conditioning, operant conditioning, and observational learning. **ch. 5 & 8**

Matthew: Portrait of a One-Year-Old. FML. 25 min. ($295). Demonstration of Matthew's motor and communication skills, who is of Chinese descent growing up in England. **ch. 5 & 10**

Newborn. With Dr. Berry Brazelton. FML. 28 min. ($295). Looks at reflexes and other abilities of the neonate. **ch. 5**

One to Three Years. IM. 16 min. (TH177; $99). Explores the toddler's search for self-reliance, reviews Piaget's theory, and discusses intellectual and physical development. **ch. 7, 9, 12**

Out of the Mouths of Babes. FML. 28 min. ($295). Traces the various events in the development of language from infancy to six years of age. **ch. 10**

Pre-Verbal Communication. FML. 25 min. Shows communication between a mother and her 8-month-old child. **ch. 10**

Toddlerhood: Emotional Development. MAG. 20-30 min. (Module 18; $35). Autonomy, shame and doubt; socialization through meeting biological needs, handling emotions, and social interactions. **ch. 11**

Toddlerhood: Physical and Cognitive Development. MAG. 20-30 min. (Module 17; $35). Physical growth and motor development; cognitive and language development; environment for language learning. **ch. 5 & 7**

Turning Two: Out of Babyhood. FML. 51 min. ($350). The accomplishments of the first two years in motor and speech areas. **ch. 5 & 10**

You Must Have Been a Bilingual Baby. FML. 46 min. ($395). Looks at toddlers that have two languages and also looks at a bilingual classroom. **ch. 10 & 18**

EARLY CHILDHOOD

Adam's Equal or Adam's Rib. RMI. 30 min. (POF-104; $99). This program explores the process of gender identification and assumption of gender roles, the evolution of self-concept, and the issue of androgyny. **ch. 13**

Child Care: Families in the Balance. PBS. 60 min. (FABA-000; $60). Looks at the lives of four families who are struggling to balance career and family demands. **ch. 15**

Day Care and the Preschool Experience. GPN. 30 min. (Module 15; $80). Looks at child care practices of the Baka and day care centers in Italy, Japan, and the United States. **ch. 11**

The Daycare Dilemma. MTI. 30 min. (DB-5818M; $80). Discusses the pros and cons of alternatives to mother care and what parents can do to minimize the hazards. **ch. 11**

Day Care Solutions. FHS. 18 min. (IL-1530; $149). Looks at effects of day care provided by employers. **ch. 11**

Dear Lisa: A Letter to My Sister. ND. 45 min. ($275). Interviews 13 women and girls and presents a multicultural look at women's hopes and dreams. The filmmaker looks at her own childhood, weaving family home movie footage, animated drawings, and a letter to her sister into the film. Can by used with this chapter, or in adulthood. **ch. 13**

Early Childhood: Behavior and Relationships. MAG. 20-30 min. (Module 20; $35). Typical behaviors; biological, performance of skills, human relationships; problem behaviors and adult responses. **ch. 6, 12, 15**

Early Childhood: Growth and Development. MAG. 20-30 min. (Module 19; $35). Physical/motor development; intellectual development; characteristics of preschool thinking; social and emotional development; early moral development. **ch. 6, 7, 9, 11, 12, 14**

Early Relationships: Habits of the Heart. IM. 60 min. (TH258; $129). Differentiates between bonding and attachment, demonstrates Ainsworth's Strange Situation Test, and looks at how early experiences channel the quality of relationships. **ch. 11**

Everybody Knows That! PFV. 15 min. Looks at the gender stereotypes of kindergartens. **ch. 13**

Friends and Foes: Peers in Development. RMI. 60 min. (WLU-210; $90). The changing nature of friendship as children progress from early childhood into adolescence. **ch. 16**

Gender, Early Morality, and the Self. GPN. 30 min. (Module 13; $80). The role of the family in the development of gender roles, moral emotions, prosocial behavior, and self-concept. **ch. 12, 13, 14, 15**

Teaching Resources

Growth of Intelligence in the Preschool Years. DAV. 31 min. ($190). Children from infancy to six years of age perform tasks designed by Jean Piaget. **ch. 7 & 9**

In the Land of the Giants (3-5 Years). IM. 57 min. (TH300; $139). Examines models of behavior and codes of discipline used to mold children to a culture's desired social image. Bronfenbrenner explains how the world affects the family and, in turn, the child's development. **ch. 2 & 15**

Interactional Styles and Attachment. GPN. 30 min. (Module 12; $80). Looks at research results concerning the attachment relationship in terms of caregiver sensitivity, predictability, and respect for children as individuals. **ch. 11**

Living the Life of the Preschooler. IM. 25 min. (TH189; $139). The camera becomes the eyes of a preschooler. **ch. 6, 7, 11, 16**

Men in Early Childhood Education. DAV. 24 min. Looks at the role men can play as preschool educators. **ch. 17**

Nurturing Capability in Children. IM. 18 min. (TH247; $119). Demonstrates how to foster skills in young children before they reach school age. **ch. 17**

Nutrition. MAG. 20-30 min. (Module 15; $35). Basic nutritional concepts; age-level nutritional concerns; infancy, childhood, adolescence. **ch. 5 & 6**

On the Home Front: The Influence of the Family. RMI. 60 min. (WLU-209; $90). Looks at bi-directional influences within the family and the changing structure of the family. Also explores the use of power assertion, love withdrawal, and induction to control one's children. Also addresses punishment, child abuse, and effects of siblings. **ch. 15**

Parents and Children: A Positive Approach to Child Management. RP. 24 min. (1958; $425). Gives an overview of how to use behavior management procedures with children. **ch. 8 & 15**

Play and Imagination. RMI. 30 min. (C25-15; $99). Looks at the developmental course of play and imagination from infants to adolescents, showing how play enhances cognitive and social-emotional skills. **ch. 16**

The Preschool Experience. IM. 30 min. (TH198; $119). Examines the advantages and disadvantages of several preschool programs, including the Montessori and Gesell approaches. **ch. 11**

Preschool Mental Development. IM. 30 min. Look at Piaget's theory, behavioristic approaches, the Head Start program, and the Pacific Oaks Schools. **ch. 7 & 11**

Preschool Personality. IM. 30 min. Includes the relationship between television watching and aggression, aggression studies with the Bobo doll, the Oedipal and Electra complexes, and conflict between initiative and guilt. **ch. 2, 8, 12, 16**

Preschool Physical Development. IM. 30 min. Includes development of bones, brain, circulatory system, and handedness. **ch. 6**

The Preschool Social Development. RMI. 30 min. (C25-14; $99). or IM (TH282; $139). The preschooler's sense of identity, gender identity, parental and peer relationships, and self-esteem. **ch. 12, 13, 16**

The Preschooler's Mind. RMI. 30 min. (C25-13; $99). or IM (TH281; $139). Uses recreated experiments and expert descriptions to look at emerging cognitive abilities in the preschool years. **ch. 7**

A Question of Quality. FHS. 26 min. (IL-3796; $149). A general overview of the benefits children get from child care and the ways parents can ensure suitable placement. **ch. 11**

Responsive Caregiving. GPN. 30 min. (Module 11; $80). Looks at the effects of variations in sleeping, nursing, comforting, and disciplining looking at examples from the United States, Russia, Japan, and the Baka of Cameroon. **ch. 2 & 15**

Risk and Resilience. RMI. 30 min. (C25-11; $99). or IM (PH285; $139). Meet abused or neglected children and observe sessions of therapy with them. **ch. 12**

The Secret of the Sexes. IM. 60 min. (PH31; $89). Investigates male and female stereotypes, explaining how adults consciously and unconsciously typecast boys and girls. **ch. 13**

Sex Roles: Charting the Complexity of Development. RMI. 60 min. (WLU-212; $90). Looks at cultural impact and cultural myths on gender roles. Covers Freudian, social-learning, and cognitive-development theories. **ch. 13**

Social Stereotyping. IM. 30 min. Looks at gender-role stereotypes and prejudices. Examines the nonstereotyped environment at the Pacific Oaks Preschool. **ch. 13**

Three Preschoolers. RMI. 30 min. (C25-16; $99). Looks at a 3-1/2-year-old who lives with both parents in a single-career home, a 5-year-old blind girl in a supportive family, and identical twin boys. **ch. 15**

Three to Five Years. IM. 14 min. (TH178; $99). The social, physical, and moral growth of preschoolers. **ch. 6, 12, 14, 16**

Turning 4—New Skills. FML. 51 min. ($350). Emerging from toddlerhood to become independent, sociable, chatty, and occasionally argumentative children. **ch. 6, 7, 10, 12, 16**

The Typical Twos. RMI. 30 min. (C25-12; $99). The life of three toddlers with varied backgrounds—a middle-class household, a mixed ethnic heritage family, and a homeless single-parent family. **ch. 3, 5, 15**

When I Grow Up. RMI. 30 min. (POF-103; $99). The changes from having prescribed gender roles to having them less defined. **ch. 13**

MIDDLE CHILDHOOD

Among Equals. IM. 57 min. (TH302; $139). Analyzes how peers work out moral dilemmas and social relationships, as well as for developing a strong self-identity. Looks at boys' and girls' interactions and types of play. **ch. 12, 13, 14, 16**

Bilingual Education. FHS. 26 min. (HI-3264; $149). Examines Latino opinion on bilingual education and attempts to increase literacy levels and English language skill. **ch. 17 & 18**

Blended Families. RP. 30 min. (4327; $95). Addresses parent and child concerns about making the transition to newly formed family structures. **ch. 15**

The Child's Mind. IM. 30 min. (TH118; $119). Explores the concrete operational stage of Piaget's theory, the information-processing approach, memory, creativity, and morality. **ch. 7, 8, 9, 14**

Child Management. RP. 30 min. (4324; $95). Illustrates techniques that encourage appropriate behavior and discourage inappropriate behavior. **ch. 8, 15**

Childhood and Adolescence (Ages 6-20). CPB. 60 min. (SOLSV; $30). In childhood, one learns skills and cultural information; in adolescence, puberty is important. **ch. 6, 7, 16**

Children of Divorce. FHS. 28 min. (IL-2012; $90). The lingering effects of divorce on children. **ch. 15**

Classification. DAV. 16 min. ($125). Uses Piagetian classification tasks to show children's ability in using categories. **ch. 7**

Cognitive Development. IM. 30 min. (TH67; $139). Focuses on the influential theory of Jean Piaget and on recent research. **ch. 7**

Concepts, Memories, and Categories. GPN. 30 min. (Module 10; $80). Examines cognitive changes between five and seven years, reviewing research on conceptual and memory development, logical reasoning, and problem solving. Uses examples from Japan, Russia, and Brazil. **ch. 7, 8, 9**

Conservation. DAV. 29 min. ($190). Children between five and twelve perform tasks dealing with quantity, length, area, and volume. **ch. 7**

Cultural Bias in Education. FHS. 28 min. (HI-3205; $149). Examines roadblocks to Latino academic advancement. **ch. 17 & 18**

Do Children Also Divorce? FML. 30 min. ($295). Shows the needs of children, especially in dealing with negative reactions, during the stress of divorce. Shows how each age group is affected differently. **ch. 15**

The Education Race. PBS. 60 min. (LEIA-101; $50). Visits American and Japanese schools to examine educational differences. **ch. 17 & 18**

The Elementary Mind. RMI. 30 min. (C25-17; $99). or IM (TH284; $139). Grade-school children in regular and special education classes and research studies help students understand the cognitive development in middle childhood, including mathematics abilities, memory, and intelligence. **ch. 7, 9, 17**

Family Influences. RMI. 30 min. (C25-19; $99). Focuses on sibling relationships, divorce, and the complexities of family context. **ch. 15**

Five to Eight Years. IM. 13 min. (TH179; $99). Investigates the changes a child experiences in school due to new social relationships and new authority figures. **ch. 16, 17**

Friends and Foes: Peers in Development. RMI. 60 min. (WLU-210; $90). The changing nature of friendship as children progress from early childhood into adolescence. **ch. 16**

Getting Along. RMI. 30 min. (C25-20; $99). or IM (TH287; $139). The development of prosocial and aggressive behavior during middle childhood, focusing on empathy, conflict at home, friendship and the possible effects of television on behavior. **ch. 15, 16, 17**

Good Intentions: Bad Diets for Kids. MTI. 30 min. (DB-5819M; $80). What good nutrition for children equals. **ch. 6**

Intelligence. IM. 30 min. (PH157; $139). Demonstrates the difference between intellectually gifted individuals and those who are developmentally disabled; shows how hard it is to define intelligence; looks at the origins of IQ tests; addresses whether intelligence is fixed or changeable. **ch. 9**

I.Q. MTI. 30 min. (DB-5247M; $80). Looks at intelligence tests and the nature of intelligence. **ch. 9**

IQ Testing and the School: Maximizing Potential. RMI. 60 min. (WLU-206; $90). or IM (PH237). Begins with a historical perspective and then moves into comparisons of ability levels in competitive or individualistic settings. **ch. 9**

Latch-Key Families. FHS. 23 min. (IL-1581; $90). A program that offers guidance to working parents with children who are on their own after school. **ch. 15**

Learning and Achievement. GPN. 30 min. (Module 16; $80). Looks at the functions of schooling, and children's orientation toward mastery and achievement. **ch. 8, 17**

Life's Lessons (5-7 Years). IM. 57 min. (TH301; $139). Examines the "5-7 shift" characteristic of middle childhood when children move away from the intimacy of home to enter school and work. Shows the first day of school in different cultures. **ch. 17**

Me and My Friends. RMI. 30 min. (C25-18; $99). or IM (TH285; $139). As children are shown playing, competing, and being friends, experts discuss self-esteem, motivation, and achievements as elements of the social and emotional development. **ch. 12, 16**

Middle Childhood: Growth and Development. MAG. 20-30 min. (Module 25; $35). Physical changes; self-concept; characteristics of thinking; acquisition of concepts; language characteristics; developmental tasks. **ch. 6, 7, 10**

Middle Childhood: Sense of Industry. MAG. 20-30 min. (Module 27; $35). Components of the sense of industry; discipline; socializing middle-years children; school curricula and teachers. **ch. 17**

Middle Childhood: Society of Children. MAG. 20-30 min. (Module 26; $35). Personality development; peer influence; society of children; emotional and social behaviors; development tasks. **ch. 11, 12, 16**

Peer Culture. GPN. 30 min. (Module 18; $80). Looks at how children and adolescents negotiate the authority of adults and the cooperation of peers. Analyzes *los abandonados,* a homeless and parentless group of children in Guatemala City. **ch. 16 & 18**

Play and Imagination. RMI. 30 min. (C25-15; $99). Looks at the developmental course of play and imagination from infants to adolescents, showing how play enhances cognitive and social-emotional skills. **ch. 16**

Preadolescence. MAG. 20-30 min. (Module 28; $35). Physical-motor development; cognitive functioning; language; emotional development; sexual awareness and behavior; sex education; relationship with parents and peers; gangs. **ch. 6, 7, 10, 11, 13, 15, 16, 17**

Prejudice: The Eye of the Storm. IM. 25 min. (PH22; $149). Documentary about a third-grade teacher's classroom experiment demonstrates how quickly people can discriminate, here on the basis of eye color. **ch 17 & 18**

Productivity and the Self-fulfilling Prophecy: The Pygmalion Effect. CRM. 31 min. Revised. The role of expectations on classroom performance. **ch. 17**

School Days. RP. 30 min. (4322; $95). Helps parents clarify their own roles and expectations of the educational system with one overriding focus in mind. **ch. 17**

Teach Your Children. PBS. 60 min. (LEIA-103; $50). Looks at textbook reform and technology and education. Concerns about the teaching of the humanities and ethical values. **ch. 14, 17**

Through the Looking Glass: The Development of Self. RMI. 60 min. (WLU-208; $90). Looks at the development of the self concept throughout childhood with Susan Harter discussing the Perceived Competence Scale for Children. **ch. 12**

Upstairs/Downstairs. PBS. 60 min. (LEIA-102; $50). The two-tiered educational system in the United States. Looks at urban versus suburban, urban versus rural, and public versus private schools. Looks at the effects of poverty, parental illiteracy, lack of nutrition, and language barriers. **ch. 17 & 18**

Using What We Know: Applying Piaget's Developmental Theory in Primary Classrooms. DAV. 35 min. ($250). David Elkind proposes educational practices that reflect thoughtful application of Piagetian theories. **ch. 7 & 17**

You Must Have Been A Bilingual Baby. FML. 46 min. ($395). Looks at toddlers that have two languages and also looks at a bilingual classroom. **ch. 10, 17, & 18**

ADOLESCENCE

Adolescence. RP. 30 min. (4325; $95). Helps parents prepare for the teen years. **ch. 15**

Adolescence: Crisis or Change? RMI. 60 min. (WLU-211; $90). Looks at the challenges of autonomy, peer relationships, and personal identity. Discusses sexual activity including issues of AIDS and teenage pregnancy. The theory of stages of individualism and vocational identity are reviewed. **ch. 6, 12, 14, 15, 16**

Adolescence: Growth and Development. MAG. 20-30 min. (Module 29; $35). Definition; puberty and pubescence; physical growth and maturation; acceptance of physical and sexual development; physical hazards. **ch. 6**

Adolescence, the Prolonged Transition. GPN. 30 min. (Module 19; $80). Through historical and cross-cultural comparisons adolescence as a period of increased autonomy, identity development, and risk taking as a social construction. The biological aspects of puberty and emerging sexuality are addressed. **ch. 1, 6, 12, & 18**

Adolescence: Relationships with Others. MAG. 20-30 min. (Module 31; $35). Relationships with parents; peer groups; influence of schools. **ch. 15, 16, 17**

Adolescence: Search for Identity. MAG. 20-30 min. (Module 30; $35). Theories of adolescence; cultural conditions influencing identity formation; identity; cognitive functioning. **ch. 12 & 18**

Adolescent Development. RMI. 30 min. (C24-17; $90). or IM (TH66; $139). Looks at the physical, social, and psychological changes involved in making the transition from childhood to adulthood. **ch. 6, 12**

Anorexia and Bulimia. FHS. 19 min. (IL-1380; $149). Looks at the addictive nature of anorexia and bulimia and the possible effects of these disorders on the cardiovascular and central nervous system. **ch. 6**

Bulimia: The Binge-Purge Obsession. BAX. 25 min. ($385). The classic chain of events leading into binge-purge behavior. Includes social uses of food in western culture, the hazards of dieting, and cultural drive toward thinness. **ch. 6**

Can a Guy Say No? MTI. 32 min. (DB-5258L; $250). Approaching the subject from a young male's perspective, the program looks at the social and psychological pressures to have sex. **ch. 16**

Close Encounters of the Sexual Kind. FML. 13 min. Looks at misconceptions and facts about sexually transmitted diseases, including AIDS. **ch. 6**

Contraception—Ready or Not. FML. 13 min. Looks at the misconceptions and facts of avoiding adolescent pregnancy. Uses a conversation with a sperm and an ovum to talk about how only some contraceptive methods are effective. Focuses more on issues than methods. **ch. 6**

Cults, Charisma and Mind Control. IM. Explores the powerful appeal of cults and their tactics. **ch. 12**

Dangerous Years. MTI. 29 min. (DB-6007M; $80). Looks at societal and psychological factors that lead to adolescent violence. **ch. 6 & 14**

Dealing with Teens: A Guide to Survival. FHS. 52 min. (IL-2721; $159). Dealing with teens and preteens in the areas of substance abuse, dating, sexuality, moods and feelings, and abnormality. **ch. 6**

The Development of Self. IM. 60 min. (TH259; $129). Self-concept, self-esteem, and self-worth, including the Perceived Competence Scale for Children. **ch. 12**

Dying to Be Thin. BAX. 25 min. ($295). Looks at the lives of several people who literally risked death to be thin. **ch. 6**

Eating Disorders. FHS. 26 min. (IL-2359; $149). Looks at both anorexia and bulimia. **ch. 6**

Eating Disorders: The Slender Trap. RP. 21 min. (4150; $385). Covers anorexia nervosa, bulimia, and compulsive overeating. **ch. 6**

The Enigma of Anorexia Nervosa. BAX. 58 min. ($850 or $325 each part). *Part I. Delusion and Discord.* 18 min. The history of anorexia, modern approaches to treatment, and the biopsychological model. *Part II. Clinical Intervention and Rehabilitation.* 16 min. The symptoms of anorexia nervosa, problems created by binge-purge behavior, some treatment techniques. *Part III. The Battle of Wills.* 24 min. Set in an inpatient eating disorders unit. **ch. 6**

Girltalk. FML. 58 min. This video portrays the lives of three runaway girls. **ch. 13, 15**

Good Girl: Exploring an Awkward Age. FML. 45 min. A re-enactment of a diary from a 13-year-old girl. Illustrates everyday activities and the underlying loneliness and self-doubts. **ch. 12**

Formal Reasoning Patterns. DAV. 32 min. ($100). Illustrates the tasks Piaget developed to probe the thinking styles of secondary students. **ch. 7**

Gender and Relationships. RMI. 30 min. (C24-13; $90). Looks at affection, sexuality, love, and commitment. **ch. 13**

The House of Tomorrow. IM. 57 min. (TH303; $139). The emotional and physical transformations of puberty and adolescence are examined in this program. **ch. 6, 11**

I Am. FML. 12 min. ($195). Yuppies, vendors, street people, and others answer questions about their own identity. **ch. 12**

Kids and Drugs. FHS. 28 min. (IL-1115; $90). Examines alcohol and drug abuse, and explores parental denial, children's denial, warning signs, and family stress. **ch. 6**

The Last Dance: Senior Prom. FML. 58 min. ($295). Looks at the hopes, dreams, and anxieties of high school seniors by focusing on senior prom at a racially mixed, economically diverse school. **ch. 12**

Nine Days of Hell: Japan's Toughest School. FML. 18 min. ($195). Japan's academic boot camp is shown in this film. **ch. 17 & 18**

Peer Culture. GPN. 30 min. (Module 18; $80). Looks at how children and adolescents negotiate the authority of adults and the cooperation of peers. Analyzes *los abandonados,* a homeless and parentless group of children in Guatemala City. **ch. 16 & 18**

The Pleasure Bond. RMI. 30 min. (POF-106; $99). Looks at sexuality from infancy to old age, including how it is affected by our self-views and our relationships with others. **ch. 6**

Rock Around Kremlin. FML. 55 min. Explores the influence of rock music on adolescents in the Soviet Union and provides a sense that disenchantment among the youth is experienced in many cultures. **ch. 16 & 18**

Sex Hormones and Sexual Destiny. FHS. 26 min. (IL-1718; $149). Looks at hormone levels' effects on masculine and feminine behavior and the anatomical structures of female and male brains. **ch. 6**

Teaching Resources

Sexism in Language. FHS. 20 min. (IL-2848; $149). Looks at sexism in song lyrics, newspaper reports, satire, written conventions, and everyday conversations. **ch. 13**

Sexual Stereotypes in Media: Superman and the Bride. FHS. 40 min. (IL-3888; $149). Looks at media images of men and women. **ch. 13**

Teen Challenges. RMI. 30 min. (C25-24; $99). Looks at teenage pregnancy, eating disorders, school dropout and delinquent behavior. **ch. 6, 17**

Teen Married Couples. FHS. 29 min. (IL-2795; $90). An adapted Donahue program that focuses on teen couples. **ch. 15**

Teenage Mind and Body. RMI. 30 min. (C25-22; $99). or IM (TH288). Focuses on physical and cognitive development, including differences between teens' abilities and interests and their parents' expectations, moral development, and physical changes. **ch. 6, 7, 14, 15**

Teenage Pregnancy. FHS. 26 min. (IL-2378; $149). Follows several teenagers through the births of their children and subsequent changes in their lives. **ch. 4**

Thin Dreams. BAX. 21 min. ($295). Explores some of the issues surrounding the drive toward thinness and looks at the need to accept physical differences due to genetic patterns. **ch. 6**

The Waist Land: Eating Disorders. MTI. (DB-4875M; $350). Looks at both bulimia and anorexia. **ch. 6**

The Waist Land: Why Diets Don't Work. MTI. (DB-4874M). Looks at the rituals of dieting and the problems of rapid weight loss and rapid weight gain cycles. **ch. 6**

Why Is It Always Me? RP. 14 min. A program for problem-solving and decision-making skills for young adolescents. Utilizes the I.D.E.A.L. five-step problem-solving method. **ch. 7 & 8**

YOUNG ADULTHOOD

Behind Closed Doors. RMI. 30 min. (POF-115; $99). Looks at the scope of family violence, the cycle of violence, and the means of escape. **ch. 15**

Being a Single Parent. FHS. 19 min. (IL-1467; $90). Looks at three different single parents exploring the effects of parenting and career as well as the psychological effects of divorce on the child. **ch. 15**

Boys Will Be . . . BAX. 33 min. ($250). Looks at a middle-class batterer's behavior and background. **ch. 15**

Children of Alcoholics. FHS. 28 min. (IL-1606; $90). Looks at how alcoholism affects the other family members. **ch. 15**

Clotheslines. FML. 32 min. ($295). Shows the love/hate relationship that women have with the task of cleaning the family's clothes. **ch. 15**

Couples Arguing. FML. 60 min. ($445). Shows actual arguments of five couples. **ch. 15**

Date Rape on the College Campus. FHS. 28 min. (IL-2792; $90). Looks at acquaintance rape at universities. **ch. 6**

Dealing Successfully with Toxic Parents. 30 min. (ARG-124; $90). Carl Whitaker and Onnolee Stevens discuss how to deal with and reconcile with the toxic behaviors of one's parents. **ch. 12 & 15**

Domestic Violence: Voices Within. BAX. 27 min. ($250). Aimed toward law enforcement and mental health professionals, this video includes conversations with an abuser and with two victims. **ch. 15**

The Familiar Face of Love. FML. 47 min. ($395). Looks at John Money's concept of love maps. **ch. 16**

Family. IM. 30 min. (SH45; $139). Analyzes different types of families including a nuclear family, a single-parent family, a homosexual family, and a family dealing with dysfunction. **ch. 15**

Families in the Balance. 23 min. (SJ259; $195). Profiles four American families in different economic circumstances trying to balance work and parenting. **ch. 15**

Family Portraits. RMI. 30 min. (POF-101; $99). A look at marriages and families by looking at four families. **ch. 15**

Fathers. FML. 52 min. ($350). Fathers of young children talk about their involvement with their children's lives. **ch. 15**

For Better or Worse. RMI. 30 min. (POF-113; $99). Handling conflict constructively in a marriage to deepen understanding and tighten bonds. **ch. 15**

Gender and Relationships. IM. 30 min. (PH155; $139). Love, affection, and sexuality, and how men and women differ in their sexual attitudes, motives, and behaviors. **ch. 13**

Going It Alone. RMI. 30 min. (POF-108; $99). Describes the trend toward being single, and the variety of single lifestyles that exist. **ch. 15**

Great Expectations. RMI. 30 min. (POF-111; $99). The beliefs and expectations individuals bring into a marriage have a direct influence on their life together. **ch. 15**

Intimate Connections. RMI. 30 min. (POF-112; $99). Deals with communications in relationships. **ch. 10 & 15**

The Japanese Family. IM. 35 min. (SJ180; $119). Looks at three contemporary Japanese families looking at changing roles for husbands and wives and the breakdown of the extended family. **ch. 15 & 18**

The Marriage Market. RMI. 30 min. (POF-109; $99). Examines the social variables that influence a person's choice of partners. **ch. 15**

Mending Hearts. BAX. 57 min. ($295). Documents two years in the lives of four people with HIV who are struggling to come to terms with reality and change their lives to accommodate their diagnosis. **ch. 6**

One Plus One Equals Three. RMI. 30 min. (POF-118; $99). The different approaches—overpermissive, autocratic, abusive—to parenting. Whether to parent as a pal, policeman, teacher, or coach. **ch. 10 & 15**

Power Plays. RMI. 30 min. (POF-114; $99). Power struggles in intimate relationships. **ch. 15**

Self-Esteem Begins in the Family. 30 min. ($295). Looks at how parents can build self-esteem in their children. **ch. 12**

Sex and Gender. IM. 30 min. (SH42; $139). Examines the lives of three women of different generations. **ch. 13**

Single, Head of Household. IM. 30 min. (SJ135; $139). Looks at how divorce affects children, joint custody, and effects of being raised in a single-parent home. **ch. 15**

Single Parenting. RP. 30 min. (4326; $95). Focuses on single parenting after a divorce. **ch. 15**

Still Killing Us Softly: Advertising's Image of Women. CAM. 30 min. Uses magazine, album, and billboard ads to illustrate effects on sexual roles, expression, and violence. **ch. 13**

Things Your Mother Never Told You. FML. 58 min. Forty women of diverse ages and backgrounds share their perceptions on what it means to be a mother. Topics include dreams during their youth, marital crises and resolutions, careers and motherhood. **ch. 13 & 15**

Three Styles of Marital Conflict. RP. 14 min. (1272; $255). Looks at patterns of the Hidden Agenda, the Passive Partner, and the Underadequate/Overadequate. **ch. 15**

To Parent or Not to Parent. RMI. 30 min. (POF-117). This program focuses on the declining U.S. fertility rate, societal views of parenthood, the personal impact of parenthood, and regulating conception. **ch. 15**

Variations on a Theme. RMI. 30 min. (POF-110; $99). or IM (SJ133; $139). Examines the variety of family configurations that exist today. **ch. 15**

Violence in the Family. IM. 55 min. (SJ101; $150). Uses still-image photography to examine the causes, characteristics, and possible solutions to family violence. **ch. 15**

MIDDLE ADULTHOOD

An American Stepfamily. FHS. 26 min. (IL-1935; $149). The program examines the problems of conflicting loyalties and rivalries, dealing with former spouses, and his/hers/ours kids. **ch. 15**

The Second Time Around. RMI. 30 min. (POF-124; $99). Looks at post-divorce courtship and remarriage. **ch. 15**

Single, Head of Household. RMI. 30 min. (POF-123). Discusses how divorce has increased the number of children living with one parent. Examines the family and personal consequences of divorce. **ch. 15**

Step Family. MTI. 13 min. (DB-80544; $245). Focuses on a woman with children who marries a single parent of a teenage boy and how their relationship is strained by disagreements among the children, and by a remarriage that involves a new baby and the husband's children from his first marriage. **ch. 15**

Stepparenting Issues. MTI. 20 min. (DB-HS05; $190). Looks at problems such as sibling rivalry, testing of authority, and emotional patterns. **ch. 15**

The Strained Knot. RMI. 30 min. (POF-121; $99). How families cope with unexpected problems and tragedy. **ch. 15**

The Survivor Symphony. BAX. 15 min. ($250). Looks at three cancer survivors. Looks at commonly held misconceptions about cancer, the role of family members, and the problems of survivors. **ch. 15**

Turning Points. RMI. 30 min. (POF-120; $99). Defines family crisis, phases of crisis, predictable crisis, and handling styles. **ch. 15**

Working Husbands/Working Wives. RMI. 30 min. (POF-116; $99). The social and personal impact of two-career marriages. **ch. 15**

Yours, Mine, and Ours. RMI. 30 min. (POF-125; $99). Looks at the complications of stepparenting and adjusting to the new family and also how to build successful relationships. **ch. 15**

OLDER ADULTHOOD

Family and Intergenerational Relationships. CPB. 60 min. ($30). Profiles older people as spouses and grandparents and looks at how elders help sustain family traditions and culture. **ch. 15**

Grandparents. ECC. 28 min. The nature and importance of grandparent-grandchildren. **ch. 15**

DEATH AND DYING

Bereaved Parents. FHS. 28 min. Deals with the overwhelming loss and guilt that parents who survive the death of an offspring experience. Also expounds on the value of talking with others who have experienced a loss, sharing happy memories of the child, and helping other children in the family. **ch. 15**

Childhood's End: A Look at Adolescent Suicide. FML. 28 min. Explores the emotional, complicated issues that surround suicide among teenagers. Includes vignettes with adolescents who have attempted suicide and with the relatives and friends of young people who have succeeded. **ch. 6**

Children Die, Too. FHS. 26 min. (IL-2374; $149). Looks at families who have lost a child and how they cope. **ch. 15**

Rachel—A Difficult Year: The Death of a Sibling. FML. 25 min. ($295). Looks at four-year-old Rachel when her baby brother dies suddenly at the age of seven months. **ch. 15**

Teenage Suicide. FHS. 19 min. (IL-1382; $90). Explores some of the reasons teenagers commit suicide and looks at the recent increase in suicide. Discusses warning signs. **ch. 6**

MEDIA DISTRIBUTOR LIST

AMB   Ambrose Video Publishing, 1290 Avenue of the Americas, New York, NY 10104. (800)-526-4663; FAX: (212)-265-8088.

BAX   Baxley Media Group, 110 W. Main St., Urbana, IL 61801-2700. (217)-384-4838; FAX (217)-384-8280.

BF   Benchmark Films, Inc., 145 Scarborough Road, Briarcliff Manor, NY 10510.

CAM   Cambridge Documentary Films, Inc., P.O. Box 385, Cambridge, MA 02139. (617)-354-3677.

CG   Cinema Guild, Division of Document Associates, 1697 Broadway #802, New York, NY 10019. (212)-246-5522.

CPB   The Annenberg/CPB Project, Intellimation, P.O. Box 1922-AH, Santa Barbara, CA 93116-1922. (800)-LEARNER.

CRM   CRM/McGraw-Hill Films, 119 15th St., Del Mar, CA 92014.

DAV   Davidson Films, Inc. 231 "E" Street, Davis, CA 95616. (916)-753-9604; FAX: (916)-753-3719.

ECC   Educational Cable Consortium, 24 Beechwood Road, Summit, NJ 07901.

FHS   Films for the Humanities & Science, P.O. Box 2053, Princeton, NJ 08543-2053. (800)-257-5126; FAX: (609)-452-1602.

FI   Films, Inc. 5547 Ravenswood Ave., Chicago, IL 60640.

FML   Filmmakers Library, Inc. 124 East 40th St., New York, NY 10016. (212)-808-4980; FAX: (212)-808-4983.

FOC   Focus, International, Inc., 14 Oregon Drive, Huntington Station, NY 11746-2627. (800)-843-0305; FAX (516)-549-2066.

GPN   GPN, University of Nebraska-Lincoln, P.O. Box 80669, Lincoln, NE 68501-0069. (800)-228-4630; FAX (402)-472-1785.

IM   Insight Media, 121 West 85th St. New York, NY 10024. (212)-721-6316; FAX: (212)-799-5309.

MAG   Magna Systems, P.O. Box 576, Itasca, IL 60143-0576. (708)-382-6477.

MIL   Milner-Fenwick, Inc., 3800 Liberty Heights Avenue, Baltimore, MD 21215.

MUL   Multi-Focus, Inc., 1525 Franklin Street, San Francisco, CA 94109-4592. (800)-821-0514.

MTI   Coronet/MTI Film & Video, 108 Wilmot Road, Deerfield, IL 60015. (800)-621-2131; FAX: (708)-940-3640.

ND   New Day Films, 121 West 27th Street, Suite 902, New York, NY 10001. (212)-645-8210; FAX: (212)-645-8652.

PBS   PBS Video, Public Broadcasting Service, 1320 Braddock Place, Alexandria, VA 22314-1698. (800)-424-7963; FAX: (703)-739-5269.

PER   Perennial Education, 1560 Sherman Avenue, Suite 1000, Evanston, IL 60201. (800)-323-9084 (ext. 113); FAX: (708)-328-6706.

PFV   Phoenix Films & Videos, 470 Park Avenue South, New York, NY 10016.

RMI   RMI Media Productions, Inc. 2807 West 47th St., Shawnee Mission, KS 66205. (800)-745-5480; FAX: (800)-755-6910.

RP   Research Press, Dept. W., P.O. Box 9177, Champaign, IL 61826. (217)-352-3273; FAX: (217)-352-1221.

SP   Starpath Productions, Box 160, Fayetteville, AR 72702.

TA   Thinking Allowed Productions, 2560 Ninth Street, Suite 123, Berkeley, CA 94710.
            (510)-548-4415; FAX: (510)-548-4275.

REFERENCE BOOKS

Adams, B. N. & Klein, D. M. (Series Eds.). *Perspectives on Marriage and the Family.* New York: Guilford.
    Volumes include remarriage and stepparenting, commuter marriage, social stress and family development, wife
    battering, and helping the elderly.
Annual Review of Psychology, Palo Alto: Annual Reviews. Excellent sources for getting caught up on various
    topics.
Bellack, A. S. & Hersen, M. (Series Eds.). *Applied Clinical Psychology.* New York: Plenum. Clinical topics with
    some relevance to developmental areas.
Blane, H. T. & Kosten, T. R. (Series Eds.). *The Guilford Substance Abuse Series.* New York: Guilford. Volumes
    include psychological theories of drinking and alcoholism, cocaine, alcohol problems in women, and children of
    alcoholics.
Chess, S. & Thomas. A. (Eds.). *Annual progress in child psychiatry and child development.* New York:
    Brunner/Mazel. Available from 1968 on.
Chilman, C. S., Nunnally, E. W., & Cox, F. M. (Series Eds.). *Families in Trouble Series.* Newbury Park: Sage.
    Volumes include chronic illness and disability, variant family forms, and troubled relationships.
Costa, Jr., P. T., Whitfield, J., & Stewart, D. (Eds.). 1989. *Alzheimer's disease: Abstracts of the psychological and
    behavioral literature.* Washington, D.C.: American Psychological Association. Contains over 1,180 abstracts
    from 1,300 journals.
Damon, W. (Editor-in-chief). *New Directions for Child Development.* San Francisco: Jossey-Bass. Volumes of
    about 100 pages published quarterly since 1978 to update a specific research topic. Recent topics include: infant
    stress and coping, empathy and related emotional responses, black children and poverty, children's gender
    schemata, how children and adolescents view the world of work, and children and computers.
Evans, B. J. & Whitfield, J. R. (Eds.). 1988. *Black males in the United States: An annotated bibliography from
    1967 to 1987.* Washington, D.C.: American Psychological Association. Provides 1,700 references to journal
    and dissertation literature.
Fiske, D. W. (Editor-in-chief). *New Directions for Methodology of Social and Behavioral Science.* San Francisco:
    Jossey-Bass. Published from 1981 through 1983, these sourcebooks include topics such as ethics of human
    subject research and single-case research designs.
Franks, V. (Series Eds.). *Springer Series: Focus on Women.* New York: Springer. A 12-volume series of major
    psychological and social issues on women's status and problems.
G. Stanley Hall Lecture Series. Washington, D.C.: American Psychological Association. Published annually from
    lectures presented at the annual APA convention; in the first nine volumes, appropriate topics for developmental
    courses include: "The structure and functions of emotions," "Coercive versus consensual sexual interactions,"
    and "The human infant."
Green, R. (Series Ed.). *Perspectives in sexuality: Behavior, Research, and Therapy.* New York: Plenum. A series
    which explores various topics of sexuality.
Hall, C. C. I., Evans, B. J., & Selice, S. (Eds.). 1989. *Black females in the United States: A Bibliography from
    1967 to 1987.* Washington, D.C.: American Psychological Association. Over 1,200 citations to journal and
    dissertation literature.
Jones, J. L., Kerby, J., & Landry, C. P. (Eds.). 1989. *AIDS: Abstracts of the psychological and behavioral
    literature. 1983-1989.* 2nd ed. Washington, D.C.: American Psychological Association. Over 650 abstracts of
    journal articles and 150 listings of books and chapters.
Kastenbaum, R. (Series Ed.). *Springer Series: Death and Suicide.* New York: Springer. Several volumes on death
    issues.
Kazdin, A. E. (Series Ed.). *Developmental Clinical Psychology and Psychiatry Series.* Newbury Park: Sage. Many
    volumes, including delinquency in adolescence, chronic childhood illness, attempted suicide among youth, infant
    psychiatry, and child abuse.
Lonner, W. J. & Berry, J. W. (Series Eds.). *Cross-cultural Research Methodology Series.* Newbury Park: Sage.
    Volumes include health and cross-cultural psychology, field methods in cross-cultural research, and intercultural
    interactions.
Master Lectures. Washington, D.C.: American Psychological Association. Includes volumes on the adult years,
    psychology and work, psychology and health, and clinical neuropsychology and brain function.

Morrison, F. J., Lord, C., & Keating, D. P. (Eds.). *Applied Developmental Psychology.* A three-volume serial publication. New York: Academic Press. Vol. 1 was published in 1984, Vol. 2 in 1985, and Vol. 3 in 1989. The third volume is called *Psychology Development in Infancy.*

Pick, A. *The Minnesota symposia on child psychology.* Minneapolis: University of Minnesota Press. Available from 1967 on.

Reese, H. W. (Ed.). *Advances in Child Development and Behavior.* New York: Academic Press. Over 20 volumes published in the last three decades on theory and research in child development and behavior.

Reynolds, C. & Kamphaus, R. 1990. *Handbook of psychological and educational assessment of children. Vol. 1: Intelligence and achievement; Vol. 2: Personality, behavior, and context.* New York: Guilford. Outstanding resource for child assessment issues in psychology and education.

Salapateck, P. & Cohen, L. (Eds.). *Handbook of Infant Perception,* vol. 1 and 2 published in 1987. New York: Academic Press. Includes color perception, taste and olfaction, depth perception, speech and sound in early infancy.

Solnit, A. J. (Series Ed.). *The Psychoanalytic Study of the Child.* New Haven: Yale University Press. This 43-volume series focuses on a wide range of psychoanalytic topics.

Sonkin, D. J. (Series Eds.). *Springer Series: Focus on Men.* New York: Springer. A five-volume series of research and theoretical perspectives on topics of significance to men.

TEACHING MATERIALS AND TEACHING SKILLS

Benjamin, Jr., L. T., Daniel, R. S., & Brewer, C. L. *Handbook for teaching introductory psychology.* Hillsdale: Lawrence Erlbaum. Selections from the first 10 years of *Teaching Psychology,* including several that can be adapted to development courses.

Benjamin, Jr., L. T. & Lowman, K. D. (Eds.). 1988. *Activities handbook for the teaching of psychology, vol. 1.* Washington, D.C.: American Psychological Association. Contains 44 classroom activities, demonstrations, and experiments including some for developmental psychology.

Bradley-Johnson, S. & Lesiak, J. L. 1989. *Problems in written expression: Assessment and remediation.* New York: Guilford. Elucidates the components essential for written communication and helps evaluate and remedy deficient writing skills.

Bronstein, P. & Uina, K. (Eds.). 1988. *Teaching a psychology of people: Resources for gender and sociocultural awareness.* Washington, D.C.: American Psychological Association. Provides minority and cultural awareness and a variety of viewpoints, research, and experiences in subjects that include development and personality.

Golub, S. & Freedman, R. J. (Eds.). 1987. *Psychology of women: Resources for a core curriculum.* New York: Garland. Provides discussion topics and demonstration projects that can help developmental psychology instructors "mainstream" women's issues into their courses. Also a good source for films and book resources. Has a whole chapter on developmental psychology, and chapters on human sexuality and history of psychology may also be valuable.

Makosky, V. P., Whittemore, L. G., & Rogers, A. M. (Eds.). 1988. *Activities handbook for the teaching of psychology, vol. 2.* Washington, D.C.: American Psychological Association. This second volume includes nearly 90 activities, including some directed toward developmental psychology courses.

McKeachie, W. J. *Teaching Tips.* Lexington: D.C. Heath. A guidebook for the beginning college teacher.

Network: The newsletter for psychology teachers at two-year colleges. Washington, D.C.: American Psychological Association. Includes resource ideas, teaching strategies, and film reviews.

Shapiro, E. S. 1989. *Academic skills problems: Direct assessment and intervention.* New York: Guilford. Step-by-step instructions for using new direct methods of evaluation and intervention of academic skills.

Teaching of psychology. Washington, D.C.: American Psychological Association. A quarterly journal directed toward the improvement of teaching of psychology courses. Includes course descriptions, film and book reviews, demonstrations, and useful articles.

Young, R. E. (Editor-in-chief). *New directions for teaching and learning.* San Francisco: Jossey-Bass. Published quarterly for more than a decade, these volumes present ideas and techniques for improving college teaching. For example:

Weaver, F. S. 1989. *Promoting inquiry in undergraduate learning.*
Stice, J. E. 1987. *Developing critical thinking and problem-solving abilities.*
Weimer, M. G. 1987. *Teaching large classes well.*
Katz, J. 1985. *Teaching as though students mattered.*
Spear, K. I. 1984. *Rejuvenating introductory courses.*
Cones III, J. H. et al. 1983. *Teaching minority students.*
Griffin, C. W. 1982. *Teaching writing in all disciplines.*

Young, R. E. 1980. *Fostering critical thinking.*
Eble, K. E. 1980. *Improving teaching styles.*

SUGGESTIONS FOR NEW TEACHERS

The following are an assortment of suggestions for new (and other) teachers. Hopefully, some of them will be helpful in organizing and teaching your child development course.

1. Do some thinking about your philosophies about teaching, grading, and interacting with students. Then think about approaches that help you translate your personal values into your course structure.
2. Prepare your course well in advance of the course starting date. It is especially important to order desirable media in advance of the course, and to construct a course syllabus in advance of the course.
3. Make your course syllabus as detailed as possible, and provide students with copies the first day of class. Make several extra copies so that you can provide students with a second copy if they lose their original. Things to consider including in the syllabus: textbook assignments, test dates and chapters covered, make-up test procedures, written assignments, grading scale, course objectives, statement about plagiarism and cheating, class attendance policy, extra credit possibilities, office hours, types of tests (multiple choice, essay).
4. Decide whether you want to lecture each class period or utilize discussion, exercises, media, and other special activities, and additions to your lectures.
5. Several test formats can be successful. Decide on the basis of goals (e.g., essay questions require more thought processing; multiple-choice and true-false questions can allow immediate feedback), and practicalities (e.g., multiple-choice questions can be quickly scored even with large classes). In classes of 30, it is possible to score multiple-choice tests as students get finished, allowing students the opportunity to immediately review their errors; if a make-up test is permitted, students can learn which topics they need to review again.
6. Know whether you believe in providing information about what will be on the test. You may prefer to let students figure out what you will emphasize on the test or to say nothing so that all material must be learned. On the other hand, the child development course contains numerous terms and concepts. In addition to those in the textbook, you might add several more in your lectures or through additional readings. You might reason that students will learn a more defined amount of material more thoroughly. In this case, tell them which pages will not be on the test, terms and concepts that won't be emphasized (or conversely, tell them which terms and concepts will be emphasized). One technique that I have used is to copy the entire test bank, have the college's bookstore sell it at cost, and therefore provide students with the entire pool of potential questions. Using this method, students looked for the answers to hundreds of questions per test and reported that they had never studied so hard for a course; they liked the technique because effort definitely translated into high grades.
7. Consider using assignments other than tests to determine grades. You might want to adopt the philosophy that all college courses should incorporate some writing. You have many options for this course: book critiques (e.g., consider having your students write about the development of a major character in a book, such as Nora in Ibsen's *The Doll House*), journal article critiques, term paper, research projects (30 ready-made research projects are included in this manual and in the student study guide), critiques and parenting guides, personal journal, and so on. You might want to allow some options for students. Consider whether all students need to do the same number of projects. I have at times adopted the policy of requiring one project toward a C, two toward a B, and three toward an A.
8. Decide on a make-up test policy. Remember that if you are on a commuter campus or have non-traditional students, the number of valid excuses is likely to be high. Develop a policy that is fair to students without buckling yourself down in piles of make-up tests during the semester. My favorite policy was to use the final exam period for multiple-choice test make-ups; students had a chance to make up tests, but those who had skipped most tests ended up with a comprehensive final test, while those who made every test were rewarded by being done with the course before the final exam period.
9. Consider using the first class period to 1) go through your entire syllabus explaining the "map of the course" and 2) make suggestions on how to study efficiently. Many college students have never been formally instructed in studying techniques. You can instead refer students to the studying section of the study guide that is available for this course.
10. Visit your campus library and see what materials (books, journals, and magazines) are available for student use. Check out the inter-library loan policy. Consider what is available in choosing class assignments. Find out how instructors can influence which books are purchased for the school library, and order books that can improve your course.

11. Include test dates on your written syllabus. As a new teacher, if you are unsure of when you should schedule tests, remember that students get more upset if you move a test forward than if you move a test back a class period.
12. Decide on your office policy. Will you be available only certain hours, or can students drop by whenever you are in the office?
13. Above all, remember that you are teaching a course to which everybody can relate. All of your students have been children, and many have or will raise children. The child development course has the potential to be a large influence in your students' lives. Some students will resolve old family issues in your course, others might discover a new concern, and many will learn of a solution to a current concern. Enjoy your course while taking it as seriously as your students will take it.
14. Know your campus resources for counseling. Your awareness will help you refer students who become distressed by topics such as child abuse or substance abuse.

Teaching Resources